WITHDRAWN

The Only Way Home is Through the Show

Performance Work of Lois Weaver

Jen Harvie and Lois Weaver

Contents

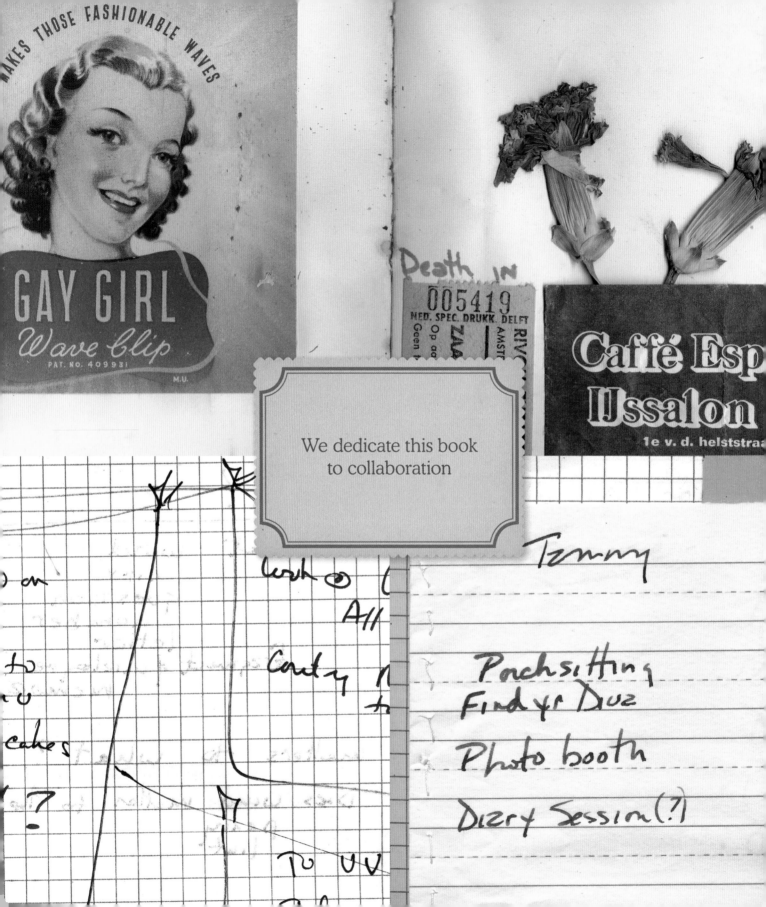

- Zip lock bags
- YouTube Video
- List of Questions
- Old ?

OTHE UK

VIRGINIA
CARSON
CODE
SHERRI
COY
DEANNA
SUDY
ROGER
TYRA
WENDY
DONALD

Jo   Stace
Clare   Vick
Cheelie   Sue
Louise   Rose
          Becca
          Al.
          Jen
          Deb

MALLORCA
TELMA
ANA

If not sex what ?

Dixie Straps

Toy Boy

Dildo joke

Check Book # 7 pink
            flag.

Old faded Rose

about the need for glas

Tammy's love of orange

Foreword

Peggy Shaw

When I want to say something, I tend to get stuck in the first letter, so the word fire comes out free or fierce or fandangle. So when I think the word Lois, I say luscious or leader or lending or light or looking.

Then I realise how much of my life has been looking at her while hundreds of other people looked at her. But I always got to see her from my own special angle, usually from the left. I could notice the glow of sweat on her face and her shoulders, because usually her shoulders and chest are exposed. Lois loves performing. She gets a giggle in her eyes. And I can tell she's there but also not really there. I know her timing. I know her body. It's like she's on display and she is all mine. All mine because I get to hold her hand when we bow as we finish, as we have for 36 years doing shows together.

This is the mine, mind, magic, making of Lois Weaver.
making love
making a plan
making a dinner
making a show
making something that wasn't there before

And that is what Split Britches, under the artistic direction of Lois Weaver, has been trying to do for 36 years. Make something and trust that the audiences will see something, see something that reminds them of a detail, an experience, a feeling that they could do it themselves if they wanted to.

This magic is very simple, really. It is a desire to connect with people. And even if you don't know it, Lois has influenced your life and what you see or what you do. You can actually see, while you are talking to her that she is waiting and thinking, that her mind is seeing a million ways of shaping what you are saying into a perfectly formed sentence, a layered story, or crazy possibility.

I have been a performer for 40 years, and I wonder if I ever would have done that if not for Lois Weaver. When I met her I was a confrontational, loud, brazen, obnoxious, gay cabaret performer. I didn't talk much then but somehow I thought I had plenty to say. I was strapping and hungry and she was accommodating and comforting. She even used to sing me to sleep at night in a loud city that kept me awake. Lois taught me to be gentle and seductive and subtle. She taught me to win an audience over rather then make them want to leave the theatre. She taught me to try not to always resist, while she celebrated my resistance. She questioned my drag, while loving me in a suit. She stood up to butch when butch needed someone with clarity of thought to stick up for it. She found words to describe me, like handsome, and mature, and tall, while still trying to find the words to describe herself. I wonder if I ever would have been a writer if Lois hadn't caught all the words I threw onto a page and lined them up in a way that would help people make sense of what I was trying to say.

She taught me to try not to always resist, while she celebrated my resistance. She found words to describe me while still trying to find the words to describe herself.

I always say, let's take a rest; Lois always says, just one more minute, one more time. She knows that we are just getting to the meaty bit, just touching the real, just about to break through.

Lois and I have always said that we make only one show, the same show over and over, just different words and songs. If I was to say what show that is, I would say a simple show with lots of images of things that make us all human: mistakes, forgetting lines, not having enough money, being queer, being lesbians, having sets that fall down or pack up in suitcases, and laughing. Always laughing because life is so beautiful and so hard. Every day is a challenge, every show is a miracle.

We always get to the theatre early to get everything calm and ironed and in place and to truly savour the evening together. We set up two separate areas, putting up favourite pictures, good luck objects, and things related to the show: a picture of Marlon Brando, a postcard of Marilyn Monroe. All preparations for the act. It's like we are not doing it for the audience but for each other. Partners in this dance, this illusion, this pretending that we are who they want us to be.

That's why we do it – besides not knowing how to do anything else. It's just plain desire. You want it, have wanted it since you sat across from each other in a rehearsal and asked, 'Ok, what are we go to do now?' And your heart starts pounding when you hear the audience come in, and the preshow music starts, and you get a 15-minute call. And no matter what, you know you have to go on. It's like sex but not sex. In sex you can stop if you have a headache or your stomach hurts or you have the flu. In shows, you have to do it. You can't call in sick.

And we always say to each other, 'The only way home is through the show!'

Introduction: welcome home

Jen Harvie

May 2015

'Performance can be a structure that allows us to do things we wouldn't normally do: it is now or never. In that now, when you insert yourself into it, you are embodying things, doing things and moving things. You change in that: it has to be now or never.'

Lois Weaver[1]

The Show

Lois Weaver is simply one of the most important feminist artists of the twentieth and twenty-first centuries. Her work has amused, informed, inspired, and influenced generations of performers, writers, directors, artists, other performance makers, audiences, participants, festival organisers, venue creators, activists, students, and academics, across the US, the UK, and beyond. It continues to influence emerging artists and new audiences now.

Lois's solo and collaborative work has pioneered some of feminist theatre's most important innovations. In 1976 with Muriel Miguel and others, she co-founded New York-based feminist and proactively diverse Spiderwoman Theater.[2] That company is still running as I write this, and it is still practising methods of what Miguel calls 'story-weaving', which Lois helped to cultivate in the company's early days and which braid together and value the personal stories of multiple performers.

In 1980 with Peggy Shaw and Deb Margolin, Lois co-founded the extraordinary Split Britches theatre company.[3] Split Britches ransacked personal stories and canonical literature to make strange and wondrous new hybrids which gleefully exposed their sources' misogyny. It mashed those textual sources together with slapstick and lip synch in joyous celebrations of pop culture and in powerful recalibrations of cultural value. It presented actors, overlaid by their characters, overlaid by their *characters*' characters in a carnival trick of disappearing mirrors that seriously questioned the location of female subjectivity in patriarchal times. Split Britches' work vaulted back and forth across theatre's fourth wall like it was the mere height of a sturdy brogue or, at most, a sassy stiletto. It staged butch/femme lesbian desire. It faced down the social inequalities fostered by Reaganomics. It was sexy and hilarious. It was so inventive, daring, surprising, often touching, and consistently funny, it became the hands-down go-to example in the great wave of feminist theatre criticism which roared through the late 1980s and early 1990s.[4] Within two or three years, Split Britches achieved near-cult status with devoted audiences, especially in the company's spiritual and most often actual home on Manhattan's Lower East Side, but also elsewhere across the States, throughout Europe, and farther afield – in New Zealand, Taiwan, Brazil, Canada, and beyond. Though Margolin has not collaborated on any of the company's new work since 1993, and regardless of Lois and Peggy's ages – mid-60s and early 70s, respectively, as I write – Split Britches is not merely still running, it's still innovating. 2013's *Ruff*, co-written by Peggy and Lois, performed by

Opposite: Lois Weaver in *Lust and Comfort* (Weaver, Shaw, and James Neale-Kennerley, choreography by Stormy Brandenberger, 1994), La MaMa, NYC. Photo by Tom Brazil.

Peggy, and directed by Lois, uses green screen technology to explore how Peggy's 2011 stroke affected her sense of memory, her sense of self and her relationships with those she's carried with her through life, from eccentric family members to favourite crooners.[5] It 'visually and verbally translates Shaw's internal experience of illness and aging into an external assemblage of her multifaceted, creatively capable, aging brain.'[6]

And it is not only Lois's group- and pair-based theatre work which is innovative. As a solo performer, she has blossomed in the persona of hyper-femme Tammy WhyNot, whose main performance form of the sing-along staged inquiry explores such topics as *What Tammy Needs to Know … About Getting Old and Having Sex* (2008 onwards). Tammy's direct interactions with audience/participants are typical of a broader strand of Lois's work: her socially-engaged or applied theatre and performance and her activism. In this work, Lois frequently appears as the chatty Tammy, whose own lack of inhibition often has a marvellously freeing effect on others too, enabling their engagement in issues that might otherwise be difficult. But Lois also appears as herself in a variety of socially engaging inventions she has collectively dubbed 'Public Address Systems'. These are designed to foster public engagement in discussion on important and often neglected social and cultural issues, such as what older people *want* from intimacy, sex, or technology; and what people have to say about, for example, feminism and live art, performance and social justice,[7] labour,[8] and performing gender.[9] Furthermore, these Public Address Systems are formally innovative, radically revising potentially exclusive forms such as the academic lecture or panel of experts by hybridising them with familiar, domestic sites and forms of conversation – around the supper table, on the porch, over a game of cards, in a sing song.[10] Familiar, 'private', domestic forms invite and enable people to engage in discussion on important social, cultural, and political issues in public fora.

Lois also co-founded New York's off-off-Broadway performance venue, the WOW Café. She is a former Co-Director of London-based Gay Sweatshop theatre company. She is a long-time teacher and promoter of live art, and a Professor of Contemporary Performance at Queen Mary University of London. Here in 2006, she was Director of the enormous Performance Studies international conference *Performing Rights* and curator of its extensive performance programme. She has been commissioned to make work by, amongst others, the Wellcome Collection, Chelsea Theatre, and Magic Me in London, P.S. 122 and Dixon Place in New York, and Out North in Alaska. She and Peggy Shaw have held residencies at the Universities of Texas, Hawaii, and Lancaster (UK), and with the Lower Manhattan Cultural Council on Governor's Island off the southern tip of Manhattan in 2014. Also in 2014, Lois was awarded a prestigious Guggenheim Fellowship in the category Drama and Performance Art.[11] Beyond all these achievements, Lois's work is important for dozens more reasons that I aim to address further below.

The Book

But before I do that, I want to address why this book is emerging only now, despite the importance and longevity of Lois's work. This may be partly because, in the firmament of artistic forms, feminist critics have probably paid more attention to forms such as fiction and visual art than theatre. Even though Split Britches generated a still-snowballing amount of criticism approaching the size of a polar ice cap (I exaggerate slightly), little has focused specifically on Lois's work. Admittedly,

Lois directs deliberately collectively, as a matter of preference and principle.

Margolin did a lot of Split Britches' writing in the first decade, and the powerful combination of Peggy's deep voice, impressive stature, and comic timing meant she often stole a scene.[12] But Lois too commanded the stage and confidently seduced her audiences, and all Split Britches' shows were and still are created collectively by the company. Furthermore, Lois was and is generally the director, sometimes named as such, frequently not. However, Lois directs deliberately collectively, as a matter of preference and principle, and in ways related to her democratic, enabling approaches to teaching. But because she doesn't direct in the domineering mode of the (frequently male) *auteur*, her directing hasn't pressed for recognition. Later in this book, feminist theatre scholar Elin Diamond reflects on her experience of a long-ago performance of Split Britches' inaugural play, *Split Britches* (1980). She writes, 'I was so overwhelmed with pleasure at what these women were doing in their apartness-togetherness, so pleased at lesbian and feminist energies swerving and swirling through rages and repetitions, shouting and kissing, that I couldn't see what Lois had done, though it was, of course, the shape of everything I was seeing.'[13]

And it is not only Lois's directing which lacks visibility – or, more correctly, has lacked attention. She is fundamentally committed to making work *for* marginalised audiences – especially of women, lesbians, and older people – and *with* groups who are socially marginalised – most often by their gender, sexuality, class, and/or age. Her work is not, therefore, habitually staged with the biggest budgets, at the most high-profile venues, for the largest audiences, for long runs, garnering masses of press attention. On the contrary, she often deliberately seeks audiences who are not 'regular theatre-goers', and she makes work in 'non-theatre spaces', for short runs or targeted one-offs, and uses the modest-but-enabling 'beg, borrow, or steal' methodologies of the School of Thrift. The ten boxes (or 9.75 linear feet) of Split Britches archival materials held by the Fales Library and Special Collections at Elmer Holmes Bobst Library of New York University[14] attest to the fact that the company's work *has* attracted a lot of attention. Nevertheless, Lois tends to work outside of places where her work might get most attention and recognition. This is not because her work lacks ambition or, indeed, is afraid to fight; it is ambitious and up for a fight. Lois makes work where and how she does because she is principally committed to exploring social and political topics that are socially repressed, and she seeks out people whose stories and priorities are socially neglected.

Finally, Lois's work has perhaps evaded more focused attention and analysis, first, because she is a world-traveller, whose career is based in New York *and* London but pops up in many other globally dispersed contexts as well; and, second, because she is a polymath, who works with equal dexterity across many forms, from performing, to directing, curating, teaching, and more. Without doubt, her practices' diversity and distribution benefit her work, audiences, and collaborators in dozens of ways; for example, her performing and teaching enhance each other; her global travels have pushed human rights up the agenda throughout her work; she not only makes shows, she can handily light, tech, promote, and tour them; and she has the fluency and facility to work with collaborators whether they're in the most elite universities or the most deprived prisons, and to facilitate discussions *between* people who are most and least privileged. But her work's promiscuous diversity does mean it resists capture and summary, especially by a single, focused audience. And her global wayfaring means she and her work are seldom directly in the eye of any particular interested party for a sustained length of time.

So, a variety of conditions have colluded to prevent a book such as this from emerging until now. But there is enormous appreciation for Lois's work, and great interest amongst audiences, academics, students, and others in her history, methods, records, memories – and phone number. I hope this book begins to satisfy the interests and appetites of those readers.

The Only Way Home Is Through the Show: Performance Work of Lois Weaver aims to convey the breadth of Lois's artistic work across its long and rich history, but more importantly across its spirit, practices, aesthetics, principles, humour, commitments, collaborations, and inspirations. It aims to document and reflect not only on the comparatively well-known work by Split Britches, but also on Lois's solo work, her work before Split Britches, and aspects of her work that are by their nature potentially less visible, mostly because they are not performance but rather thinking, directing, organising, teaching, and theorising. The book is structured chiefly thematically, not chronologically, though to facilitate contextualisation, it ends with a timeline of Lois's work and life. The book's form is partly inspired by the commonplace book, a kind of scrapbook used historically to compile knowledge. The scrapbook format resonates with many aspects of Lois's aesthetics, and the apparently banal but actually rich and evocative term 'commonplace' captures her commitment to the 'common' and/or democracy as well as to the specifics of particular, local places and the people gathered there. The book's six main sections address: Lois's early life and work until she co-founded Split Britches in 1980; her work as a lesbian femme feminist; her approaches to making performance; her practices of facilitation, curatorship, and leadership; her work as alter ego Tammy WhyNot; and some of her less well-known performance and activist work. Inevitably, there is some overlap across these sections, and given that the book offers different perspectives on shared stories, there is some repetition. *The Only Way Home* has been designed by our great collaborator David Caines, who painstakingly photographed many of Lois's most decrepit (and beloved) old props and writings and created stunning settings and panoramas for each section of this book with them. Each one of the six sections features writing by Lois and by me; a wealth of images from Lois's and Split Britches' vast archives, many by such extraordinary photographers as Eva Weiss, Lori E. Seid, and Christa Holka; and writings by artists, critics, and academics who have worked with Lois, been inspired by her, and/or written about her work. These contributors number over 30 in total and include other WOW Café alumni such as Moe Angelos and Holly Hughes; younger artists such as Rosana Cade, Jess Dobkin, Lauren Barri Holstein, and Johanna Linsley; long-time collaborators such as Muriel Miguel, Stacy Makishi, and Lois Keidan; critics such as C. Carr; ground-breaking feminist scholars such as Sue-Ellen Case, Jill Dolan, Lisa Duggan, Gerry Harris, Joan Nestle, and Peggy Phelan; plus members of a next wave of feminist scholarship such as Dee Heddon, Erin Hurley, and Kim Solga. Most often we asked these contributors to write on an aspect of Lois's work which was important to them because it inspired them, or it provoked them to respond. In planning, Lois and I both wanted this book itself to be beautiful, moving, and inspirational.

Going Home with Lois

Before a performance, 'standing backstage and on the edge of the unknown',[15] Lois and her collaborators have regularly, even ritually, long said versions of the phrase, 'The only way home is through the show', 'The only way to the bar is through the show', or, in a very early iteration articulated by Split Britches fellow member Deb

'The only way home
is through the show'
suggests theatre
can offer a kind of
restorative, comforting
power, like a coming
home. But also, theatre
is a job that must be
laboured through.

Margolin, 'There's no way home but straight through the show. It's part of the way home.'[16] These phrases encourage Lois and her collaborators to cross that familiar threshold of adrenalin and nerves that sometimes manifests as all-out stage fright. As Lois has observed, stage fright can be a lot like 'age fright', 'a feeling of anxiety that most of us experience from time to time as we enter different phases of our lives and readjust notions of our own identities', for example during puberty, at midlife, or at retirement.[17] The phrases capture some of performance's most powerful feelings, of longing, fear, drive, resignation, warmth, kindness, and comfort. They might convey a sexual innuendo. The reference to home highlights how important in the work of Lois and her collaborators are personal and apparently 'mundane' stories, hospitality, and feminism, given the centrality of debates about domestic labour both to feminism and to Split Britches shows such as *Split Britches, Upwardly Mobile Home* (1984), *Little Women* (1988), *Lust and Comfort* (1994), and the adaptation of Tennessee Williams' *Streetcar Named Desire* they co-created with Bloolips, *Belle Reprieve: A Collaboration* (1991). The phrase suggests theatre can offer a kind of restorative, comforting power, like a coming home. But it also insists that theatre is a job of work that must be laboured through. It acknowledges theatre can indeed be 'magic', but it proposes theatre must also be sustaining; it must offer a livelihood. The critique of labour that Lois and her collaborators propose, therefore, doesn't stop in domestic contexts; it addresses the vast field of creative contexts too. Lois and I chose the phrase 'the only way home is through the show' as the main title for this book, therefore, because it goes a long way towards capturing her priorities, commitments, and attitudes, as well as her fun and her humour, from the cheeky to the bittersweet.

The images and writing in this book also capture those aspects of Lois and her solo and collaborative work, and many more aspects beyond them. For me, the book conveys Lois's passion, her politics, and their inherent connection for someone who, like bell hooks, challenges the ways that 'all too often our political desire for change is seen as separate from longing and passion in our daily lives'.[18] It shows her commitment to making work from desire, impulse, and fantasy, and the licence she takes and offers her collaborators to do what they want. It shows her as an out and proud lesbian, femme, middle-aged woman, ageing woman, and a changing body. It shows how she has worked to face down shame and to put her identities into global visibility and how she has powerfully hitched her feminism to many other important issues and practices of social justice and human rights. It shows her commitment to local issues. It conveys her inspiring imagination and her empowering belief that, if you can imagine something, you can make it, and if you can make it, you can change it.[19] It reveals her capacious and magnanimous curiosity, especially about things that are repressed in dominant, patriarchal, heteronormative, and ageist cultures. It shows her commitment to exploring ways to enhance democracy. It shows what various contributors to this book refer to as her joyous energy, spirit, wonder, and commitment to entertainment. It captures her love of pop culture but also her commitment to challenging its potential heternormativity. It demonstrates her preparedness always to break and remake her own work and canonical work. It displays her intolerance for pretentiousness. It shows her intellect and love of language and word play. It shows her beauty and sexiness. It shows her charisma, love of talk, and willingness to be boldly opinionated. And it shows how she listens and is humble, supportive, and patient when necessary. ('I really enjoy patience', says Lois. 'That's why I've had the girlfriends I've had.')[20] It shows how the performances she and her collaborators make usually prioritise characters and relationships over stories or resolutions, and the fact that they are often packed with a weird and wonderful miscellany of treasures in their commitment to honouring every contributors' desires and telling everyone's stories. It shows her fun and inspiring leadership. It shows her profound commitment to collaboration, and to kinship, over community – recognising the value of 'chosen families' and of attachments which may be profound if only temporary because they are formed on the basis of shared commitments.[21] It shows her fear but also her fearlessness.

On with the show.

A Few Additional Notes about the Book

First, because the names Lois Weaver and Peggy Shaw are repeated so many times throughout this book, other authors and I tend to refer to Lois (rather than the more formal Weaver) and often to Peggy (rather than Shaw).

Second, much of Lois's work has been deliberately and powerfully collaborative, and we aim to recognise that explicitly throughout the book. However, to avoid excessive repetition of the mouthful 'Lois and her collaborators', sometimes a reference in my writing to Lois's work stands in for what is more precisely the work of Lois and some collaborators. Third, how and why am I am the lucky co-editor of this book? The practicalities: Lois and I co-conceived the book's structures; she devised its original sections titles in collaboration with me; I have been the principle textual editor, and she has been the principle visual editor, in collaboration with our designer, David Caines. Why am I the co-editor? I have admired and been inspired by Lois's work (and that of her collaborators!) since I was a feminist theatre student in the late 1980s and early 1990s; I saw my first Split Britches show *Anniversary Waltz* at the Drill Hall in London in 1990 though I was living between Guelph and Toronto, Ontario at the time and wouldn't move to London until 1994, after three years in Glasgow, where I saw *Lesbians Who Kill*. Lois and I have been working on (in my case) and on and in (in her case) political, feminist and queer theatre in London since the early 1990s. We probably formally met in the late 1990s. Since 2004, we have been colleagues in the Drama Department at Queen Mary University of London (QMUL). She is one of my most important people and my dearest friends. I have been keen for a while that more of her innovative and inspiring practices should be effectively documented and widely shared with more audiences. I am an academic writer and editor, and a few years ago Lois and I started collaborating on a different book about her practices; I hope that will follow in future. Lois Keidan and CJ Mitchell of the Live Art Development Agency and Dominic Johnson, another QMUL colleague and co-editor with Keidan and Mitchell of the series Intellect Live, approached us about doing a monograph for that series on Lois's work. This is it.

1   Lois Weaver in Weaver and Caoimhe McAvinchey, 'Lois Weaver: Interview and Introduction by Caoimhe McAvinchey', in *Performance and Community: Commentary and Case Studies,* ed. by Caoimhe McAvinchey (London: Bloomsbury, 2014), pp. 21-32 (p. 32).

2   The company website is *Spiderwoman Theater*, <http://www. spiderwomantheater.org> [accessed 23 May 2015].

3   The company website is *Split Britches* <https://splitbritches. wordpress.com>; extensive Split Britches material, including performance videos, is archived online at 'Split Britches', *Hemispheric Institute of Performance and Politics* <http://hemisphericinstitute.org/ hemi/en/modules/itemlist/category/245-britches> [both accessed 23 May 2015]. Seven of the company's plays are anthologised in *Split Britches: Lesbian Practice/Feminist Performance*, ed. by Sue-Ellen Case (London: Routledge, 1996). Split Britches' material archive from 1978-2000 is held by the Fales Library & Special Collections, Elmer Holmes Bobst Library, New York University; see, 'Guide to the Split Britches Archive, 1978-2000, MSS 251', The Fales Library & Special Collections <http://dlib.nyu.edu/findingaids/html/fales/splitbritches/index.html> [accessed 23 May 2015]. All subsequent references to this archive will cite Split Britches Archive.

4   For some details of this criticism, see the bibliography and the concluding section of my chapter below, 'Lois, Love, and Work'.

5   Some details on *Ruff* are available on its Facebook page, 'Peggy Shaw: RUFF', *Facebook,* 10 April 2013 <https://www.facebook.com/ events/403777483050902/> [accessed 19 May 2015].

6   'Professor Lois Weaver', *School of English and Drama, Queen Mary University of London*, <http://www.sed.qmul.ac.uk/staff/weaverl.html> [accessed 23 May 2015].

7   'Long Table on Social Justice and Performance', Stanford University, 8 November 2012. See: *Facebook*, <https://www.facebook. com/events/516491255044999/> [accessed 19 May2015].

8   'Long Table on Labour', Queen Mary University of London, 10 February 2012. See: *Labour Live Art*, <http://labourliveart.blogspot. co.uk/p/london-long-table-discussion-with-lois.html> [accessed 19 May 2015].

9   'Long Table on the Performance of Gender', City of Women – Association for the Promotion of Women in Culture, Ljubljana, Slovenia, 12 October 2013. See: *City of Women* <http://www.cityofwomen.org/en/ content/2013/project/long-table> [accessed 19 May 2015].

10   For more on Lois's Public Address Systems, see Lois Weaver, 'About', *Public Address Systems*, 2013, <http://publicaddresssystems. org/about/> [accessed 19 May 2015].

11   'Lois Weaver', *John Guggenheim Memorial Foundation*, 2014 <http://www.gf.org/fellows/all-fellows/lois-weaver/> [accessed 23 May 2015].

12   Later in this book, for example, Elin Diamond admires Peggy's 'throaty urgent syncopated phrasing' in *Split Britches* and calls it 'one of her gifts to performance for the next 40 years' (Diamond, 'Lois', p.161). As Lois points out to Peggy Phelan in Phelan's entry, below, the butch often upstages the femme (see, below, Peggy Phelan, 'A Femme on Her Own').

13   Elin Diamond, 'Lois', p.161.

14   'Guide to the Split Britches Archive, 1978-2000, MSS 251'.

15   Lois Weaver, email correspondence with Jen Harvie, 17 June 2015.

16   Deborah Margolin, email correspondence with Lois Weaver, 17 June 2015.

17   Lois Weaver, Helen Paris, and Leslie Hill, *Getting On: A Backstage Tour: An Open Source Workshop Template*, 2014, p. 3.

18   bell hooks, *Reel to Real: Race, Sex and Class at the Movies* (London: Routledge, 1996), p. 29.

19   See, for example, Lois Weaver in Split Britches workshop for the Women's Writing for Performance Project (2003-06), Lancaster University, 12-15 January 2006, referenced in Elaine Aston and Geraldine Harris, *Performance Practice and Process: Contemporary [Women] Practitioners* (Basingstoke: Palgrave Macmillan, 2008), p. 2 and p. 105.

20   Lois Weaver, unpublished interview with Jen Harvie, New York, 12 October 2014.

21   For more on Lois's ideas on kinship, see Weaver and McAvinchey, 'Lois Weaver', p. 30; and Lois Weaver, 'Kinship', *Contemporary Theatre Review*, 23:1 (2013), 43-4, reproduced below, pp. 214-15.

Lois Weaver in 1950.

Ask a question
Just say the word
Exhibit tendencies
Work with what you got
Act on an impulse
Pay attention to accident
Tangle a few stories
Have faith in detail
Perform a fantasy

How do you start?

Lois Weaver

Getting started is the hardest part and I tend linger on the threshold where I feel both tempted and terrified by the unknowns that are patiently waiting for me in the rehearsal room, anxiously occupying a workshop space, or hungrily stalking an empty page.

So I start with questions, any question. It can be personal or professional; painfully exquisite or extremely mundane, trusting that the smallest bait could catch the biggest fish.

I attempt to answer the question with the first thing that comes to my mind, acting on impulse and remembering to believe that my first thoughts are, by definition, my most original.

I may or may not tell the truth, maintaining a creative privilege of mixing fact and fiction.

One by one, I turn to everyone – friends, collaborators, students, ancestors – and ask them to ask me any question. It helps me get a measure of the voices in the room, the personalities at the table and reminds me that I don't do this alone.

Red pajamas

Lois Weaver

This is how I got my start. One day the sixth grade teacher came into my class just after lunch. She had lost her lead character and was looking to replace her with a fifth grade girl who could speak the loudest. We all assumed that the sixth grader who was supposed to play Vesta, the fire goddess, was ill and could not continue with rehearsals and therefore couldn't be in the production. Now, I suspect that her Bible Belt parents did not approve of anything that proposed a mythology that contradicted their 'In the beginning God created heaven and earth' version of creation. The play was full of Roman gods and goddesses and the title had something to do with Rainbows.

I was still suffering from not being able to be in the first grade Christmas play. The only criteria seemed to be ownership of the necessary wardrobe. My teacher asked anyone who had a pair of red pajamas or even a pair of red long-johns to raise their hands. I didn't put my hand up because there was not a single pair of solid colour pajamas in my household and besides I was once-removed enough from a farming background to know not to admit to the ownership of a pair of long-johns, let alone red ones! However, the kids who raised their hands got to be the main characters in the play. I was devastated. Was that all it took? I spent a month dwelling on the unfairness of this particular kind of audition. Finally, when I saw three child-sized mannequins in red pajamas in the window of the local department store, I collapsed in tears. 'Well, Lois,' my mother said. She always said, 'Well, Lois', when I was sick or crying, as if the salutation 'well' was somehow self-fulfilling. 'Why didn't you go ahead and raise your hand? We could have managed to get you a pair of red pajamas.' It had never occurred to me to lie. Not then anyway. I hadn't learned how to employ the useful lie or creative truth as I call it now. But I did, after that, learn how to make the most of every opportunity.

When it was my time to read, I was fortunately all the way on the other side of the room. I knew I was backlit by the Virginia afternoon sun streaming through the row of windows behind me so everything depended on the voice. I practically bellowed and made damned sure she could hear every single syllable. I got the part. I was Vesta, the fire goddess, at the age of ten and no longer in need of red pajamas.

Opposite and clockwise from top left: Daughters of the Revolution Good Citizenship Award, 1968; Lois Weaver as cover girl for *The Religious Herald* (Virginia Baptist newsletter), 20 January 1972; Lois Weaver in freshman rush for Alpha Sigma Alpha sorority, Radford College, 1969; Letter from the Department of Sociology at Virginia Tech on Lois Weaver's speech on Women's Liberation, 8 May 1972; Weaver family. Clockwise from centre: Coy, Virginia, Judy, Lois, and Russell, Roanoke, Virginia, 1953; Mill Mountain Playhouse, Roanoke, Virginia, 1970; Lois Weaver practising as mascot for William Byrd High School cheerleading squad, 1954.

The **RELIGIOUS HERALD**

January 20, 1972

VIRGINIA POLYTECHNIC INSTITUTE

COLLEGE OF ARTS AND SCIENCES

BLACKSBURG, VIRGINIA 24061

8 May 72

To Whom It May Concern:

   Miss Lois Weaver presented to two sessions of my

Minority Group Relations a speech on Women's Liberation.

It was well prepared and dramatically delivered. Further,

it was received by the students with enthusiasm.

   I am most grateful to her for sharing her knowledge

and experience with us.

21

Pink Tornado (from *Faith and Dancing*)

Lois Weaver[1]

I want to go home but I can't find my way.
I left a trail of corn bread but the wind has come
    and scattered the crumbs.
It was more than a wind. It was a tornado,
    a pink tornado.
It wasn't pink to start with when it hovered
    over Virginia.
Virginia is a state, you know. But it is also the
    name of my mother.
And I think this tornado had something to do
    with her because I haven't seen her since.
It started over the west ridge. I should have
    known this was different.
Storms usually come from the east.
Do their dance of terror and temptation
    on the east ridge.
Appearing from the back door to be just beyond
    the lilac and the clothesline.
But this one came from the west, from the end
    of the day, a winter's day.

Winter is an unusual season for tornadoes
    but there had been blizzards
then the warm spell
then the terrible ice storms
then the flood
so a tornado was odd but not impossible.

It was at the end of the day.
Just after the sun had dropped behind the nearest
mountain beyond the west ridge,
a halo, no, more like a tiara, appeared on the
    head of the mountain.
So we were expecting it. We were waiting.
The air stilled. The hawk took off and I pretended
    everything I could.
But then I would you see because my name is Faith.
Faith, who had always lived in the state of Virginia
until the tornado.

It looked like an ordinary tornado.
You know what that looks like don't you? Fuzzy grey
    and blue, even though it isn't.
Like the Blue Ridge Mountains look blue even
    though they are not.
Tornadoes start out as colourless droplets
    of moisture and turn blue
from all the debris that gets sucked up into their
    souls, like white clothes in a dark wash.
And they dance on one leg, on one pointed toe.
They only have one leg, tornadoes and yet they
    can be such good dancers.
Spinning on one toe... What is that called in dance?
Pirouetting.
Pirouetting down the road they can, like
    discriminating neighbours, destroy all the houses
    on one side while leaving those on the other side
    completely unscathed.

I never studied dance although I did pay a lot
    of attention to the weather.
I looked it up in the yellow pages once, dance that is,
and marked the place with a pencil.
Just like I looked up the word lesbian in the
    dictionary
after I heard two boys spelling it out behind me
In a voice that made me think it must be written
    on my back.
I was only ten and couldn't find the definition.
    But I got my answer.
Without asking I got my answer.

'How can you be a good Christian and think
    about Dancing?'

What Virginia meant is that she didn't know
    how to manage this.
How would I get there for a start?
Besides the only dancing she knew about had
    been prohibited,
not by God but because of economics.

She'd grown up in the depression when all such
    social gatherings had been cancelled.
And to put the record straight it wasn't God or the
    Baptist preacher she cared about really.
She just didn't know what else to say.
She would have had to admit then and too soon that
    Faith had a body
and that body could take flight and leave the state
    of Virginia.

Which brings me back to the tornado and how I lost
    my way home.
So the tornado was heading east
They always do you know.
They always head east and they blow in counter
    clockwise spirals
because they are deflected by the rotation
    of the earth.
That is if you happen to be in the Northern
    Hemisphere.
Otherwise your spirals will be clockwise.
So heading east and slightly south, it came down
    our dirt road just like I had many times.
And like me it stopped for a split second,
    just long enough
to be late for dinner
or considered missing
or possibly even long enough to get a naked switch
    across the back of the leg.
It stopped like me at Ame's house.
Ame's other name was Lucy
but I called her Ame because she had one.
The main one I think was to tempt me away
    from Virginia.

She tempted me with cornbread. Hard, course,
    crunchy cornbread.
Not that cakey sweet kind.
Oh, she had nothing against sugar.
Put sugar in just about everything
including a handkerchief tied in a knot so I could
    suck on it.
A sugar tit she called it.
But she never put sugar in her cornbread
and it's that recipe for cornbread that always helped
    me navigate my way home
until the tornado.

Headed down our dirt road and sidestepped just
    when it got to Ame's house
although now we might call her Aunty Em.
Because this mighty tornado stopped at her house,
danced delicately around the African violets in her
    basement
and turned a violent pink when it pulverized her
    yard full of geraniums.
That's the last thing I remember, the tornado
    turning pink
and the sky full of the smell of geraniums.

When I came to, Virginia was gone and I was looking
    for a way back home
Which is why in spite of my dyslexia, I have taken
    up cartography.

Places to start

Jen Harvie

'Place – where we were born, where we grew up, where we work
and perform – influences the things we say and how we say them.'
Lois Weaver in material for a class on 'Re-inventing the Southern Voice'
the College of William and Mary, Williamsburg, Virginia, 1997[2]

'One of the most interesting things about maps is that they lie. I come from
a family of liars. That's because we are optimists. In the face of most things
we either imagine a way out or tell an untruth. In fact I have already told you
a lie and there will be six more before the performance is over. […]
[M]emories, like maps, lie about shape and distance.'
Faith in *Faith and Dancing* by Lois Weaver, 1996[3]

Tangled Roots

Lois Weaver was born in October 1949, the final and significantly youngest child
of three, to Russell and Virginia Weaver in Roanoke, Virginia, USA. As she likes to
put it, she is the daughter of two Virginias: the State and the woman.[4] Lois's roots
lead firmly back to her upbringing in Virginia in the 1950s and 1960s. But they are
tangled, happily untidy, queer roots.

Clearly amongst them are the stark lines drawn by political and social
contexts in an historically Confederate State with its deep, encrusted histories
of slavery and racial segregation, acute economic inequality between wealthy
land-owners and an impoverished working class, and proud, committed Baptist
Christianity. All of these contexts clearly contribute to Lois's sense of social
justice, and the last perhaps especially to the ways she performs social justice both
with and *as* love and compassion, as Holly Hughes suggests later in this book.

But those public, social factors that so strongly affected Lois grafted
inextricably with influences from her personal and domestic background. Chief
amongst these are the strong and often eccentric women in her family, as well
as the attractive women just beyond it. Such tantalising outsiders include the
neighbour 'aunt' Ame/Lucy who features in Lois's autobiographical solo show
Faith and Dancing and inadvertently seduces an impressionable child-Lois/Faith
with the delicious prospects of being messy, gossipy, and socially inappropriate.[5]
They include the Avon Lady, with her bag of disappearing mysteries and magic
as conjured by Lois in her 2005 collaboration with the company Curious, *On
the Scent*. And they include the preacher's wife, whose position both within
and beyond Lois's grasp unwittingly instructed her in the thrills and chills of
femininity and seduction.[6] Other domestic influences include a resourceful
thriftiness necessitated by modest means in her working class home but
instrumental in forming her lifelong ability and eagerness to improvise, have a go
and take risks. And they include her desire to stand on the dining room table at
five years old to sing 'How Much Is That Doggy in the Window'.[7]

Opposite: Lois Weaver with her
father, Russell Weaver, in their
Virginia backyard, 1950.

In these complicated, spliced together roots we can see the foundations that will later become the Lois Weaver who is at once committed social activist *and* proud, risk-taking, queer, exhibitionist performance-maker. This section tells some of the story of Lois's Southern, semi-rural background. It explores her upbringing in a working class Baptist home; her life as a child, sister, cheerleader, student, church leader, trainee teacher, summer theatre ingénue, new-theatre-seeker, social justice community worker, and emerging feminist before she moved to New York in 1973, just before she turned 24. And finally it looks at her early years in New York, before she co-founded what is likely the most influential, though deliberately never large, feminist and lesbian theatre company Split Britches in 1980.

It tells this history because Lois and I agree that it is important to who she is and what she does; it is important to her character, her performance making, her loves and her fantasies. In other words, this history profoundly influences Lois's voice, as she notes in a different context in the first epigraph to this section, above. But I also try to recognise here that background and biography did not and do not entirely determine Lois. For one thing, as my second epigraph observes, history-telling is fallible, and the stories I tell here are both necessarily partial and knowingly partisan. For another thing, Lois is committed to telling *creative* truths, truths fused with fantasies, ultimately making 'better' truths that can help us realise our fantasies. Surely it would be disingenuous not to take a bit of that creative license here, in telling Lois's stories.

Lois, Childhood, Social Justice, and Pleasure

Given all the inequalities that might have first sparked Lois's care for political and social justice in mid-twentieth century Virginia – especially inequalities to do with gender, race, and class – I asked Lois where she thought her commitment to social justice initially came from. Without hesitating, she replied, 'stress over my father's working conditions'.[8] Near the beginning of *Miss America*, Lois and Peggy's 2008 show and lament for the USA in the aftermath of Hurricane Katrina, Lois circulates amidst the audience, taking photographic portraits of them and intoning a series of things beginning, 'You never told me....' One of these is, 'You never told me... that your sense of justice came from a father who worked too hard.'[9]

Class and Labour

As a milkman, Russell Weaver worked six days a week, year-round, including Christmas day.

His pay was docked when he had to take time off, whether because he was sick, snowed in, or on holiday, or whenever some other unpreventable incident occurred. Like so many others employed under such repressive conditions, economic necessity meant that Russell rarely took sick leave, the Weavers seldom took holidays, and unavoidable circumstances such as heavy snow jeopardised the already modest family income. Although her childhood household was by no means a site of radical activism, young Lois was incensed by the injustice of what we might now call this precarious, exploitative working class under-employment that conflicted directly with a key Baptist teaching she was raised to believe in: equality. Young Lois would invent excoriating speeches to deliver to her father's

It was on *Gunsmoke* that an impressionable young Lois first met and developed a crush on Kitty, the sultry, powerful saloon manager.

Opposite and clockwise from top left: Postcard of Mill Mountain Star, ca. 1950s; Lois Weaver, Brownie school photograph, 1959; Newspaper clipping from *Roanoke World-News* (now *The Roanoke Times*), featuring Lois Weaver in upcoming TV performance, 1957; Touring van for Virginia Baptist Drama Team, 1969; *Gunsmoke's* Miss Kitty, Lois Weaver's early femme influence, ca. 1960s; Lois Weaver on float with Miss Virginia, William Byrd Homecoming Parade, Vinton Virginia, 1957.

ROANOKE, VA.

"PUT ON YOUR SHOES, LUCY"—The "Six Notes", five of whom are shown, will appear on the "Cactus Joe" program Feb. 17 at 8:30 a.m. on Ch. 10. They will present their version of "Put on Your Shoes, Lucy". The girls are, left to right, Diane Payne, Lois Weaver, Sharon Sutphin, of Mt. Pleasant School, and Margaret Chisom, of Riverdale School. Sitting is Judy Waldron, Donna Dudley and Nancy Kanode are not shown.

HOW TO MAKE MILLIONS WITHOUT REALLY WORKING
see page 4

RICHARD GEHMAN SUMS UP STEVE ALLEN

employers, speeches she would then imagine delivering to those bosses as they cowered before her and succumbed to her demands for fair employment. Already, Lois's compulsion to address social inequalities was finding expression in that powerful pairing of fantasy and performance that would come to inform so much of her future work. And she was motivated by disagreements with inequalities of labour, income, and opportunity, all of which would return as concerns in such work as Split Britches' inaugural play *Split Britches: The True Story* (1980) as well as their *Upwardly Mobile Home* (1984) and *Little Women: The Tragedy* (1988).

Race in Virginia

A second social inequality which pervaded and influenced Lois's early years in Virginia had of course to do with race. For the sake of readers (like myself) less familiar with American history than most Americans will be, I offer a bit of historical context, with apologies for its necessary brevity. One of the Virginia area's deepest and cruellest racial fault lines concerns its natives or Indians. Native peoples are thought to have been living in what is now named Virginia from 17,000 years ago,[10] their chiefdoms including the Powhatan and Patawomeke and their tribes including the Chickahominy and Rappahannock.[11] The region was one of the first parts of North America invaded and colonised by Europeans (from England), in the early seventeenth century. It is estimated that within a century of that invasion and settlement, the local native population had been decimated by about 90 per cent, partly from warfare, but especially from diseases such as smallpox brought by the invader-settlers.[12] The Virginian Racial Integrity Act passed in 1924 'prohibited marriage to whites by people of color, including Indians.'[13] This Virginian law was overturned as unconstitutional by the US Supreme Court, but not until as late as 1967. And Virginia treated native peoples grossly unequally in a number of other 'everyday' ways. Public schooling, for example, was 'not made available to Virginia Indians until 1963',[14] meaning either they received no state schooling or had to travel miles to obtain it.

Virginia's history of racial relations has also of course been profoundly damaged by its early adoption of, and long engagement with slavery. Indentured workers from Africa are reported to have begun arriving in Virginia as early as the second decade of the seventeenth century, but slavery was enshrined in law there from the early 1660s. By the 1770s, Virginia had a larger population 'than New York and Pennsylvania combined'[15] and reportedly 'two out of every five Virginians was a black slave.'[16] Slavery contributed enormously initially to Virginia's agricultural economy, including tobacco, corn, and grains, but also, later, to other industries such as iron production, mining, and shipbuilding.[17] In the American Civil War of 1861-65, Virginia was a key partner in the Southern Confederate States of America which fought to preserve slavery against the forces of the Union in the North. Of course, the North won, and slavery was technically abolished. But racial segregation and its pernicious effects persisted, not least because it was legally enforced in the Jim Crow laws which mandated and legitimated Southern states' ongoing racial segregation of public facilities, from water fountains to bathrooms, buses, and schools. Virginia's Racial Integrity Act cited in the paragraph above of course pertained to African-American Virginians as it did to the state's native population, forbidding interracial marriage. And, though a 1954 US Supreme Court legal ruling forbade school segregation, this ruling wasn't properly enforced until 1964,[18] when the Civil Rights Act also

American race relations were evolving rapidly and radically – Lois's expectations around social equality were directly informed by living through these times.

outlawed discrimination in such public places as restaurants and workplaces. Finally, the Voting Rights Act of 1965 legally equalised access to voting – though, as ensuing decades have shown, that Act has neither sufficiently *enforced* equal voting rights nor done much to redress other structural causes of voter exclusion and disaffection.

The point I want to emphasise in offering these brief histories is that in Lois's childhood, the USA, and particularly the State of Virginia though it was not the 'deep South', were sites of acute, vicious, and deeply historically embedded racial discriminations. How much were these racial inequalities something Lois was aware of growing up, and how much did they influence her? Born in late 1949, Lois was in primary school as laws around school segregation were changing and in high school when they were finally being properly enacted and the black civil rights movement was finally gaining substantive ground. She remembers watching television reports in 1957 of the nine African-American students being escorted by the United States Army into Little Rock High School against the wishes of Arkansas's segregationist Governor, Orval Faubus. She also remembers television reports from Birmingham, Alabama in 1963, when civil rights campaigners were bombed by racists, prompting protests which were aggressively repressed by Birmingham police. By the time Lois performed in the Lions Club Annual Review at Roanoke's Mount Pleasant Elementary School in 1964, it had only been a matter of about five years since the Review no longer featured a segment of black and white minstrel performance.[19] This was despite the fact that 1964 was the same year civil rights campaigner Martin Luther King Jr delivered his legendary 'I Have a Dream' speech imagining complete racial equality. Lois's own high school had few African-American students, but she was friends with some who were there, and she remembers a flirtation with a black boy when she was about sixteen[20] – around when the Voting Rights Act of 1965 was being passed. Despite her school's small black population, Lois experienced more integrated environments through the YWCA-run Y Teen group which she joined around age 14, and through which she travelled to Virginia's capital city, Richmond, where she roomed with girls both black and white.

American race relations were evolving rapidly and radically while Lois was growing up, and her expectations around social equality were directly informed by living through these times and through the commitments to equality that she learned from Baptist Christianity. When she became the first female president of the Virginia Baptist Student Union in her last year in College and she gave speeches at their annual Assemblies, she advocated social equality. This foundational commitment to human rights would later lead to Lois's advocacy of human rights through performance, as in her Public Address Systems described later in this book; through her work as Director of the major conference and festival, Performance Studies international #12: *Performing Rights*, in London in 2006;[21] as co-founder and co-curator of the Library of Performing Rights;[22] and, following the example of bicultural partnership demonstrated by performance colleagues at the International Festival of Women's Performance in Aotearoa/ New Zealand,[23] through the custom of starting performances sited on land with an indigenous history – and present – by thanking the relevant local native tribe(s).

Women and Femininity

Evidently, Lois's sense of social justice was not just about class and race. It was and is, perhaps most importantly, about gender and sexuality, and these concerns too have recognisable roots in her childhood. The 1950s and 1960s were also decades of radical social change around gender and sexuality in the USA, as in many places elsewhere. Perhaps most famously, the era ushered in sexual liberation facilitated by the advent of the contraceptive pill in 1960, opening the way for second wave feminism to demand greater equality for women, especially in the workplace. But, as with other kinds of social change, change around gender and sexuality was uneven across the US. On one hand, the overwhelming dominance of Baptist Christianity in Virginia reinforced sexually repressive beliefs such as the risks of dancing. In *Faith and Dancing*, young Faith hints to her mother that she'd like to take dance classes by pointing out 'FLOYD WARD SCHOOL OF DANCE' in the *Yellow Pages*.[24] 'Without asking I got my answer. "How can you be a good Christian and think about dancing?" she said.'[25] On the other hand, some women couldn't afford to lose time merely *advocating* for equality, especially the right to equal work, because economic necessity forced them simply to *enact* such rights. This was at least partly the case for Lois's fierce female ancestors, sisters Della Mae and Cora Jane Gearheart and their aunt Emma Gay Gearheart, who would come to inspire and populate Split Britches' first play, *Split Britches: The True Story*. It was also partly true for Lois's mother Virginia, who worked in the school cafeteria from about when Lois went to high school, giving young Lois both a working role model and a lot of childhood independence.

Likewise, many of the Virginian women Lois encountered as a child could *appear* straightforwardly to be throwbacks to an earlier age of conservative feminine propriety – the Avon Lady with her beauty products; the preacher's wife with her gender-subservient role and her repressive costuming. But Lois's later writing and performance reveal how she was intrigued by the mystery and, effectively, the power radiated by these women. As Helen Paris observes later in this book, young Lois was beguiled by the flirtations of the Avon Lady, who would reveal potions' secret powers, seduce with their promises, and then spirit those potions away, leaving Lois (or her mother) waiting for some deferred delivery at an unknown future date. The pastor's wife was both available to Lois – as a spiritual and piano instructor and confidante – but also thrillingly beyond her reach, loftily ensconced in some complex echelons of social power which Lois had yet to learn to navigate.[26]

Surrounded by such complex and often contradictory models of femininity, Lois was learning both what she didn't like – women's unfair constraint – and what she did like – women's power, and powerful women. This understanding of women as complex and powerful has continuously informed all the female characters and personae Lois has subsequently created for performance, from her Salvation Army Sergeant Beauty in *Beauty and the Beast* (1982) to her infamous alter ego, country 'n' western star turned lesbian performance artist, Tammy WhyNot, first performed in 1977 in Spiderwoman Theater's *The Lysistrata Numbah!*. It also informed Lois's childhood performances of femininity, characterised by a combination of enthusiasm, success as conventionally understood, partial failure, a keenness to please, a not-always-compatible desire for power, and a growing independence of spirit. She eagerly followed her sister into cheerleading

Surrounded by complex and often contradictory models of femininity, Lois was learning both what she didn't like – women's unfair constraint – and what she did like – women's power, and powerful women.

Opposite and clockwise from top left: Review of *Carousel*, Mill Mountain Playhouse, Roanoke , Virginia, 1971; Review of *Winnie the Pooh*, Mill Mountain Playhouse, Roanoke, Virginia, 1970; Article on talk given by Lois Weaver at Southern Baptist Convention, St Louis, Missouri, 1971; Lois Weaver in Frank Marcus's *The Killing of Sister George*, Radford College Theatre, 1971.

Mill Mountain Cast Sparkles in 'Carousel'

A Review
By DICK EURE
Times Staff Writer

Rogers and Hammerstein's classic musical "Carousel" took a highly successful maiden whirl at the Mill Mountain Playhouse Tuesday evening, and a good time was had by all.

A comfortable opening night audience of more than 200 followed the ups and downs of this mid-century hit still bright and sparkling after twenty-odd years, and it was a lovely ride by anyone's measure.

Much of the credit for the show's success goes to Mona Hanes, playing the leading role of Julie Jordan. Lovable and lovely, she is mistress of the stage from her first moment on it.

While her lilting, beautiful voice, considerable acting talent, and a set of expressions that could make any audience weep or sing at her whim, she makes the carousel go round.

Costumer Shelley Brian and set and lighting designer Richard H. Graham Jr. deserve considerable credit for outstanding jobs. Miss Brian's costumes, in particular, are stunning.

Paul Corman has choreographed several exceptionally entertaining pieces for a show that gives a choreographer a chance to show off a bit. The music, directed by Dodie Matze and performed by Ron Northrup and Doug Higgins Jr., is highly competent. With numbers like "June is Bustin' Out All Over," "A Real Nice Clambake," and "You'll Never Walk Alone", how can you lose?

Producer-Director James L. Ayers is to be commended for a tight and enjoyable performance by the entire cast. The few rough spots will smooth themselves out, and some of the characters will jell more with time, but with a leading lady like Miss Hanes, one really could really care less.

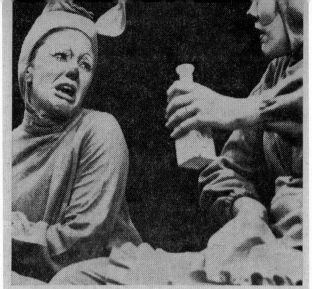

Lois Weaver (left) and Celia Watson In a Scene From 'Winnie-the-Pooh'

'Pooh' Is Delight For Old and Young

THE NASHVILLE TENNESSEAN, Saturday, June 5, 1971

ate Religion News

'Hope in Youth,' Baptists Told

By W. A. REED
TENNESSEAN Religion News Editor

S — A young Baptist told 13,000 aptists, "there is u would not look ty, angry students nal demands, but d Christian stu-

ker, Miss Lois Radford College old an applauding ednesday, "young to go out of their raise money to nger or to gain black culture and

AVER was one of g Baptists who, a musical youth ought 13,000 SBC to their feet ramatic persenta- Auditorium. She her Baptist

an opportunity to st racism, pollu-

—Photo

Studying Religion's Future Cours

ST. LOUIS — Miss Lois Weaver, a Radford College student, and B leader of the youth group that challenged Southern Baptist Convention here discuss future plans.

IN AN INTERVIEW after   MISS WEAVER added.

'Sister George'

BBC executive, Mercy Croft, right, played by Mary Browning,   Luxembourg. Performances are November 5-8 in McGuffy Hall

Touring Drama Troupe 'Points' Finger At Religion Hypocrites

By GENE McCLELLAND
Times-News Gate City Bureau

GATE CITY — Taking a backhanded slap at the hypocritical "Christian," the Virginia Baptist Student Union Quintette is touring the state with religious drama.

This week the group is appearing in Gate City First Baptist Church. Tonight's show is at 7:30 p.m.

Religious drama, as a part of missions, is relatively new, and this group of rising sophomores from four different colleges has worked together only since March.

The drama they present is designed to tear into some of the "accepted ways of thinking" with bitter sarcasm.

"Hopefully the people who see us will try to right what's wrong," Lynda Brooks of Madison College says. Alluding to a line from one of the plays, "The people look to me," Lynda explains:

"In the drama, the people look to us and see themselves or somebody they know. We talk of war and hate, and love, and race against race. It forces them to see the way things are. They can't run away, because they're cornered on that bench and they can't get away. Hopefully it will make a difference in their lives as it already has in ours."

"Dust of the Road," one of the plays the Quintette portrays, manages to stick pins in the self-righteous, by showing there is a great deal of pretense in the world.

In this particular drama,

"USE ME, LORD," Mike Hawkins, center, has implored all his life in the play—"but, not just now." Here, dying, he's surrounded, left to right, by Lynda Brooks, Philip Chenault, Lois Weaver, and Alice Martin, who join him in pleading with God to "use me now."

It's a question of whether or not a person should practice what he preaches, because while the church teaches love, all the couple in the play have to offer is hate.

Only one member of the Quintette is a drama major, Lois Weaver of Radford College. She tried out for the team at the urging of her college

be something I'd like to go into."

Michael Hawkins, a student at the University of Richmond, became a member of the Quintette "because a friend knew I was involved in drama in high school." The friend urged him to try out, and he did because "there's something up inside me that's inside a lot of young people. I want to protest against a

least 18 to 19 hours a week-end since mid-March while the try-outs were held for students all across the state, and the five players were chosen. Some days they were on the stage as long as 18 hours in one day, stretching their week-end work to more than 30 hours.

It's worth it, Phillip Chenault, a student a University of Richmond, says.

"I want to make personal contacts growing Hopefull me, and I war counseling now I d

"There satisfyin thing sa i' and Lois We

"Dram element. fellow God. situation possible real. W and shak even k because of what the pla satisfact done on Hawkins the mini

"This whole o Martin enthusia many p The g more summer end the a speci to Coll Eagle R

Roanoke Student To Star in Play

RADFORD — Lois Marie Weaver, daughter of Mr. and Mrs. Russell C. Weaver, 1901 Mayfield Dr., S.E., Roanoke, will appear in Radford College's production of "The Killing of Sister George."

Lois is a junior at Radford College, majoring in dramatic arts and speech. She is the winner of the college's 1969 award for best actress in a leading role for her performance in the title role of "Antigone."

Performances of the Frank Marcus comedy are scheduled for Thursday through Sunday in McGuffey Hall Auditorium. Curtain time is 8 p.m. nightly, with two performances on Sunday at 2 p.m. and 8 p.m.

Admission is 50 cents for Radford College students and one dollar for others.

"The Killing of Sister George" concerns the problems created for actress June

Buckridge when Sister George, the character she portrays, is eliminated from a radio soap opera series.

Lois plays "Childie" McNaught, June's roommate. With a combination of childlike cuteness and womanly allure, Lois reveals the motherly concern and gentleness of Childie, George's comfort and antagonist.

Lois returned this fall following a summer season with the Mill Mountain Playhouse, where she was in "The Eiffel Tower Wedding Party," "The Impossible Years," "Summer and Smoke," and "Winnie the Pooh."

The dual role of Sister George and June Buckridge is played by Alice Swiney, a senior from Bristol. Mary Browning, a junior from Luxembourg, is BBC executive Mrs. Mercy Croft.

Madame Xeniea, a fortune teller, is portrayed by Linda Powell, a senior from Arlington.

It's Called 'Alternative Theater'

By ENID SEFCOVIC

Theater Project styles itself "alternative" theater.

It is a booking house for itinerant professionals; it is an arena for drama students from the Baltimore Antioch College Learning Center; it is a community service, offering its resources free to the public.

As alternative theater, it exists somewhere between the restrictive definitions of professional theater and student (or community) workshop theater, says Phil Arnoult, director of Theater Project in Center Stage's former location at 45 W. Preston St.

Personality Spotlight
RC Actress Really Enjoys Life

by Beth Teall

What do Antigone, Childey, and Abigail Williams all have in common? Underneath the make-up and costumes, they are all Lois Weaver as she portrayed them in *Antigone, The Killing of Sister George,* and *The Crucible.* These are only a few of the dozens of characters Lois has played, on campus and off, during her four years at Radford.

Lois is a dedicated woman. Theatre is her life, her abiding interest. As a Dramatic Arts and Speech major, she feels fortunate to have chosen Radford, citing the small size of the Department, and its

Lois loves the audience contact of live theatre. Serious drama is by far her favorite. She would not feel true to herself, she says, in the theatre that "sells itself", such Broadway musical comedies or TV, preferring instead the atmosphere of drama found on a college or community theatre level. Here she can receive the audience contact so necessary to an actor, for "the loneliest thing in the world is to give all you've got on stage, and then have the curtain close and the audience go home, without your ever having felt them."

After grad school, Lois has two options, to teach or to act professionally. She is determined

level, but the theatre is her first love.

Lois's devotion to the theatre has not cut her off from the world, however. She is currently the president of the State BSU, the first female elected in over 15 years. Driving from speaking engagement to committee meeting to seminar in her borrowed van, she urges Baptists young and old to minister rather than preach their religion. Her strong feelings on the subject were aired to 13,000 Baptist leaders meeting in St. Louis last year.

Lois Weaver could be Radford College's chance at real fame. When Lois appears on the

Part of social justice _was_ pleasure, and both would be important and often inextricably joined up for Lois.

and became the high school cheerleaders' mascot when she was a little girl. As a teenager, she was the first female president of the Virginia Baptist Student Union. Twice she delivered speeches at Southern Baptist conventions to audiences of over 20,000 congregates of preachers and, as she puts it, 'their wives', addressing issues of social injustice such as racism, hunger, poverty, pollution, and the church's investment in the military-industrial complex. She also organised protest fasts at these conventions.[27] But Lois has recently reflected that activities like being cheerleading mascot, and engaging with such zeal in church events, were at least partly about trying to fulfil what she thought were her parents' expectations and desires.[28] I write 'at least partly', because one of _Lois's_ chief desires from a very young age was to perform and command attention. Cheerleading fulfilled this desire, as did singing and dancing on the dining room table aged five, lifted there by her admiring father. By 16, Lois was 'outfitted with the first and only Mary Quant mini dress and pair of white Courreges Go Go boots the Blue Ridge Mountains had ever seen'.[29] And in a speech about women's liberation titled 'Beyond the White Picket Fence' delivered to the Baptist Student Union when she was around age 21, Lois specifically rejected domestic constraints.

Popular Culture, Passion, and Pleasure

In other ways too, Lois's childhood was not all about social justice, but also about pleasure. Or perhaps it is more accurate to say that Lois was already discovering that part of social justice _was_ pleasure, and both would be important and often inextricably joined up for her throughout her life. Lois's generation was experiencing not only the civil rights and women's movements, but also rapidly expanding access to popular culture. Though only 3.9 million US households had television sets in 1950, by 1960, the figure was 50 million.[30] While Lois was watching civil rights news stories, she and other children were more typically watching other 'adult' (as distinct from children's) programmes, including 'crime, variety, westerns' and sitcoms.[31] One of Lois's favourite westerns, _Gunsmoke_, was first broadcast in September 1955, destined to run for 20 years.[32] It was on _Gunsmoke_ that an impressionable young Lois first met and developed a crush on Kitty, the sultry, powerful saloon manager and (likely) sex worker. Through popular cultural references – to songs by the Boswell Sisters, Perry Como, or Justin Timberlake – Lois continues to draw on her own powerful early attractions, and also to draw out her audiences' cultural connections. Similarly, while the church instructed Lois about the pressures and demands of social justice, it also introduced her to the pleasures of poetry. In a segment of _Faith and Dancing_ reproduced below as 'Virginia Started Over' (see page 69), Faith recalls 'the first time I really heard the words to the third stanza of _Amazing Grace_' and sings, 'When we've been there ten thousand years,/ bright shining as the sun, / We've no less days to sing God's praise/ than when we first begun.' She observes, 'That was my first awareness of poetry, or infinity for that matter. But then maybe that is the power of poetry. It pulls up the skirt of infinity.'[33]

Mixed into all of these influences was and remains Lois's slightly absurd perspective on the world, a perspective she attributes partly to her dyslexia, and through which it is logical to her to make connections and sometimes redemptions which others might resist. In _Faith and Dancing_, Faith reflects on her attractive neighbour/aunt Ame.

Opposite and clockwise from top left: Article on Virginia Baptist Drama Team, 1969; Feature on Lois Weaver in _The Killing of Sister George_ in _Roanoke World-News_, 1970; Feature on Lois Weaver in _Grapuchat_, Radford College newspaper, 1971; Article on Lois Weaver's work with Baltimore Theatre Project, in the _Baltimore Sun_, 1973.

Ame's house was different [from ours]. It teetered on the edge of disaster. It was a mess and wouldn't go to church to clean itself up. 'Sorry' was what [my mother] Virginia would say. That girl or this man is 'sorry' which means they wouldn't pick up after themselves. If you look it up in the dictionary, sorry means apologetic, repentant, asking forgiveness. When Virginia said someone was sorry they weren't usually the kind of person who would apologize for their behavior. You wouldn't find them on their knees except maybe for sex, and I'm not sure they would care to have your forgiveness, let alone ask for it. So these sorry people were the opposite of sorry. Although in the dictionary sorry also means worthless, just like Virginia meant it. Then the opposite of sorry could be worthy. So to me, if these sinful people are not sorry for their sins, if they are not sorry, then they are worthy. That's how dyslexia functions.[34]

There is no black and white for Lois. There may be bad and good things, but they are seldom entirely distinct, and the tricky places where they overlap mobilise Lois with curiosity and desire.

The College Years

Radford College

In autumn 1968, Lois went to Radford College in the Blue Ridge Mountains, about 50 miles west of where she'd grown up. Founded in 1910 as a women-only institution that would not become co-ed until the year she graduated, 1972, over half the 4,000 students attending at Lois's time were Physical Education majors. Lois majored in Drama, not realising, as she puts it in her publication and subsequent performance lecture included at the end of this book, 'Still Counting', 'that most of the drama took place in dormitory hallways where volleyball players wooed the future primary school teachers of America'.[35] For Lois, Radford had many rich benefits. It surrounded her with women. It consolidated her knowledge of drama and theatre and developed her skills in theatre production, as her teacher Charles Hayes notes in his reflection in this book, 'Lois Weaver: The College Years'. Her practice in 'converting the Home Economics lab into a theatre'[36] enhanced her skills in making theatre wherever and however possible. And despite its location in the Blue Ridge Mountains, hundreds of miles and, in some respects, light years away from the radical alternative theatre and culture happening at the time in New York and elsewhere, Radford nevertheless did introduce Lois to an astonishing range of emerging social ideas and new and experimental forms of performance, not to mention women and lesbians. Beyond that, it provided her with opportunities to lead the theatre experiments she was encountering. At the same time, stark public events that occurred during Lois's College years, including the Kent State University shootings of 1970 and ensuing US-wide anti-Vietnam War protests, contributed to her ongoing human rights awareness and politicisation.

At Radford in her late teens, Lois was already playing interesting female characters in very recently written plays. For example, in autumn 1970, she played 'Childie' or Alice McNaught in British playwright Frank Marcus's 1964 *The Killing of Sister George* (first produced in London in 1965). The play and its 1968 film version, with a screenplay adapted by German Lukas Heller and directed by American Robert Aldrich, were notorious for depicting a sadomasochistic butch/

femme relationship. The relationship was intimated as lesbian in the play and was explicitly so in the film, with Childie, as the name suggests, portrayed as the childish femme to her often aggressive older butch partner June, aka George. 'I wasn't a lesbian', Lois reflects in 'Still Counting', 'but my heart skipped a beat each time I heard Sister George describe how she felt when she stepped into the wet and talcum powdered footprints left by Childie after her bath.'[37] The play immersed Lois in lesbian desire, but also in a depiction of lesbianism as both punishing and deserving punishment: George loses both her job as a soap opera star and her life partner Childie; Childie can be seen as weak and dependent, moving somewhat passively from one domineering partner, George, to another, BBC executive, Mrs Mercy Croft. This was the kind of penalising representation of lesbianism that Split Britches would later reject – though by no means would Split Britches make what Lois and fellow Split Britches member Peggy Shaw refer to as goody-goody characters,[38] nor what writer Cynthia Carr refers to later in this book as 'prissy'. The play also allowed Lois to explore playing the power of femme. George is much more blatantly aggressive than Childie, but Childie's behaviour is often passively aggressive: when she sees that George is jealous of a male neighbour, Childie taunts her, 'Yes, I do fancy him – he's a dish'.[39] In the film version, when George punishes Childie by making her eat the butt of a cigar, Childie gradually turns the scene to her advantage, appearing to relish the task, even to find it sexually gratifying. It is also possible to interpret some of Childie's behaviour according to Lois's dictum for a femme: 'a highly competent woman who just *looks* like she needs a little help'.[40] Mercy Croft 'rescues' Childie, but Childie actively seeks rescuing:

> ALICE: I can't stand it any more.
> MRS MERCY: I know dear, I know. You've been under a terrible strain.
> ALICE: You've no idea, Mrs Mercy –
> MRS MERCY: I can imagine.
> ALICE: She's been *terrible*!
> MRS MERCY: Hush, dear. She'll hear you –
> ALICE : I was praying you'd come.[41]

Finally, the play and film focus on George as an ageing actress whose employment and sense of identity are profoundly jeopardised in a fickle entertainment industry that discriminates freely on the bases of both gender and age, and on Childie who appears to be both emotionally and certainly financially dependent on more powerful women. *The Killing of Sister George* thus explored issues of making a living, livelihood, and outright survival that Split Britches would work on in detail in *Upwardly Mobile Home*, and it explored connections between acting and ageing which Lois would later connect in her work on stage fright and age fright.[42]

At Radford College in spring 1970, Lois played the title role in Sophocles' *Antigone* (c. 441 BCE). Polyneices has been killed at war and his sister Antigone's aim is to give him a decent burial, though King Creon of Thebes, their uncle, forbids it. Antigone defies the King, is sentenced to burial alive but hangs herself first. Creon's son Haemon, who was engaged to Antigone, also kills himself, as, then, does his mother and Creon's wife, Eurydice. Creon loses all those he most loves, while Antigone stands by her commitments to her brother and her principles and is proved both right and effectively more powerful, though 'only' a niece, a sister, and a young woman. *Antigone* gave Lois an extraordinary opportunity to play female power. Furthermore, during Radford's production period for the play, unarmed Kent State University students and anti-Vietnam War protesters were notoriously shot by members of the Ohio National Guard, spurring a nationwide student strike and amplifying *Antigone*'s rage against the costs of war and the apparent wisdom of an arrogant male warlord. The play's portrayal of King Creon as misguided and ultimately out of touch with his people's sense of morality and justice chimed powerfully with growing dissatisfaction with US engagement in the war in Vietnam under the leadership of Presidents Lyndon B. Johnson (1963-69) and Richard Nixon (1969-74).

Perhaps even more important for Lois than these opportunities to play iconic women were the opportunities she had to make performance that was formally experimental, whether because it explored feeling and relationships more than narrative; movement and image more than speech; or process more than product. Also at College, she co-directed Samuel Beckett's *Come and Go* (first performed in 1966), a short 'dramaticule' for three female characters, Vi, Flo, and Ru. The play's short text of less than 130 words hints at relationships: the women schooled together, they share some nostalgic feelings, and they know secrets about each other. But it withholds key information: what secrets do they whisper to each other? And the women's relationships are perhaps most vividly portrayed not through text so much as movement, for example, whom they sit beside, in what order, and how they (ritualistically) hold hands at the play's close. A play about long-term female relationships, *Come and Go* is affecting while nevertheless unsentimental, and it makes rich if ambiguous intimations of these women's complex connections while actually speaking very little.

In 1972, for her final BA show, Lois elected to direct – rather than perform – and her show was presented on Radford's main stage, with a capacity of about 150. The play she chose to adapt was the experimental script *The Serpent*, described in its 1969 publication as 'a ceremony written by Jean-Claude van Itallie in collaboration with The Open Theater under the direction of Joseph Chaikin'[43] and was first produced in Rome in 1968. Chaikin's Open Theater experimental method rejected dominant theatre's naturalism and its requirement that performers interpret established roles according to received methods. Chaikin wanted performers to do more creative work, to improvise, to respond to their impulses, to be more expressive, especially physically, and to devise performance that was immediately meaningful to them and responsive to current political and social issues.[44]

The Serpent developed out of Open Theater improvisations on the Bible's story of Genesis but was also, according to Chaikin, '*a repudiation of its assumptions, thus forming a dialectic*'.[45] Chaikin proposed that assumptions arising from biblical mythology 'are even now the hidden bases of a lot of our making of choices'.[46] Partly to highlight this, *The Serpent* portrayed not only biblical scenes but also current events such as the Kennedy and King assassinations.[47] It also included contemporary commentary. Two scenes titled 'Statements I' and 'Statements II' feature a chorus of four women. Amongst other things, they reflect on the often gendered oppressions and violence of apparently polite society.

Her practice in 'converting the Home Economics lab into a theatre' enhanced her skills in making theatre wherever and however possible.

FIRST WOMAN:
I went to a dinner.
The guests were pleasant.
We were poised,
Smiling over our plates,
Asking and answering the usual questions.
I wanted to throw the food,
Ax the table,
Scratch the women's faces,
And grab the men's balls.[48]

The women also reflect on the gendered aspirations of their younger selves:

THIRD WOMAN
When I was thirteen
I wanted a house of my own.
The girl I was then
Would say to me now:
'What have you done with your advantages?
You could have married a rich man,
And had a big house.
Instead, you're a freak.[49]

The Serpent depended fundamentally on group collaboration: 'It would be difficult to overstate the importance of the group effort', observed Chaikin.[50] And the play was mostly made up of ritualistic movement and mime.[51] In an introduction to the play, van Itallie wrote,

> Theater is not electronic. Unlike movies and unlike television, it does require the live presence of both audience and actors in a single space. This is the theater's uniquely important advantage and function, its original religious function of bringing people together in a community ceremony where the actors are in some sense priests or celebrants, and the audience is drawn to participate with the actors in a kind of eucharist.[52]

For Lois, *The Serpent* offered opportunities to try out the kind of ritualistic movement-based theatre that was then erupting in New York, to direct, to explore and follow impulse in performance making, to pursue her emerging feminist politics, and to use performance to interrogate her Christian upbringing. It also fed her growing interest in performing while not being in character and her increasing commitment to devising as a group and to working to articulate the shared – and sometimes conflicting – feelings and desires of a group. One of the original members of the Open Theater, who performed in its original *The Serpent*,[53] was Muriel Miguel, with whom Lois would work in New York and then co-found Spiderwoman Theater.

Mill Mountain Playhouse

In the summers of 1970 and 1971, Lois performed in summer stock theatre at the Mill Mountain Playhouse (now Theatre) established in a vacant resort on the highest hill in Roanoke. Despite being a commercial summer theatre in a smallish town, the Playhouse, like Radford, exposed Lois to some plays and roles that were radically experimental. In 1970, she was cast as the Bride in avant-garde French

Summer and Smoke immersed Lois in the Southern Gothic style and overblown language of a writer who would become one of her favourites.

writer, playwright, and filmmaker Jean Cocteau's *The Eiffel Tower Wedding Party* (1921), a libretto for a ballet in which a Bastille Day wedding party on an Eiffel Tower platform is invaded by a murderous child, a cascade of radiograms, and a lion. The characters enter through a camera, and two on-stage phonographs played by actors 'comment on the action and recite the lines of the characters'.[54] As the 'phonographs announce the members of the wedding party, [they] enter in pairs, strutting like trained dogs in an animal act.'[55] In the play's Preface, Cocteau offered provocative explanations for what he was attempting.

> Here, I renounce mystery. I illuminate everything, I underline everything. Sunday vacuity, human livestock, ready-made expressions, dissociations of ideas into flesh and bone, the fierce cruelty of childhood, the miraculous poetry of daily life: these are my play, so well understood by the young musicians who composed for it.[56]

He concluded: 'The fact is that I am trying to substitute a "theater poetry" for the usual "poetry in the theater".'[57] He sought a poetics of *theatre* and performance, perhaps what would later come to be known as total theatre, following the publication of Antoine Artaud's *The Theatre and Its Double* in 1938. Lois enjoyed the play's physicality, rich images, and absurdity, all three features which have subsequently grounded her performance creation indefinitely. Perhaps the play also drew her to Cocteau's 1946 visually opulent film version of the fairy tale *Beauty and the Beast*, which Split Britches too would adapt in 1982.

In 1971, Lois played Nellie Ewell in Tennessee Williams' 1948 play *Summer and Smoke* at Mill Mountain. Nellie Ewell is a comparatively small but important part in the play. The main focus is on a tormented and turbulent attraction between upstanding young society lady Alma Winemiller and her more dissolute neighbour John Buchanan. Alma cannot accept John... until it is too late, at which point he is already engaged to naive, young Nellie. As with Childie, Nellie gave Lois the chance to play with youthful girlishness. The role also gave Lois another opportunity to play a young woman attuned to same-sex desire. 'Don't you know why I took lessons?', Nellie asks Alma, who trains Nellie's voice.

ALMA: I'm afraid I don't
NELLIE: I had a crush on you!
ALMA: On *me*?[58]

Nellie reveals, 'Those were the days when I had crushes on girls, but those days are over with now and I – have crushes on – *boys*...'.[59] Performing in *Summer and Smoke* also immersed Lois in the Southern Gothic style and overblown language of a writer who would become one of her favourites, and whose Stella from *A Streetcar Named Desire* she would play in *Belle Reprieve* (1991). Not all Lois's Mill Mountain roles were as experimental and influential as The Bride and Nellie. For example, in 1971, Lois played Baby Roo in *Winnie the Pooh* – but even that role offered fantasy, outrageous make-up, and fake fur, three things the future Lois would exhibit fondness for.

For Lois, the Mill Mountain Playhouse was inspiring because it took risks – the risks of having a youth ensemble, staging avant-garde plays and, even, making devised work. In 1970, Lois collaborated on a Mill Mountain devised show, *US*, which included a sequence where the performers recounted their dreams. Lois told about a dream in which she had sex with Jesus.[60] Faith recounts

Clockwise from top left: Lois Weaver in Jean Anouilh's *Antigone*, Radford College Theatre, 1970; Members of the Virginia Baptist Drama Team, 1970; Lois Weaver in Tennessee Williams' *Summer and Smoke*, Mill Mountain Playhouse, 1970; Lois Weaver in Jean Cocteau's *The Eiffel Tower Wedding Party*, Mill Mountain Playhouse, 1970.

a version of the dream in *Faith and Dancing*. The Playhouse also taught Lois about professional theatre. A female choreographer there took Lois on a walk one night and eventually cautioned her that she needed to be more ambitious to succeed. The conversation was sobering for Lois. At the time, she took it as an instruction to lower her expectations. In retrospect, she has seen it as a sorry commentary on the internal competitiveness between women in professional theatre, a competitiveness which she has challenged through her work as an events leader and curator, a facilitator, a teacher and a deviser of Public Address Systems aimed at facilitating democratic discussion. By Lois's own account, 1971 and 1972 were the years she became properly politicised.[61]

After College

Dropping out

After she graduated from Radford College, Lois applied to postgraduate acting programmes at Florida State University, Yale, and New York University at the Tisch School for the Arts. She attended one of the three auditions – at Florida State University – then no more, changed her mind about studying acting, and, for the summer, as she puts it, dropped out.[62] When I asked her why she dropped out, she explained that there were a number of factors. First, since she could barely afford to travel to Florida for her audition, let alone Yale and New York, how would she afford to go to grad school? Second, she experienced a number of personal traumas at this time that made her reflect on what she was doing with her life. One of her friends from the Folk Team at College died of a heart condition, and her 38-year-old brother, Coy, with three kids, had a massive heart attack (from which he recovered). Third, Lois increasingly recognised that some of what she had been doing – especially with church – had been about satisfying what she saw as her parents' expectations. She wanted to find her own. Lois's turning away from a route through conventional theatre training and possibly into a conventional theatre career may be a loss to that theatre, but it has been a huge boon to experimental and feminist theatre.

Going to Baltimore

Instead of going to study acting in the autumn after she graduated from Radford, Lois went to Baltimore, Maryland, to work in the inner-city peace and justice movement. Certainly the 'peace and justice' elements of this period of Lois's life connect with her future as a human rights activist, performance maker and facilitator. But Lois's time in Baltimore offered her two other important and unpredictable points of instruction. First, alongside her peace and justice work, Lois spent time at Baltimore Theatre Projects where she did workshops on the practices of Jerzy Grotowski with Lynn Norris, and the Open Theater with Mark Samuels, and learned more about the kinds of experimental, physical, non-character-based performance strategies that had begun to inspire her at College. She knew she wanted to learn more. Second, though she was committed to the principles of the peace and justice movement, 'the unbridled patriarchy of the Left'[63] that she encountered made her feel alienated, and provoked her to seek alternative forms of organisation, leadership, and feminist solidarity. 'I soon left Baltimore in search of sisterhood,'[64] Lois reflects. She moved to New York.

Though she was committed to the principles of the peace and justice movement, 'the unbridled patriarchy of the Left' that she encountered made her feel alienated.

Coming to New York

Lois moved to New York in 1973, its appeal to her was its theatre and its opportunities to learn about emerging theatre-making methods, but also its social and cultural variety, its women and its opportunities for feminists. It took her a little while to get into theatre, and longer still to get into lesbian theatre (Split Britches was founded in 1980). Given our shared interests in how artists make a living, or what Lois refers to as artists' 'livelihoods' – happily situating the core idea of survival in an implied lively neighbourhood – I asked Lois how *she* made ends meet in those early years in New York. The answer is: she worked a lot at many jobs. She was a bike courier for the *Village Voice*, worked in catering and babysat. She had a few gigs as an 'artist in a school' in a 'gifted and talented programme'. For example, with her then-boyfriend Cuban immigrant Cristobal Carambo, she co-directed *Bustin' out the Box: A Folk Play of Stereo-types*, conceived and written by The Company (of participating children), produced by the Children's Theatre Video Workshop, presented by the American Folk Theatre and, coincidentally, with a set designed by Moe or Maureen Angelos, who writes about Lois's influence on her later in this book.[65] Lois assistant directed and did a few performance projects. She also had her first job at a University, Emerson College. For a fee of $1000, which she describes as good for the time, she led a beginners' acting course. The class was scheduled directly after lunch, when, Lois remembers, students would arrive drowsy and slow. Lois immediately instituted a 20-minute nap at the start of each class, after which students were ready to work.[66]

Most continuously in her early months in New York, Lois worked in a fish market – until one day when the male proprietor was extraordinarily rude to her, and she simply left. Experiences like this were destabilising but also helped Lois realise that she could in fact survive on very little and she could and should take that risk to make performance. In 1975, Lois taught at a residential school for girls with emotional disorders[67] – experience which, in name at least, would chime with her future performance workshops for 'The School for Wayward Girls' at the WOW Café. In spring 1975, she was cast in a production of African-American playwright Amiri Baraka's play *The Sidney Poet Heroical* directed by Baraka himself and about Sidney Poitier's appropriation by/sell-out to a white-dominated Hollywood. Though the play itself explored political tensions, Lois recalls that the contexts of production felt even more politically febrile: Lois had the invidious position of playing almost all the white women's roles Poitier had ever come up against in his Hollywood career; as an 'out' politicised black person, Baraka was shadowed by body guards; and Lois recalls that, on occasion, tensions within the production team nearly mounted to outright fights.[68]

Spiderwoman Theater

In January 1975, Lois participated in a workshop with Muriel Miguel, who had trained as a dancer and worked in Chaikin's Open Theater. The workshop resulted in the show *Storyweaving*, performed by Muriel, Lois, and native weaver and storyteller Josephine Mofsie. Early in 1976, with Muriel and her sisters Lisa Mayo and Gloria Miguel, Lois was a co-founder of Spiderwoman Theater, a company devoted to telling the stories of its members as women who were native or Indigenous, African American, and white working class.[69]

As is clear in the interview between Lois and Muriel conducted at the meeting of the Hemispheric Institute of Performance and Politics in Montreal in spring 2014 and reproduced later in this book, Lois learned many things from Muriel, about both what stories to tell and how to tell them. One of these lessons was the practice and formal structuring of story-weaving, which they describe as integrating two or more stories not through a single, amalgamating narrative but through sound, movement, and shared visual imagery, such as the river that ran through the three performers' narratives in *Storyweaving*.[70] A second lesson was not to denigrate or 'simply' overlook the everyday and personal as trivial and irrelevant, but to recognise and emphasise in them the foundations of everything important – relationships, desires, ways of surviving, everyday acts of violence, everyday moments of triumph, and more. Lois put into action this commitment to the everyday, personal, and often socially overlooked or outright repudiated in Spiderwoman's first play as a company, *Women in Violence* (1975). Here, she devised for herself a bag lady character based on a woman she saw regularly on the streets of her Manhattan neighbourhood, the East Village. She enacted this commitment again by focusing on her farming ancestors in *Split Britches*. A third lesson Lois honed through work with Muriel was to foreground fantasy, to practise the belief that in performance, certainly, one can be anything she or he wants to be. This was an important principle for Muriel, whose body had not fit the long, thin mould of dance conventions she'd encountered as a student. But it was equally empowering for all the members of Spiderwoman, whose shared working class backgrounds meant that, despite the myths of the American Dream, none of them had received the kind of routine affirmation often encountered by those who are more privileged. Lois would continue to interrogate the class privileges of the American Dream across her performance-making career, from *Split Britches* in 1980, across *Upwardly Mobile Home, Beauty and the Beast* and *Belle Reprieve*, to *Miss America* in 2008. In *The Lysistrata Numbah!*, Spiderwoman's adaptation of Aristophanes' comedy from 411 BCE in which the women of Greece go on sex strike to coerce Greek men into ending the Peloponnesian War, Muriel's insistence on fantasy compelled Lois to face what she describes as 'my childhood distaste for country music and my fear of my trailer trash roots'.[71] Here, she performed her *fantasy* of a country western singer in the first incarnation of her infamous persona Tammy WhyNot who would create the remix 'Stand ON Your Man'. A fourth thing Lois learned from Muriel's leadership was the power of humour. As Muriel and Lois describe in their interview, Spiderwoman's irreverent play with misogynist humour in *Women in Violence* met with disapproval from other feminists.[72] With the benefit of critical hindsight, we might say the play deconstructed that humour and misogyny. Lois describes this effect as a kind of turning inside out; Muriel portrays it as an act of radical tickling. Drawing together Muriel's celebration of the everyday story and her commitment to the

A lesson Lois learned with Muriel Miguel and Spiderwoman Theater was not to overlook the everyday as trivial, but to recognise in it the foundation of everything important.

Opposite: Lois Weaver in Spiderwoman's *Women in Violence* (1977), Festival of Fools, Amsterdam. Photo courtesy of Spiderwoman Theater.

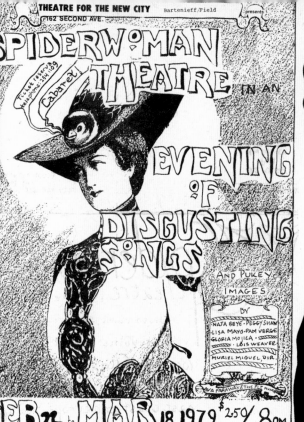

THEATRE FOR THE NEW CITY   Bartenieff/Field   presents
162 SECOND AVE.

SPIDERWOMAN THEATRE IN AN

EVENING OF DISGUSTING SONGS

AND PUKEY IMAGES
BY
NAJA BEYE · PEGGY SHAW
LISA MAYO-PAM VERGE
GLORIA MOJICA ·
· LOIS WEAVER
MURIEL MIGUEL DIR.

VIVA FARAWAY & THE NEW

FEB 22 to MAR 18, 1979 $2.50/ TDF   8PM

THEATER FOR THE NEW CITY
162 Second Ave.
New York, N.Y. 1000

SPIDER WOMEN

NON-PROFIT ORGANIZA

U.S. POSTAGE
Paid
New York, N.Y.
Permit No. 8404

photos : jean-louis sternotte

Storyweaving

New York Womanspace
Theatre Workshop

Lynne Norris
Josephine Mofsie
Lois Weaver
Muriel Miguel

Weaver

New Wilderness
Preservation Band

Charlie Morrow
G. Richardson Cook
Carole Weber
Paul Abels
with Philip Corner
Bill Fontana

River from
River Archive
maintained by
Anna Lockwood

THURSDAY JAN. 16, , 8:30 P.M.
Washington Square Church
135 W 4th Betw 6th Ave & the park.
HOST: REV. PAUL ABELS
FREE WILL OFFERING

44

SPIDER WOMAN Theater t.m.
AT NEWFOUNDLAND
6 WEST 18 st
FEBRUARY
m/sun. 8 P.M.
in moon & feather
split britches
Fri & Sat 10 P.M.
Cabaret

Spiderwoma
theatre is an exhib
dissonant, sataric, m
violent, vulnerable, burle
occaisionally pornograph
theater ensemble that to

Another thing Lois learned with Spiderwoman was the practice of storyweaving – integrating two or more stories through sound, movement, and shared visual imagery.

power of irreverence, a final performance practice Lois learned from Muriel was to play with popular culture, especially music. For Spiderwoman as for Lois ever after, popular cultural references were never misplaced in pleasurable and powerful politically engaged feminist work; they simultaneously grounded it and got it up laughing and dancing.

Other important things Lois gathered from her time with Spiderwoman were practice in touring, strong networks formed while touring across north eastern USA and north western Europe in particular; and an introduction to Peggy Shaw, Lois's future lover and lifelong collaborator and one of the other co-founders of Split Britches. When Spiderwoman Theater was born, there were growing audiences in North America, Europe and elsewhere hungry for feminist performance and the company toured a lot. Split Britches would go back to many of the venues and festivals Lois had first visited with Spiderwoman. Famously, it was while on tour in Europe that Spiderwoman began touring on the same circuit with the drag company Hot Peaches, featuring Peggy Shaw. As told by feminist theatre folklore – and Lois in 'Still Counting' – Spiderwoman arrived on tour in Berlin to discover their costumes had gone missing in transit. Having learned another New York company, Hot Peaches, was in town, Spiderwoman promptly asked if they could borrow costumes. Hot Peaches' 'feather boas, sequined gowns, vast wigs and sparkling platform shoes'[73] became part of Spiderwoman's repertoire and transformed their style and work. 'As we began to dress in this finery', says Lois, 'we secretly knew we would never be the same again. We would never make a show that did not involve glitter, false eyelashes and real attitude.'[74] Before long, Spiderwoman's *Evening of Disgusting Songs and Pukey Images* (1978) included its usual members alongside Peggy Shaw. Working with Peggy and then Deb Margolin, Lois co-produced the first professional production which she would direct. This would become Split Britches' first, eponymous play, it would launch Split Britches, and it would lead to Lois and Peggy moving on and out of Spiderwoman.

Opposite: Posters for various Spiderwoman performances, 1975-1980.

Lois Weaver: the college years

Charles L. Hayes

Lois graduated from William Byrd High School in Vinton, Virginia, where, among other activities, she was a cheerleader. The following fall, she entered Radford College (now University), which was then all female. Lois was very active in the Department of Dramatic Arts throughout her time in college.

Her first involvement in the department was when, during her first year, she worked props for the production of *Three Sisters*. The properties for this show were demanding and the faculty members were amazed when she produced whatever was asked for: a silver tea service, porcelain dolls, etc.

In *Three Sisters*, she also had her first acting role, that of a fiddle player who crosses over in the background. The director had not cast that part and Lois said that she was free at that particular moment. So, dressed as a man, she mimed playing a fiddle as she crossed up stage.

From that small beginning she took on larger roles and became a student leader in the department. She served in several positions, including president in Alpha Psi Omega, the honorary theatre fraternity. On a larger level she was state president of the Baptist Student Union. Lois was a leader from early in her career.

Among leading roles that Lois played in college were the title role Anouilh's *Antigone* and Childie in *The Killing of Sister George* by Frank Marcus. She also directed *The Serpent*, by Jean-Claude van Itallie, for the main stage.

An interesting insight into Lois's later theatre career was gained during an all student-directed performance that occurred monthly and allowed theatre, music, and dance students to exhibit their skills, independent of classes and faculty-directed productions. These were performed in a large dance studio with a raised stage.

During performance, after the first act, Lois entered from stage right, carrying a jar of peanut butter and a kitchen knife. She plopped down on the stage, opened the peanut butter and proceeded to slather it generously on her hand as one would a slice of bread. She admired her work, popped up, and skipped happily off stage.

After the second act, Alice Sweeney (a frequent collaborator), entered from stage left with a jar of grape jelly, plopped down and proceeded to slather her hand with jelly. When she finished, she admired her handiwork and skipped happily off stage.

After the next act Lois wandered slowly across the stage admiring her peanut butter hand.

After the act that followed Lois's cross, Alice wandered across the stage admiring her jelly-smeared hand.

They then alternated their separate stage crossing between each of the following acts. In each subsequent cross they looked at their peanut butter or jelly smeared hands with increasing concern.

Just before the last performance, Lois stumbled on from one side and Alice from the other, each focused on her own hand. About mid-stage, each noticed the other and they began to slowly circle one another. Then one noticed the hand of the other and vice versa. They smiled, slowed their circling and cautiously approached each other and carefully extended their peanut butter and jelly hands. Smiling, they joyfully grasped hands in a good squishy handshake and jubilantly skipped off stage together to great applause.

It was a fully realised improvisation with a definite beginning, middle, and end, a climax and a conclusion.

Lois graduated from Radford College in 1972.

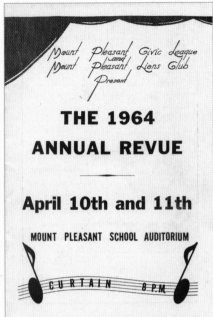

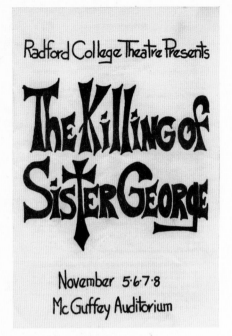

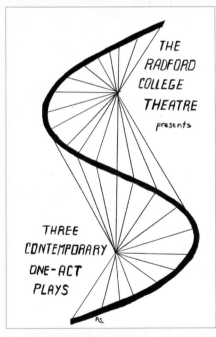

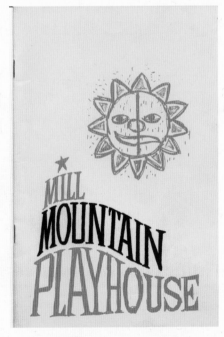

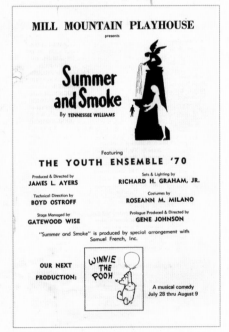

Programmes, clockwise from top left: *The House of Blue Leaves*, Radford College Theatre, 1972; Mt. Pleasant Community Revue, 1964; *The Killing of Sister George*, Radford College Theatre, 1971; *Summer and Smoke*, Mill Mountain Playhouse, 1970; Mill Mountain Playhouse programme cover; 'Three Contemporary One Act Plays', Radford College Theatre, 1971.

Jen Harvie interviews Lois Weaver

Jen Harvie and Lois Weaver

This is an edited version of an interview conducted in Lois's apartment in the East Village, Manhattan, New York, on 13 October 2014.

JEN: I'm interviewing you about the history of your work. You've talked about your work with the Baltimore Theatre Project. What did you get out of working with them?

LOIS: When I left college I think I was in a bit of a confused state. I had become politically active, or at least politically aware, and I wanted to do something that meant something. I thought I wanted to do social and political activism. I was invited to Baltimore – I didn't know what to do. I had given up on going to grad school for various reasons; one of them was that I had realised that wasn't the kind of theatre I wanted to do. I've spoken about this before, but it's really true. I thought: 'Is playing Nora going to be my fate?' That was the only kind of feminist view of – certainly dramatic – literature that I had encountered, although I knew a bit about experimental theatre. So, I went to do political activism. I went with the church. There was an inner city Baptist church that had an inner city home; a bunch of us were going to live there, restore that home, and then work in some of their social action projects. One was a halfway house for 'restored' mental patients – that's what they called it. It was a house for people coming out of mental institutions. Also, as a member of the church I worked a little bit in their inner city day care and breakfast programme for kids. The other thing I did in collaboration with a peace and justice group I was working with was set up a soup kitchen for alcoholics, basically, our homeless people in the neighbourhood. It was a really dire kind of neighbourhood we were living in. The church was in that neighbourhood, the house was across the street, so we worked in that community. Aside from that church work, I started working with Peace and Justice Center, which is really active in Baltimore mainly because that's where the Berrigans were. They were big peace activists and pacifists who had been put in prisons for their activism: the Catonsville Nine, Daniel Berrigan, and his brother [Philip Berrigan] – priests. So

it was a kind of ecumenical peace and justice movement; I was doing peace and justice work with them, and social justice work with the church. I saw an advertisement in the paper for free workshops at the Baltimore Theatre Project with someone who had worked with the Open Theater, and somebody who had worked with the Grotowski theatre. Those were big key words for me in my last couple of years at university; so I went to the workshop. I realised that I had tried to sort of go away from the theatre, and the moment I went to those workshops I was hooked back in. I realised that was my priority, and that political and social justice was a part of what I wanted to do, but I wanted to do it with theatre. It was there I learned how to do that. I had started to learn that, but it was at a distance, and out of a kind of academic study at university. I had been introduced to experimental theatre that had politics at its heart, but this was my opportunity to actually take workshops and learn the techniques of how to do it.

JEN: What were the techniques you learned there?

LOIS: Working with impulse, and also working with what they called 'worlds', which is where you set up a world but it's not necessarily linear improvisation. It allowed for more abstract, non-linear, non-psychological interventions. It was image making. Also, there was a lot of physical work, like 'machines', physical and vocal conducting – stuff like that.

JEN: And those things felt viable or valuable to you as ways of doing the politics you wanted to do?

LOIS: Yes – I didn't make that connection, but by the end I was making it. We took two classes: one, on the Grotowski technique, and one on the Open Theater technique. We created an ensemble out of that Open Theater class that actually produced some work at the end. So it was in that trajectory of the whole year that I understood exactly how to do it. I don't think I would have understood just taking the

classes. Along that journey we also started doing workshops with people who were freshly out of prison. I quickly started teaching the things I was learning. It was in the teaching that I started to think, 'Oh, this is how I would make this work', or figure out how to make this work for me, or adapt it. I started adapting it quite quickly.

JEN: It sounds like some of the principles of it that worked for you were things like impulse?

LOIS: ... Impulsive – the physical element was what you brought to it. It wasn't until I started working with Spiderwoman that I actually started to trust the value of the personal. But then, of course, [Spiderwoman director] Muriel [Miguel] had worked with the Open Theater, so that came from the same place, but I think it was just the difference in the two teachers. Mark [Samuels] was much more intellectual, more philosophical, a man, you know. His take was to bring texts for us to work through, and bring our personal [stuff] to those texts – but we didn't go into that totally autobiographical place until I worked with Spiderwoman.

JEN: And Mark Samuels was the leader of the Open Theater workshops in Baltimore?

LOIS: Yes, and Lynn Norris was the leader of the Grotowski workshops. They were a couple, and were residents at the Baltimore Theatre Project for a while.

JEN: I'm curious about your relationship to religion at that time. Up to that point, probably the church – as distinct from religion – had been important to you. Tell me what religion and the church meant to you then.

LOIS: I think I had already understood by the end of my time in college – a year prior – that, for me, the church was primarily a platform and an audience. While I adhered to certain Christian principles, I wasn't really a Christian in the sense of thinking that Jesus was my saviour and that everyone else was doomed. I don't think I ever really believed that. I did believe in peace, love, generosity, and responsibility for your neighbour – all these things that I think were rooted in Christianity. I knew early on at university that I was using this as a platform both for my feminism as it was budding, and also for my social justice work. That was 1972. What happened also was that we had managed as students to make a shift in the Southern Baptist Convention to pay more attention to social issues. But, there was a backlash, the Jesus Freak movement.[75] Once the Jesus Freak movement took hold nationally, it meant the Southern Baptists, I think, really grabbed on to that as a way to backtrack and think, 'Oh good, we can stay with

our proselytising and conservative principles'. I knew, even as I was walking into the situation in Baltimore, that I was in some sense walking away from the church, and again I was using it as a structure. Even though that church was a fairly liberal Baptist church, I didn't really engage. In fact, I started to kind of get in trouble because I wasn't coming to the services and, when I did, sometimes it was after being out late at night doing naughty things. [JEN laughs] I think it became clear between the Baptist preacher and me, at a certain point, that we were parting ways. That also coincided with me getting more and more involved with the theatre, and less involved with some of those projects.

I mention this in *What Tammy Found Out*: those projects were the first time I had set something up and started working on them, where I actually felt like I couldn't succeed. I kept pushing against something; not in the church, it was fine in the church, and not necessarily in the theatre, but it was in the sort of left political realm. Once, I organised a film screening to raise money for North Vietnamese hospitals, and actually that was the one thing I felt like I pulled off really well. I remember the men who ran most of these organisations sort of congratulating me in a way that made me realise what the problem had been all along: they didn't expect me to succeed. There was that stereotypical sexism of the left. They thought I was cute and nice to have around; I was a great assistant, I helped them, fed their egos, whatever, but for me to actually be a leader? They had never seen me as a leader. I thought, OK, so this is what has been going on. That, and probably the fact I had started to split my focus and my focus was going more into the theatre than the real hardcore organising of getting a soup kitchen going in the middle of inner city Baltimore.

JEN: Can you tell me what you think had started making you a feminist, and when?

LOIS: I was the baby of the family by ten years, and a child of the 1950s, born in 1949. We were, as a generation, told that we could do and be anything we wanted to be. It didn't come down to me as a gender-specific possibility; I really did think I could be anything I wanted to be. My parents encouraged that, and not because they were particularly liberal. My mother used to talk about how independent I was. They saw an independence in me and they wanted me to do the things I wanted to do. And I was surrounded by women. I grew up around all my mother's sisters, my own sister, there were very few men I interacted with. My brother was in the air force and my dad was very mild-mannered, a very gentle and unconfident male; consequently, he was not very macho. I've told this story too, that I learned my first lessons of

non-violence through him, because as a milkman he carried dog biscuits in his pocket, whereas everybody else carried Mace. That had a huge impact on me when I realised what it took to make that decision, and what a simple decision! They would come and bark at him and he'd pull out the dog biscuit and it would be over – whereas everybody else had a very aggressive approach. He was a very non-violent, gentle, and shy man. My mother and my sister were kind of everything to me – and my mother's sisters: my aunt Edna, my aunt Vesta, my aunt Carrie, they were big role models. Not because they did anything other than being housewives, but they were pretty fierce – just strong country women. Then, I don't know, I succeeded in high school...

JEN: ... You won awards, you were the first woman to do certain things....

LOIS: I won awards, I don't know if I was the first woman so much, but I was a cheerleader.... There weren't that many options. I was the editor of the yearbook the year I graduated, and I took leadership roles. I enjoyed being in leadership positions. Again, it never occurred to me that there was a limitation on that because of my gender. Then when I went to college, out of a certain kind of laziness and a lack of guidance, I ended up going to this women's college nearby, and it was all women! We had a theatre department of around 13 majors, two really non-sexist, gentle male professors, one into contemporary theatre, and one into the classics, and we had to do everything. We had to build the sets, direct the show, be in the show, publicise it, and re-build the theatre out of an auditorium in an old elementary school each time we did the show. I thought that was all normal. So, back to your question of how did the feminism wake up.... In 1970 it started to proliferate through the mass media, really mass media. There was no other contact with any on-campus organising or anything like that; this was a fairly conservative girls' school. They were all going to college to either get married to someone at Virginia Tech, or to be elementary school teachers – except for the 2000 women who were Physical Education majors, who were probably all lesbians, but I didn't know about it then! Half the student body were Physical Education majors.

I think also wanting to be the first woman president of the BSU [Baptist Student Union], wanting to lead and succeed, and moving into positions of leadership.... It wasn't pushing against what I thought I couldn't do; I was moving forward with what I thought I *could* do. My feminism started with supporting that. Also, there was my idea for this talk I gave when I was a junior in college, 'Beyond the White Picket Fence'; I was starting to think that what I see my sister

Previous page: Lois Weaver as the bag lady in *Women in Violence* (1977), Vondel Park, Amsterdam. Spiderwoman Theater photo.

Top: Lois Weaver and members of Virginia Baptist Drama Team, 1969.

doing, or my friends doing, is not something I'm going to do. I'm not going to get married, settle down and have kids. So, I think it all just came out of that, and it was supported by some limited reading.

JEN: After Baltimore, you went to New York City. I know it's kind of an obvious question, but why did you go to New York?

LOIS: I was sort of on my way to New York. I had only been to New York once before and fell in love with it. Of course, there was all it represented in terms of theatre. I had worked with people from New York in the summer stock days, and I had almost auditioned for NYU [New York University]. So, New York was a goal. Not a very clear goal, but a goal. I think if I had been braver I might have just gotten on a train, come here, and checked it out. But, this Baltimore opportunity, and that other side of myself that wanted to do social activism, pushed me in the Baltimore direction. At the end of this year of working at the Baltimore Theatre Project, several of the people were moving to New York, and these teachers were going back to New York. So, it was kind of natural to come. Having spent one year in an urban environment, it was easier. But, it was kind of a conflictual situation because the reason for coming to New York would be to try to get into theatre – audition, get headshots, do all those things I had understood the theatre to be. But we were coming as these little initiates in experimental theatre at a time when all the theatres were falling apart. Performance Group was breaking up. The Open Theater had broken up. So there wasn't a substantial experimental theatre scene happening at that moment. This was lucky for all of us in that little group, because a lot of the people were teaching workshops, because they weren't working; they were trying to figure out how to make their own work. Paul Zimet, for instance, and Tina Shepard who had been massive members of the Open Theater, were starting to work together and do these workshops. That ultimately became the Talking Band, which still exists. Elizabeth LeCompte was starting to do workshops around the use of deconstructing texts – I think she said that – which then ultimately became the Wooster Group. Joe Papp from the Public Theater organised an event, kind of like a smorgasbord of workshops where all these young practitioners would show up, and there were five or six different leaders, and each of those leaders gave a spiel about what they were going to be working on, and then you could work with them. LeCompte was one, and Zimet another. Some people became members of those companies. It was good in that way; the historical intention is to get here, get into a show, get known, and make print

Company photo of Spiderwoman Theater, 1980.
Top; Muriel Miguel, Gloria Miguel;
Middle: Peggy Shaw, Lois Weaver, Pam Verge, Lisa Mayo;
Front: Eva Bauman.
Photo by Pamela Camhe.

advertisements and commercials. But then there was this other thing, which we had been involved in – ensemble, political, alternative theatre. So how could you do that?

JEN: Did you have to pay for the workshops?

LOIS: No. Well, some of them we did, but this Joe Papp thing, no. I think he probably got funding. Then I continued working with Tina Shepard and Paul Zimet. A lot of those artists went to Boulder, Colorado – that was [around] 1975 – and worked with Chögyam Trungpa Rinpoche, a Tibetan Buddhist who established this place called Naropa Institute. [Allen] Ginsberg and a lot of that group of poets and alternative theatre people went there and taught classes. I went out there for a summer, or a month. I took mime and yoga classes – and also acting classes. I even auditioned a couple of times.

JEN: How did you support yourself?

LOIS: My first job when I got to New York was working in a fish market. This is a very upscale, up on the Upper East Side, fish market. My job, alongside the wife of the man who owned it, was to take telephone orders, and be the cashier. That was very interesting because Woody Allen would call – or, he wouldn't call, his cook or house person would call, who could barely speak English, and you could hear him in the background shouting the instructions; I thought, *just fucking get on the phone!*

JEN: So it was interesting because of the social hierarchies you were exposed to?

LOIS: Yeah. Edward Albee came in to set up an account, but it was this pretty young boy who came to the [counter]. I wasn't paying attention and he said, 'I want to set up an account.' I said, 'What's the name?' He said, 'Albee.' I said, 'First name?' He said 'Edward.' I looked up at him and he was 20 or so. I looked and there was Edward Albee behind him. Things like that happened.

JEN: And it was flexible enough it allowed you to keep doing the workshops?

LOIS: This was probably in my very first six months in New York. I had this arrangement that I could leave early and take classes at night. But I left because the guy who owned it became really paternalistic towards me. But he was also a bit of a monster. I had arranged to leave early to go to this class, and one day when I did that he started screaming at me, asking me what I thought I was doing – and this was a very clear arrangement we had. I never went back. I went, *nope, I'm not going to do that.* Also, I felt really uncomfortable about how the family aspect of it had started to infiltrate the working. They were treating me like family, which had its perks, but I didn't like it. So, I quit that, and then I got a job as a messenger for the *Village Voice*. This was before it became this high-powered, very competitive 'get on your bike', kill everybody kind of thing. They just had their own messenger. It was print messages, so you had to pick up the print-ready advertisements – this is before the Internet – and you just had to be on call. I loved that. I really enjoyed that.

JEN: What did you love about it? Being out and about, talking, meeting people?

LOIS: Yeah, I had my little bike, I met people. I met some real weirdos – that was OK, I felt alright about that. It was flexible and it was active; I enjoyed it. I also had gotten a few gigs, 'artists in the schools' type gigs. There was a big 'gifted and talented' – I hate that, but anyway – initiative. There was a lot of money putting artists in schools to identify kids who had talent. My boyfriend and I got hired to do some of these. We would go into the classroom and do workshops. We started also working with some of the teachers to create curriculum-based performance. I did this *Bustin' out the Box* [performance with children], in 1974 or 1975. I was still of the working class, I had to have a job; I didn't understand how to be freelance, quite. So after the fish market job I did a few things. I was a 'para', a teacher's assistant, at a residential home for emotionally disturbed adolescent girls. It was a diagnostic centre. After six months, the Board of Education said that, because I had a teaching degree, if I studied, took an exam, and got a certificate as a special education teacher, I could get an actual teaching job and not a 'para' job. So, I took the test and got the certificate, but god only knows why they gave it to me. I didn't know anything about testing. Anyway, I got a job. I finished up that year as a teacher, so I got more money. But then the city went bankrupt and we got laid off. Then I went on unemployment. It was after that I understood how I could piece together a living. Some of it was through these 'artists in the schools' programmes, directing youth projects, going on tour with Spiderwoman a little.

JEN: So you discovered a way of committing yourself full-time to your art and performance practice?

LOIS: And finding ways to support that, yes.

JEN: And you discovered how to feel safe, because you could be on unemployment and pick up multiple jobs?

LOIS: Yes, I think my brain changed, and that idea of the 'livelihood' – it was scary and risky. I would come home from being on tour with Spiderwoman and think, *oh my god, what am I going to do?* But usually then there would be some offer of teaching, or other things. I did catering; that really filled in some gaps.

JEN: Were you the cook?

LOIS: No, I had a friend. I also assistant directed, making a little money doing that. I did a few performance projects where you could get paid, and add that to your employment, so you could extend your unemployment; I learned ways to work the system.

This catering job, there's a great story of that. Peggy and I were catering, and we mainly worked in the kitchen, assembling hors d'oeuvres. The waiters had it easier and made more money. [The woman who ran the catering] was our friend so we talked her into letting us be waiters. She said, 'OK, if you get a good haircut, I'll let you be waiters.' So we both went and got good haircuts. We were working on the WOW Festival at the time, and we showed up, and we were going to wait this particular event the night before the Festival opened. We got out of the cab (we took a cab I think because we helped her bring this stuff up from the kitchen), and there was a Women Against Pornography picket in front of the event. The event was the *Penthouse* Pet of the Year Awards.... Peggy and I looked at each other: *oh my fucking god.* [JEN laughs] We had no choice, we had no money, we had to do the job. Besides, we had committed; it wasn't her fault. So, we said, 'OK, you're going to have to put us in the kitchen, we're not going to wait!' So, she put us in the kitchen. She made the most beautiful food. One of the things we had to do was scoop out these mussels, do something to them, put them back and garnish them. There were oysters, prosciutto, beautiful wines. And these people showed up and they would rip off a hunk of bread, make themselves a ham and cheese sandwich, and get a bottle of beer. I was like, *oh my god.* They announced the *Penthouse* Pet of the Year, and the woman stood up and she said that was very nice but she didn't want to do it! She said, 'I've got my own career now, my own business. I just think it would interrupt me'....

JEN: Wow!

LOIS: Peggy and I were backstage in the kitchen, with boxes full of her picture on the front page of the *Penthouse*, because they had already chosen her and published her picture. When it was over, there were tonnes of prosciutto hams, bagels, all sorts. So, we brought huge bags of food home, and we catered the opening night of the WOW Festival. That would have been 1981.

JEN: That's a great story. You've mentioned Spiderwoman. Is that the first theatre company you really joined, and how did that come about?

LOIS: Well, Lynn [Norris], who I mentioned did the Grotowski work with us, I maintained a connection with her. She had been asked by Muriel [Miguel] to join a group of women who were getting together regularly, not really to make a theatre company but to think about taking control of their own work. Muriel, as well as a few other women who had worked in the Open Theater, really suffered – it's a strong word but I can't think of anything else – because they were always the assistant director, the dramaturg; they didn't get any of the credit that the men did, like Jean-Claude van Itallie and Joseph Chaikin. That was a really good early lesson for me to see what happened when people worked collectively on a piece and one person takes authorship of it. They all complained of that. Roberta Sklar had worked with Joeseph Chaikin as an assistant director, as well as Megan Terry, and initiated a lot of the techniques. Megan Terry in particular pushed it on its political path, but didn't get any of the credit. So, that kind of thing was happening and Muriel wanted to get together a group of women and talk about that. Muriel had also been part of a group that had gotten a small grant to do some investigating around women's issues in theatre. She called together this group: Lynn, her best friend Josie [Josephine Mofsie], this Native American rights advocate – a wonderful woman, powerhouse, terrifying person – and a few other people. Lynn proposed me and told me they were having to have a conversation about that, because I would have been the youngest one and they weren't so sure about that. Anyway, they let me in the group.

JEN: How old were you?

LOIS: I was 25 when we actually started making work as Spiderwoman, so I would have been 23 or 24. We met once a week and did hardly any theatre work. We all talked about husbands and partners, situations and directors that we had worked with. Once in a while we would do one exercise. Then we'd go out and eat. I thought, *what is this?* But I was fascinated! [JEN laughs] Somewhere along the line, I thought this was a consciousness-raising group, actually. I thought, *why are they talking about their children, or their uncle?* But that was the nature of the way they talked, and worked. Then, Muriel got an invitation. It was a new music ensemble I was doing in the evening, and they wanted Muriel to contribute some performance. She said, let's do something called 'story-weaving', let's put together these stories, and let's call ourselves Spiderwoman. She described

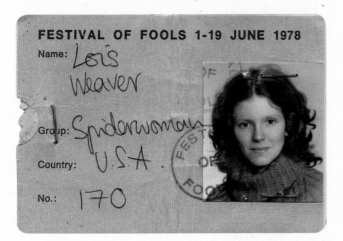

Lois Weaver festival passes, 1977 and 1978.

the reference to the Hopi goddess Spiderwoman. We did this one evening. It was me, Josie, Muriel, and maybe one other person. People liked it, and we liked it. Then Muriel got another little grant, and at that point she said, 'OK, I'm making a company.' In the meantime, her friend Josie had died, and the other one went off to advocate for Native rights in Washington, DC. So, she asked her two sisters [Lisa Mayo and Gloria Miguel], me, a student she had been working with at Bard College, and one other person to make this company, and we called it Spiderwoman. We started working on this piece called *Women in Violence*. That was the summer of 1975 because I went away for Naropa. By the time we started doing *Women in Violence* in the spring I'd already made this commitment to go and I really wanted to do that. I needed to get away from my boyfriend, I wanted to learn more about theatre, I'd spent a lot of money, so I went. I had to plug back in [when I came back], which was a little bit tricky but it worked. We made the show and performed it.

JEN: What do you feel you learned working with them?

LOIS: I definitely learned the value of the commonplace detail, and mundane aspects of people's lives, that talking about, sharing, and working through those things with a group is another way of working. It can produce material. I'm the kind of person, still, I don't say my sister's name. I say, 'oh, my sister', or 'my mother', whereas they were like, 'oh, Judy'. The familiarity with family, and detail, and the importance of that, it took me a long time to trust that. I learned that. I also learned how to work with fantasy. It was Muriel who taught us how to take our performance fantasy, and turn it into something we could make, that would fit into and build on the performance. I'm sure there are some other things, to do with how not to structure a theatre company around this structure of the family.... [laughs] Again, there's great comfort in that, but when it comes down to it, family is family; there were the three sisters against us. The power dynamics are never straightforward.

JEN: What were the highlights and some of your best memories of working with them?

LOIS: Well, finally being able to identify myself as a working performer in New York. I don't know if I'd even been able to articulate it as a dream, but it was. The next biggest highlight would be that we toured Europe. It had never occurred to me that we would be able to do that. Muriel said, 'I'm going to get us a tour of Europe, because that's how Open Theater survived; we're going to do that too.' I thought, *she's nuts, we're never going to get this*. She invited the director of the Nancy Festival to come and see a run-through of this tacky little performance group. He loved

Top: Spiderwoman's *An Evening of Disgusting Songs and Pukey Images* (1979). Left to right: Peggy Shaw, Lois Weaver, Lisa Mayo, Pam Verge, and Gloria Miguel. Photo courtesy of Spiderwoman Theater.

Bottom: Lois Weaver in Spiderwoman's *The Lysistrata Numbah!* (1977) with Pam Verge, Lisa Mayo, and Gloria Miguel. Photo courtesy of Spiderwoman Theater.

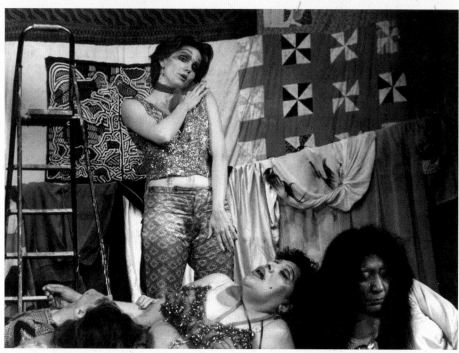

us and booked us for the Festival. From that one gig we toured, as a company, I think, a good five times. There was one devastatingly long, totally dysfunctional tour, but yeah, we toured a lot. I obviously built my system for how I got to London, based on Spiderwoman.

JEN: Then you joined up with Peggy.

LOIS: Yeah, one of the members of Spiderwoman Theater, who was not Muriel and not functioning as the director, Lisa, who happened to be the older sister, decided to invite Peggy – unbeknownst to the rest of us – to join the company for this performance of *An Evening of Disgusting Songs and Pukey Images*. Her reasoning for doing that was, supposedly, because it was a cabaret and Peggy, in Hot Peaches, had a lot of cabaret experience. And she probably had a little crush on Peggy. So, Peggy joined Spiderwoman.

JEN: Then you started collaborating more with Peggy?

LOIS: Well, we became lovers, while we were on her first tour. This is another documented story, I'm sure, because I've done it in performance. I had met Peggy myself two years before and she'd said, 'I'll give you two years to come out'. When she joined the company I was really thrilled because I was trying to come out, but I was going to bars, getting drunk, and it wasn't much fun. Once Peggy joined the company, a lot of lesbians started hanging around, her friends, her gang from the East Village. I met a friend of Peggy's and was able to have a short, but a good little relationship. So, I came out as a lesbian. We went on tour and of course we fell in love, finally. I think I was chasing her. I had been chasing her for years, probably! [JEN laughs]

But we had to keep it secret, because there was a rule in Spiderwoman that you couldn't shit where you eat. That rule, I remember the moment it came about; it would have been much earlier, when we were on tour in Amsterdam. The three sisters kind of had a crush on the same guy, who was this really fantastic Argentinian clown – it was kind of a professional crush. In all this talk of working with him, Muriel would say, 'You can't shit where you eat.' That became the edict of the company. Of course, it had never been a problem because there had never been any lesbians or lesbian activities within this woman's company. It wasn't a problem... but that was what it was, and we knew it would be really frowned upon. So, we kept it secret. Keeping it secret was probably a really good thing for us, because the whole reason for not 'shitting where you eat' is because your personal life interferes with your work. Peggy and I were determined not to let anything interfere with the work. The work always came first, and the relationship second. That just became a muscle that

we developed and maintained – sometimes probably to our own detriment. We kept it secret for quite a while.

JEN: There seems a double standard. Spiderwoman's sisters obviously had relationships, as sisters. So, their biological relationships were permitted, but your family of choice, your lover...

LOIS: You're absolutely right. I don't think I was sophisticated enough to think about it in those terms. Also, I think there was an intense power dynamic, partially to do with age (I was much younger), partially to do with that Muriel was the director, and also something to do with the racial aspect of being white in a primarily Native company. That's probably really low down on the list, but it was there. You couldn't challenge Muriel, because if you challenged Muriel the other two would come after you – and they were formidable women. Lisa, bless her heart, has passed... but whew.... I'll never forget the time when Peggy and Muriel were naked in the dressing room, and they came at each other [as though to fight]. When I looked up, there was Lisa and Gloria behind Muriel. I thought, *this is what they mean by the phalanx*, you know? Then there were others of us sort of ... [standing by feebly]. Anyway, they didn't come to blows. Me and the others, not quite the same size, not quite sure what the hell to do...[laughter].

JEN: You and Peggy ended up going a separate way from the others, and setting up WOW. Can you narrate that?

LOIS: It kind of happened simultaneously in a weird way, because we'd been touring so much with Spiderwoman, and there was real growing cultural energy in Europe around feminism – there were lots of women's festivals. On the tour where Peggy and I got together in 1979, there was a really big women's festival at the Melkweg in Amsterdam. That's where we met Pamela [Camhe] and Jordy [Mark] and we started to talk. Peggy said, 'I've always wanted to do a lesbian festival in New York.' I started saying how I didn't understand why we didn't have a similar structure around theatre, where you can go and have a drink, see one show, stick around and see another, go to a movie, go dancing, all in the same venue – which was a European thing we'd seen everywhere in the festivals. I wanted to bring that to New York. Peggy wanted to have a lesbian festival in New York. These two other women were, I think, very excited by what they had encountered, and wanted to do stuff too. We got together, and started fantasising about this. And at the same time, I guess for that first festival I wanted to work on this idea, *Split Britches*, that I'd been thinking about for a while. I never thought about starting my own company, I just wanted to do a project. So, the first WOW Festival, and the very first, fragile little showing of *Split Britches*, happened in 1980. For the second festival, I had worked on the play, and that's when Deb [Margolin] got involved. We presented it under the auspices of Spiderwoman, but that's when we knew we couldn't do it any longer, because we'd already begun to split the power, and change aesthetically. I wanted to do something different from what I'd been doing with Spiderwoman.

JEN: How was it different?

LOIS: I wanted to play with different kinds of subtleties. Certainly everything we did with Spiderwoman was very episodic. It was fabulous, shouty, rude, big, vulgar, *obvious*, you know, in ways that I did love, but I wanted to find ways to make something a little more subtle. I was interested in ideas of *relations*. I would have called it relationships then: relationships between women obviously, between family members, but also between women and their environment, women and their objects.... I was interested in *moments*, and also portraiture, and *layering*. We had talked about layering with Spiderwoman, but I wanted a deeper kind of layering. For instance, when I first started working on *Split Britches*, that was because I had read this book *Hillbilly Women*,[76] and I thought, 'Oh my god, if she's going to tell that story, I need to tell my story!' Suddenly I got competitive and I would go, '*No*, I have to tell this story.' That set me in the direction of wanting to work with material from my family. But I also had this fascination with bag ladies, and how the bag ladies looked the same. Then around about that time *Grey Gardens*[77] came out and I started thinking about how we could make those associations across different environments – working with personal story (which I had learned to work with in Spiderwoman), weaving that into the context of a bigger story (which was something we hadn't really done with Spiderwoman).

JEN: Could we backtrack a little to WOW? WOW was two festivals, but then also a venue that had longevity....

LOIS: Yes; we did two festivals. In 1980, we were in Andy Warhol's old Electric Circus on St. Mark's Place. It had already been turned into something else, but we were kind of thrilled by that. We did what we said we were going to do, which was to put together pieces that would inspire people to come and see one, and then happen to see another. We were trying to broaden the lesbian palate slightly. It was international, we brought people from all over, and

we worked with a sort of 'party', clubby aspect of it. We did lots of extra things in the bar; kissing booths, stuff like that. We had lots of events leading up to it to support it, because we had no funding. Then we did another one in 1981, where, again, we had no funding, but we got different kinds of support because international artists could get their governments to get them here. That was in another venue, the old Ukrainian Home on 2nd Avenue, and several other venues. Several theatres were willing to put stuff on.

After that second festival there was a collective of about 10 or 11 women who had really volunteered to make it work. We wouldn't have called ourselves a collective, but we kept meeting and having brunch, because we had such a good time. We talked about what would happen if we had an ongoing storefront space. At that point I was more interested in that than this big 'one off'. We got a storefront and established that with probably about eight or 10 people, and started to run it as a collective – sort of. It took us a while to learn how to do that. So, we finished the festival in autumn 1981, and it wasn't until 1983 that we got it together and opened and became established as WOW Café.

***

Jen's note: We took a break at this point in the interview. When we reconvened for another half hour, I failed to record us properly. Maybe this is the flaw in the weaving, the puncture Muriel and Lois refer to in the interview that follows. While I didn't record what came next, I did take notes. I asked Lois what her principles were as a director, and she said she was interested in collaborating, responding, and orchestrating. I asked her the same about being a performer and actress and she talked about not wanting to be in character. Regarding the importance of word play in her work, she spoke of her love of 'overblown language from Southern Gothic writers such as Tennessee Williams'. On the differences between performing solo, in a duet, or in a group, she said that solo work was not her preference, that she was more interested in group work for its processes than its products, and that work on timing with Peggy was 'a complete pleasure'. Projects she had most enjoyed included *Belle Reprieve*, because she wanted to collaborate and work on that area with that team, and *Ruff* and *Lost Lounge*, where she had trusted her impulses and fine-tuned them. My final question was, what would you like to make or do that you haven't yet made or done? Her reply: 'Something virtuosic.'

Top: Lois Weaver in Spiderwoman's *An Evening of Disgusting Songs and Pukey Images* (1979), The Melkweg, Amsterdam. Photo courtesy of Spiderwoman Theater.

Bottom: Spiderwoman's *The Lysistrata Numbah!* (1977). Left to right: Lois Weaver, Pam Verge, and Lisa Mayo. Photo courtesy of Spiderwoman Theater.

Lois Weaver interviews Muriel Miguel

Lois Weaver and Muriel Miguel

This conversation between Muriel Miguel of Spiderwoman Theater and Lois
Weaver took place at the Library of Performing Rights, conceived and curated
by Lois, on 26 June 2014, during the Hemispheric Institute Encuentro IX at
Concordia University, Montréal.

> I remember when we started working I didn't think my stories were interesting. And you encouraged me. You encouraged all of us to talk about the everyday.

Lois: I've been wanting to sit down and have a conversation with you for a long time. To talk about process and the kind of things I learned from you, the kind of things we were doing at the time and how that might've progressed for you and how I might've taken them forward. And about the creation processes that I think both you and I depend on now. Storytelling and layering are the two terms that come to mind first.

Muriel: Storytelling to me is layering. You know, you put one layer upon another layer, upon another layer. And you dip down and you pull out a colour that goes through all of it. I bring this up all the time.... Before Spiderwoman there was Josephine Mofsie and Lois Weaver and myself, and we did a piece at this church and we talked about... we didn't talk about creation stories, we talked about revelation. And we put together a piece that put Josie up on these blocks – Josephine was a real artist in beadwork and weaving and she was wonderful and she had this piece of finger-weaving that she dropped down and she sat on this stool. Remember?

Lois: I remember it was part of a new music evening. I didn't even know what new music was at that point... or what I was doing.

Muriel: You came in with a dream about making love to Jesus.

Lois: Oh, right... that old thing. That story, that I walked up to Jesus and he put these great big arms around me and sort of lay me down. I realised later that it was probably a big, tall butch woman, with big arms, and who crumbled into all these big stones and fell on me.

Muriel: And I did a story about a butterfly and the butterfly talking to me. So we had these three pieces together: I had this big river flowing through and I was on one side, Lois was on the other side, and Josephine up there finger-weaving. She told spider-woman stories, which are creation stories, with finger-weaving. And it was the first time I started to think about this, and we used the sound and the movement to figure out who came next -

Muriel: And so now that's what I use all the time. Sound and movement. What comes next? How do you make that creation story? How do you support that creation story? How do you support the dream or the butterfly...?

Lois: We called it story-weaving. And that became the basis of the Spiderwoman method – how to weave these three stories together. Because that was how my dream ended... Jesus was on one side of a river and I was on the other and we were waving. I remember the river turning into yours. So we wove, not just the sound and movement and text, but the visual. But it was the story that we always started with. That's something I wanted to ask about too. You have absolute faith in the story. I remember when we started working I didn't think my stories were interesting. I thought they were very mundane or incredibly personal. And you encouraged me. You encouraged all of us to talk about the mundane, to talk about the everyday. To use those details. And sometimes we'd come together to work, tell stories, and I'd think, 'I don't have a story.' Then as we began to talk it would be the story of my day, or the story of our nights. Sometimes that would lead to a more painful or more in-depth story.

Opposite: Spiderwoman's *The Lysistrata Numbah!* (1977). Left to right: Lisa Mayo, Lois Weaver, Gloria Miguel, Pam Verge, and Muriel Miguel. Photo courtesy of Spiderwoman Theater.

Muriel: I remember my older sister saying, 'Oh, I don't have any stories about violence,' and I'd say, 'Do we come from the same family?' But a lot of those stories came out in that first piece, *Women in Violence*, that we did in 1975.

Lois: Where do you think you developed such faith in the everyday?

Muriel: From under the kitchen table. I think about it in terms of how my family, and plenty of Native families tell stories. Whether it's a bad story, a sexy story or whatever, it's like, 'Oh boy, you know what happened?', and you act it out. Kids are not supposed to know about these stories, right? And I remember being under the kitchen table hearing a story and I went back and told my aunts and uncles. It was a real sexy story. I had no idea what I was saying. And I remember my mother coming in and my aunties and uncles jumping on her. 'HOW DARE YOU TELL STORIES LIKE THAT IN FRONT OF THIS CHILD? WHERE WERE YOU? WHAT KIND OF FRIENDS DO YOU HAVE?' But it was a great place to hear these wonderful stories. And they can be how Uncle Joe met Aunt Lizzie. They're very little stories that are about your family. They're who you are. And I think of that circle, the family. And then I think who that family is within the tribal community. And then in the whole community – who are they across North, South, Central America. And every one of these places has stories. So you see, I never think of them as mundane.

Lois: I knew you were going to pick up on that word. I have learned, through you, to love the word mundane. Let's think of it as everyday. And while I learned to love the everyday, what I really learned from you was to trust the personal, what it meant to tell my story and to trust the detail of my day and to use that personal detail as material. Is there something else besides family that helped influence your ability to talk personally on stage or to use that personal material?

Muriel: Well, Open Theater certainly was helpful. It was funny because in a way they thought they 'discovered' storytelling, that storytelling was like a new invention. And the director Joe Chaikin would say, 'Muriel, you're such a great storyteller.' But I understood storytelling from my toenails up. Everybody in my family told stories. So when people come into a group, I really expect them to tell stories.

Lois: I think one of the things I learned from you through story-weaving is how to use listening. In terms of composition, you helped me learn to listen to the thing that comes next and not to think through the logical thing that might come next. That's something we worked a lot with – how to slam one thing up against the other to create a different type of meaning.

And another thing that I consider one the foundations of my practice is the use of fantasy, something that you brought into the Spiderwoman collective when we were starting to work together. That for me is the bedrock of my practice at the moment, and I wondered where you think that came from for you, because I remember the day that you said, 'OK, what is it that you want to do on stage?' And I said, 'Ah, no one's ever asked me that before.' Or you'd say to Gloria, 'What do you want to do?' And Gloria would say, 'I want to be Juliet.' And you'd say, 'Fine. You can be Juliet.' Or you'd say to Lisa, 'What do you want to do?' And she would say, 'I want to sing opera and levitate.' And you'd say, 'Fine, go do that.'

They put their hands down the grizzly bear's mouth and pulled it inside out. And so the bear tickled himself to death.

Muriel: I think it goes back to dancing, you know. When I was dancing at the Henry Street Playhouse[78] – everything I did was wrong. My breasts were too big, my hips were too big. One of the teachers would say, 'Oh, you know when Muriel is coming on.' So, I felt like I was always trying to be a tall, thin dancer. And everyone was dancing to Vivaldi and Bach and I wasn't interested in that. I liked it, and when I'm working as a teacher I bring it in. But I wasn't interested; I was interested in pop culture. I remember doing a dance to Reggae on a yellow chair. I remember doing a dance with a trombone – I can't play a trombone. I always felt like everyone was going downstream, and I was going upstream. That's the way my head worked. So, my fantasy is that I can do – I can be anything. I can put on false eyelashes and be Liza Minnelli.

Lois: You absolutely brought that into the company and established that as our starting point: we can be anything and do anything. And you encouraged us to work with our flaws. Flaws because you said that the Hopi goddess Spiderwoman always left flaws in her creative work so that the spirit could come and go.

Muriel: Reality is the big flaw. I'm fascinated with that. I'm fascinated with *The Real Housewives*.[79] There are these women with perfect noses talking about their teeth or their stuff.... It's so opposite to who I am and it's fascinating to think that this is what these people think about all the time. It's so not real that you feel like if you're looking for the flaw in there that would let the spirit out, you'd have to puncture the TV.

Lois: That's another thing that I learned – not just to allow for the mistake but to actually capitalise on the mistake.

Muriel: That's what I was talking about. It's that these people are so perfect there's no mistakes. There's no room for anything. And that's what we are all proud of, that we all have these mistakes. You know? Our voices aren't perfect. We're fat. Skinny. Funny.

Lois: Yes, including being funny. We started early on as a feminist theatre company when women weren't supposed to be funny. And you were determined that we were going to be funny.

Muriel: I went to so many feminist events where I was going, 'Oy, my head.' They just kept hitting you on the head and you're like, 'OK, OK, I get it, I get it.' So I was determined that we were going to be funny. So for *Women in Violence* we hounded my older sister's husband for dirty women jokes. He gave us all these awful jokes, and we put them into the show. You know, like, 'Hey, hey [whistles] pretty.' And she'd turn around. 'Not you, ugly.'

Lois: Yes, in *Women in Violence* we decided to look at violence through the lens of the male prerogative of the offensive jokes. Not the dirty jokes, the offensive jokes.

Muriel: One of the early things I remember from when I was a kid, is a story of somebody facing a grizzly bear. They put their hands down the grizzly bear's mouth, all the way down till they got its tail and pulled it inside out, so it was reversed. And so the grizzly bear tickled himself to death. That was the whole idea.

Spiderwoman's *Women in Violence* (1975).
Clockwise from top left: Lois Weaver, Muriel Miguel
and Pam Verge, Lisa Mayo, Gloria Miguel.
Photo courtesy of Spiderwoman Theater.

I wasn't sure you really wanted me in the group because I was too young – too white probably – a little too Southern...

Lois: That was a really good representation of the kind of the thing that we were trying to do with popular culture. I think we were trying to get inside and pull it out by the tail.

Muriel: I mean we polarised many a festival.

Lois: I remember on one of our first tours out of New York we went to Boston where we were produced by some academic feminists... this was in 1975. And I remember how upset they got with us, because after the show we sat around putting our make-up on. They started to challenge us and questioned our 'dialectical thesis'. We went home and stayed up all night trying to think what's wrong with us. 'Something must be wrong with us, because they don't like who we are, they don't think we're feminist.' And we came to the conclusion that they were the feminists and we were the women that they thought needed to be liberated. And we were fine with that.

Muriel: I also remember going to Philadelphia, and you were performing as a bag lady. And you started outside in the crowd, while the rest of us were inside. And as you were walking around these ladies – this is, the NOW convention, you know, the National Organization for Women – they got really anxious and wanted to make sure that you behaved yourself. They didn't want to let you in the performance space. I was thinking the other day about CR [consciousness-raising] groups. Remember the CR groups? No one refers to them anymore.

Lois: We kind of started out that way. Although, we wouldn't have used those words. Muriel, you got together a group of women because you wanted to make theatre with women and about women and women's stories. We were all sort of outsiders in our various ways and we found a way to work that embraced the outsider-ness. We didn't come together as feminists to make work. We came together as artists to make work that was feminist. And the focus was always on the work and the creation and if you tried to get one definition of feminism out of all of us, it wouldn't have happened

Muriel: No. It wasn't going to happen.

Lois: That was a survival thing and our strength was that we embraced our difference and we didn't focus on the politics; we focused on the work and let the politics come through. Anyway. We got together once a week and basically we'd talk about our partners and complain about husbands and talk about children and then go out to eat after we did maybe one exercise – one creative exercise together, and then we'd meet up the next week and do something like that again. And it was like a consciousness raising for me, although we would never have said that. And I remember thinking that I had gotten in by the skin of my teeth, remember? Because I wasn't sure you really wanted me in the group because I was too young – too white probably – a little too Southern.... And it was only because we got this new music gig where we did the story-weaving that we sort of brought it round from just meeting once a week and complaining about things and talking about things and telling bad jokes and -

Muriel: - and warming up to -

Lois: - we warmed up to do nothing, usually, but it was fun and it WAS the beginning of Spiderwoman because after the story-weaving you wanted to start a company.

Muriel: That started because Josephine Mofsie passed. So I was determined to start a group and do what I wanted to do and I got this small grant and I started to ask people I wanted to work with to join me. I wanted to work with my sister. Gloria wanted to work with me. My older sister Lisa didn't want to at first because she didn't want to stand on her head. She would come to see all the stuff that I was doing and she would say, 'Muriel does wonderful things but I can't stand on my hands.'

Lois: You asked your two sisters, Gloria Miguel and Lisa Mayo and then you asked me and a couple of other people, Brandy [Penn], and Pam Verge, and we started to work on *Women in Violence*, and after we did a piece called *The Lysistrata Numbah!*, where we actually made a vow that we wouldn't have sex until we got the show made.

Muriel: I still have that vow at home. I think I lied.

Lois: You always thought I lied! I didn't stand a chance in that group. They always thought I was lying. And sometimes I was. You don't know what it was like being confronted by the three of you. 'No, no, really I didn't.... OK, maybe I did.' And that was how Tammy WhyNot was born, in *The Lysistrata Numbah!*

Muriel: And then after that we did *An Evening of Disgusting Songs and Pukey Images*.

Lois: It was a cabaret about romance, and we did that in 1978 and then we went on a six-month European tour. We had a gig in May and September and we mistakenly thought we could fill the in-between. And there were by then 12 of us on the road.

Muriel: Lisa brought in Peggy -

Lois and Muriel: [simultaneously] She didn't tell us.

Muriel: She wanted Peggy to be in the company so she invited Peggy and we all showed up for our first rehearsal and Peggy was there. We said, 'What's Peggy doing here?' And Lisa said, 'I invited her.'

Lois: And she became a member of the company. And on that tour, we had to beg and borrow and divide. We couldn't afford for all of us to go to London, so half of us stayed in Amsterdam while the others went to London and we made smaller pieces so that we could move around and survive. We made a piece called *The Fittin' Room: One Size Doesn't Fit All*, which was our 1979 response to a feminism that was trying to put us all in the same category. Then the other small pieces that we made were – *Friday Night* -

Muriel: - *Friday Night*! Date night, date night -

Lois: - which was a piece about loneliness, and I remember we wrote a punk song.

Muriel: ... that punk song... oh my God. That's so funny.

Lois: And that brings me back to popular culture. I think that's something that is big in my practice and something that you're still doing in yours.

Muriel: Pop culture. Well, recently, I've been working mostly with Native people... the last 15 years or so. And I remember one time I was at a big pow-

The focus was always on the work and the creation and if you tried to get one definition of feminism out of all of us, it wouldn't have happened.

wow, and there were these guys breakdancing. And, I was thinking, I've seen breakdancing in New York, but how did it get here? They had these big satellite dishes and these kids were seeing a lot that they had never seen, because these reservations were pretty isolated. But now that they are seeing all of this, what does it mean to them? In the same way, what did it mean to me when I was 20 and choreographing to Little Peggy March or The Chiffons? And I saw the same thing happening here with these kids. They were, you know, wiggling across their little piece of cardboard and I realised how important it was. It's not going to go away. None of this is going to go away, this part of the pop culture that people are telling you is low-brow, and because it's low-brow you shouldn't use it. But we use everything we can. I remember once we were at a Sun Dance and we were trying to get in and Dennis Banks, who was a big activist as I was growing up, came in and said, 'I'm sorry but this is for Native people. This is our Sun Dance. This is our tradition. This is only for Native people.' And this man said, 'Well, you're speaking English. If you're speaking English, you're not really traditional.' It was like, here we go again. So Daniel got on the PA system and he talked to all of us. It was really early in the morning – you know we start sun-dancing at 6am. He said, 'We use everything. If we have to use English, we'll use English. If we have to use Spanish, we'll use Spanish. We'll use everything we can to fight for what we think is right.' That's how I feel about pop culture. We're using, I'm using, everything for that reason.

Lois: Maybe here's a good place to wrap up.

Muriel: There's one more thing... sometimes when you're feeling so down and so blue and you didn't get the grant that you wanted, nothing's coming through... but I see that Split Britches is working and I go to see Split Britches. And I say, 'That's why I'm working.' Because I see it right there... thank you for being that encouraging.

Lois: And thank you for the legacy, the lineage. We are connected in that way. Thank you for giving me all the tools that I use to make it possible to make the work that I make and make it possible for other people to make the work they make. I feel really, deeply connected to that lineage and that legacy and that's why these conversations are important... to talk about where things come from and also think about where they might be going.

Muriel: And to pass it on. You know, Split Britches is passing it on. Spiderwoman's passing it on, and that's so important. There's no point in hoarding it, you know? We started out the same way with Split Britches – and I have to say this – the big split-up that happened with Spiderwoman, right? My sister said, 'They wanted to be lesbians; they wanted to turn us into lesbians.' And Peggy was going round saying things about my sister.... In a group like Spiderwoman, there was all this thinking and talking and wondering, and out of it we became mentors... but then people have to go their own ways. And even if the mentor is saying, 'No, you're going to stay with me, you're going to do what I want', it doesn't matter. You have to know that mentors are there for a while, and you change mentors. And the ones that were being mentored become mentors. You have to be aware of that at a certain point and let go. And it doesn't mean you're losing. That's one of the things I learned from Spiderwoman; at that point we thought we were losing these people. But it wasn't that we were losing them, it was that they were going on to do something else.

Lois: We felt we were losing too. There were huge amounts of grief and loss in that split-up. And mainly because we worked as a family. But right up until we broke up, it worked. We were a company of eight to 12 women of all ages, from 20-something to 60-something – although we didn't know it at the time, because they were lying about their ages. We were working class and Native and white and African-American people who were together for a particular period of time and it worked for that time.

But then we reached a point where we couldn't sustain it. We had to reconfigure. I learned a lot from that experience. I found new ways to think about community. Community has all sorts of connotations associated with family and permanence. I learned to think of it as more temporary, that we could be a group of people who come together for a particular period to accomplish something but then disperse and reconfigure into something else. You're talking about passing on, but I like to think of it as a reconfiguring.

Muriel: Yeah. I was really excited about that time. We were young, we were mothers, grandmothers. You know... gay, straight, everything. We were so different, it couldn't last.

Lois: People grow at different times. We had to grow and do our thing. And you guys were doing a different thing. But after that period we looked down at the *Village Voice* one day and there were four different ads on the page, an ad for performances by Spiderwoman, Split Britches, Hot Peaches (who Peggy had started with), and Bloolips, a group that grew out of Hot Peaches. All of that lineage was sitting right there on that one page. Peggy said, 'The main thing is that we all keep working.'

Muriel: Yes.

Lois: Just keep working no matter what. And that's the big lesson. We keep working and we're still going.

Muriel: Yeah.

Lois: Strong.

Muriel: Kinda. [Audience laughter]

Virginia Started Over (from *Faith and Dancing*)

Lois Weaver[80]

Before the tornado,
I would sit on the swing
I would look up and deep into a blue that you hardly ever get on a map
Although sometimes you might see it on a globe
but then it's the ocean and not the sky.
I would go out after supper and wait for the first three stars to come out
and think about the first time I really heard the words
to the third stanza of Amazing Grace.

When we've been there ten thousand years,
bright shining as the sun.
We've no less days to sing God's praise
than when we first begun.

That was my first awareness of poetry, or infinity for that matter.
But then maybe that is the power of poetry. It pulls up the skirt of infinity.
I saw this from the swing. I realised so many things while swinging on that swing.
Almost too tall to make you believe it would stand on its own.
But not so tall that I couldn't imagine swinging high enough
to gain enough centrifugal force to wrap myself around the cross piece at the top.
It was in those fantasies of flight or actually orbit that I had thoughts.
I thought for instance, both suddenly and surely, that
I must have been an accident.
I am not sure why I thought that.
While swinging I might have imagined letting go.
Unwrapping my fingers from the chain and catapulting
through the air
over the rose bush,
toward the back steps.
Virginia would be standing at the door.
She would have on her hat and coat and gloves. It was her fortieth birthday.
She had just killed the pigs and made the sausage.
And it had been ten years last July since she finished canning an acre of peas
on her way to the hospital with her second and
what she thought would be her last child.
So she was going out. She was going to learn to drive.
And just as she pivoted on the cement step turned back
to make sure the coffee was off,
I landed in her arms. But she didn't fall.
She simply went back in the house and started over.

1   This text is adapted from Lois Weaver, *Faith and Dancing: Mapping Femininity and Other Natural Disasters*, an excerpt of which is reproduced in Lizbeth Goodman (selected and introduced by), *Mythic Women/Real Women: Plays and Performance Pieces by Women* (London: Faber and Faber, 2000), pp. 287-300 (pp. 289-92).

2   Lois Weaver, 'Theatre 479: Re-inventing the Southern Voice', College of William and Mary, 1997, unpublished class syllabus, cited in Ann Elizabeth Armstrong, 'Building Coalition Spaces in Lois Weaver's Performance Pedagogy', *Theatre Topics*, 15:2 (2005), 201-19 (p. 203).

3   Faith in Weaver, *Faith and Dancing*, in Goodman (intro.), *Mythic Women/Real Women*, pp. 292-3.

4   This is a claim of her alter ego Faith in Weaver, *Faith and Dancing*, in Goodman (intro.), *Mythic Women/Real Women,* p. 289.

5   Weaver, *Faith and Dancing*, in Goodman (intro.), *Mythic Women/Real Women,* p. 292.

6   Lois Weaver, 'Still Counting', published in Del LaGrace Volcano and Ulrika Dahl, *Femmes of Power: Exploding Queer Femininities* (London: Serpent's Tail, 2008), pp. 140-5 (p. 142), age 19. Lois has performed this text – and updated versions of it – widely since she created it; an updated version appears in the Afterwords to this book.

7   Weaver, 'Still Counting', in Volcano and Dahl, p. 141, age 5.

8   Lois Weaver, unpublished interview with Jen Harvie, New York, 12 October 2014.

9   Peggy Shaw and Lois Weaver, *Miss America*, in *Theatre in Pieces: Politics, Poetics and Interdisciplinary Collaboration, An Anthology of Play Texts, 1996-2010*, ed. by Anna Furse (London: Methuen, 2011), pp. 317-51 (p. 322). This 'You Never Told Me' section of *Miss America* also appears later in this book, p. 173.

10   Karenne Wood 'Virginian Indians: Our Story', *The Virginia Indian Heritage Trail*, 2nd edn, ed. by Karenne Wood (Charlottesville, VA: Virginia Foundation for the Humanities, 2008), pp. 12-23 (p. 12); available at <http://virginiaindians.pwnet.org/lesson_plans/Heritage%20Trail_2ed.pdf> [accessed 24 November 2014].

11   Wood, 'Virginian Indians', p. 14.

12   Wood, 'Virginian Indians', p. 15.

13   Wood, 'Virginian Indians', p. 20.

14   Wood, 'Virginia Indians', p. 22.

15   David Brion Davis, *Inhuman Bondage: The Rise and Fall of Slavery in the New World* (Oxford: Oxford University Press, 2006), p. 135.

16   Davis, *Inhuman Bondage,* p. 125; Davis cites Philip D. Morgan, *Slave Counterpoint: Black Culture in the Eighteenth-Century Chesapeake and Lowcountry* (Chapel Hill and London: University of North Carolina Press, 1998), pp. 659-60.

17   Davis, *Inhuman Bondage*, p. 125.

18   Peter Wallenstein, *Cradle of America: Four Centuries of Virginia History* (Lawrence, KS: University Press of Kansas, 2007), pp. 340-1.

19   Lois Weaver, unpublished interview with Harvie, New York, 12 October 2014.

20   Weaver, unpublished interview with Harvie, New York, 12 October 2014.

21   PSi#12: Performing Rights, 14-18 June 2006, at Queen Mary University of London. See 'PSi#12', *Queen Mary University*, <http://www.psi12.qmul.ac.uk/> [accessed 26 November 2014].

22   The Library of Performing Rights was co-created by Lois Weaver and the Live Art Development Agency. See 'The Library of Performing Rights', *Public Address Systems* <http://publicaddresssystems.org/projects/the-library-of-performing-rights/> [accessed 26 November 2014].

23   Lois Weaver, unpublished interview with Jen Harvie, New York, 10 October 2014.

24   Weaver, *Faith and Dancing*, in Goodman (Intro.), *Mythic Women/Real Women,* p. 290.

25   Weaver, *Faith and Dancing*, in Goodman (Intro.), *Mythic Women/Real Women,* p. 291.

26   Weaver, 'Still Counting', in Volcano and Dahl, age 11, p. 141.

27   Lois Weaver, unpublished interview with Jen Harvie, New York, 6 October 2014.

28   Weaver, unpublished interview with Harvie, New York, 10 October 2014.

29   Weaver, 'Still Counting', in Volcano and Dahl, p. 142, number 16.

30   Elliott West, *Growing Up in Twentieth-Century America: A History and Reference Guide* (Westport, CT: Greenwood Press, 1996), p. 183.

31   Elliott, *Growing Up in Twentieth-Century America,* p. 184.

32   Elliott, *Growing Up in Twentieth-Century America,* p. 194.

33   Faith in Weaver, *Faith and Dancing*, in Goodman (Intro.), *Mythic Women/Real Women,* p. 294; a similar but fuller version of this text is held in Split Britches Archive, MSS 251, Series 1, Box 1.

34   Weaver, *Faith and Dancing*, in Goodman (Intro.), *Mythic Women/Real Women,* pp. 297-8.

35   Weaver, 'Still Counting', in Volcano and Dahl, p. 142, age 19.

36   Weaver, 'Still Counting', in Volcano and Dahl, p. 143, number 19.

37   Weaver, 'Still Counting', in Volcano and Dahl, p. 143, number 19.

38   See Elaine Aston and Geraldine Harris, 'Imagining, Making, Changing: Split Britches', in *Performance Practice and Process: Contemporary [Women] Practitioners* (Basingstoke: Palgrave Macmillan, 2008), pp. 100-18.

39   Frank Marcus, *The Killing of Sister George* (London: Hamish Hamilton, 1965), p. 47.

40   Weaver, 'Still Counting', in Volcano and Dahl, p. 144, number 44.

41   Marcus, *The Killing of Sister George*, p. 81. Italics original.

42   For example, at Stanford University with Curious (Leslie Hill and Helen Paris) in 2013.

43   Jean-Claude van Itallie, *The Serpent* (New York: Atheneum, 1969), p. ix.

44 Joseph Chaikin, *The Presence of the Actor*, 2nd edn (New York: Theatre Communications Group, [1972] 1991).

45 Joseph Chaikin, 'From the Director' in van Itallie, *The Serpent*, xii-xviii (p. xiii). Italics original.

46 Chaikin, 'From the Director', p. xiii.

47 van Itallie, *The Serpent*, pp. 9-15.

48 van Itallie, *The Serpent*, p. 53.

49 van Itallie, *The Serpent*, p. 69.

50 Chaikin, 'From the Director', p. xv.

51 Short filmed extracts of the Open Theater's production of *The Serpent* are available on YouTube: 'The Open Theater "The Serpent" Part I', *YouTube* <https://www.youtube.com/watch?v=FB2OHclka5o>; 'The Open Theater "The Serpent" Part II', *YouTube* <https://www.youtube.com/watch?v=tzCXVvjxg6k>; and 'The Open Theater "The Serpent" Part III', *YouTube* <https://www.youtube.com/watch?v=WHtVcHwePNE> [accessed 25 May 2015].

52 Jean-Claude van Itallie, 'From the Playwright' in van Itallie, *The Serpent*, ix-xi (p. ix).

53 Loose Change Productions, Press Release for *Red Mother* by Muriel Miguel, New York, n.d. [2010], p. 2. <http://www.loosechangeproductions.org/PR_PDFs/RedMother_PR.pdf> [accessed 4 December 2014]; see also Anne Fliotsos and Wendy Vierow, 'Muriel Miguel', in *American Women Directors of the Twentieth Century* (Champaign, IL: University of Illinois Press, 2009), pp. 287-95 (p. 288).

54 Jean Cocteau, *The Eiffel Tower Wedding Party*, trans. by Dudley Fitts, in *The Infernal Machine and Other Plays by Jean Cocteau* (Norfolk, Connecticut: New Directions, 1963), pp. 151-78 (p. 161).

55 Cocteau, *The Eiffel Tower Wedding Party*, p. 164.

56 Jean Cocteau, 'Preface', in *The Eiffel Tower Wedding Party*, pp. 153-60 (p. 154).

57 Cocteau, 'Preface', in *The Eiffel Tower Wedding Party*, p. 156.

58 Tennessee Williams, *Summer and Smoke*, in *Period of Adjustment and Other Plays* (London: Penguin, 1982), pp. 95-175 (p. 123). Italics original.

59 Williams, *Summer and Smoke*, p. 123. Italics original.

60 Weaver, unpublished interview with Harvie, New York, 10 October 2014. Versions of this story also appeared in *Storyweaving* with Muriel Miguel and Josephine Mofsie (see Weaver and Miguel interview later in this book), and in Weaver, *Faith and Dancing*, though not in the excerpts in Goodman (Intro.), *Mythic Women/Real Women*.

61 Weaver, unpublished interview with Harvie, New York, 6 October 2014.

62 Weaver, unpublished interview with Harvie, New York, 6 October 2014.

63 Weaver, 'Still Counting', in Volcano and Dahl, p. 142, number 25.

64 Weaver, 'Still Counting', in Volcano and Dahl, p. 142, number 25.

65 Some details on *Bustin' out the Box* are held in the Split Britches archive in the Fales Archive and Special Collections at New York University, MSS 251, Series 1, Box 3.

66 Weaver, unpublished interview with Harvie, New York, 6 October 2014.

67 Weaver, unpublished interview with Harvie, New York, 6 October 2014.

68 Lois Weaver, in conversation with Jen Harvie, London, 19 May, 2015.

69 Spiderwoman Theater's website uses the word Indigenous: 'About Us', *Spiderwoman Theater*, <http://www.spiderwomantheater.org/SpiderwomanAboutUs.htm> [accessed 10 February 2015].

70 Weaver and Miguel, 'Lois Weaver Interviews Muriel Miguel', later in this book, p. 61.

71 Weaver, 'Still Counting', in Volcano and Dahl, p. 143, number 28.

72 Weaver and Miguel, 'Lois Weaver Interviews Muriel Miguel', later in this book, pp. 63-64.

73 Weaver, 'Still Counting', in Volcano and Dahl, pp. 142-3, number 28.

74 Weaver, 'Still Counting', in Volcano and Dahl, p. 143, number 28.

75 The Jesus Freak movement was a Christian subculture of the 1960s and 1970s with links to hippie cultures.

76 Kathy Khan, *Hillbilly Women: Mountain Women Speak of Struggle and Joy in Southern Appalachia* (New York: Doubleday & Company, 1973). Republished with new material as Skye K. Moody (Kathy Khan), *Hillbilly Women: Struggle and Survival in Southern Appalachia* (New York: Anchor, 2014).

77 *Grey Gardens* (Portrait Films, 1975) is an American documentary film by Albert and David Maysles (and others) featuring a reclusive upper class mother and her adult daughter, both named Edith Beales, who are near relations of Jacqueline Kennedy Onassis and live in a decaying mansion in East Hampton.

78 Muriel studied dance here with Alwin Nickolai, 'Creative Time Bios', *Spiderwoman Theater*, <http://www.spiderwomantheater.org/RM_Creatives.htm> [accessed 16 June 2015].

79 *The Real Housewives* is an American reality television franchise first broadcast by Bravo in 2006.

80 This text is adapted from Weaver, *Faith and Dancing*, in Goodman (intro.), *Mythic Women/Real Women*, pp. 294-5.

What does it mean
to be Femme?

Embrace your stereotype

Show your slip

Sleep with the enemy

SEP 5 5

Page 72: Lois Weaver, portrait for *Faith and Dancing: Mapping Femininity and Other Natural Disasters* (1996). Photo by Eva Weiss.

Above: Lois Weaver in early femme pose in her backyard in Virginia, 1955.

Virginia was the East (from *Faith and Dancing*)

Lois Weaver[1]

Virginia was the east.
She was that harsh reality of morning light.
Her face and arms were creased by the sunlight
But under her cotton dress she wore the moonlight white skin of a city girl.
Her breasts were strong, her feet were bare and her legs could have been dancing
if her knees hadn't failed her from too much kneeling.
Not from praying
but from planting beans and waxing hard wood floors
And the desire was there.
I found it in the debris of the tornado
She had wrapped it in newspaper to keep it from yellowing.
Foolishly I never noticed the date. I didn't develop those skills.
I confined my research to the out of doors
and never learned to look for facts in print.
Probably because the Bible had been such an unreliable source.
So I guessed about the dress. It was Virginia's prom.
Virginia was the baby of the family of Angells by birth
and carpenters by trade who worked and saved to buy their baby a long lace dress.
Because although her hair was red
they knew she could be the Jean Harlow of her senior prom.
I have no idea what she intended to wear under that dress.
Maybe something like Harlow's pink satin skin
that made you wonder is that real or just the colour of flesh.
Just like the use of different colours for different areas on a map
give the mistaken impression those areas are that colour.
Green and yellow for land black or red for boundaries and the works of man.
And that was Virginia's first disappointment.
After the men in her family had worked so hard to dress her
in lace and satin the colour of skin,
the market crashed.
And while men in other places threw themselves out of windows and off bridges,
Virginia silently wrapped her lace gown in newspaper
and packed it in her hope chest.
It was 1929 the year the dance was cancelled.

Opposite: Lois Weaver's early 'femme on her own' photos. Clockwise from top left:
Her first stage, standing on the family barbecue built by her father, 1951; A solo visit to her
grandmother, Blanche Gearheart Weaver's house, 1954; Standing amongst the front yard
ornaments, 1956; Coming home from a Sunday drive, ca. 1952; Practising her bathing suit
competition for Miss America Pageant, 1955.

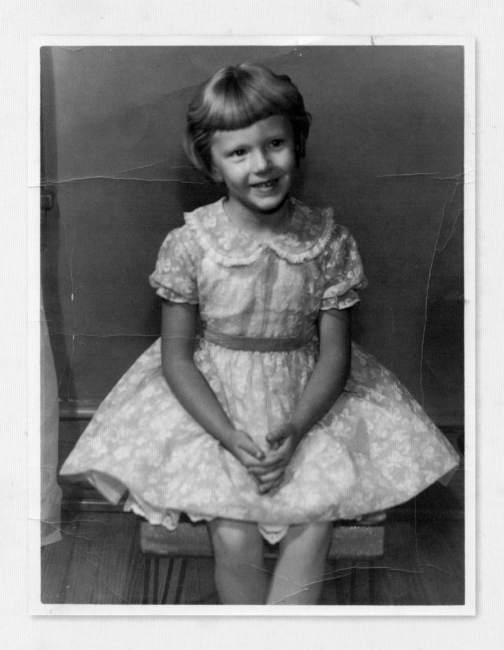

Subject and Object (from *Faith and Dancing*)

Lois Weaver[2]

What is it about perspective that makes it an old idea?
Is it the vanishing point? The one viewer, the one eye, the one story?
Once upon a time there was a dancer named Faith
who was the apple of her mother's eye, the object of her affection.
Let's talk about subject and object.
I'll diagram that sentence.
You the subject, look at me the object, who is the dancer,
Subject or Object?
Who has taken off her objects, her clothes.
But what about the dancer?
Is she the subject or object?
If she is the subject of this story what is the object?
Does that mean what is the point?
And if so doesn't that elevate the position of the object
to the entire reason we are here?
And in that case why wouldn't you want to be objectified if it meant
you were the very reason for living?
So what is the subject?
The dancer or the one who is danced round?
Did you know that if you put oestrogen in a lab dish
it immediately begins to dance to web to spread to connect?
If you put testosterone in a lab dish it stands still?
But it's the stress that confuses me.
To subject I think is to force your will on someone else.
To object is to refuse.
A subject is something you study.
An object is something you value or throw away.
An object is also a goal, like the object of this performance.
What is the object of this performance?
You see, that is the thing about dyslexia.
Each word is its own individual object.

Jesus Wept (from *Faith and Dancing*)

Lois Weaver[3]

Oh please, please brush my hair I would ask most anyone.

Especially the younger ones up the road.
I would ask my mother to brush my back.
I would lie across her lap and she would stroke my back with a hairbrush.
It's like that story of Brandon Teena or Teena Brandon
The girl who must have been dyslexic like me
because she reversed her name and gender.
She was a favourite among her girlfriends who thought they were going out with a boy.
She was their favourite because HE would brush their hair.
Brushing is a favoured feminine activity.
Like in church, my girlfriends and I would take turns brushing,
or combing if it was less conspicuous, the hair on each other's arms.
I could barely wait to be the one brushed.
Oh, I would brush but only if it meant that I could get brushed.
I would close my eyes as the preacher talked about how 'Jesus wept.'
We all knew THAT because it was the shortest verse in the bible.
It was a handy thing for an adolescent mind
who could only focus her mind on things short
like a pair of cut off Levis that she had waiting back home.
Perhaps that's why Jesus wept.
He wanted to be touched, brushed.
He wanted to be driven home after church
on a summer night with the crickets beggin' for it
and the honeysuckle choking back every desire,
pushing it back down the throat so it would last longer
so it would hurt more
so it would gather force for later
when the night cooled just past midnight
and the car windows were down
and you were already in and out of those cut off Levis.
On a night like that Jesus would have wept.
Would have fallen apart in tears
like he did in my dream.
I dreamt he came down off the cross,
fucked me
and then fell to pieces around my feet.
But what I remember are the arms.
These were not the arms of god or the father or the Baptist preacher
but the arms of a tall woman
with big hands that smelled of geraniums.

Lois Weaver as mascot for William Byrd Cheerleading
squad, 1954. Her sister Judy is on the far left.

Citizen femme

Jen Harvie

'She's sweet, complex and shadowy...'
Partial description of Lois's character Cora Jane Gearheart in *Split Britches: A True Story*.[4]

Dynamic Femme

Being and performing femme are fundamental to Lois Weaver's life and work. This may sound simple, but Lois's femme certainly is not. Femme is her dynamic identity, her persona, her politics, her erotics, and her playground. Femme is her career-long challenge to others, a secondhand satin glove thrown down gauntlet-style to second wave feminism's widely held suspicion that femininity inevitably capitulates to heteronormative patriarchy. Femme is also Lois's lifelong challenge to herself. It is a role she has fought to keep visible and independent in the long shadow cast by the towering butch in lesbian culture, in lesbian performance, and in her long-lived relationship with almost-six-foot-tall Peggy Shaw. In societies that are endemically sexist and ageist, where ageing women face ever-increasing and paradoxically simultaneous invisibility and scorn, Lois sustains a femme role that is sexually engaged, publicly visible, and simply powerful.

Some of the potency of Lois's femme is implied in the title she initially created for this section of the book: State of Femme. For Lois, femme is a big, lush idea and a dynamic, complex state of being. The phrase invokes a particular geo-cultural history of femininity, drawing on her background in the Commonwealth of Virginia in the American South, a region populated by Southern Belles such as Georgia's Scarlett O'Hara in *Gone with the Wind*[5] and Lois's fellow blondes, Californian actress Marilyn Monroe and Tennessee's singer-songwriter Dolly Parton. Like others in a long genealogy of human and mythical Belles, none of these women is ever simply a pawn of her femininity; all of them strategically *play* it, and they play it in ways that are impressively – though not unequivocally – in control. One of Parton's biographers calls her a '*smart* blonde',[6] and Lois is one too, both of them challenging the misogynist myth of the dumb blonde. Lois's femmes, like her Cora in *Split Britches: A True Story*, are frequently 'sweet' but almost always 'complex and shadowy' as well.

'State of femme' also suggests that femme is a kind of citizenship which brings particular affiliations, loyalties, beliefs and, frankly, rights. Citizen femme has subjectivity. She is never simply sexist patriarchy's object, its redundant 'spare rib', or its plaything. She is never reductively 'to-be-looked-at-ness', the passive object of a putatively active heterosexual male gaze.[7] She is always her own self-determining subject. In lesbian culture, femme is a self-consciously adopted role that actively values beauty, elegance, female power, femme eroticism, and many other characteristics besides. It does not assimilate the femme or, for that matter, the butch, to heteronormative gender and sexual roles; it troubles those roles.[8] As femme pioneer Joan Nestle writes in her 1992 article, 'The Femme Question',

Opposite: Lois Weaver marching with WOW and the Lesbian Herstory Archives in NYC Gay Pride March, 1986. Photo by Morgan Grenwald.

Butch-femme relationships, as I experienced them, were complex erotic and social statements, not phony heterosexual replicas. They were filled with a deeply lesbian language of stance, dress, gesture, love, courage, and autonomy. In the 1950s particularly, butch-femme couples were the front-line warriors against sexual bigotry [...]. The irony of social change has made a racial, sexual, political statement of the 1950s appear today a reactionary, nonfeminist experience.[9]

Femme is not entirely synonymous with femininity, and especially not heteronormative femininity. Lois performs the identity not just as adjectival femme *characteristics*, but as '*the* femme' – an active femme subject.

'State of femme' also implies that being femme is a *state* of being. Neither intractable nor permanent, it is instead dynamic, ever-changing, and likely to be only one of many simultaneous and sequential shifting states of being. The phrase aligns too with a state of mind, casting femme as an important way of thinking. In Lois's work, this mode of thought operates not so much along the lines of a 'feminine intuition', which manages to be both biologically determinist while nevertheless evasively unspecific. Rather, her work suggests that there are distinctive and important female ways of experiencing the world and therefore understanding it. It suggests that these female processes arise from the specificities of women's social experiences and bodies, through, for example, the particularity of female desire. Furthermore, like Lois's home state of Virginia, femme is curvy, and she is replete with femme memories of beauty queens and cheerleaders who 'observed' feminine categories, but were also physically active, artistically creative performers.

For Lois, femme is culturally constructed and dynamic; femme is compellingly informed by a long history of her performance; femme is wittingly adopted and deployed; and femme is powerful – as a social actor and a set of feelings. She is also who you are as a woman in the Virginia of Lois's youth. Within these contextual understandings of femme, I elaborate in what follows on Lois's performance of the power of femme, the challenges that femme presents for feminism *and* for Lois, the particular dynamics of butch/femme pairing and collaboration, and the implications of the enduring butch/femme relationship and the ageing femme. Throughout Lois's life and work, she performs and is femmes who are powerful and inspiring.

A Woman Who Just *Looks* Like She Needs a Little Help: The Power of Femme

Lois refers to her femme as a 'resistant femme'. This is a femme who occupies, enjoys and deploys femme attractiveness and its inherent power while refusing any intimations of subordination that are conventionally attributed to femme. As I noted in the introduction to the previous section of this book, Lois's working definition of her resistant femme is 'a highly competent woman who just *looks* like she needs a little help'.[10] Her femme uses others' perceptions of her as dependent as a subterfuge to get what she wants. Especially as Tammy WhyNot, Lois also uses femme as a catalyst for the social empowerment and inclusion of others who, like her, are often sidelined from positions of cultural authority. Her apparent naivety and dependence encourage others kindly to help her and, in so doing, to speak up for themselves.

Lois's femme performance does not rely on masculinity, it exploits it, ignores it, or, more powerfully, negates it.

Though to some the femme's sweetness may come across as naive, weak, and guileless, Lois actively deploys those features in order, wittingly, to get what she wants from those who would patronise her. '[P]retty is as pretty does and pretty doesn't have to tell the truth', asserts Lois's semi-autobiographical character Faith in *Faith and Dancing*,[11] summarising Lois's pick-and-choose approach to expectations of the good woman or girl. As Lisa Duggan and Kathleen McHugh put it in their 1996 'Fem(me)inist Manifesto', the femme 'occupies normality abnormally'.[12] In *Split Britches*, for example, 'simple' Cora appears to dote obsessively on such 'feminine' distractions as china dishes, handicrafts, and social visits. But Cora is neither *simply* simple nor entirely distracted: she is focused and ambitious and she repeatedly defeats self-styled leader Della (played by Peggy Shaw) in various contests of will.[13] Cora's aunt Emma Gay Gearheart (played by Deb Margolin) defends her naivety; 'That child don't even know what she's saying, really.' But Della counters, 'Like Hell she don't, Emma! Like HELL she don't!'[14] In *Belle Reprieve*, Lois's Stella, like Tennessee Williams', is confident in her own sexuality and commands her husband Stanley (played by Peggy Shaw), despite his masculine bravado. 'I don't have to spend long on the likes of you', Stella/Lois tells Stanley/Peggy, 'not one as experienced as I am. I know that your tension is sexual, it's a desire that I share in, but not for your pleasure, for my own.'[15]

Despite the power of Lois's various incarnations as femme, however, the man, and to a lesser extent the butch, continue to hold authority in patriarchal culture. As Peggy Phelan explores in her essay in this section, Lois herself has bemoaned the butch's easy visibility in contrast to the femme's struggle for respect and independence, especially when the femme is on her own. Nevertheless, Lois's femme is formidable, and she commands and manipulates attention. She deliberately exploits masculine gallantry, coaxing it in those who are well-mannered and cultivating at least a grudging respect for her ability to give as good as she gets in those who are not. For example, however reticent about performing or singing in public audiences might be when they initially see Lois's persona Tammy WhyNot, once they are exposed to their hostess's persuasive charm and coquettish coaxing, she soon has them joining in. Before they know it they're singing Holly Hughes' lyrics, 'She puts the cunt back in country',[16] from *Dress Suits to Hire*. Tammy charms her admirers beyond mere polite participation into proclaiming a kind of plain-speaking, county and western gynophilia. As this example suggests, much of Lois's femme performance does not rely on masculinity, it exploits it, ignores it, or, more powerfully, negates it. Flirting happily with their female audiences, Lois and Tammy daintily step out of a patriarchal cultural economy. To propose that either the butch or the man could ever be *more* powerful than Lois's femme is therefore far too simple, because she cunningly stirs up gendered power dynamics and audaciously recomposes them.

Certainly part of what Lois's femme wants is sexual attention. As she persuasively demonstrates, being femme does not mean a woman is sexually submissive, always responsive, or never proactive. On the contrary, being femme allows Lois to express her sexuality, flaunt her attractiveness, take the proverbial 'top' position, and flirt. Lois deploys this flirtatiousness onstage, especially in relation to Peggy Shaw's various roles, for example in *Lust and Comfort, Beauty and the Beast, Anniversary Waltz, Dress Suits to Hire*, and *Lesbians Who Kill*. But she also deploys it in her relationships with audiences. As Peggy Phelan recounts in her essay here, audiences revelled in Lois's titillated and titillating response to the play of Phelan's dancing red light on Lois's naked body in *Femme Lecture Dem*. Here and elsewhere, Lois's beautiful, sexy femme commands her audience's attention, celebrates female power, and both has and is sexual potency.

Lois plays the femme hostess. She is charming and welcoming, she attends to her guests' needs, she is flirtatious. But she is always prepared to pull the trump card command that she has spirited up her hostess's capacious sleeve, or concealed in her bra: 'be nice or leave'. The hostess's apparent subservience is a polite, pleasant, and even pleasing mask that perches lightly on the profound authority she actually commands in her role.

Lois's femme is powerful. She is powerful as a tool – for getting what she wants and for empowering others whom she conscripts as her gallant aides and fellow naives. And she is a powerful message. The femme is not supporting actor to the male or butch lead. She has her own, distinctive, enthralling authority.

Independent Femme: The Challenges of Femme

Lois has commented many times on the fact that organisers of women's performance festivals and feminist conferences who hosted Spiderwoman Theater in the late 1970s and early 1980s were frequently surprised, shocked, and even angry when the performers put make-up on *after* the show. For example, in interview with Kate Davy for Davy's history of the WOW Café,

> Lois Weaver recalled an incident backstage at a performance by Spiderwoman at a New England college. She was removing her stage makeup when a group of feminists arrived in the dressing room to lavish praise on the performance. The mood in the room changed completely, however, when she began to apply her *street* makeup. She could feel the visitors' disapproval of an act considered male identified. Weaver remembered, 'For the first time I understood the feminists thought I was one of those misguided women who needed to be saved.'[17]

In her performance lecture 'Still Counting', Lois remarks that 'by the time I was 30, I had been pushed up against the wall by a few prominent lesbian feminists asking me didn't I realise that Tammy's push-up bra was offensive, that I was just titillating and tempting the men in the audience and wasn't I *really* a lesbian?'[18] For those feminists who castigated Lois, glamming up like this reinforced patriarchal conventions about how women should look and behave, what position they should occupy in society, and therefore what power they should – or more precisely, should not – have.

From the perspective of the twenty-first century, such feminist attitudes may seem cruel and censoring, but also self-punishing and self-defeating, since they did – and still do – fuel misogynist dismissals of feminists as ugly, humourless, uniformly man-hating, and paradoxically *un*sisterly. It is important to remember, though, that this strand of feminist thought and action did important, pioneering work challenging oppressive behavioral restrictions on women. Without that work, women would not have the kind of freedoms to choose how we behave that so many of us enjoy today. Furthermore, the censure that these feminists' actions encountered demonstrates the necessity of their work precisely in challenging patriarchal control.

The femme is not supporting actor to the male or butch lead. She has her own, distinctive, enthralling authority.

Lois Weaver and Sheila Dabney in movie stills from
Shelia McLaughlin's *She Must Be Seeing Things*
(1987). Photos courtesy of First Run Features.

That said, the femme was something of an anomaly in the context of 1970s and 1980s western feminism, perceived by many feminists as an unsisterly sell-out to patriarchy. As several of the writers in this section of the book note therefore, the work of Lois and others to make the case for the femme was challenging, and remains so. But it is vitally important. It expands the range of what women can be beyond the conventions broadly accepted by both feminists and others from the 1970s on. As Lisa Duggan observes in her essay in this section, though butches audaciously cross gender lines while femmes have to 'massage' them, both lesbian butches and femmes challenge gender categories. As Lois observes, 'Butch and femme are words that give us some distance from the ideas of male and female.'[19] The work with femme that Lois and others practice *reclaims* femininity *from* patriarchy *for* women, so that a femme woman is understood not as an object in patriarchal culture but as an active, powerful subject. This work foregrounds not patriarchal but *femme* genealogies, including those between mothers and daughters. It asserts the femme as attractive to the butch in a lesbian economy that does not require men, but it also poses her as attractive to other women beyond butch lesbians and, importantly, it asserts the femme as attractive to herself.

Lois makes this range of powerful cases for femmes in myriad ways across her work. As I've discussed above, Lois's femme has demonstrated that she is by no means an inert tool of patriarchy; she shows the room for manoeuvre within the femme role and she demonstrates that it can be tactically deployed for women's advantage. Playing femme allows Lois and others to explore and promote the advantages of what Duggan calls in her essay 'femme-ininity': beauty and sexiness as well as charm, fun, and playfulness. Lois is by no means pious or arrogant about femme glamour; her femme enjoys cheap jewellery, false eyelashes, and big wigs. In this femme incarnation, Lois reveals and embraces the social construction of femininity. This is part of what Lois's characters discuss in a piece of her writing staged as a dialogue between two femmes named Sheila.

> SHEILA: I think that a resistant femme can embrace traditional images of femininity and resist them at the same time.
>
> SHEILA: Sounds like a lot of work. Just *being* femme is high maintenance.
>
> SHEILA: I like to think we can play the part and comment on it at the same time. That we can put on femmeness in a way that signals the fact that we *know* we are playing femme. There is a space between the photographic image and the real thing. It's in that misfit or crack that I like to think you can see the resistance. Sometimes for me it's the dirty fingernails or, thankfully now, the unshaved legs.[20]

Lois's resistant femme demonstrates that femininity is to-be-played-with and that such play is accessible, given the cheapness of so many of its accessories, the ease of creating misfitting features such as unshaved legs, and the welcoming openness of both Lois and Tammy. But the 'cheap' or slightly dishevelled femmes are not Lois's only femme personae. In incarnations rendered in plays such as *Belle Reprieve*, *Miss Risqué*, and *Miss America*, and captured in so many of Eva Weiss's hand-tinted naturally-lit photographs, Lois's femme is also sultry, thoughtful, and even weary. Lois's femmes actively engage with gender clichés in order to play with them, but at the same time these femmes fundamentally challenge the clichés.

'I struggle against my invisibility as a woman and a femme and yet there is a part of me that wants to keep it a secret.'

Importantly, throughout the work of Split Britches, Lois's femme is also a partner to Peggy Shaw's butch. This pairing both lampoons heterosexual and gender normativity while it values the queer alternatives that Lois and Peggy perform and it repeatedly shows lesbian desire for butch and for femme. Again, the femme is not just an object of desire within patriarchy; she is an object of desire between women, within lesbianism, and she is an active desiring subject herself.[21]

Given the dominance of the butch-femme dynamic in so much lesbian culture as well as so much of the performance work Lois and Peggy Shaw have made together, as Lois herself repeatedly observes (see Phelan's essay in this section), it can be very difficult to be 'a femme on her own' and to claim the value of femme *without* the contrasting presence of the butch. This is one of the challenges that femme poses to Lois: to show that the femme is never simply dependent on or an accessory of the butch, and that she has independent meaning. Lois likes a challenge. In *Femme Lecture Dem*, a collaboration with Peggy Phelan which Phelan discusses in her essay here, Lois performed her own independent pleasure in herself, lasciviously and delightedly playing with the red dot of light directed by Phelan on the landscape of Lois's naked body. As Phelan recounts the scene, Lois seems to be in charge of the dot; she is certainly in command of her audience. Phelan recognises that despite the fact she is directing the dot and delivering the lecture, she becomes somewhat superfluous – to Lois and the audience. Lois is on her own, with the dot and the audience; she is also demonstrably self-loving, playfully and sexily. Lois also proudly performs the femme's independent meaningfulness in *Faith and Dancing*. As Jess Dobkin observes elsewhere in this book, the performance stages 'a Heroine's Journey that can only be accomplished unaccompanied [...] without the butch companion to help or hinder'.[22] Lois's heroic behaviour in that performance is to foretell the social and natural disasters that women face and to ride those disasters, as she rides the red dot of light – independently and with spirit. Lois makes the case for femme, and for the femme on her own, while she also treasures the femme's semi-visibility. One of her Sheilas comments, 'I struggle against my invisibility as a woman and a femme and yet there is a part of me that wants to keep it a secret.'[23]

Butch/femme collaboration continues

Having noted the importance – to Lois and beyond – of recognising the femme's independence, negotiating the *real*, lived, butch/femme, mutually dependent, creative partner dynamic of her lifelong collaboration with Peggy Shaw is a crucially important part of what Lois does. Lois is absolutely committed to working for femme independence. But she is also committed to collaboration; and her most sustained and likely most sustaining collaboration continues to be with Peggy Shaw.

The two first worked together in Spiderwoman, then split off to form Split Britches with Deb Margolin in 1980. Lovers since the late 1970s, Lois and Shaw shared a small apartment in Manhattan's East Village for many years, where they also shared the raising of Shaw's daughter, Shara. Eventually, they got two apartments – about two blocks away from each other. Over time and increasingly separated by space since the early 1990s, when Lois started working about half-time in London, their romantic relationship receded, but their working partnership and their life partnership did not. They are both grandmothers to Shara's son. They co-own what they affectionately call 'the shack', a small cottage in upstate New York, and they spend a lot of time there together. They are each other's family. They remain indefatigable creative partners. They are in more than one long-term relationship with each other.

So, when I write that collaboration with Peggy Shaw is a crucially important part of what Lois does, I mean that 'collaboration' as artistic, emotional, material, social, and ongoing. Fundamentally, Lois is committed to collaboration, in love and in work. And across both spheres, in varying measures at various times, her collaboration is loving, charged, fulfilling, and difficult. As the title of Split Britches' 1994 play puts it, collaboration requires negotiating lust *and* comfort. Lois and Peggy are in it for the long haul; not just when it is thrilling, fresh, and sexy all over, but also as it shifts and its pleasures become perhaps less immediately obvious or perhaps simply more continuously comforting. Collaboration requires caring adjustment. It merits continuous effort, and it rewards it.

For Lois, the pleasures of collaboration are many. In developing performance, collaboration expands the sources of ideas and enriches their exploration. In performance, it offers diverse possibilities of comic and tragic timing and demands dynamic responsiveness to each other and the audience in the moment. Lois and Peggy have been inspired by vaudeville in this respect, and by couples from 1950s television programmes such as *Show of Shows*' Sid Caesar and Imogene Coco. In 'Still Counting', Lois says Peggy 'was George Jones to my Tammy WhyNot, Spencer Tracy to my Katharine Hepburn and I was Barbra Streisand to her Neil Diamond.'[24] These pairings come from importantly popular cultural sources, drawing on material familiar to both Lois and Peggy and to any of their audiences. These sources also feature couples united in conflict, where the power flits back and forth between the man and woman or butch and femme. But these are also couples who are, of course, *collaborating*. Together, these partner performers expertly balance the powerful shifting energy and humour of their scenes on a knife-edge with precise, delicious timing. They offer support; each partner is always there to spot the other. As longtime collaborators, Lois and Peggy have developed a vast shared vocabulary and a repertoire, not to mention an intricate, elaborate but second-nature rapport. They have also used butch/femme dynamics as stimulating creative elements to inhabit and play with across their careers and throughout their shared lives. This dynamic offers both keen attraction and powerful contrast. Butch/femme's proximity to male/female allows them to hijack conventional gender and sexual dynamics, only to drive those dynamics into places that inherently – and humourously, irreverently – challenge the prescriptiveness of heteronormative male/female cultural roles and rules. Collaborative performance also offers excitement, even lust, its energy and achievements indicating ever-expanding and thrilling possibilities. 'We played and displayed butch-femmeness in order to disrupt the norm, unsettle the status quo', says Lois. 'It was both sex toy and work ethic and the key to the theatrical success of the company. Playing femme mixed my business with my pleasure.'[25] As much as Lois enjoys solo work and sometimes finds collaborative work challenging, she thrives on the dynamism, mutuality, and frankly erotic thrill of collaboration.

In *Miss America*, the wisdom but visible fatigue of Lois's ageing femme leveraged critical insight into the ageing of her fellow traveller, the American Dream.

Enduring Femme

The femme has been and continues to be Lois's role throughout her life and, in particular, her performance career. Ageing in role has presented challenges, not least that of social intolerance for the ageing woman, the 'old crone' whom Lois describes in *Lust and Comfort*, with her 'brittle bones, faded lips, sagging tits, laugh lines, crow's feet, frog's legs'.[26] However, as ever, Lois converts challenges into opportunities, here, opportunities to explore bittersweet experiences. In *Faith and Dancing*, for example, the collapsing distance between Lois herself as a middle-aged woman and her experience of her mother Virginia allowed her to explore her relationship with her mother, and mourn her mother, with gentle sensitivity. In *Miss America*, the wisdom but visible fatigue of Lois's ageing femme leveraged critical insight into the ageing of her fellow traveller, the American Dream. *Miss America* showed the Dream's evolution as erosion, even as a betrayal of its principles. And it showed Lois and Peggy expressing a keen sense of loss and disappointment, as well as a subtle rebuke. These attitudes were conveyed through Peggy's diminished stature in her too-small suit and her repeated placement high upstage, where her proportionality with downstage Lois was skewed. They were also characterized through Lois's costuming as a faded, slightly fragile Beauty Queen, the paleness of her face and blue clarity of her eyes highlighted against a black dress and a bobbed black wig crowned with a sparkly tiara. Her age was emphasised by a string of pearls and an old fur coat, which she clutched around her, as though this ageing femme felt the chill of the wake evoked by her evolving America. Despite these intimations of despair or at least disappointment, *Miss America* also expressed a resilient hope for the future, epitomised in the photographic portraits of audience members which Lois-the-hostess takes in the show's opening sequence as she wends her way up close through the seating and which play back in a magnificent, huge slide show at the performance's close. Similarly, in *Lost Lounge*, Peggy and Lois's pleasure-filled play as the vaudevillian duo allows them to display what is squandered as such acts and their habitats become extinct with the rapid gentrification of Lower Manhattan. Such gentrification, Lois and Peggy suggest, is symptomatic of a world where neoliberal capitalist values increasingly crowd out other social values epitomised by so much of the duo's work and the values it models, such as mutual support and cooperation.[27]

Lois's femme has always claimed power, but aspects of the terrain of that power have shifted across the decades of her career. Her femme has always allowed her to express and explore her sensuality and sexuality. Over the many years when some feminists have viewed the femme as a tool of patriarchy, Lois's resistant femme has been part of important work which redresses that suspicion and recognises the multiplicity of the femme's many, often exciting, meanings. And as Lois and her femme-ininity age, her femme has combined fragility and authority in repeatedly bittersweet reflections on relationships between desire, pleasure, loss, sadness, and resilience.

A femme on her own

Peggy Phelan

Fall 2014

I thought this would be a very easy essay to write: a summary and appreciation of one of Lois Weaver's spectacular nights as a performer. I am a total fan and I loved the show. No problem, I thought. But each time I sat down to write about that night, a night lived long ago in London, I kept getting snarled up. No doubt memory distorts, but the knots aren't caused by accuracy of recall. The basic facts are clear enough. And yet, in recalling the performance now I feel deeply – and surprisingly – confused about where to locate myself. I was 'in' the performance and yet I write now, inevitably, from a position external to it. It occurred a long time ago in the early 1990s – when both Lois Weaver and I were different than we are now. In this account, Lois and I are characters, ciphers refracted through the language my present tense writing self brings to bear on the event as I recall it here.

Perhaps, as Walter Benjamin argued, this chasm between two distinct nows defines history itself. 'History is the subject of a structure whose site is not homogenous, empty time, but time filled by the presence of the now.'[28] I have written about this sentence on other occasions and have spoken about it in classes for almost 30 years. And yet, as I reach for this familiar sentence now, I feel both its explanatory power and its stark avoidance. Yes, history hazards forgetting the irreducible gap produced by the interval that divides this now from that one. *Yes, yes, yes.* But the pain caused by this chasm also comes from remembering it all too clearly. It is the strange rub between these two risks – forgetting completely that time has altered the past or remembering the time all too vividly – that perturbs me here. Additionally, Benjamin's smooth claim avoids the wounding bruise that accompanies our efforts to remember who we have forgotten to be even as we recognise why we no longer want to be as we once were.

In my attempt to celebrate one extraordinary performance event, I see anew how rare it was, how lucky I was to be part of it. And yet I have no regret about departing from it. 'Perhaps my best years are gone. When there was a chance of happiness. But I wouldn't want them back. Not with the fire in me now. No, I wouldn't want them back.'[29]

Thus, the recollection recorded here is an effort to release the performance that took place then into this other now – the now of my writing and the now of your reading. These words birds in search of the twigs that once held a nest in which we briefly sang. Performed under the wonderfully arch title, *Femme Lec Dem*, in the early 1990s, the piece was part of Queer School, a week-long set of pedagogical performances about queer sexuality and identity that Lois organised while she was co-artistic director of Gay Sweatshop.

Lois Weaver in *Retro(pers)pective*
(Lois Weaver and Peggy Shaw, 2007),
The Hemispheric Institute's
Encuentro, Buenos Aires.
Photo by Marlène Ramírez-Cancio.

Origins

('Any beginning in narrative cunningly covers a gap, an absence at the origin.')[30]

Lois and I were walking to a bus on a rainy night in London. It was late October or early November, 1992 or 1993. I had given a talk earlier in the evening and Lois attended. After the talk, there was a typically English reception – coffee, tea, and biscuits. A robust, somewhat shy crowd milled around politely. After a time, a smaller group of us left and went to an Italian restaurant. After dinner, a yet smaller group went to a pub where we had some pints. Then it was just me and Lois walking to the red bus. We had spent several hours together, but we had not spoken to each other much at all. We were pleasantly elevated, buzzy, but not drunk. As we walked through the slow grey drizzle, I was beginning to feel tired and was thinking about jet-lag and worrying if I would sleep so I was not utterly attentive to the beginning of the conversation. Lois was complaining that she was fed up by her current life and wanted to do something that would signal her independence, celebrate her creativity and allow her to claim the full complexity of her relationship to her work and life. After many years of entwining both her erotic and professional life with Peggy Shaw, Lois and 'the other Peggy' were beginning to explore different modes of attachment. I was mainly nodding and doing mild cheerleading, but was slightly distracted by worry about sleeping. Lois got my full attention, though, when her complaints produced the full-throated pronouncement that she wanted to be 'a femme on her own'. I found the idea immediately striking - rich in its contradictions and entrancing in its comic and erotic possibilities. Like many of Lois's ideas, it was rooted in the epistemology of desire and as such it was simultaneously alluring and troubling.

How might it be possible to conceptualise femme, without butch's shadow falling across its meaning? And beneath that puzzle, another issue: why would one want to? Wasn't the whole point of (butch) femme – as concept and as performance – to expose the dynamic structures of the sex-gender apparatus *tout court*? No one I knew ever referred to a 'femme butch couple'; it was always a 'butch femme couple'. Placing butch first in the appellation enforced a more extensive prioritising of butch generally. The idea of exploring femme without the shadow of butch ghosting it was, therefore, wonderfully enthralling. I agreed with Lois's claim that butches seemed to get a lot more attention than femmes in the academy but I was not convinced, despite her maniacal insistence, that butches also got 'way more attention' in lesbian bars.[31] With a hint of impatience, I told Lois that if she were determined to discover 'a femme on her own', we need not settle our disagreement about who gets more attention in bars. As 'a femme on her own', I suggested, social rivalries with and without butches would cease to matter. But secretly I thought her insistence that butches attracted more erotic interest in bars stemmed from her wounded sexual ego. As was my (appalling) habit at that moment in my life, I viewed Lois's injury with some compassion, but I was determined to keep it out of what I considered the cleaner arena of the argument. (I do not want to justify or apologise for my younger self. At the time, I simply thought I was doing honour to the clarity of the argument. Now, of course, the injury seems much more interesting than the argument). For me, the idea that erotic attention was quantifiable was a dead-end. Some femmes would get more erotic attention than some butches in some bars in some places sometimes. All these sums made for unreliable equations. I was unpersuaded by Lois's claims that butches 'always' got

If she wanted to declare herself a femme on her own, why would she want to share the stage with anyone?

more attention in bars. 'From whom?' and 'it depends' and 'give it a rest Lois' were the phrases that kept ricocheting around my head like balls on a pool table. But I thought the proposition of 'a femme on her own' was brilliant.

I loved that Lois did not say she wanted to be 'a femme on MY own'. By avoiding the proprietary pronoun, a conceptual ground for Lois's desire was clear. Femme functions as a fundamental category of performance rather than a category of being. Looking back, I think my enthusiasm for Lois's aspiration stemmed from the safety I registered in the philosophical and political challenge of disentangling femme from butch. I could see in a flash that the disentanglement would also benefit other uneasy couples that also functioned as hierarchies – queer and straight, man and woman, black and white.

The next day Lois brought the topic up again, this time in the dim twilight of London's dying autumn light. We were sitting at a long brown table in a large Victorian house, drinking tea. What, Lois asked, was the status of femininity in the academy? I was a bit befuddled. Did she mean how were women treated in the academy? No, she said impatiently. What defines femininity? Is there a theory of femininity? I mentioned Freud and said that he was intrigued by the question, 'What does woman want?' She was dismissive. She said she wanted to know how femininity looked in the academy. How is femininity performed? How is it regarded? I realised I rarely thought about these questions. Groping, I hazarded that thinness sometimes functioned as a cipher for intelligence among younger women scholars. I said I thought there was a 'will to thinness' as strong as Nietzsche's will to power. Thin women, I said rather miserably, tend to use their bodies as a way of conveying discipline, mastery, and competency. Academic women in tight black dresses with leather belts were saying, 'Since I can handle my weight, I can certainly handle a class. Look at these results.' We laughed, uneasily.

There were a few more conversations that ran in this line. Then maybe on the third or fourth day, Lois asked me if I would join her in creating a performance that would explore her desire to be a femme on her own. I laughed and said she should do a solo show. If she wanted to declare herself a femme on her own, why would she want to share the stage with anyone? Wasn't the whole point of being 'on her own' to be, well, on her own on stage? Deflecting her request, I stumbled into the thicket of another foreboding. I knew Lois was engaged in necessary psychic work in relation to the other Peggy and I did not want the accident of our shared first name to confuse things. There was an awkward silence. And then (again) we moved on to other things.

A few days later we returned to the thicket.

Lois: I've thought about it and I still want to do the performance with you.

I had also thought about it and had decided that if she asked again I would say yes. (Although had she not asked again, I would not have mentioned it). I had spent the intervening days reading Winnicott and Lacan. As I read, I began to think that perhaps the commonality between my name and the other Peggy's could be psychically useful. Perhaps the signifier 'Peggy could function as a transitional object for Lois, a way for the signifier to be both reassuring in its familiarity and releasing in that it was attached to a different person. Performing 'with' me was not the point; the point was to fashion a new attachment to her history of performing with the other Peggy. The signifier 'Peggy' was key but I was incidental – a place-holder for Lois as she discovered creative ways to hold and create her (singular) name.

PP: OK, sure. What do you want me to do?

LW: Do that thing you always do.

PP: What thing I always do?

LW: You know.

PP: No, I don't know.

LW: Just be yourself.

PP: OK. So I just have to stand there?

LW: Well, you have to talk of course. That's what I mean when I say do what you always do – talk!

PP: Oh. OK. What should I talk about?

LW: Something interesting. Say facts about femininity.

PP: OK. I can pretend to be Freud and explain his theory of femininity.

LW: That sounds good. Also say some facts about it.

PP: What do you mean by facts?

LW: Say things that are actually true about femininity. How long do you think the facts, plus Freud, will take?

PP: I don't know. Eight minutes, maybe ten if I go slow. But not much longer than that.

LW: Well we'll need more. What else can you do? We need about 45 minutes to an hour.

PP: Lois, this is about your desire, not mine. Tell me again why do you want to make this performance? What comes to mind when you think of 'a femme on her own'?

LW: Well I have always wanted to have a red dot travel across my body in a big lecture hall.

PP: [*Totally baffled*] Really? What do you mean? Why a red dot? I don't get it.

LW: [*Confidently, with precision*] I'd like to be a living slide. You can give a lecture about painting and I can pose like the model in the painting and then you can use a red laser dot to point to different parts of my body.

PP: [*Laughing*] Wow. OK, sure, I can do that. But does it have to be figurative painting? Can I talk about abstract expressionism?

LW: You can pick any painting you want as long as the red dot moves on me when you say different things about the painting.

Long pause.

PP: What will you wear?

LW: I will do my reverse strip tease so sometimes I will have my clothes on and sometimes I will have my clothes off. It will be something sexy. But something I can move around in; something I can get on and off easily.

PP: OK. What should I wear?

LW: I don't know. Let's talk about that later.

Long pause.

PP: We still don't have 45 minutes.

Lois Weaver performing her 'reverse strip'
at the Hemispheric Institute's Encuentro,
Buenos Aires, 2007. Photos by Marlène
Ramírez-Cancio and Julio Pantoja.

LW: I know. What else should we do?

PP: I think we need to say something about theatre and performance. Right now just having painting and psychoanalysis in focus lets theatre off the hook.

LW: The reverse strip tease is theatre. And everything we do on stage will also be theatre and so the whole thing will be 'about' it too.

PP: Good point. Sorry I forgot you were going to do the reverse strip tease. I still think though that we should say something explicit about theatre. If I am going to be all scholarly about painting and Freud, it will be weird not to be the same way about theatre and performance.

LW: [*Unconvinced*] I guess.... What were you thinking of?

PP: I don't have a specific idea. I just think doing a critique of the construction of white femininity in western painting and psychoanalysis while saying nothing explicit about the construction of that same femininity in theatre is unfair. Western theatre's participation in and contribution to femme as performance is really important. While painting obviously influences how women look, theatre and performance influences how women are.

LW: OK, but remember this is not an academic talk. It's a performance. I am a performer you know!

PP: Right. Sorry again. This is your thing, not mine. But if I am up there, it is going to be some kind of talk. I'm not a performer! I will do my best not to be boring. I want it to be fun too. What do you think the piece needs?

LW: I know! I will do Lady Macbeth's 'unsex me here' speech and you can lecture about Shakespeare. Actually, this will be great. We'll call it *Femme, Lec, Dem*. You do the lecture and I'll do the dem!

PP: Ha. OK, yes, sounds great. Just keep in mind though that Lady Macbeth is not really a key figure in the construction of femme or femininity. Really, she is very aggressive – indeed, she might even be kind of butch.

LW: Not the way I will play her.

PP: [*Laughing*] OK. I guess I can talk about her as a sort of other to the construction of femininity that was already rooted in Renaissance England. It's all fictive though because neither Elizabeth I nor Mary Queen of Scots was a femme. I guess a lot of it really emerges from the iconic construction of the Virgin Mary. I am hesitant to get into religion, but maybe I should say a few words about Mary because she does play a big part in the construction of idealised femininity. I will keep those references brief though.

LW: Hmm... I am not sure I want you to talk about any Virgins at all. I want the whole night to be sexy and fun. No references to Virgin Mary. Let's do it at the ICA as part of Queer School.

PP: What's Queer School?

LW: Oh it's a one week intensive course we're doing at Gay Sweatshop. We want to teach everyone how to be queer. Each day of the week there will be different lessons in queer life, queer performance.

PP: I should probably take that course and not be part of the curriculum.

LW: Don't worry. I will do all that part. You just have to talk and point the laser at me.

And with that I returned to New York, worried only about the dangling Virgin.

> When Lois did her reverse strip tease, I felt embarrassed and suddenly terribly over-dressed. I had not anticipated that her nakedness would underline the heavy materiality of my tuxedo.

The Event

We did not rehearse because we could not get into the ICA until about an hour before the doors opened. I wore a tux, with long black tails. I was trying to look like a cross between a Viennese analyst, a Sotheby's auctioneer, and a sober art historian. I was trying to be formal and full of authority: professorial. I wanted to be emotionally neutral, unmarked by gender or desire. I had written down some notes on a yellow legal pad and I tore them off right before we went on stage and placed them in my breast pocket. My notes did not add up to a formal talk, but they were specific and rife with facts.

The room was crowded. I had forgotten how popular Lois was in London. The temperature with all those people jammed in was stifling and the stage seemed small. The lights were bright and hot as I began reading 'as' Freud. I stood at a narrow lectern on the side of the stage while Lois improvised responses in the manner of a silent film star to each of Freud's claims. I remember one moment in particular: I was explaining that Freud argued that women lack moral judgment and Lois pretended to be scandalised. It was so interesting to see her show both the expression of scandal and the quotation marks around that expression. She was dramatizing the irony involved in 'being' scandalised. Maybe all expressions of scandalised feeling are performances – maybe they are fundamentally theatrical responses. Insofar as sexuality is itself a scandal[32] perhaps there is something intrinsically ironic in it as well, an irony carried especially overtly within femme performance. Perhaps it is this irony, this knowing wink, which is constitutive of a femme on her own.

When Lois performed Lady Macbeth's 'Unsex me here!' monologue, she got so riled up she threw the book. She was both calculating and calculated. And as her passion rose, she blushed rose-pink all across her neck. I tried to stay calm and lecture on Renaissance England, Shakespeare, the revenge plot, and concepts of power articulated by Castiglione and Machiavelli, and performed by Elizabeth I and Mary Queen of Scots. But mainly I was drowned out by Lois's rousing run through Lady Macbeth's denunciation of the link between femininity and moral conscience.

When Lois did her reverse strip tease, which I had seen before but only as a member of the audience of an earlier performance, I was the one to blush. I felt embarrassed and suddenly terribly over-dressed. I had not anticipated that her nakedness would underline the heavy materiality of my tuxedo. Although I was standing off to the side when Lois performed her reverse strip tease, I was nonetheless in the audience's visual field. Lois was focused on the crowd but as she vamped and got dressed as the strip-tease music played, I felt engulfed within a performance that was absolutely not mine. The beautiful gap I had been drawn to when Lois said 'femme on her own', and not 'femme on my own', was now absolutely lost; there I was, exposed, not as an incidental transitional object taking the place of the other Peggy, but fully there as my all-too awkward, all-too formal self. I began to sweat regret.

When Lois performed the reverse strip tease, she climbed atop a small set of steps and threw her arms up triumphantly. The whole thing was wonderfully brassy and loud, with audience members offering hilarious cat-calls and sharp wolf-whistles. When I began the lecture on western painting, Lois returned to that mini-stage again. She was now, after the robust exhortations of Lady Macbeth and the reverse strip tease, remarkably silent. The lights went down and for the first time during the performance I felt safe and confident behind my lectern. At ease in my professorial role, I spoke about the distinction between figure and ground and tried to employ the red laser dot in a way that would strengthen my argument. But as I spoke I began to realise that no one was interested in my argument – everyone was enjoying the red dot, or more precisely, everyone was enjoying Lois's pleasure in the red dot. Suddenly I saw the huge auto erotic game Lois was performing; she was wittily and seductively weaving between 'being' the living slide and responding (appreciatively) to the red dot bouncing about her body. I was supposed to be guiding the laser based on my 'lec', but her 'dem' was so powerful that the dot was travelling on a vector I could not pilot. The shadow of the butch was gone; in its place, a red dot scored to the living slide of a femme's (public) expression of desire. Her performance did not 'illuminate' my lecture; her performance undid my lecture entirely.

After

When it was over, we sat in wooden folding chairs and people talked and laughed. Del LaGrace asked me outright if I identify as butch. Cherry Smyth mentioned my affectlessness. Lois talked beautifully, elegantly, fluently. I mainly stuttered and paused. I wanted desperately not to be there and at the very same moment I was so happy I was. As I twiddled with the laser pointer in my pocket, I realised that Lois was sliding beyond us, into her own.

In the bar later, she had them lined up around her like picture frames: queer, trans, straight. Femmes, men. Techies, students. Pints and shots. Red dots.

Her performance did not 'illuminate' my lecture; her performance undid my lecture entirely.

Opposite: Opening image from Lois Weaver's 'reverse strip' at the Hemispheric Institute's Encuentro, Buenos Aires, 2007. Photo by Marlène Ramírez-Cancio.

A woman disguised as a woman: Lois Weaver's fem(me)inist performances

Lisa Duggan

In a 1990 collaboration with the UK performance group Bloolips, Split Britches staged a queer appropriation of Tennessee Williams' *A Streetcar Named Desire* titled *Belle Reprieve*. The players were identified as:

> Mitch (Paul Shaw) – *a fairy disguised as a man*
> Stella (Lois Weaver) – *a woman disguised as a woman*
> Stanley (Peggy Shaw) – *a butch lesbian*
> Blanche (Bette Bourne) – *a man in a dress*

In one significant exchange, Blanche provides what might be a *cri de coeur* for the queer femme (though not playing one in this production):

STANLEY: If you want to play a woman, the woman in this play gets raped and goes crazy in the end.

BLANCHE: I don't want to get raped and go crazy. I just wanted to wear a nice frock, and look at the shit they've given me![33]

Lois Weaver's femme performances, evolving over more than three decades of work in queer feminist theatre, have never proffered any kind of static, stable, or even coherent vision of femme-ininity. As she advocates in her performance pedagogy, as a director and teacher of an actor-centered creative practice, Weaver presents the historical body in context. The performing body is layered, contradictory, fragmented with literary references, pop culture icons, mythological figures, multiple story lines and strands of autobiography. But this postmodern mix is situated in time and space, history and geography. Its reference points are not free floating, but specific. Weaver does not attempt to transcend the cultural specificities of the body, but puts pressure on the historically located contexts of race, class, gender, sexuality, religion, and region to reveal themselves as layered embodiments of character.[34]

Weaver's femme performances appeared and transformed in this historically and culturally specific way, from the 'sex wars' of the 1980s through the queer 1990s and into the interconnected growing global performance context of the twenty-first century. For Weaver, there is no general or universal definition of femme to be abstracted from changing social conditions. As the social construction of gender shifts over time and place, there are multiple strategies deployed to 'take back the girl' from dominant forms of the masculine/feminine binary.[35]

The performing body is layered, contradictory, fragmented with literary references, pop culture icons, mythological figures, multiple story lines and strands of autobiography.

Opposite: Lois Weaver and Peggy Shaw in 'butch/femme steamy book cover shoot', 1984. Photo by Eva Weiss.

Lois Weaver began producing embodiments of the then controversial high femme of the butch/femme lesbian couple during the early 1980s. She emerged as a solo performer of the femme on her own in the 1990s, then continued on to develop collective projects for femme-inizing masculinist institutions in the present. In each context, her femme performances never aspired to establish a fixed location. Her only consistency has been an expressed yearning to escape conventional femininity ('I don't want to get raped and go crazy') while holding on to her desire for the powers and pleasures of 'a nice frock' despite the 'shit' they give us.

Beyond a Binary

Lois Weaver studied theatre at Radford College in Virginia, her home state, then left to pursue acting, writing, and directing in experimental theatre in New York – with the Open Theater, as a founder of Spiderwoman Theater, and as a co-producer of the Women's One World international theatre festivals and the WOW Café productions of the early 1980s. With Peggy Shaw and Deb Margolin in Split Britches theatre company, she developed her actor-centered creative practice as a performer, writer, director, and teacher. She rose to prominence and notoriety in the midst of the feminist 'sex wars' as the embodiment of femme performance, both on and off the stage, in her butch-femme personal and professional relationship with Peggy Shaw.

The sex wars, lasting from the late 1970s through the 1980s, generated mountains of writing and heated debates over proper feminist sexuality, specifically about whether pornography, butch-femme lesbian roles, and BDSM could ever be considered 'feminist' at all. The performers of Split Britches and the WOW Café fell decidedly on the 'pro sex' side of these extended brawls, creating staged enactments alongside the political organising and academic theorising that proliferated during the 1980s. Weaver walked past and wandered into the infamous Barnard Conference on sexuality held in 1982, where she heard Amber Hollibaugh (another high femme) deliver a powerful lecture advocating sexual freedom as feminist anti-pornography protestors attacked the speakers in leaflets distributed outside the hall.[36]

During the 1980s, feminist pro-sex art, politics, and performance represented the butch-femme lesbian couple, rather than any single figure; that couple embodied and enacted a critical restaging of heterosexual gender. Weaver and Shaw together performed extended commentaries on this coupling through multiple shows over more than a decade. Weaver's embodiment of femme performance in this context was always complex – drawing from her own white Southern rural-to-urban history, as well as from a plethora of images, texts, and stories to create multi-layered characters.

Let's face it – the femme performance challenge has always been more slippery than the butch project. Butches cross gender lines, femmes must massage them, making room for dissident desires and practices within an apparently conventionally 'feminine' frame. Butches take more or less direct aim at gender and sexual normality; femmes sucker punch it, coming at it without warning, biding their time, displaying craft and exploiting opportunity. The couple form disguises a very differentiated and uneven playing field with apparent

> **Butches take more or less direct aim at gender and sexual normality; femmes sucker punch it, coming at it without warning, biding their time, displaying craft and exploiting opportunity.**

equivalence. Weaver confronted these challenges with evolving strategies, working to get beyond the binary from within it.

The femme challenge became especially clearly visible in *Belle Reprieve*, as Weaver's Stella dramatised the 'woman disguised as a woman' alongside the non-drag 'man in a dress' – Bette Bourne as Blanche. The Split Britches/Bloolips collaboration opened up the form of butch-femme coupled performances like *Anniversary Waltz* (also 1990) to such illuminating non-equivalences. A fairy and a butch, a non-drag queen man in a dress, and a femme – together they created a grid through which Weaver's performance challenge could appear in relational context yet singular, rather than always-already paired. But Weaver went on to complicate the more tightly paired performances as well. In *It's a Small House and We Lived In It Always* (1999) the couple form comes under pressure, and the femme performance is less enmeshed in a binary contrast and more defined through a struggle for autonomy. In *Lost Lounge* (2009), Weaver and Shaw draw their cabaret show from a range of historical acts – Keely Smith and Louis Prima, Imogene Coco and Sid Caesar, Sammy Davis Jr and Dinah Shore. In her revision of Keely Smith's performance mode, Weaver enacts an exhausted and emotionally flat refusal of femme seductive excess. Still in the nice frock though! With her voluminous skirts in tow, Weaver embodies ambivalence, fatigue, and withdrawal from the intensely interdependent butch-femme couple of the 1980s sex wars, as her performances evolve over 30 years.[37]

Femme Sole

Weaver developed a solo version of her femme performances all along as well, beginning with her alter-ego, country music star turned lesbian performance artist Tammy WhyNot, who evolved as a parodic character and a cabaret hostess at WOW Café events from the early days. Tammy is an uncoupled and uncorked uber-femme character, still based solidly in Weaver's white Southern context as well as in popular culture. Tammy gave Lois some comedic range, with the stage to herself now and then. But it was during the 1990s that Weaver developed her solo performances, her strip and reverse-strip becoming modes of staging a 'female-to-femme' transitional embodiment without reference to a butch partner.[38]

In *Faith and Dancing* (1996), Weaver emerged as a fully developed solo artist of exceptional range and depth. Drawing directly on autobiographical fragments, and centrally thematizing the puzzle of femme embodiment, Weaver focuses on the mother-daughter relation rather than a butch-femme partnership. In *Mother Camp*, Esther Newton interprets the gay male drag queen as a kind of magical illusion of merger between mother and son – a merger that both honours and distances the mother. *Faith and Dancing* offers us a vision of a particular femme in a similar register. The femme daughter deeply honours the mother through re-enactment, but at the same time flees the confinements of her femininity to be at one, yet far, far away at the same time. Weaver's performance in no way universalizes this portrayal – this is a time-and-place, culturally specific representation of generational ambivalence and change.[39]

Weaver staged other solo performances from the mid 1990s forward, several as Tammy WhyNot. She also appeared with Peggy Shaw in roles, like *Miss Risqué* (2001), that left her on stage to go forward alone. These performances developed as queer politics and theory emerged alongside lesbian feminism

Creative activism brings her vision of femme performance into a set of projects designed to re-imagine public life.

in the 1990s – another site of political and theoretical contention. The queer conceptual frame left the couple aside, to focus on multiple genders in an array of non-normative social relations. Lois Weaver's solo femme performances queered femininities along multiple axes as well, anchoring her vision beyond the butch-femme couple form.[40]

Absolute Practice

Always a director, teacher, and writer as well as an actor/performer, Weaver has been branching out into an even wider range of creative activities across broader geographical spaces over the past decade. In 2006 she became Artistic Director for Performing Rights, an international festival held originally in London, with subsequent events in Vienna, Glasgow, and Montreal. She has been a principal artist for Democratising Technology, a research project using performance techniques to illuminate issues of technology design. She has taught in women's prisons in Brazil and the UK. And she initiated a range of experiments in public communication documented on her website publicaddresssystems.org – including the *Long Table*, the Card Table, and the Porch Sit. This creative activism brings her vision of femme performance into a set of projects designed to re-imagine public life and public institutions, from a femme standpoint critical of masculinist modes of institutional life. As Tammy WhyNot she inaugurated The FeMUSEum, a performance installation connected to the travelling Library of Performing Rights. With Carmelita Tropicana, Bird La Bird, and Amy Lamé, Tammy honoured historical femme muses, from seventeenth-century Mexican lesbian nun Sor Juana to Dolly Parton, with the goal of establishing a femme presence, creating a repository of femme materials within the male dominated institution of the museum.

In some ways this collective femme performance, lodged in critical relation to material institutions and their concrete practices, is an innovation. But in other ways, Weaver is utterly consistent. From the 1980s to the present, her theatrical labours have always combined entertainment with illumination of the material structures of inequality – of class, poverty, and gentrification, of region, religion, and race. Hers is a grounded zany practice, a critical project performed with music and in costume; it is theory in her own mode of *absolute practice* – the performance not an object or conclusion but a structure that allows us to 'do things we wouldn't normally do'.[41]

From couple to solo to collective femme performances, Weaver's creative practices and embodiments have consistently combined contradictory elements – the material and historical with the fantastic and farcical, the autobiographical with the pop cultural. A brazen iconoclast at the centre of controversy, she is a populist, democratic, and a deeply ethical activist and pedagogue. Wearing that nice frock, she flings the shit they give us right back into the faces of the powerful.

Opposite: Lois Weaver in *Faith and Dancing: Mapping Femininity and Other Natural Disasters* (1996), La MaMa, NYC. Photo by Tom Brazil.

For Lois: femme glorious

Joan Nestle

Somewhere in the cleft between parody and portrayal, Weaver makes us see the rich and humane possibilities the femme imagination offers the world.

For all my writing life, I have tried to find the right words to bring femme alive in all its complexities, in its ironies and desperations, in its textures of skin and thought, in its laughter and bone-deep desire, in its historical settings and new inventions. Femme is the outlier in both pre-liberation days and after, so close to being 'woman', so touched by other histories.

Where my words fall short, the body of Lois Weaver – the body of her work and her body – never does. Whether in persona, clothed or naked, Weaver magnifies the femme discourse, through parody, portrayal, or simply walking across the stage. Weaver is a femme Mother Courage, hauling in her wake theatrical and cultural stereotypes of femininity – Southern and poor, sassy and resistant, blonde and full of shadows, feminist and queer and real. Somewhere in the cleft between parody and portrayal, Weaver makes us see the rich and humane possibilities the femme imagination offers the world.

In the earliest days of lesbian feminist theatre in the 1970s, from It's Alright To Be A Woman Theatre Group to Women's Experimental Theatre, the femme-gendered performance remained invisible, its inherent dramatic tension unexplored, almost wilfully so. And yes, I sat entranced by the 1970s experiential-experimental theatres, where actors sat on plastic milk crates and brought vignettes from their lives centre stage, painful sincere revelations of abuse and broken dreams. But it was the performances of Lois Weaver that brought into the light the complexity of femme desire and attitude in its many shifting terrains, from explosive comedy to hesitant exchanges of identity. Weaver gives body and voice to what a femme gender politic and aesthetic looks like, shows how essential this performance is to telling the full human story, the woman who loves in her own way, who is not simply the complement to performed masculinity but a feminist queer force all her own. Using the femme delight in play, in costume, in seduction, and its interrogation, Weaver invokes an older femme history while employing the aesthetics of a new one, a community that has survived the hard knocks of belittlement and exile from the clearly known. To us, femmes of all ages and all genders, Weaver gives the gift of her charisma and her humility, her stunning beauty which she mocks and illuminates, all in the service of a radical dramatic vision, where community-as-audience radiates hope.

Opposite: Lois Weaver in 'the lesbians in the woods' photo shoot, near Weaver and Shaw's upstate retreat in Beaverkill, New York, 1995. Photo by Eva Weiss.

Lois's is a femme energy of the body and spirit, dedicated to the wonders of community theatre, the most subversive vision in such a time as this.

The image that stays with me through all these years is the almost empty stage, littered with small props. Stage lights go up, Weaver walks out naked centre stage. She stands for what felt like decades, never flinching from full view, holding her ground. How does a naked body denote femme, its story of self-possession and yet complex offerings? But of course, Weaver is dressed in her past performances, in her politics of gender and theatre. In this, the moment of her now-famous reverse strip, she clothes herself in garments that for centuries have hindered the full wonder of women's possibilities and then she refuses their imprisonments.

Weaver travels the world now, educating and listening, her Tammy WhyNot persona asking questions of age, isolation, and community building. All these years – I am 74 now – I have been inspired by her appearances, in Split Britches' innovations, New York's Gay Pride Marches with other WOW performers strutting their politics, and on a myriad of small and large stages. I have been delighted with so many others to be in her theatrical presence, to receive her joyful challenges, her femme delight an offering to us all to do more with our imagings of another kind of world. Hers is a femme energy of the body and spirit, transformative, funny, demanding, and dedicated to the wonders of community theatre, the most subversive vision in such a time as this.

Talking about Lois: An Excerpt from an Oral History, Melbourne, 2014

The downtown off-Broadway theatre was packed as always, our scruffy community audience and the lucky others. Lois walked onto the lit stage totally naked. Theatrical and real, stunning and known, she was the femme incarnate taking us on her journey of character and politic. Slowly, she dressed herself until she was in a full nun's habit. She wore reversals of expectation on her body. One of the great batch of wonders of my life has been watching Lois Weaver perform, teach, play, invent. She brought the depth of femme dramatic possibilities out of the shadows and I, a femme from the 1950s, so used to disdain, to the belittlement femmes endured in both the old world and the new, whispered, 'You have got it! You have got it!'

Opposite: Lois Weaver in a reading for Lesbian Herstory Archives, NYC, 1992. Photo by Morgan Grenwald.

Lois Weaver has great hair

Moe Angelos

The woman has style. The woman has hairstyles, many. Am I being a bad feminist if I write about how ~~hot amazing~~ HOT she looks all the time? Am I objectifying her, reducing her to her physical self? Would she mind?

In the spirit of innate hotness that Lois teaches by example, I think she would be happy to be defined by her gorgeous hair and its many moods. Because Lois has harnessed the powers of her hair/hotness as forces for good. She and her allures are doing the lordess's work, as she has been since I first saw her more than 30 years ago.

In the prosaic 1980s setting of a disused furniture showroom at the corner of Avenue A and 7th Street in Manhattan's decaying/thriving East Village, Lois greeted me at the headquarters of the second WOW Festival. Her hair was red with blonde accents, thick like a sheaf of the most brilliant ruby-coloured wheat, with little white spots of paint. She explained that she'd gotten those flecks 'painting an ashram, upstate' to pay for the festival. Curious.

As one of the four founders of the festival, she enthusiastically put me to work immediately, installing me at the information table, a 20-year old know-nothing volunteer tasked with customer service. 'Just make it up if you don't know', was Lois's advice for my new job.

This offhand instruction is the first lesson Lois taught me on that warm fall day in 1981, when Ave A still smelled like boiled cabbage, and trash can fires burned across the street in Tompkins Square Park. Making-it-up is the simple-profound lesson for art, and maybe even for survival itself. We all emerge into this life as I did at the information table, without knowledge, and we must learn so much to negotiate living. There is a whole lot of not-knowing in existence and Lois, in her one-sentence training session, schooled me: just make it up.

I did make it up. I took Lois at her word that day and I am still making stuff up. Her guidance and deep, fierce teaching over the decades has often been carried out through her performances where I have had the extremely pleasurable privilege of watching her, in many shows, absorbing what it means to be a woman, Lois-style. During our shared time at WOW, she steeped me in her processes and thoughts, always rigorously feminist while at the same time so sparkly in other ways: humour, smarts, sexiness, glamour (and anti-glamour), and just plain old fun. She has taught legions of us how to be better artists, better thinkers, better people.

And that hair. It has been red, blonde (both clean and dirty), brunette, sometimes a little of all. It's been long, bobbed, wedged, fringed, layered, side-parted, centre-parted. And let's not even start with the wigs. All that hair, all these years, has been fantastic, a thing of Lois that can do no wrong.

Thus, wisdom: have trust in your hair and just make it up.

'Just make it up' is the first lesson Lois taught me on that warm fall day in 1981, when Ave A still smelled like boiled cabbage.

Opposite: Lois Weaver in photo shoot for the remounting of *Dress Suits to Hire*, 2005. Photo by Eva Weiss.

A view from the bottom

Sue-Ellen Case

It was an uncharacteristically hot night in San Francisco, sometime in the 1990s, when most of the members of the ATHE (Association for Theatre in Higher Education) conference gathered to watch the new play by Lois and Peggy. This audience looked forward to another humorous, warm take on butch femme relations. What they saw, instead, was *Lust and Comfort*, perhaps Split Britches' darkest play, exploring uneven power relations between two isolated people. Lois played the manservant Barrett, whose anger at the author and resentment of her subordinate role was direct, simple, unadorned. After the play, the audience was quiet, discussing in hushed almost frightened tones, the change in the actors. It was watching Lois in this transgender role that helped me to recognise the power of femme that she always played, but laced with the artificial sweetness of the Coca-Cola she thirsted for in *Belle Reprieve*. As Barrett, she withdrew the humour with which she typically served up her critiques and assertions of power that created her threatening, edgy, seductive, and socially critical performances of feminine stereotypes. I was forced to see now, what before I had resisted knowing. Lois had always scared me. Even in her sweetness, in personal encounters, I could sense that she did not play by the rules – she might do just anything, like when she rushed the audience in *Lesbians Who Kill*, gun in hand, saying 'up against the wall, motherfuckers', or when, as the Salvation Army Lady, in *Beauty and the Beast*, she recited, with glee, Lady Macbeth's power-hungry, violent monologue. In these instances, she played the righteous anger that the history of the oppression of women could inspire and granted it to characters who had been denied its resistant power. Politically, I always knew she was doing that, but emotionally, I always felt somewhat guilty, caught out by her, in my own unthinking participation in the dominant order. Maybe all of us academics were called out by Lois to stop delivering on the promises of security and whatever else that kept us from continually performing the violence of that history, though we certainly produced what we could in writing and resisted, in our own ways. But we did not signal that there were no bounds, that we could rush out of the script at many minute, with gun in hand, and shove them up against the wall. And maybe that's why we invited her to perform in our institutions, over and over, to bring that threat into the secured space of the campus.

I first met Lois on a plane, accidentally seated next to her, and although I had seen her perform the night before, I didn't recognise her. A few nights later, I attended her performance at WOW and she called me up on the stage. I can't remember why, but I remember that I was terrified to be up there with her – this was a stage where anything might happen and I would need to match her strength, directness, energy, seductive power, and quick intelligence. She saw the panic on my face and, bewildered, apologised. Always kind, always supportive, but always a challenge.

> I could sense that she did not play by the rules – she might do just anything.

Overleaf: Lois Weaver and Peggy Shaw in opening dance of *Lust and Comfort* (Weaver, Shaw, and James Neale-Kennerley, choreography by Stormy Brandenberger,1994), La MaMa NYC. Photo by Tom Brazil.

A view from the top

Lois Weaver

When Peggy Shaw and I travelled for work we always sat together on the plane and requested at least one aisle seat because Peggy was tall and claustrophobic. One time on a flight to New York from Seattle, we arrived at our allotted seats to find someone already sitting in the aisle seat. Peggy politely said, 'I think this is my seat.' The woman sitting there barely looked up and said, 'No it isn't, this is my seat.' Showing her our tickets Peggy repeated, 'This is my seat.' To which the woman replied, 'No, it's my seat, I always book aisle seats.' Peggy then said, 'I always book aisle seats.' Eventually it was clear that the woman was not going to move, so Peggy went looking for somewhere to sit and I took my place next to this disgruntled passenger. I knew she was disgruntled and I thought she might be dangerous so I started to wonder what polite conversation I could muster in order to make it through the five hour flight. Shortly after take-off she pulled out a book and started reading. My recollection of the title was a combination of words like... 'my mother, my mirror, my self'. Ah, I thought, this is my opener. So I casually looked over her shoulder and said, 'Oh, I've seen that book.' She abruptly put down the book, turned her head to me but leaned away to get a fuller view. She looked me up and down, from head to toe and back again from my bleached hair to my red lipstick to my high heels then back to the lipstick. Then she said, 'Where would *you* have seen this?' The emphasis on the YOU flustered me. What part of my appearance made her doubt my interest in such things? I responded with, 'Oh, I must have seen it reviewed in some journal somewhere.' At which point she leaned back again, fixating again on my red lipstick, and said, 'What do you do?', and I said, 'I'm in the theatre.' Now she seemed flustered and replied, 'I am in the theatre,' with the same tone she used when she said, 'This is my seat.' She continued, 'What kind of theatre do you do?' I said, 'I have my own company called Split Britches.' She jolted upright, 'Split Britches?', and then she nearly stood in spite of her seatbelt and she started to flip her head around violently shouting, 'Peggy Shaw! That was Peggy Shaw!' We became good friends with this woman, who is a leading feminist scholar and has since supported our work in many ways.

But the snapshot of that first encounter is pasted in my scrapbook under, 'This is what it means to be femme.'

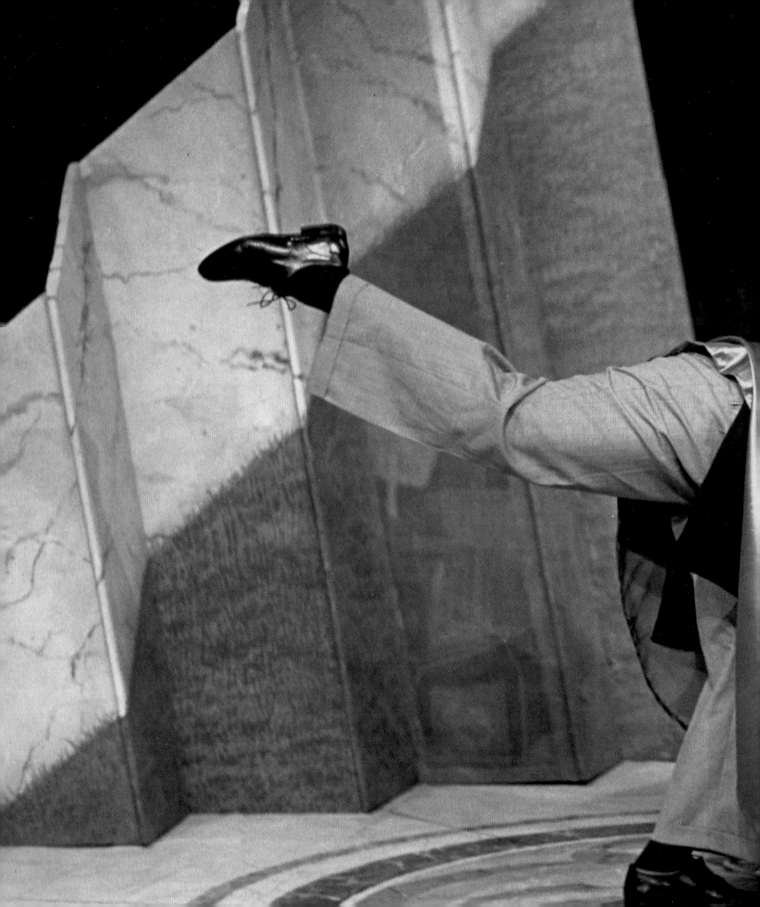

Femme Cha-cha (from *Lust and Comfort*)

Lois Weaver[42]

LOIS

I just wanted to see if you were paying attention. Are you paying attention?

Can you see me? How do I look?

I'm dressed. I'm ready. Shall we dance?

Cha Cha Cha

You are going to dance with me now

You're going to lead and I will follow.

I will relinquish, surrender, yield, submit.

I will be seized in a state of following, in a state of two steps and high heels.

I will gaze into your eyes and you will know me.

You will see something in the roundness of my shoulders

and you will think it is yours

But I will know they belong to me... even if they are reflected in your eyes.

But watch carefully

Cha Cha Cha

Pay close attention as I glide across the floor in a cloud of sequins

that appears to be hanging on the arm of a dinner suit.

Observe carefully as my foot retreats to leave space for yours.

Put your foot there. No. There.

Put your hand there in the small of my back. No. One hand.

You're going to lead me.

Don't you know how to lead?

Don't make me have to tell you.

Can't you read my mind?

Try listening. Can't you hear it?

Cha Cha Cha

PEGGY

How much floor have we covered? An inch? How long have we been dancing?
A second? A minute? Fifty years?

LOIS

Fifty years! And all I got was roses. I wanted pearls and you gave me roses.

PEGGY

Red is not my favourite colour.

LOIS

Colour me blue.

PEGGY

I sent me your blue note –

LOIS

It wasn't perfumed. I was surprised.

PEGGY

Maybe it wore off crossing the Atlantic.

LOIS

So much lost at sea. They say the band played on when the Titanic sank.
All those notes lost at sea.

PEGGY

When I get old I'll still slick back my hair.

LOIS

When you get old you'll be distinguished, mature, greying around the temples.

You'll have on sensible shoes and comfortable clothes.

When I get old I'll be cold in my stockings and bare legs.

I won't be so steady on my feet and I'll feel foolish in my lipstick.

Move a little closer. Listen to it. Feel it. See it.

Look how round... I am...

how perfectly formed...

I wilt at the slightest compliment.

I swoon at the sound of my own voice.

My mother always said I would need something to fall back on

a couch or a pair of arms and even when I was at my best

she said I would have to look like I needed a little help...

but pay close attention...

Cha Cha Cha

1   This text is adapted from Lois Weaver, *Faith and Dancing: Mapping Femininity and Other Natural Disasters*, an excerpt of which (not containing the section printed here) is reproduced in Lizbeth Goodman (selected and introduced by), *Mythic Women/Real Women: Plays and Performance Pieces by Women* (London: Faber and Faber, 2000), pp. 287-300.

2   This text is adapted from Weaver, *Faith and Dancing*, an excerpt of which (not containing the section printed here) is reproduced in Goodman (intro.), *Mythic Women/Real Women*, pp. 287-300.

3   This text is adapted from Weaver, *Faith and Dancing*, an excerpt of which (not containing the section printed here) is reproduced in Goodman (intro.), *Mythic Women/Real Women*, pp. 287-300.

4   Peggy Shaw, Deborah Margolin, and Lois Weaver, *Split Britches: A True Story* (1980), in *Split Britches: Lesbian Practice/Feminist Performance*, ed. by Sue-Ellen Case (London: Routledge, 1996), pp. 35-57 (p. 36).

5   Margaret Mitchell, *Gone with the Wind* (New York: Macmillan, 1936); *Gone with the Wind*, dir. by Victor Fleming, George Sukor and Sam Wood, adapted by Sidney Howard, (Selznick International Pictures, in association with Metro-Goldwyn-Mayer, 1939).

6   Stephen Miller, *Smart Blonde: Dolly Parton* (London: Omnibus Press, 2006).

7   See Laura Mulvey's classic article, 'Visual Pleasure and Narrative Cinema', *Screen*, 16:3 (1975), 6-18; reprinted widely, including in Laura Mulvey, *Visual and Other Pleasures*, 2nd edn (Basingstoke: Palgrave Macmillan, [1989] 2009). See also Kim Solga, *Theatre & Feminism* (Basingstoke: Palgrave Macmillan, forthcoming 2015).

8   For more on Split Britches' work with what Paul Menard calls 'dyke camp', see his article, 'The (Fe)Male Gays: Split Britches and the Redressing of Dyke Camp', in *We Will be Citizens: New Essays on Gay and Lesbian Theatre*, ed. by James Fisher (Jefferson, N.C.: McFarland & Company, 2008), pp. 185-93; see, for example, p. 191.

9   Joan Nestle, 'The Femme Question', in *The Persistent Desire: A Femme-Butch Reader*, ed. by Joan Nestle, (Boston: Alyson Publications, 1992), pp. 138-46 (p. 138).

10 Lois Weaver, 'Still Counting', in Del LaGrace Volcano and Ulrika Dahl, *Femmes of Power: Exploding Queer Femininities*, (London: Serpent's Tail, 2008), pp. 140-5 (p. 144), age 44; an updated version of 'Still Counting' appears in the Afterwords to this book.

11 Lois Weaver, *Faith and Dancing: Mapping Femininity and Other Natural Disasters*, cited in Deanna Shoemaker, 'Pink Tornados and Volcanic Desire: Lois Weaver's Resistant "Femme(nini)tease" in *Faith and Dancing: Mapping Femininity and Other Natural Disasters*', *Text and Performance Quarterly*, 27:4 (2007), 317-33 (p. 330).

12 Lisa Duggan and Kathleen McHugh, 'A Fem(me)inist Manifesto', *Women and Performance*, 8:2 (1996), 153-9 (p. 155), cited in Shoemaker, 'Pink Tornados and Volcanic Desire', p. 317.

13 See, for example, Peggy Shaw, Deborah Margolin, and Lois Weaver, *Split Britches: A True Story* (1980), in *Split Britches: Lesbian Practice/Feminist Performance*, ed. by Sue-Ellen Case, (London: Routldge, 1996), pp. 35-57 (p. 45).

14 Shaw, Margolin, and Weaver, *Split Britches*, p. 47.

15 Bette Bourne, Paul Shaw, Peggy Shaw, and Lois Weaver, *Belle Reprieve: A Collaboration*, 1991, in *Split Britches*, ed. by Case, pp. 149-83 (p. 169).

16 Holly Hughes, Peggy Shaw, and Weaver Lois, '*Dress Suits to Hire*: A Collaboration between Holly Hughes, Peggy Shaw, and Lois Weaver', *TDR: The Drama Review*, 33:1 (1989), 132-52 (p. 147).

17 Kate Davy, *Lady Dicks and Lesbian Brothers: Staging the Unimaginable at the WOW Café Theatre* (Ann Arbor: University of Michigan Press, 2010), p. 50; italics original; Davy quotes Weaver from an interview with her on 14 August 1993, in New York. Lois mentions this incident again in her interview in this book with Muriel Miguel, p. 64.

18 Lois Weaver, 'Still Counting', in Volcano and Dahl, p. 143, age 30. Deanna Shoemaker writes; 'Weaver recalls in the early seventies being thrown against a wall by a feminist who accused her of titillating men with her high femme performance.' Shoemaker, 'Pink Tornadoes and Volcanic Desire', p. 325.

19 Lois Weaver, 'Performing Butch/Femme Theory', *Journal of Lesbian Studies*, 2:2-3 (1998), 187-99; and simultaneously in *Acts of Passion: Sexuality, Gender and Performance*, ed. by Nina Rapi and Maya Chowdhry (New York and London: Haworth Press, 1998), pp. 187-99 (p. 190).

20 Lois Weaver, 'Sheila Dances with Sheila', in *Butch/Femme: Inside Lesbian Gender*, ed. by Sally R. Munt (London: Cassell, 1998), pp. 66-73 (71-72). Italics original.

21 Sue-Ellen Case has written an important library on butch-femme subjectivities and representations in theatre, performance, and culture, much of which is collected in her book *Feminist and Queer Performance: Critical Strategies* (Basingstoke: Palgrave Macmillan, 2009).

22 Jess Dobkin, 'The Permanence of a Performance', in this collection, p. 156.

23 Weaver, 'Sheila Dances with Sheila', p. 73.

24 Weaver, 'Still Counting', in Volcano and Dahl, p. 143, age 31.

25 Weaver, 'Still Counting', in Volcano and Dahl, p. 143, age 31.

26 Peggy Shaw, Lois Weaver, and James Neale-Kennerley, *Lust and Comfort*, 1995, in *Split Britches*, ed. by Case, pp. 225-72 (p. 257).

27 For my more sustained analysis of performance's relationships to neoliberalism and sociality, see Jen Harvie, *Fair Play – Art, Performance and Neoliberalism* (Basingstoke: Palgrave Macmillan, 2013).

28 Walter Benjamin, 'Theses on the Philosophy of History', in *Illuminations*, ed. and introduced by Hannah Arendt, trans. by Harry Zohn (New York: Shocken Books, 1968), pp. 253-64 (p. 261).

29 Samuel Beckett, *Krapp's Last Tape*, 1958, reprinted in *Krapp's Last Tape and Other Dramatic Pieces* (New York: Grove Press, 2009), p. 28.

30 J. Hillis Miller, *Reading Narrative* (Norman, OK: Oklahoma University Press, 1998), p. 58.

31 Sue-Ellen Case's influential argument, 'Towards a Butch

Femme Aesthetic', originally published in late 1988, framed much of the conversation about lesbian bars at the time. See Case, 'Towards a Butch-Femme Aesthetic', *Discourse*, 11:1 (1988-89), 55-73.

32   See Shoshana Felman, *The Scandal of the Speaking Body, Don Juan with J.L. Austin, or, Seduction in Two Languages*, trans. by Caroline Porter (Ithaca: Cornell University Press, 1983).

33   See the full text of *Belle Reprieve* in *Split Britches: Lesbian Practice, Feminist Performance*, ed. by Sue-Ellen Case (New York: Routledge, 1996), pp. 149-83. Blanche and Stanley exchange also cited in Jill Dolan, *Theatre and Sexuality* (New York: Palgrave Macmillan, 2010), p. 79.

34   See Lois Weaver, 'Performing Butch/Femme Theory', *The Journal of Lesbian Studies*, 2:2-3 (1998), 187-99. For my own version of this way of conceiving of 'femme' performance in the context of a personal history that uncannily mirrors Weavers, see Lisa Duggan, 'Escape Velocity, or There Must be 50 Ways to Queer "The Family",' *Bully Bloggers*, 19 February, 2015 <https://bullybloggers.wordpress.com/2015/02/19/escape-velocity-or-there-must-be-50-ways-to-queer-the-family/> [accessed 23 June 2015].

35   Shoemaker, 'Pink Tornados and Volcanic Desires', p. 317.

36   Davy, *Lady Dicks and Lesbian Brothers*, pp. 51-52.

37   Nicole Eschen, 'Pressing Back: Split Britches' Lost Lounge and the Retro Performativity of Lesbian Performance', *Journal of Lesbian Studies*, 17.1 (2013), 56-71.

38   Shoemaker, 'Pink Tornados and Volcanic Desires', p. 319.

39   Kate Davy, 'Fe/Male Impersonation: The Discourse of Camp', in *Critical Theory and Performance*, ed. by Janelle Reinelt and Joseph Roach (Ann Arbor: University of Michigan Press, 1992), pp. 355-71 (pp. 234-5).

40   See Catherine Fowler, 'Performing Sexualities at Lancaster', *New Theatre Quarterly*, 10.38 (1994), 196-97; Geraldine Harris, 'Double Acts, Theatrical Couples and Split Britches', *New Theatre Quarterly*, 18.3 (2002), 211-21.

41   Lois Weaver in Lois Weaver and Caoimhe McAvinchey, 'Lois Weaver: Interview and Introduction by Caoimhe McAvinchey', in *Performance and Community: Commentary and Case Studies*, ed. by Caoimhe McAvinchey (New York: Bloomsbury, 2014), pp. 21-32 (pp. 21-32).

42   This is a version of text from Peggy Shaw, Lois Weaver, and James Neale-Kennerley, *Lust and Comfort* (1995), in *Split Britches: Lesbian Practice/Feminist Performance*, ed. by Sue-Ellen Case (London: Routledge, 1996), 225-72 (pp. 255-6).

ornment and material
nsulation.

ELISABETH ENDRES

RUE MERCELIS 91 - BTE 14
1050 BRUXELLES

 HATTEN

IN

Oh, for the Love of Work!

FESTIVAL OF FOOLS 1984

groep
group **Split Britches**
groupe

naam
name **Lois Weaver**
nomme

PASS

Edinburgh Rock Festival

This pass must be displayed at all ti...
or access will be withdrawn
Stewards are entitled to withdraw

EDINBURGH
ROCK
FESTIVAL 79

Love the one you are with
Compete
Respond to necessity
Exploit eccentricity
Make up a title
Spread a rumour
Do what scares you
Take something apart
Reveal a guilty secret
Ease a pain or two

BEAUTY
AND THE
BEAST
A
FAIRY TALE

For love and work

Lois Weaver

When I was in my late twenties, a younger woman took my hand and with the wisdom of an old psychic read the lines of my palm. She said, 'You will have a long life, full of work. You won't have much money, but you'll have lots of work and you will love your work and be happy.' Now when I think about this thing I call my work, it is intertwined with the thing I call love. Peggy Shaw and I worked together in Spiderwoman and we fell in love. Peggy literally fell on the floor of the lobby in a hotel in Germany after *An Evening of Disgusting Songs and Pukey Images*. She fell on the floor and said, 'I think I'm in love with you.' I had been in love with Peggy for some time, while carefully and patiently tending a place of friendship where she could land between girlfriends. She had several in several cities and, at the time, was travelling with another one on the road. From the moment of her fall, we interlocked friendship, passion, and work.

For the first year, Peggy and I had to keep our relationship a secret. Spiderwoman had an odd rule that prohibited her members from mixing sex and work. It was easy enough to keep because up until Peggy's arrival in the company in 1978, we were all women and all heterosexual. With her came an entourage of lesbians and the inevitability that I and a few other members of the company would finally and thankfully come out and, with that, the probabilities shifted.

The secrecy of our relationship formed the infrastructure for our collaboration but it also informed the content of our work. We worked hard to keep our passion for each other under wraps and under our skin in order to strengthen the muscle and bone of our work. I became obsessed with what was hidden, unearthed and untold. I used the unspoken nature of relationships and the invisible connections between things - between women, women and their survival, women and their teacups – to replace plot and story line. And I had been opened to a world of desire that gave me the confidence to utter the phrase, 'I want.'

The thing I *wanted* was to create a living portrait of my three Blue Ridge Mountain aunts, Cora, Della, and Emma in a performance that I wanted to call Split Britches. I remember saying in our very first rehearsal that I wanted this piece to start out like an old-fashioned sepia family picture, and if you tore that open it would reveal these women singing and dancing like in a 1930s colour cartoon. If you scratched even further you would expose the sweat and disappointments of three women engaged in a struggle for survival on a post-Depression farm in rural Virginia.

When we produced the final draft in 1981, we got a review for that production by Marilyn Stasio, in the *New York Post*. She said 'Emma, Cora and Della are like figures in a primitive painting, trying to crack through the canvas to come alive.'[1] A quiet desire had survived months of exploration and uncertainty and been heard by someone who had been nowhere near its first utterance. And there it was stated again, this time in hard print and in public. This was a delicious moment, marking the beginning of a life-long creative partnership and a delightful tangle of love and work.

Photo p. 122 Publicity portrait for *Split Britches* (Weaver, Shaw, and Deb Margolin, 1981). Photo by Pamela Camhe.

Photos p. 124 Top left: Publicity Photo for *Lesbians Who Kill* (Weaver, Shaw, and Deb Margolin, 1993). Photo by Amy Meadow; Bottom right: Peggy Shaw in 1983. Photo by Eva Weiss.

Lois, love, and work

Jen Harvie

'I love I love I love my art'
Final line sung by all performers in *Belle Reprieve: A Collaboration*[2]

'I Love My Art'

The longevity and variety of Lois's career make it challenging to summarise. But the title she originally devised for this section of the book – 'For the Love of Work' – begins to do the trick. Love is at the core of all her work. Another way of putting that is to say that her work *is* love. For one, Lois finds love *in doing* the work. Most importantly, she finds and generates love in collaborating with others, in negotiating complex relationships with them, and in discovering, exploring, and mining the shared energy and dynamics they create. Secondly, Lois makes performance work that often *operates as* love. This includes love for the frequently misunderstood and marginalised subjects of her performance, to whom her work tenders attention, sympathy, generosity, and good humour as well as, sometimes, the kind of affectionate mockery often shared between friends and within families, be those families biological or chosen. And it includes love for her audiences, to whom her work extends a range of intimate engagements, from riotous flirtation, by way of good-humoured teasing, to the gentle *tête à tête* sharing of secrets. Lois's practice of work as love tends to mean that there is often little separation between her 'life' and 'work': she works almost continuously; her friends and intimates are her collaborators, and vice versa; and her work encompasses both the banality of the everyday – even if that 'everyday' is love – and the extraordinary that is also love.

In what follows I will not attempt to 'cover' Lois's work across the whole of her career.[3] But I will attempt to map four key ideas and motivations that are distinctive and in many ways innovative about it: instinct and desire; work; humour and irreverence; and love and care. I'll trace these ideas through analyses of her work as *outcomes* or aesthetics and her work as *practices* of making performance. By describing Lois's work as love I do not mean to portray it as, either, prioritising moral virtuousness or disappearing into some sort of self-indulgent emotional vortex. If anything, Lois does *the opposite* of both of these things. Despite her youthful religious interests, Lois is not pious or self-denying. Her pleasures in promiscuous self-indulgence and moral ambiguity are evident, for example, when she flirts indiscriminately with anyone and everyone in an audience, individually, serially, and/or collectively. They are also detectable in the way she takes audiences on rollercoaster rides through huge ranges of emotional registers, where she is ribald one moment, then erotic, sensual, playful, stern, and/or kindly the next. And she consistently explores not so much herself – though there are many autobiographical elements to her work – but instead relationships and identities in social and cultural contexts. Her love is not

Opposite: Lois Weaver Peggy Shaw, Susan Young, Vivan Stoll, and Stormy Brandenberger in rehearsals for the remounting of *Dress Suits to Hire* (Weaver, Shaw, and Holly Hughes), La MaMa, NYC, 2005.
Photos by Lori E. Seid

exclusive and isolating; it is precisely about relationships and the conditions that affect them. By calling Lois's work love, I aim to capture something of the social engagement, social value, generosity of spirit, carnal pleasure, sensual appeal, caring friendship, and downright huggable warmth that characterises both Lois and her work.

Instinct and Desire

Following instinct is one of the most important elements of Lois's principles for making performance – as well for living her life.[4] By following instinct, she tries to get beyond the self-censorship that she has internalised within predominantly patriarchal, heteronormative, ageist cultures, and that would have her be a 'good girl', 'do the right thing', 'be quiet', and, often, acquiesce to other people's desires, instead of identifying, acting on and satisfying her own. Clearly, this approach is feminist in that it prioritises her desires as a woman rather than self-denyingly subordinating her labour and life to anyone else, be that a spouse, children, parents, employers, colleagues, or friends. Her approach is also queer because it recognises and enacts her queer desires, both sexual queer desires and a broader range of desires that are simply culturally different. It is also fundamentally creative, since it aims to identify and fulfil what she *really* wants to do, rather than simply executing something she feels she *should* do.

It's an approach informed by the open, democratising spirit of 1960s and 1970s hippy culture when Lois was becoming an adult, and by the practices of the Open Theater that Lois learned about through directing Jean-Claude van Itallie's *The Serpent* at Radford College, practising story-weaving with Muriel Miguel in Spiderwoman Theater, and experimenting with collectively devised work at Mill Mountain Playhouse, as discussed in the 'Places to Start' section of this book. Lois has explained in interview with Kate Davy the genesis of this approach at WOW Café which Lois co-founded with Peggy Shaw in New York. Shaw, Lois says, came out of Hot Peaches [performance company] and then we both came out of Spiderwoman [multicultural, feminist theatre] where the encouragement was to do whatever you wanted to do, where you could be how you want to be on stage. All you needed was a fantasy and you could make it happen on stage. My vision for WOW was that it would be a place where anybody could do anything; my particular nature is to encourage anybody to do anything.[5]

This approach has proved enabling not only for Lois but also her collaborators and students, all of whom she encourages to name their desires and to fulfil those desires in performance. 'When we're making a show', says Peggy Shaw, 'we get together in a room and we list everything that we hate, that we love. And we think, what's our fantasy? "Okay, this time, this show, I want to be a girl, and I wanna be bad, and I wanna sing the blues." You just make all your lists of fantasies, and then you practice every morning.'[6] In the same interview with Davy quoted above, Lois describes the workshops she ran at WOW: 'I did workshops called "acting on impulse". It was all about freeing up the associative part of the brain and the associative creativity within us.'[7] Later in this section, Lois's collaborators on the three-handed performance for domestic spaces *On the Scent* (first produced in 2005), Helen Paris and Leslie Hill, single out 'openness' and 'fearlessness' respectively as features of Lois's work that have impressed and inspired them.

Following instinct is one of the most important elements of Lois's principles for making performance – as well for living her life.

Opposite: Lois Weaver and Peggy Shaw in original version of *Dress Suits to Hire* (Weaver, Shaw, and Holly Hughes, 1987), Vesleka Performance Festival, P.S. 122, NYC. Photo Uzi Parnes.

The cabaret-like performances pay homage to the messy but delightful treasure-trove cacophony of thrift shops.

Famously, Lois's advocacy of pursuing everyone's individual desires in group performances produces some wonderfully absurd results. In *Beauty and the Beast* (1982), for example, Lois followed her desire to play a Salvation Army Sergeant; Peggy Shaw pursued hers to perform as 'Gussie Umberger, an 84-year-old vaudeville hoofer'; and Deb Margolin fulfilled her yearning to play 'a Jewish Rabbi in toe shoes'.[8] This advocacy of desire also means that Lois and her collaborators' performances are frequently full of *stuff* they love, even it if doesn't 'match'. Formally, the work is often episodic, vaudevillian, perhaps chaotic, jumping from a scene, to a song, to a reference to a favourite film, to an image, to a slapstick sequence, to another song. *Little Women: The Tragedy* (1988), for example, starts with the three performers – Weaver, Shaw, and Margolin – circulating in the audience. Lois enters as the writer Louisa who plays Jo from *Little Women* to introduce the show. There's an 'excerpt' from the novel, then the performers ogle the audience; there are intermittent fanfares and 'heavenly music',[9] then the performers are confused angels; there's a slapstick scene involving mixed up luggage, and sudden, tantalising glimpses of the performers naked, then equally sudden, caught-you-looking blackouts – and that's all within the first seven pages of the printed script. As that 'summary' begins to indicate, stylistically, the frequently cabaret-like performances pay homage to the messy but delightful treasure-trove cacophony of thrift shops. *Little Women's* characters suddenly have plastic binoculars, then fake wings, suitcases, wooden cut-out clouds, and water guns disguised as cameras, with which they mischievously squirt the audience.[10] They have costumes of dressing gowns, then hospital gowns, wings, kimonos, and for Margolin/Khurve/Amy, 'a skimpy red showgirl costume'.[11] (Peggy Shaw recalls, 'I learned theater from competition, and from the street, and from garbage. I got all my costumes from the garbage.'[12]) Tammy WhyNot, likewise, is often surrounded by large, plastic carrier bags festooned with polka dot patterns and images of 1950s pin-up girls; the bags contain costume changes, accessories, a mechanical poodle, back-up wigs – anything and everything a girl could ever desire. The shows' lost-and-found, assembled-by-a-magpie aesthetics patently reveal the workers' low budgets; but those aesthetics also gleefully promote the performers' rights to indulge their desires to be who they want to be, play who they want to play, and play with whatever and whomever they want to play with.

A focus on instinct and desire also informs the narratives Lois and her collaborators tell. This is obvious with Split Britches' eponymous inaugural play, based on Lois's female ancestors who lived in extreme poverty in what Split Britches identified as a 'world without men'[13] in Virginia's Blue Ridge Mountains. The piece started from the assumption shared by Lois and *Split Britches*' initial collaborators, Peggy Shaw, Pam Verge, Naja Beye, and Kathy Gollner, that 'these lives were worthy of exploration',[14] despite being perceived by others as, in Split Britches' words, 'unforgivable', embarrassing' and 'eccentric'.[15] Vivian M. Patraka writes, '*Split Britches* is about women too old, too poor, too dumb, too lesbian, or too insistent on controlling their own lives to be visible.'[16] For Charlotte Canning the play was therefore about women who were 'at risk of being forgotten or erased'.[17] Split Britches' aim was to tell these women's stories, but also to tell their own, as women who were also culturally marginalised by their lesbianism in the case of Lois and Peggy, and her Jewishness in the case of Margolin. Lois has stated that 'When we worked on *Split Britches*, we wanted to create characters that people would identify with and like, and then realize..."Oh my God, I like a lesbian!"'[18]

Opposite: Deb Margolin, Peggy Shaw, and Lois Weaver in Split Britches' *Beauty and the Beast* (1983). Photo by Eva Weiss.

Even when Lois and her collaborators 'tell' canonical narratives such as *Beauty and the Beast*, *Little Women*, and *Streetcar Named Desire*, those stories act principally or at least in parallel as vehicles for the personal stories and agendas of Lois and company. In *Little Women*, when Lois speaks words as Louisa's left 'more intimate, more seductive, more passionate... more culturally marginal'[19] hand, her words might equally be Lois's: 'I was drawn to more earthquakey and volcanic themes. I wanted to be the sharp-tongued master of racy, unladylike American vernacular'.[20] Later, she turns to the audience and *'Asks for and answers questions from the audience... She must attempt to answer the questions as truthfully as possible either as the character of Louisa or as the performer herself.'*[21] Similarly, in Split Britches and Bloolips' adaptation of *Streetcar Named Desire*, *Belle Reprieve*, Lois could not simply enact the role of Stella; she *had* to tell the story of how the play oppressed her and Stella. 'Look', she says, 'I'm supposed to wander around in a state of narcotized sensuality. That's my part.'[22]

'Look', she says, 'I'm supposed to wander around in a state of narcotized sensuality. That's my part.'

This commitment to telling their own stories shared by Lois and her collaborators is not gratuitous self-indulgence, though Lois and her characters frequently approve of self-indulgence, since it rebuffs the accusation that women with any self-interest are 'dreadfully selfish'[23] and rejects the expectation that women should be self-denying.[24] This commitment to telling one's own stories demonstrates the importance of subjective perspectives. This approach which prioritises subjective perspectives is valuable in itself, for example, in telling the stories of marginalised women such as Lois's impoverished forebears in *Split Britches*, or for expressing Lois's frustration in *Belle Reprieve*. As Lois has commented, the approach pays attention to 'details that are often forgotten or stepped over in male-dominated work. But little parts of our lives are as important as the big climactic events that usually make dramas.'[25] The approach is also important because it challenges would-be objectivity, revealing it as a mask behind which male-dominated cultures conceal their own subjective desires and agendas. In Tennessee Williams' *Streetcar Named Desire*, for example, an apparently objective, fictional perspective contains Stella and degrades her sister Blanche as 'mad', all the better to give Stella's husband character Stanley full range to tyrannise her and rape Blanche. (Admittedly, Williams' play does acknowledge many of the structural conditions that produce women's oppression.)

In terms of process, this desire-led approach is perhaps more about the *processes of pursuing* desires or making the work as it is about arriving at satisfying conclusions or the final performance as a finished piece, which partly explains why Split Britches' and Lois's other performances often evolve over several years. Her performance piece 'Still Counting', for example, also takes the slightly different form of *What Tammy Found Out*, and both accrue more material as time passes and they are performed at different ages and for different contexts and audiences.[26] *Dress Suits to Hire* was first performed in the mid-1980s, then worked through in workshops in Taiwan in 2004 and at the University of Texas at Austin in 2005, then re-staged in 2005. As Lois recounts, she and her collaborators would 'bring the show to its knees, and then invite an audience to help us stand up. Or sometimes, we'd say, 'We invited people for dinner. We went to the grocery store. On the way back, we met them on the doorstep. We hadn't quite cooked the dinner.'[27]

Opposite: Lois Weaver and Peggy Shaw in *Belle Reprieve* (Weaver, Shaw, Bette Bourne, and Paul Shaw, 1991), Drill Hall, London. Photo by Sheila Burnett.

This emphasis on ⟨fly-by-the-seat-of-your-pants⟩ process also means that Lois and her collaborators resist objectifying and commodifying their work. For them, box office takings are important for making the work and paying the workers, but likely more significant is the work's processes, including processes of making, but also processes of audience-performer interaction and audience reception. Even the forms of performance the work ultimately does take might be described not as conventional dramatic narratives, with crises, resolutions, and denouements, but as process-based patchworks, assembled from asides, duets, solo moments, comic numbers, lip synch sequences, songs, and sudden turns which are not necessarily motivated by narrative. This emphasis on collective process also values what Sue-Ellen Case has identified as collective subjectivity, which she calls 'the most forward construction in the feminist field' because it resists the inbuilt dualism and conflict of conventional drama, suggests a kind of 'transpersonal subject', and claims subjective agency for women even while it emphasises women's heterogeneity *and* values collectivism and mutuality.[28]

Work

A second key element of Lois and her collaborators' performance is that it is often about work, and it often explicitly shows that it is itself work. Instead of attempting to naturalise or disguise the labour and effort that go into making it, as so much theatre does, Lois and her collaborators repeatedly foreground the material challenges, practical labours, and interpersonal negotiations that go into creating anything, including performance. Fundamentally, this makes the work's form Brechtian and its effect, like Brecht's, social critique. By exposing and denaturalising the processes of production, the work shows those processes and their outcomes as the result of choices that are influenced by material and social conditions. Lois and collaborators show that gender is produced, not natural, and that its oppressions, too, are produced and reproduced. They show that art and

Lois Weaver in original version of
Dress Suits to Hire (Weaver, Shaw, and Holly Hughes, 1987), Vesleka Performance Festival, P.S. 122, NYC. Photo by Uzi Parnes.

They make work that they want to make and, as feminists, that they need to make.

Peggy Shaw, Lois Weaver, and Stacy Makishi in *Salad of the Bad Café* (Weaver, Shaw, Makishi, 1999), La MaMa, NYC. Photo by Tom Brazil.

creativity are not some romantic form of magic which happens without effort or finance, but rather labour produced in a 'factory' (as Peggy Shaw called the WOW Café in interview with Kate Davy)[29] by artists who have to pay the rent. And they show how collaborations, like other relationships, also need work – attention, nurturing, care, and love.

Across their work, Lois, Split Britches and her other collaborators stage the construction of gender, showing how social attitudes towards gender violently constrain women. In *Belle Reprieve*, Lois has to play a woman who is continuously 'narcotized', a construction of femininity which demonstrably aggrieves Lois. In *Salad of the Bad Café*, Peggy Shaw is required to wear a dress because Lois wants to appear in masculine clothes but her femme politics (discussed in the previous section) insist that lesbian feminist performance must not exclude or erase the kinds of female identity that dresses can signify. The play stages the labour of producing different articulations of femininity as well as the labour of negotiating conflicting desires. In *Little Women*, Louisa May Alcott has to repress the racy, volcanic themes she really wants to write about in order to support her family by producing writing which falls within suitably saleable, conventional ideas of femininity.

Split Britches' choices make a stark contrast to Alcott's: they make work that they want to make and, as feminists, that they *need* to make, but they barely scrape a living doing so. In *Little Women*, their props are virtually all handmade or cheap, plastic toys. And in *Upwardly Mobile Home*, the three characters' continuously disastrous efforts to make a performance are shown to be the consequences, at least in large part, of their extraordinarily precarious living conditions: they have to brew coffee on a Coleman stove, they hand wash their clothes, they do multiple jobs, and they go without the 'clown white' and face cream they run out of.[30] Similarly, as Vivian Patraka has observed, the very title of

She advocates performance as work, and encourages everyone she collaborates with to see it as work they too can do.

Split Britches focuses on the adapted clothing the women wear to continue working in the fields even while urinating, and the play itself features the repetitive labour of cooking biscuits, fetching wood, tending the fire, delivering eggs to market, and sewing quilts.[31] In both *Split Britches* and *Upwardly Mobile Home*, the characters' experiences of labour and a needs-based frugality merge tellingly with those of the performers, Lois, Peggy Shaw, and Deb Margolin, who are also making a performance/a living in a small space, with rudimentary scenery and thrift shop costumes which are mismatched in ways at once joyously playful and starkly articulate about the company's constrained circumstances.

Split Britches' shows are also generally explicit about the labours and negotiations their creation entails, especially in what the company refers to as the 'Split Britches Breakdown' scenes.[32] Here, 'everything' the company 'has been going through' in devising the show 'is brought up'.[33] In a production drawing on Euripides' *Alcestis* at Hampshire College in 1993, the 'breakdown' scene included Peggy's protests against playing a man, Lois's ambivalence about playing a woman who dies for a man but wanting to do so in order to come back singing an aria, and Deb Margolin's argument that women's choice of clothing shouldn't be censored according to ideas of putative 'respectability' if those ideas sacrificed her sexual expressivity.[34] As Lois observed, the scene allowed audiences to 'see us struggling with the issues. . . , [to] see that we don't have any answers, necessarily, to some of the questions'.[35]

What this repeated foregrounding of conditions of work does is make visible the material and cultural conditions that enable some – those with privilege – and restrain or discourage others. This discouragement internalised as self-doubt and self-censorship is part of what Lois tries to teach her students, collaborators, and audiences to cast off by encouraging them to commit to desire and instinct.

Work is not only an important subject and an important formal aesthetic in Lois and Split Britches' performance-making, it is also an important feature of their creative practices. Of course all performance makers work. But Lois has a disciplined, committed, hardworking approach to work, she advocates performance *as* work, and she encourages everyone she collaborates with to see it as work they too can do, despite art's mythic exclusivity. This pro-work approach demystifies ideas of being an artist as the protected preserve of only those with natural-born talent or personal (financial) resources. For Lois, anyone can be an artist; she shows it is never so mysterious as to be beyond anyone's reach. In echoing the slightly vexed phrase 'for the love of god', the title Lois created for this section of the book, 'For the Love of Work', chivvies people to get on with it and make work, despite their self-censorship, self-doubt or apparent lack of resources. This approach is one Lois takes across her work as a director, teacher, co-writer, performer, facilitator, and more. It is enabling, generous and, indeed, loving, and it is a main pillar of her commitment to – and achievement of – human rights and democracy through its democratising effects for performance, public discourse, and social life.

Deb Margolin, Peggy Shaw, and Lois Weaver in two different scenes from *Upwardly Mobile Home* (Weaver, Shaw, and Margolin, 1984), WOW Café, NYC. Photo by Uzi Parnes.

Humour and Irreverence

A third key feature that is pervasive across Lois and her collaborators' performance-making and that again informs its content, forms, and practices is the work's fun, humour and jolly, often cheerfully vulgar, irreverence. As Peggy Shaw has said in interview about the WOW Café that she and Lois co-founded and co-ran with others in New York for many years, 'At WOW, it's funny. It's an aesthetic.'[36] This commitment to humour continues the mission of Lois and her collaborators – especially Peggy Shaw – to challenge conventional cultural hierarchies, especially those that privilege patriarchy, in order to queer culture and thereby democratise it.

Formally, this humour includes slapstick sequences, such as when Lois/ Stella and Peggy/Stanley debate what's funny in *Belle Reprieve*. The scene is appropriated from a famous vaudevillian turn and culminates in Lois approaching Peggy with a 'cream pie' (shaving foam in a pan), only for Peggy/ Stanley 'unexpectedly' to tip it into Stella/Lois's face and pronounce, 'Now *that* was funny.'[37] The conclusion *is* funny, but it also highlights how the butch/man habitually dominates the femme woman and makes her the butt of his joke. Another humorous form Split Britches adores is lip-synching. In *Anniversary Waltz*, a femme-y, chirpy Lois lip-synchs Barbra Streisand's lines in 'You Don't Bring Me Flowers' while (badly) manipulating Peggy's body like a ventriloquist's dummy to make her 'sing' Neil Diamond's part. Comedy arises immediately from the queering of Barbra and Neil's apparently heterosexual and certainly canonical duet. In Split Britches' sassy democratising crusade, nothing – not Louisa May Alcott's novels, nor Tennessee Williams' plays, nor Barbra and Neil's duets – possesses the kind of canonical inviolability that puts it beyond irreverent ransacking and redeployment. Humour in this duet sequence also comes from the dissonance produced by tiny Lois's attempts to maintain both a 'bubbly and spunky'[38] femme hostess's attitude *and* the attention of her adoring audience, while simultaneously controlling Peggy's large, passive, dead-weight, and ultimately disobedient body, which starts to keel over several times before Lois manages to upright it. Sequences such as this stage the oppressions of dominant gender roles while never letting those oppressions have the last, miserable word; Lois, Peggy, and their audiences take the last, gleeful laugh.

Especially as Tammy WhyNot, Lois also often adopts a tone of cheerful naivety that cunningly allows her to treat social taboos with acute irreverence. In the on-going performance series *What Tammy Needs to Know*, Tammy asks all kinds of 'inappropriate' questions, regarding, for example, *What Tammy Needs to Know... about Getting Old and Having Sex*, first staged in 2008. Tammy's apparent naivety allows her to pass under the radar of propriety to ask difficult, often neglected but crucially important social questions, here about intimacy in older age, while also massaging those questions' difficulty with the grease of wonder.

Lois frequently interjects what is apparently inappropriate to challenge unwritten rules of propriety, especially in situations which claim their own authority through elite and exclusive rituals. Later in this book, Johanna Linsley writes about how Lois and Tammy practise 'subversive expertise' in the context of the ritual of the British university inaugural lecture which marks an academic's promotion to the rank of full Professor and is usually framed by the pomp

They stage the oppressions of dominant gender roles while never letting those oppressions have the last, miserable word.

Lois Weaver and Peggy Shaw in *Anniversary Waltz* (Weaver and Shaw with sets by Paul Shaw, 1990), Drill Hall, London. Photo by Sheila Burnett.

and circumstance of a procession of academically-robed Principals and Vice-Principals, a series of ceremonial introductions and responses, and a formal wine reception in what is often an inhospitable institutional space. Lois's inaugural lecture at Queen Mary University of London in 2012 was titled *What Tammy Found Out: A Front Line Report from the Back Porch, the School Yard and the Dinner Table*. It was indeed a lecture, but it was punctuated with two sets of important interjections. One of these was her act of slinging cupcakes into the initially unsuspecting crowd. Another was the fact that several times, without warning, commentary or apparent 'motivation', she occasionally 'fell down', stricken into temporary silence, only to rise again a moment or so later and continue where she left off with her lecture. For me, the flying cupcakes staged Lois's consistently ambivalent relationship to being a femme hostess, at once a role she idolises and fetishises and one she defies and rejects, as I discussed in the earlier section on Lois and femme. The falling down was funny and unsettling, an unpredictable series of moments when Lois ludicrously punctuated the event. But it also literalised her 'falling out' or 'passing out' of the event, her ostensibly inarticulate (but actually very clear) response to the self-proclaimed, secure authority of both the event and the institution.

Across her work Lois again and again promotes and relies on comedy, play, and irreverence. She values popular tastes such as slapstick in gestures of democracy but also of love, as she affirms forms that she herself loves and that she finds her collaborators and audiences loving too – like the water-squirting plastic cameras in *Little Women*. Split Britches co-founder Deb Margolin once described the collective vision she, Peggy Shaw, and Lois discovered while making *Split Britches* as the 'overlapping point of Sapphic poetry, MAD magazine, the Talmud, and the Marx Brothers'.[39] Lois deflates authority-protecting attitudes of canonical superiority. She addresses would-be 'taboo' topics that are simply socially censored topics. And perhaps most importantly, she welcomes her collaborators and audiences to play and laugh with her, flying in social change on the wings of a soaring cupcake and the holler of a dirty laugh.

Love, Care, and Loss

Finally, Lois and her collaborators' work is about love, and it is love. It stages all kinds of love: love between women in *Split Britches*; one woman's lust for another woman in shows such as *Belle Reprieve*; love for the disappearing lounge acts of the 1950 and 1960s in *Lost Lounge*; love of fun and experiment with Tammy; and much more. It's not always joyous love. Quite often it's ambivalent, marked by distrust and the lurking possibility that Lois and Peggy will mock each other *as well as* love each other, marked, in other words, by the reality that love *includes* violence. In *Lust and Comfort*, for example, they dance violently to 'The Ten Commandments of Love'.[40] The love is also often bittersweet, noting the *loss* of something still loved but achingly missed: Lois's mother after her death in *Faith and Dancing*; or the American dream before the beatification of selfishness in *Miss America*. Whether joyous or saddened, the work's expression of love is a testament to its commitment to emotional instinct and honesty, despite the fact that its slapstick cavorting is decidedly *not* the sincere, realist form that usually makes such claims to truth. And even when the love is sad or longing, the shows themselves perform efforts to retrieve and redeem what's lost, even while recognising the loss. Love's pleasures and love's pains are the messy emotional terrains of the work.

A tendency to put the same kinds of love and effort into work as she does into personal relationships means she has little life/work separation.

Again, love is not only the subject of much of the work of Lois and her collaborators; it is the form and the practice. As collaborator Stacy Makishi observes in this section of the book, Lois's work is always about collaboration, friendship, and love. As I noted above, Lois's tendency to put the same kinds of love and effort into her work as she does into her personal relationships means she has little life/work separation. It also means she works in ways that could be seen as polyamorous, or at least not monogamous, or perhaps poly-caring. She always has more than one important project on the go. If I meet to talk with her about research, we inevitably also discuss friends we mutually care about and students for whom we share some responsibility. For me, these are all features of Lois's feminist practice, which is intrinsically collaborative, led by human relationships, and nurturing of those whose voices are marginalised, not least performance makers who are at early stages in their careers. The love in Lois's work also reveals its social commitment; even – or perhaps especially – at its funniest, this is work with social purpose for social intervention. Throughout much of Split Britches' work, the aims have been to promote women, lesbians, and feminism. Some aspects of Lois's later work, especially through her Public Address Systems (discussed in more detail in part four, 'How Do You Make Things Work'), have been about other important human rights issues globally. Her most recent work has been about ageing. All of the work is about listening to those who are least heard, entering into conversation with them, and building relationships with them.

'I Love I Love I Love My Art'

Over the years, critics have taken many approaches to analysing the work of Split Britches in particular, as well as other aspects of Lois's work. This analysis has focused especially on butch/femme role-playing and feminist subjectivity in the work of Sue-Ellen Case,[41] audience address in the analyses of Kate Davy[42] and Jill Dolan,[43] and desire in the writings of Dolan, Vivian Patraka, and Deanna Shoemaker.[44] Case, Davy, and Paul Menard have explored the work as camp,[45] Elin Diamond has examined its formal experiments with mimesis,[46] and Lynda Hart focused on its representations of lesbianism.[47] Patraka has also explored its engagements with nostalgia, vaudeville, and the everyday.[48] Gender is at the centre – or at least boldly on the periphery – right across the critical literature. I have chosen to emphasise the four key elements of instinct/desire, work, humour, and love partly to build on the existing critical literature, and to attempt to draw out what are for me some of the most important elements of the work, all of which resonate in powerful ways with what I see as the overarching commitment, logic, ethos, and pleasure of Lois's work: love.

Looking back from behind

Deb Margolin

May 2015

I like it when people make fun of me! Now that I'm not a little kid, I find it delightful; it's a way of being seen that's tender and somehow full of care and specificity. No one ever teased me the way the members of Spiderwoman Theater did. I met them through my friend Ginny Mayer who, after a year's radio silence in the middle of our deep and enduring friendship, returned to my life and told me she'd become their business manager. She brought me to see one of Spiderwoman's wildly comical, profoundly personal, radically theatrical shows, and I felt a movement in the tectonic plates of my life. I'd just seen a bunch of wildly diverse women accredit their own lives with artistic validity and narrative viability, and it made me think my life might have valence in a similar way. I didn't really understand this yet. My work with Lois Weaver was my rigorous training in the disciplines and liberties of artistic self-respect.

When Lois stepped out of Spiderwoman, with her partner Peggy Shaw, to work on a piece about her ancestors, three strange women, invisible in the ways that women have always been invisible, she interviewed relatives about these three women and brought back tapes and notes. She and Peggy, along with another woman from the Spiderwoman company, began to play with and explore images of these women – who they may have been, what their lives may have looked like from the inside. This was, of course, an inherently feminist investigation, and comes back to the accreditation of the lives of women not considered 'attractions' in the conventional sense. They had a scriptwriter lined up to assist in capturing improvisations in the form of a written text, but this person apparently disappeared, and Lois asked my dear friend Ginny if she might not bring me around to see if I could help. Spiderwoman knew I loved to write, and Lisa Mayo, one of that company's three Native American founders, had already tried me out to write some cabaret patter-type stuff.

I didn't really understand what I saw on the day Ginny brought me. It just seemed, that afternoon, like a lot of cackling, pie dough-throwing, and a humorous and fertile kind of frustration and grief. I promised to try to help, and I remember Ginny saying, as we were leaving, 'That's going to be a brilliant piece of theatre someday'.

Lois tracked me down later that week, and I lied and said I'd written quite a bit of material and hung up. It was a weird, prescient, tremulous, and unprecedented kind of lie; the kind of lie a part of yourself you don't know yet tells. That night, sleepless, I got up and locked myself in the bathroom and wrote for hours: songs, monologues, dialogues. It was before the days of computers and tablets and iPhones. It was all just in pen on lined paper. Something unlocked for me: I realised we have collapsible boundaries; that my experience of YOU belongs to ME and vice versa; that love is a form of invention; that fiction is the redistribution of autobiography. I realised my long love of language was most at home in the theatre. I could tell that theatre was a torn-open place for the writer

I was a student, through Lois, of the feminist theatre, a theatre that sees conflict and resolution within the slightest human gesture.

Publicity photo of Peggy Shaw, Deb Margolin, and Lois Weaver in *Little Women, the Tragedy* (Weaver, Shaw, and Margolin, 1988). Photo Amy Meadow.

with all the margin of error that comes with bumbling, honest efforts to speak. I understood that images from my life could find poetic homes in the mouths of characters with whom I had nothing in common other than my humanity. I realised that this humanity varies from person to person, when you get down to the deepest levels of it, in only the tiniest and most exquisite of ways.

I brought this text to the gang, who were getting ready to open this show under great duress, and they found almost all of it useful. The headline of a review of the piece, which became the eponymous play called *Split Britches*, used a phrase I'd brought to the mouth of the character of Della from a previous part of my life, and I was sold on writing for theatre right then and there. When someone dropped out of this play, Lois contrived to take a look at me in an acting workshop taught by Polina Klimovitskaya in her loft on Leonard Street, and I seemed, I guess, through this unannounced audition process, like a potential company partner. I'm kind of weird, love comedy, love language, am outrageously clumsy and passionate, and I have always considered it a tribute to Lois Weaver's cool, detached intelligence that she was able to see in me the possibility of an actor and collaborator. Lois, Peggy, and I tried out performing together, calling ourselves Weaver, Margolin, and Shaw. The next thing I knew, I was in this play, this *Split Britches*, and we became the Split Britches Company, and we were touring Europe, and I was learning what the theatre actually is, how it functions from the inside; and more specifically, I was a student, through Lois, of the feminist theatre; of the non-Aristotelian theatre, a theatre in which an emotion is a plot point, a theatre that sees conflict and resolution, the traditional model of drama, within the slightest human gesture.

When Split Britches was on tour, which happened pretty often in the early days, we were often teaching master classes as well as performing. Some of Lois's most refined skills were in evidence in the laboratory of the classroom,

and by watching her I've studied pedagogy with someone I consider to be among the most excellent. Lois modelled a way of teaching that I think works most effectively: she was able to show her humanity at absolutely no expense to her authority. Students in any classroom, and especially a room where theatre is being studied, need to know who's in charge of the room, so they can be free to make the kinds of recondite personal inquiries that acting requires. Lois always led a room of students with her tenderest humanity visible and invulnerable at once. This alchemy is not easy to describe really. It worked miraculously to invite students out, to invite them into the room, to give them the wild fright and joy of the roller coaster ride that comes of making a self-scripted theatre piece. When you are in an ensemble, creating a piece of theatre that is at once collective and profoundly and intimately personal, having someone at the helm who understands these complexities and can curate the investigation with such calculated warmth and authority is brilliant. It is invaluable. I sought to emulate this technique for the next 30 years.

I watched Lois direct for 15 years; she taught me that acting is just being. Directing is a specialised form of teaching, and Lois managed to guide our company to the core of its purposes, ever conscious of theatricality and spectacle, but never at the expense of depth. How she managed to both direct and be in the shows at once I'll never fully understand. Part of it was demanding of Peggy and me that we watch her as acutely as she watched us, and support her in going to the most vulnerable emotional places in rehearsal. One of the few ways I always felt myself Lois's equal rather than her student was in our ways of looking at people and quickly understanding who they are; what their struggles and pretensions are; where their beauty resides, where the cracks in them must be mended rather than called out or stepped upon. We'd look at each other sometimes, in great moments of understanding, in the presence of a person in whom we both saw the same things. I watched Lois lose her father, then her mother. I learned ineffable things from this.

Lois once said to me: *You see everything from BEHIND.*

In addition to striking me as wildly funny, there was something very accurate about this observation; it implies that I'm slow, which very few people see about me because I talk so much and so quickly; but it also implies that I see people's asses! That I see things that other people aren't seeing because they're moving on without retrospect! Retrospect literally means looking back. When I look back at my 15 years with Split Britches, I see the enormous expenses and tremendous rewards of education. Lois Weaver and Peggy Shaw were teachers of mine, and I could have asked for easier teachers, but not really for better ones.

Publicity photo of Peggy Shaw, Deb Margolin, and Lois Weaver in *Upwardly Mobile Home* (Weaver, Shaw, and Margolin, 1984). Photo Eva Weiss.

Fire in My Pocket (from *Split Britches*)

Deb Margolin[49]

Della: Fire... see it ain't just a thing, it's
a person... I mean it ain't a person... it's
a living thing... got a mind of its own...
I seen Fires... I felt little fires on my
skin and I heard 'em cracklin' in my ear...
even in the rain... ~~once~~ fires think! they got purposes...
once I saw a farm burn down and all
the chickens and ~~two~~ cows... and the fire
called in other creatures... they was
big black birds! ~~Donna,~~ these birds flew
upside down next to the fire and they
came from miles around and ~~I seen~~
strings attached to 'em... *to their wings...* cause the
fire held ~~them~~ there to scare ~~the~~
animals to death. I seen a chicken fall
over... and the fire comes right over
and eats her whole body and burps out
big white smoke... there was dogs barkin'
but there wasn't no dogs! And I got
fires eatin inside of me only they don't
show themselves so as to make me be a
person with some kind of secret... ~~that is the only~~ and so
so I just feel 'em but nobody sees.
and I feel 'em in my eyes and in
my chest... and other places... I
feel like that farmhouse... and dry, and
the fire's so smart it could make ashes
outta me if I ain't careful... one
of the fires was in my pocket once... I
put my hand in there and I pull it out
real quick... and then I don't know
why I did that so I look in and there!

the fire, actin' real shy and cute like
a pretty girl, but then it starts to hurt
me and it could kill me and so I beat
it and beat it and beat it and beat
it and beat it and killed it, Emma!
I put it out! But it keeps comin'
back in other places, so I watch out!
I listen for it... I beat it before it
leaps up like that... the fire comes
like as if the whole earth was bored
and so it comes to entertain 'em
but it hurts to laugh... and by the
time the men come to put it out its
too late and there's nothin' left... its
fire steals the land for real.

Weaver's web

Stacy Makishi

Weaver. I take her name literally. It's no coincidence that she was a Spiderwoman. She's a master weaver and her web is alive. It's not science fiction. Researchers have discovered that spiders lure insects by using the mutual 'electrical attraction' of their web to catch their prey. Flying insects' wings create an electrical charge, which in turn acts as a magnet for the spider's web – sucking them towards a most glorious death. I'm getting dramatic here, but nothing's more compelling than being drawn towards destiny.... to believe we are inextricably interconnected by something continuous and alive.

Have you ever read *Charlotte's Web*? If you haven't, put down Proust and read this. It's about friendship and connection... about a wise spider named Weaver, and a lucky pig named Makishi. The pig's life is spared because of miraculous words that appear in the spider's web. The web pronounces messages of love, like 'Some Pig', 'Radiant', 'Terrific'. The spider has the pig's back, as he begins to believe, and aspires to live up to the vision that she holds for him.

I find that whatever I do well can be traced back to Weaver's web.

I met Lois Weaver in 1993, while Split Britches were teaching at the University of Hawaii. The class was full but I was convinced these women came just for me... to rescue me from paradise, so I clung on to the web. Weaver's workshop changed my life. I am just one of many who have made such claims. Weaver's web expands across the globe and extends across many contexts. 21 years have passed, and Lois has continued to be my teacher, my mentor, and friend.

In 2012, I took part in *33 x 3* – a festival celebrating the legacy of Split Britches. The festival paid tribute to both the elders (Spiderwomen) and the 'progeny' (me!) of Split Britches. During Lois's *Long Table*, I not only sat with my mentors, but alongside my mentor's mentors. I remember saying something stupid like, 'Oh, I'm nearly 50, and I don't know if my work holds any relevance...'. Gloria Miguel, who was in her eighties, interrupted, 'I didn't even *start* making work until I was 50!' Then Peggy Shaw added, 'I'm still making work and I've just had a stroke!'. Then Lisa Mayo trumped us all by saying, 'Look! I'm almost 90 with Alzheimer's, and I'm still trying to memorize my lines for my show!'

Now I am a teacher, a mentor, and an independent artist. I also have students who have grown to become teachers and mentors too. I love to think of a world of more weavers who continue to spin their egg sacs containing their progeny, or what Charlotte the spider referred to as her 'magnum opus'. We are all interconnected, radiant, and terrific. We all need someone who's got our backs and who is willing to reinforce their beliefs into us, to say that we are, indeed, Some Pig. Weaver's web saved my bacon. Her web is continuous, alive, and ever-expanding.

Stacy Makishi and Lois Weaver's
legs in a performance created by
Weaver and Makishi for Gay Sweatshop's
Club Deviance, WOW, NYC, 1996.
Photo courtesy of Gay Sweatshop.

On Lois, for Lois, because of Lois

Jill Dolan
26 November 2014

Lois Weaver has long established herself as one of the foremost practitioners and theorists in feminist and queer theatre and performance. I first saw her perform in the eponymous *Split Britches*, the three-woman Split Britches company's signature performance, at its very first presentation, in the auditorium at Bellevue Hospital sometime in 1981. I had just arrived in New York for graduate school, and fancied myself a feminist critic, whatever that meant at such an early moment in our then non-existent field. *Split Britches* used utterly innovative methods to stage lives I'd never before seen on stage; watching that performance cracked open my world.

As many well know by now, *Split Britches* concerns the lives of Lois's relatives deep in the Blue Ridge Mountains of Virginia. The three women on whom the performance focused lived in extreme rural isolation, in a small cabin in which their lives could have been mistaken for nineteenth, rather than twentieth century examples. Watching Lois perform as the odd, naive little Cora, Peggy Shaw as the volatile, sexually repressed Della, and Deb Margolin as the querulous old woman perpetually waiting for her dinner made an impression on my young feminist mind that forever reshaped how I think about theatre and performance. Lois, Peggy, and Deb presented these characters with great humour and compassion, understanding from what seemed the inside out their wealth of passion and longing, despite their simple, constrained circumstances. Such insight and empathy became a trademark Split Britches style. While the troupe's work was always funny, they never laughed at their subjects, but always understood them, sympathised with them, and truly loved them. This, I think, came from Lois's deep compassion for her origins and her ability to theorise what lives very different from her own might mean.

Lois and Split Britches established a new form and formula for feminist theatre. At a time when those two words tended to mean didactic agitprop performance with excellent politics but terrible aesthetics, Lois, Peggy, and Deb offered eager spectators a whole new way to experience theatre that addressed women's intimate public and private lives. They used popular culture motifs. (Seeing the three women stumble through a Yiddish version of 'I Like To Be in America' from *West Side Story* in their third production, *Upwardly Mobile Home*, remains one of the highlights of my theatre-going experiences.) They cast off the well-made realist play form and refused all dominant cultural assumptions about appropriate performances of gender and sexuality. Split Britches taught us (and modelled for us) that women could take pleasure in their bodies and desires without dieting ourselves out of existence and without acquiescing to dominant standards of social behaviour. Perhaps more importantly, they took seriously the complexities of women's relationships with one another and with the world, even as they explored them with great good humour and cheer.

Lois organised Split Britches' vision into a performance experience that left its spectators with a palpable sense of how our lives might be different.

Lois was the impresario-director-pedagogue on the Split Britches team. While Deb was the primary writer and Peggy perhaps the troupe's most galvanizing performer, Lois directed their productions and made theatrical alchemy from their abundance of collective performance-making metals. Lois organised Split Britches' vision into a performance experience that cohered and sang, that left its spectators with a palpable sense of how our lives might be different, along with a tactile image of how we were living now, crafted from imaginative metaphors that rang true even as they delivered their commentary in rich theatricality. Lois's meticulous sense of craft and style, and her ability to articulate a methodology for feminist performance practice, quickly made her invaluable to the by-then growing subcultural marketplace for new theatre aesthetics and ideas.

Along with directing and performing in Split Britches' work, Lois has always run workshops in which she taught other feminist performers the tricks of the trade. With Peggy, she planned two international women's theatre festivals, and hosted them in New York, events that prompted the establishment of the WOW Café on New York's Lower East Side. With Peggy and others, she ran WOW, which became, under her stewardship, a laboratory for some of the most important feminist work of the 1980s and 1990s in the United States and beyond. Lois's vision for theatre and performance has always been international, well before 'globalisation' was a buzzword of the academy. She's always endeavoured to extend the reach of performance and artistic practice that many were content to let languish in the ghettos in which it began. Lois, on the other hand, has always aimed for larger audiences, has always believed that feminist and queer work speaks universally of what it means to be human.

I'm now co-editing – with Holly Hughes and Carmelita Tropicana – a collection of plays, interviews, and conversations about the first ten years of the WOW Café, where Lois began to have her dramatic effect as an artist. I'm struck again and again in this process by how often people testify to Lois's ability to instruct them in deeply generous ways. These, after all, were typically people who'd never performed, whose participation in this deeply amateur project was driven by love – of women, of community, of the kind of ecstatic zaniness that WOW privileged and promulgated. But few of those key early players would have found the courage to perform without Lois's generative and unstinting guidance.

I've seen Lois teach in numerous venues, from university classrooms to community-based workshops, where she's instructed eager acolytes in the methods that made Split Britches so vital. In fact, Lois's roles as a teacher and as a performer have always seemed intertwined. Her approach to spectators, too, has always been pedagogical. I recall an early post-performance conversation at a Women and Theatre Program conference meeting at which Lois and Peggy talked about wanting audiences to 'like' them so that spectators could leave the theatre and say, 'Gee, I learned how to like a lesbian today.' In her own persona as 'Lois Weaver', and in her built character 'Tammy WhyNot' and the numerous roles she's played with the Split Britches trio and with Peggy as a duo over the years, Lois's on-stage aspect always presents as something of the teacher. She's not at all didactic in her presentations of self; on the contrary, she's almost casual in how she instructs spectators and fellow performers about what it means to be present together and different from yet similar to one another in space and time and history. Lois is *there*, as the facilitator, co-conspirator, chief cook and bottle-washer, master- and mistress-mind, with a thoughtful nod and vigilant eye that tells us someone is watching over the insanity, someone who takes the long view on how and why this will all pan out. She's part of what's held the WOW aesthetic together all those years, on stage and off.

Lois's pedagogical performance practice has yet to be codified which, in the best feminist tradition, leaves it nimble and fluid, responsive to the particulars of each community with which she works. Her teaching strategies embrace their own orality, as they're handed down among the students and faculty who host her campus workshops, and across the communities that produce her performances. As unlikely as it seems, even feminist practices can ossify and out-stay their usefulness, but Lois has been able to resist the canonisation that too often fixes methods and risks turning them into museum artefacts. Lois's teaching continues to respond to the moment, transforming itself alongside the feminist, queer, and critical race politics with which it's so deeply imbued and to which it's indebted. She's willing to stay out there, engaging, colliding, and sharing more and more of herself, offering more and more points of contact, even as her own flesh wears the accumulation of wisdom and the marks of time. Lois won't let those of us who've learned from her sit at her feet, because she insists on the impact of co-presence and sharing knowledge across an equal plane. But she enters our hearts as a teacher who instructs by example, who passes the learning stick back and forth, who asks as much as she shares, and who shows us how to follow our own desire.

Over the years, Lois has also taught us how to age with grace. As a public personality and persona (as herself and as Tammy WhyNot), she's made her own growth and ageing visible where others of us (who write or constitute audiences) stay comfortably out of the public eye. Her performance of ageing, too, has been pedagogical. After Split Britches stopped performing as a trio, Lois created original work as a duo with Peggy and presented her own solo work under the evolving auspices of *What Tammy Needs to Know*. In the early 2000s, Peggy and Lois revived *Dress Suits to Hire*, the two-hander they first performed in the late 1980s, which was written by performance artist Holly Hughes. The remounting of the piece 20 years later allowed Lois and Peggy to revisit one of their most important performances and, without changing a word of the text or revising much of the blocking, to inquire into the effects of time and its passage on a specific piece and its performers. The revival proved a moving, elegiac affair, partly because how time had changed these two iconic lesbian bodies was distinctly on view. Even in the poster created for the production, Lois and Peggy simply look older; their bodies, drawn together in a near embrace, their faces close enough to one another to kiss, show more wrinkled skin, lowered jaw lines, and more rounded flesh. They're clearly middle-aged and astoundingly beautiful. The sepia-toned poster offers an implicit comment on how the new production looked back, inviting a not quite nostalgic return to an earlier work that still, presciently, spoke into the present.

Lois and Peggy have also devised new performance pieces in the last decade, which capitalise on their long-term professional and personal relationship to inquire into contemporary intimate and social politics under the patina of ageing. *Lost Lounge*, first presented at Dixon Place in New York, uses snippets of video, interspersed with monologues and stand-up comic 'shtick' to explore

The revival proved a moving, elegiac affair, partly because how time had changed these two iconic lesbian bodies was distinctly on view.

Lois Weaver as Michigan in the remounting of *Dress Suits to Hire* (Weaver, Shaw, and Holly Hughes), Off Centre Theatre, Austin, Texas, 2005. Photo Lori E. Seid.

They are adept at juxtapositions that accrue meaning through the unexpected proximity of ideas, written across the bodies of middle-aged women daring to command the stage.

how we can resist the encroachments of capitalism when it's presented as social progress. Time here ticks down inexorably as we watch, moving toward what Lois and Peggy hint is already gone: humanity, love, youth. As in the *Dress Suits* revival, the duo revels in their advancing age, thinking across their personal and public history to make critical claims on the present. Their *Miss America*, which debuted at LaMama E.T.C., engages the double meaning of its title to address beauty pageants, Hurricane Katrina, and the battered remnants of the American dream. Lois and Peggy are adept at juxtapositions that accrue poignant meaning through the unexpected proximity of events and ideas, all written across the bodies of middle-aged women daring to command the stage.

Likewise, *What Tammy Needs to Know about Getting Old and Having Sex* continues Lois's 30-year construction of the Tammy WhyNot persona, an affectionate parody of the country music sensation Tammy Wynette. In this piece, Lois collaborates with older adults, using interviews and collective research to describe how ageing influences intimacy. The performance is personal and public, asking audiences to meet her more than halfway in their willingness to be vulnerable to the effects of time on bodies. And as always, she's fearless about how much she's willing to expose of herself, physically and emotionally.

Lois has always been an itinerant artist, despite her half-time position as Professor of Contemporary Performance Practice at Queen Mary University of London, a long way from the ad hoc workshop teaching she began at WOW on the Lower East Side of New York. She's travelled the world over, bringing her unique and powerful vision for performance and social change to people who've found their lives transformed by her presence, her practice, her politics, and her creativity. She's collaborated with artists and with scholars, determined to build and extend the community of feminist performance practice into those committed to all forms of social justice, in which her performing and teaching methods find renewed purchase and purpose. Her impact on performance has been profound and global, and her commitment to spreading the ever-renewing gospel of her artistic practice is deep and abiding. Her impact on me has been indelible and on-going; my gratitude remains immense.

Lois Weaver, Peggy Shaw, and Vivian Stoll in *Lost Lounge* (Weaver and Shaw, Skirt by Johann Stegmeir, 2009), Dixon Place, NYC. Photos by Lori E. Seid.

The permanence of a performance

Jess Dobkin

I saw Lois Weaver perform *Faith and Dancing* at La Mama in 1999. I had to go see it a second time because the performance changed my life. When I watched her dance, tantrum, strip, and (silent) scream to Billy Joel's 'She's Always a Woman to Me', I witnessed a person achieving greatness, discovered a lesbian being divine. I care to put Lois Weaver on a pedestal. As lesbians, sometimes in our fight for equality we neglect to acknowledge the extraordinary. We forget to be as affected by beauty and power as we are by injustice and discrimination.

Performance is considered an ephemeral form, but this Billy Joel number proves its permanence; it is lodged, solid in me, and I carry it with more weight and form than a standard memory. We talk of trauma living in the body; a great performance can, too. They cohabitate where the Venn diagram intersects at that juncture of Things That Happen to a Person. They are the things that are transmitted, the most ugly and the most beautiful.

1999 was a long time ago, yet my thoughts often return to the potency of that Billy Joel number. I toss and turn with it, wanting to explain its mystery and magic, its power over me. It makes me step back and then lean forward to peer in to question the nature of performance itself. How is performance transmitted? How is inspiration shared? How does art transform us? Beyond Weaver's craft, intellect, and hotness, beyond giving voice to unspoken issues of our time, there is her spirit. We witness the embodiment of another way of being; we see aliveness in action. This is what art can do, what it can be, in freedom and in difficulty and dignity.

Weaver brilliantly recruits Billy Joel, the messy piano man-child who can't get his act together, can't get it right with the ladies, as an unknowing accomplice for her radical lesbian feminist agenda. She starts the scene as her younger self, a girl playing with matches in a dress made of paper, a girl who holds knowledge of natural and social disasters.

We are all aware of the dangers, and she isn't naive in her course of action, as she teases the open flame in a cramped, crowded East Village theatre. She channels Dorothy Gale, in her glittering ruby slippers, on her cornmeal Yellow Brick Road, a girl/woman on a courageous journey to understand her mother, her sexuality, and herself. It's significant that this is one of Weaver's very few solo works. It is a Heroine's Journey that can only be accomplished unaccompanied, without the three stunted sidekicks to hold her back, and without the butch companion to help or hinder.

Her strip is anything but a tease. It is self-possessed and of absolute necessity. The dress comes off, the ruby slippers come off, and she performs what Dorothy dared not: she rejects the paved road and declines the return home to Kansas (in Weaver's case, the mother and the state called Virginia). Her process moves from questioning authority to questioning reality. She is consciously homeless, a real and naked renegade.

When middle-aged women take off their clothes, there's habitually some remark commending their vulnerability and bravery, reinforcing patriarchal values that prescribe these bodies as undesirable and unwelcome. Yet when Weaver rips her dress and underwear, she performs visibility, not vulnerability. She performs power and presence, the embodiment of the tornados and volcanoes she ponders.

Her tantrum has the compulsion of a child, and yet, unlike the futile rage of children, hers is effective. She conjures up adult sexual energy while simultaneously depicting childhood, exploring the taboo connection between adult and child sexuality. She's dancing naked at the junction of girl/woman, daughter/mother. She's stomping and swinging at the intersection of wisdom and spirit. From this liminal space she offers a new, multidimensional reality, a prismatic view of the world.

Opposite: Lois Weaver in *Faith and Dancing: Mapping Femininities and Other Natural Disasters* (1996), La MaMa, NYC. Photo by Tom Brazil.

A queer family tree

The Famous Lauren Barri Holstein

The first time I met Lois Weaver was in 2010 during Fresh AiR, a London-based platform for emerging artists co-directed by Weaver, where I was asked to present my work. I was paired with performance maker Stacy Makishi as my mentor, Weaver's renowned mentee. Immediately a lineage of loud, queer, American, cunty ladies was conceived. While Lois may not be aware that I consider her a sort of grandmother to my work, I certainly revel in our illustrious family tree.

Lois Weaver, among others, has laid the groundwork for contemporary feminist performance, engendering a genealogy, a family tree, to nurture 'newcomers' like myself. Weaver's work has consistently challenged established forms and ideologies, providing not only a political lineage, but a formal, or strategic, one as well. The queer, feminist politics of her work are mobilised by her forms and techniques. The strategy of troubling mimesis, of appropriating and destabilising the familiar, is central to Weaver's practice, as well as to the subsequent history of feminist performance practices, including Makishi's work and my own.

As Rebecca Schneider points out, 'it seems to be often forgotten that the core of much feminist performance-based work of [the 1970s] was *already* a kind of re-performance – a repetition, a remimesis not concerned with purity or authenticity– through acts engaged in re-acting against the stultifying dilemma of the "second" sex'.[50] Weaver's work re-inscribes a poignancy, a politic, around the representation of lesbian desire and the power structures of gender and sexuality through miming the recognisable and recycling its use – both through content, and through form. Split Britches' transformations of canonical texts – *Little Women* (1988), *Beauty and the Beast* (1982) – mime the predecessor, and in doing so, produce a queer update, a contemporary recontextualisation, of a recognisable story. Weaver's work re-enacts representations of lesbian desire, but in its re-enactment, it is strategically redeployed – through the use of parody, drag, and 'poor' aesthetics – pointing to the problematic representation it mimes, but also re-inscribing it with a new politic through its subversive appropriation.

Equally, her art-daughter, Stacy Makishi, reclaims popular films and television series – the acclaimed Coen Brothers film *Fargo* (1996) in her piece *The Making of Bull: The True Story* (2011) and the popular HBO series *The Sopranos* (1999-2007) in her work *The Falsettos* (2013). Makishi hilariously redistributes queer, feminist reconstructed narratives in her work though these appropriations. Similarly, I rehash, reuse, and generally make a mess of recognisable pop songs, fairytales, celebrity tabloid drama, and even historical feminist performances in my work in order to 'update', re-imagine, and reanimate the central feminist politics underlying the work.

The strategy of appropriating and destabilising the familiar is central to Weaver's practice.

Tammy WhyNot, Weaver's beloved Southern persona, 'famous country music singer turned lesbian performance artist', is another manifestation of this mimetic strategy. Weaver's adoption of Tammy Wynette, a famous country singer in the vein and era of June Cash or Dolly Parton, again, is a queer update, a feminist appropriation. Wynette, most famous for her songs about the hardships of (heterosexual) relationships, is re-imagined in the body of WhyNot – WhyNot a lesbian? WhyNot a feminist? WhyNot a performance artist? But in this case, the mimetic appropriation is not a parody – it is a destabilising homage. Like my own appropriations of canonical feminist performance, including the work of Weaver, the strategy of destabilising mimesis can be both a tribute and a subversion.

When 'repeating it' is a political move towards recontextualisation, when 'copying' occurs within a different set of socio-cultural-political circumstances, it can be re-categorised not only as an honouring of the past, but of political moves towards the future. As WhyNot nods to Wynette, The Famous curtsies to Weaver/WhyNot – and to Finley, to Schneemann, to Wilke, to Lunch – revealing yet another (metaphorical and/or literal) cunt to the audience, but also a recontextualised contemporary politics around the well-known image.

Weaver's strategic refusal of 'authenticity', of 'the original', provides a model of feminist performance that constantly regenerates itself, that updates itself, in its own reproductive mimesis. Her canon of work can be situated not only as a political and strategic progenitor to contemporary feminist work, but also as its own descendant, as she continues to develop and evolve her practice. And as she moves forward, she further establishes a lineage of queer, feminist performance that recycles its own motives, aesthetics, and strategies in order to call into question, continually and contemporarily, problematic representations of gender and sexuality.

Lois

Elin Diamond

To write on Lois Weaver is to pour through two big file folders crammed with programmes, notes, letters, and reviews dating from 1983, when I arrived in New Jersey to take a job at Rutgers, until, well, yesterday, when I saw *What Tammy Needs to Know About Getting Old and Having Sex, The Concert Tour* at La MaMa in New York. How did I hear about the 1983 show? Maybe from *The Village Voice*. Maybe from Vicki Patraka or Lynda Hart, both of whom I met before coming east. I remember sitting at a theatre with a broad stage when someone called Lois Weaver walked on and spoke in a honey-coated Southern voice that had an edge to it. Apparently *Split Britches: The True Story* would be an homage to Lois's ancestors who survived the Depression on an isolated Blue Ridge Mountain farm. Good actor's diction, I thought, and something else. As the play started, with its hilarious faux-ethnographic slides (staged tableaux) and endless talk of biscuits, I understood that notwithstanding the play's autobiographical premise, performers Lois Weaver, Peggy Shaw, and Deb Margolin were utterly unique stage presences and neither they nor the script sought to rationalise or disguise their differences. Each woman had solos that fit and didn't fit with 'character development' – like the references of tall Della (Peggy) to Catholic girls and short Emma (Deb) to 200 girls swatting flies. None of these odd images added up to an identity. Instead it seemed that the performers' histories and raw desires were emerging from behind the granny specs and aprons (and those invisible crotchless work pants or split britches, designed for easier peeing).

Split *Britches: The True Story* was her 'roots' project and Lois, as director, created a production ecology of soft turf for playing and an open sky for verbal fireworks and song. No linear action but rather powerful acts of expression, connection, and comical disconnection. Doubtless Lois's experiences with Spiderwoman Theater taught her how to carry out open-form performance storytelling yet her stage images for *Split Britches* were distinct and memorable. The one I remember best is Peggy in profile upstage, her straight back slightly stooped over biscuit batter. When the three Virginia women took their places in a final tableau, narrating the facts of the deaths of the actual women they played, Peggy/Della, without warning, delivered a beautiful monologue, written by Deb: she 'had fire eatin' inside of me. I can feel it but you can't see it. And that makes me a person with a secret. [...] It's fire steals the land for real.'[51] Peggy's throaty urgent syncopated phrasing (one of her gifts to performance for the next 40 years) made the speech catch fire: the longing and mystery of tall Della singed us as we listened there in the audience. At that long-ago performance of *Split Britches* I was so overwhelmed with pleasure at what these women were doing in their apartness-togetherness, so pleased at lesbian and feminist energies swerving and swirling through rages and repetitions, shouting and kissing, that I couldn't see what Lois had done, though it was, of course, the shape of everything I was seeing.

Opposite: Lois Weaver in Split Britches' *Miss America* (Weaver and Shaw, 2008). Photo by Lori E. Seid.

Misprision is the term for comic misunderstandings, coming from the old French *mes-prendre*, to mis-take. It refers to farcical plot twists that let audiences feel superior to the characters' mis-takings and misrecognitions. Audiences like to laugh at misprision but I was laughing at what *I* didn't recognise – the uncorked poetry of fire and bugs ('fire in the pocket' would be a favourite trope of Deb's) and a kind of acting that I couldn't name until Lois explained it in a much later solo show, *Faith and Dancing* (1996): an acting that consists of 'practising my personality'. Peggy's version is simpler: 'I always play myself.' If you're a sexual woman, if you're a sexual *queer* woman, playing yourself is a complicated and political thing to do, especially in Reagan's America in the 1980s with its reverence for a 'new traditionalism'. In response, Split Britches[52] cultivated the old traditions, putting down roots in popular culture, parody, and cabaret satire. They tossed a feminist glance in Brecht's direction not to reveal the historical contradictions of capitalism but to reveal the contradictions in their own lives – for laughs. They vacuumed up and reassembled gender roles, camp styles, and the extreme political conservatism of the era both to mock and to take seriously the patchwork of traits, styles, yearnings, identifications, and hungers that women dramatise every day as 'personality'. It turns out that in flaunting their poor-theatre pedigree, their cabaret flair, and their personalities, Split Britches was giving us another kind of history – the unofficial history of feminists and queers trying to survive capitalism – all the while inviting their audiences to laugh at platitudes, presidents, and the nonsensical misprisions of gendered reality.

Of all the Split Britches collaborations, my favourite is *Upwardly Mobile Home* (1985), an experiment in feminist dada: anarchic, confrontational, and sharply political. With a triple-character schema (performers playing themselves, playing a family of actors, playing parts from a Depression-era film in the hopes of winning a new mobile home), Weaver, Margolin, and Shaw take aim at the economic and gender politics of the mid-1980s. We had an actor playing a president, one who pushed through neoliberal 'reforms' that squeezed the middle class, attacked organised labour, and nearly destroyed the poor and the striving. New York City has always generated catastrophic rent stories but, as Sue-Ellen Case observes in her introduction to *Split Britches: Lesbian Practice/ Feminist Performance*, lower Manhattan in 1985 was in the midst of a gentrification rush that displaced thousands from the subsistence-living rentals they'd occupied for years.[53] Artists like everyone else looked for ways to peddle their skills and struggled to keep alternative theatre venues like WOW, the women's performance space of which Lois and Peggy were co-founders, up and running. Under Lois's direction the frustrated trio of *Upwardly Mobile Home* produced unforgettable images: Mother Goddam (Peggy) methodically washing their dirty underwear, Mother snarling at the audience, 'You have paid to see me. You will not get your money back'[54]; LeVine (Deb) addressing an unseen crowd: 'I know what you're thinking. You're thinking this woman's not normal. [...]Well I am normal, I drive a car. [...] And I am talented. Didn't you hear that song I just sang? It was very good, and I am upwardly mobile'.[55] Then there was *West Side Story*'s 'I like To Be in America' translated into Yiddish by Margolin and sung with gusto by all three inside a gigantic hoop skirt.

I was so overwhelmed with pleasure that I couldn't see what Lois had done, though it was, of course, the shape of everything I was seeing.

Opposite: Lois Weaver, Peggy Shaw, and Deb Margolin in Split Britches' *Upwardly Mobile Home* (Weaver, Shaw, and Margolin, 1984). Photo by Eva Weiss.

Upwardly Mobile Home also marks the (re)appearance of Tammy WhyNot, who was born in Spiderwoman's *The Lysistrata Numbah!* in 1978. Lois's Tammy puns on the name of country music singer Tammy Wynette but is inspired by the wit, generosity, and (knowingly deployed) naiveté of another country music megastar, Dolly Parton. Unlike the multiply married and chronically ill Wynette, Parton is very much alive, successful, and queerly beloved. In *Upwardly Mobile Home*, Tammy emerges from the family van with blonde hair in curlers, dreaming of Burger King coffee. She often speaks to an imaginary buyer of belongings that she's trying to sell out of a suitcase, cooing half apologetically, 'We're usually on the road and we just couldn't hold on to our apartments.[...] And I also had this other place... it used to be a warehouse and now it's TriBeCa'.[56] But her marketing contradicts her desires: she doesn't want to sell her stuff. In one of the play's most searching monologues about the invisibility of the poor, Tammy worries that '[s]ometimes I'm afraid we're just too far gone. I'm afraid we just slipped through a crack somewhere...'.[57] In the styling of Split Britches, however, deep emotion is never far from comedy; the tone quickly shifts and Tammy enacts the happy fantasy of starring in a country music spectacular complete with canned cheers. The all-women audience at WOW soon join in, overwhelming the canned cheers with its own applause and admiring whistles, especially when Tammy sings, 'Your good girl is gonna go bad.' Tammy brought us *in* during that mini-performance – a sexual seduction where the audience embraced Tammy publically and noisily and amused *itself* in the process – all orchestrated, of course, by Lois.

Behind Tammy's sweet seduction is a distinctly femme seduction. Tammy's increasing importance in Lois's professional life has a lot to do with how much Lois can accomplish in her exploration of femme sexuality, behaviour, and politics by embodying her. 'No one sees the femme,' Lois has said, 'unless she's on the arm of a butch'. And: 'What is a femme alone? What is a femme's resistance?' With one

Left: Publicity photo of Peggy Shaw, Bette Bourne, Lois Weaver, and Paul Shaw for *Belle Reprieve* (Weaver, Shaw, Bette Bourne, and Paul Shaw, 1991). Photo by Sheila Burnett.

Right: Peggy Shaw as Stanley and Lois Weaver as Stella in *Belle Reprieve* (Weaver, Shaw, Bette Bourne, and Paul Shaw, 1991). Photographer unknown.

In *Belle Reprieve*, Lois throws down a femme gauntlet on the very ground of queer performance.

foot in the straight world and both feet in the feminist one, I saw these questions play out in *Belle Reprieve*, Weaver and Shaw's inventive collaboration with Bloolips performers Bette Bourne and Paul Shaw in 1990/1991. A mocking, loving implosion of Tennessee Williams' *Streetcar Named Desire*, a play that has been a repository for queer gender send-ups for decades, *Belle Reprieve* gives audiences a reprieve not only from Williams' tragic plotting but also from stale parodies of his characters. The performers collaborated to devise a script that honours theatre's capacity to disrupt gender stereotypes *and* to reinforce them. As usual Lois directed, airing out Williams' toxic fatalities with vaudeville numbers, comic bits, and recycled theatrical props (old trunks). Quip-ready drag queen Bourne played Blanche with vaguely exhausted elegance; ripped-t-shirted Peggy Shaw gorgeously inhabited and thus undercut Stanley's boorishness; Paul Shaw as Mitch was a 'fairy disguised as a man,' but Lois Weaver wins the tautology prize: Stella's description in the cast of characters reads 'a woman disguised as a woman'. Freud thought straight women, wanting daddy, were forced into a gender masquerade; gay women, wanting to *be* daddy, only more so. And the lesbian femme? Nowhere, as Lois remarked, to be seen. In *Belle Reprieve*, then, Lois throws down a femme gauntlet on the very ground of queer performance: Split Britches and Bloolips already had deep reputations as contemporary gay performers, and of course drag queens like Bette have a long history of playing women better than women do. So who is Lois's Stella?

In theatre, identity questions are inevitable but absurd. Much better to ask: what is she doing? At the opening of *Belle Reprieve*, a blonde-coiffed Stella in high heels and a belted flared 1950s print dress saunters onstage chugging a bottle of Coke. It's hot out. She cocks an eye at the audience and begins her seduction and – typical of Split Britches' style – she undercuts the seduction with real questions: 'Is there something you want? What can I do for you? Do you know who

I am, what I feel, how I think?'. Stella worries about her gender script and Mitch suggests, 'Change the script.' Stella replies: 'Change the script. Ha ha. You want me to *what* in these shoes? The script is not the problem. I've changed the script. [...] Look I am supposed to wander around in a state of narcotized sensuality. That's my part.'[58] Lois's femme repertoire for acting this part soon encompasses more than Tammy's sweet confusions; she summons a famous woman 'disguised as a woman,' Marilyn Monroe. Of course Marilyn is also a drag cliché, so it's a gamble, but Lois decentres Marilyn (and the brilliantly comic Monroe would have enjoyed it), by preceding her entrance with an old vaudeville routine: one (Lois/Stella) beats up on another (Peggy/Stanley) because 'that's funny'. The beaten one replies 'that's not funny', so more extreme things are done – Stella tears off Stanley's sleeves, squirts him with seltzer and whacks him with a big powder puff. Still Stanley replies 'that's not funny'. Then Stella brings out the classic cream pie. Before she can blast him, Stanley tips it into Stella's face and says, 'Now that's funny.' With pie remnants spoiling her make-up Stella stands in front of a drop cloth painted with a butterfly-like vagina and delivers a set-piece, an invocation to the prophetess Cassandra, the abused prisoner from Troy whom nobody believes.[59] Lois unravels her 1950s housedress to reveal a black 'tight strapless dress' and summons Marilyn's sexual styling. She sighs, crouches, moves her hands between her thighs with come-hither self-arousal; simultaneously she cries out in the martyred voice of Cassandra, 'I'm nailed to this story. Cut me down.' Soon Stanley emerges from the audience clapping loudly ('Hey, isn't she great?') drops to his knees and, after verbal jousting, the lights come down and they enact extravagant noir-movie gestures of love-making. The femme will seduce and be seduced (that's her part), but there's so much more.

Yet while watching the performance back in 1991 I didn't see the more. What I felt was Stella's aloneness, made worse (and obscene) by the remnants of cream pie stuck to her chin. I saw the Stella in Marilyn (a career based on playing up to the Stanleys) and Marilyn in Stella (an enormous yearning that transcended the Stanleys). I emailed Lois after the show and told her what those Marilyn shudders meant to me and she replied that she was glad to hear it because 'nobody sees the femme'.

That's where Tammy comes back into this story. As a 'country music star turned solo performance artist' Tammy practises her big femme personality in her big blonde country music star wig. *Everyone sees this femme.* Because 'she needs to know', Tammy is never alone; her audiences have to participate, not just watch. In *What Tammy Needs to Know About Getting Old and Having Sex, The Concert Tour*, Lois worked with senior groups in London, Zagreb, and now in New York. In the performance, Tammy walks through the audience with a hand mic asking in her humble Tammy way whether anyone is having sex, and if so, how is it going? The 17 seniors sitting in the first rows, women and men ranging in age from their seventies to their nineties dressed in spiffy colourful outfits, join Tammy onstage to tell their stories, dance a choreographed routine and sing a rousing final number. Devising and directing as usual, Lois ventures into new territory here: she opens her show to others, creating a community performance that is also very much her own. Lois co-wrote all Tammy's lyrics and was sole author of a beautiful ballad with these lines: 'Mend a broken cup...set a broken bone...fix up an old house...right a wretched wrong.'

Lois readjusted the volume on the domestic terrorism debate by insisting on the value of domestic life – of a woman's life.

So many wretched wrongs these days it's no wonder Tammy needs community help. But Lois Weaver has been on the case for human rights for more than a decade. She directed Performance Studies international #12: *Performing Rights*, an international conference and festival on performance and human rights in London, 2006. She is founder of The *Long Table*, a forum that gets people talking about democracy. She has taught innumerable workshops, mentoring students in theatre making and script devising, giving them outlets for, and the means of, expression. (This too spreads democracy.) And when Lois/Tammy proposed to talk about sex with seniors to the Guggenheim Foundation she won a Fellowship for 2014-15, spectacular recognition for a US artist. Under Tammy's generous wig, art, politics, and community organising come together. Of course Tammy gets the last word: human rights for seniors and for the rest of us can't be separated from the sighing-between-the-thighs blessings of sex.

I admire Tammy but I'm probably too not-Southern to get her whole vibe. Another solo performance from 2011 has moved me more: *Domestic Terrorism: Hang Your Laundry in Public* is part of an 'Art in Odd Places' project. Dressed in a bright red coat and black wellies, Lois's Lady in Red strings clotheslines between scaffolding poles or street signs and hangs out her laundry – large-sized women's underwear and other white linens – on the street. Of this conceptual piece, Lois writes that it makes literal the crossing of boundaries between private and public, and engages audiences with questions of what and why we hide [...]. The intimacy and materiality of washing is also a social marker of class and gender. It can disclose the population and income of a household, reveal personal taste and bad habits; [...] elicit shame or shelter the good in good dreams. It can be a form of communication between neighbours, a violation of housing codes in some communities or perceived as a national threat in times of national insecurity. The act of hanging laundry is a daily yet resonant gesture that holds the memories of mothers' hands. It's a local ritual that translates globally in both rural and urban landscapes.[60]

Audio recordings of the Lady in Red's chats with passersby and photographs (by Lori E. Seid) of these encounters 'were placed alongside the airing laundry in a growing public installation'. Lois concludes: 'This gentle disruption of the everyday was a generative act of dialogue on the nature of what is public and what is private.'[61] I saw an early iteration of *Domestic Terrorism: Hang Your Laundry in Public*[62] not on a public street but at an international theatre conference in Helsinki in 2006. In a beautiful old hall with semicircular plush seating Lois readjusted the volume on the domestic terrorism debate by insisting on the value of domestic life – of a woman's life. On lines strung around the speaker's area, she hung her laundry. Then she addressed the members of the august assembly... would all the feminists please stand? We did, and those in the Feminist Research Working Group stood shoulder to shoulder. Then she asked, would everyone who supports a feminist please stand? This was a funny moment – even without a cream pie. After some shuffling and backward glances everyone else stood up. Lois had given them a second chance to look good. It was smart politics. For one moment we stood together as a large community of feminists and supporters. Smart performance politics. Lois passed out 'domestic terrorist' clothespins as a memento of the event. Smart *and* funny. That's Lois. I still have my clothespin.

On the road

Helen Paris (Curious)

When I think of Lois Weaver I think of velocity. I think of this in terms of her approach to her work and in terms of her approach to her life: a life lived on the road, open to all possibilities, destinations known and unknown, territories unfamiliar or revisited over and over. Constant motion – physical, intellectual, creative. Even when she finally sits down there still a tapping foot, the shimmy of a bangled wrist.

For over ten years Lois, Leslie, and I have been touring a piece together called *On the Scent*, a performance about smell and memory that takes up residence in domestic spaces. Our individual props and costumes for the show fit in to each of our suitcases. When Lois opens her case, sitting rooms across the globe are suddenly transformed – lacy negligees tossed over sedate coffee tables, kitten heels kicked under the sofa, trails of creamy face powder spilling on the mantle piece, exotic cobalt blue perfume bottles crowding on net curtained window sill. Sometimes, during a break I come down to Lois's room. She will be sitting in a sheer black negligee (her costume) Skyping or typing or texting or chatting. Working, engaging, moving forward.

Velocity. Constant motion.

And then she 'goes back to work', casts her spell over another audience, teasing, provoking, capturing.

In the performance, Lois blames her addiction to scent on the Avon Lady. She leans back seductively, her eyes half closed as if suddenly transported to another place, another time, and confesses,

I blame it on the Avon lady. What got to me was her bag. It was so compact, so organised and so full of bottles shaped just to make you want to hold them, stroke them and explore the miracles of their cures. But you couldn't have them right away. You had to order them. And she could never tell you exactly how long it would take. Then the space between that immediate craving and the possibility of satisfaction was packed up inside her bag and carried down the sidewalk to her car and driven home to a place I didn't know and couldn't imagine. What would she do at night with all those little bottles and jars? I just had to get my hands on that bag. But she never came back. They don't last, Avon ladies. They are temporary. Itinerant. Door-to-door...

I think of Lois Weaver herself as the Avon lady, constantly on the move, arriving suddenly, unexpectedly with her intoxicating gifts, her magic potions, vintage, collectable. Then she disappears, always leaving us wanting more, longing for her to return, knowing that she is on the move elsewhere – on to other places, other audiences, leaving them forever altered by the encounter.

Opposite: Various photos from *Retro(per)spective* (Weaver and Shaw, 2009). Photos by Marlène Ramírez-Cancio and Julio Pantoja. *Dress Suits to Hire* (Weaver, Shaw and Holly Hughes, 2005). Photos by Lori E. Seid. *It's a Small House and We lived in it Always* (Weaver, Shaw and Clod Ensemble, 1999). Photo by Marlène Ramírez-Cancio *Lost Lounge* (Weaver, Shaw, and Vivian Stoll, 2009). Photo by Lori E. Seid.

Staying on the road

Leslie Hill (Curious)

Several years ago at one of the *Everything You Wanted to Know About Live Art* events, Lois gave a talk about staying on the road. Her advice to young practitioners was not to worry so much about going directly uphill in their careers. The road doesn't always go uphill, sometimes it goes downhill or takes an unexpected turn or there's a terrible accident and the best you can do as an artist is just to *stay on the road*. I've thought about this a lot in the years since and think it is great advice though my personal associations with Lois are not of cars and roads but of airplanes and airports. I normally assume that if she isn't in the room, she's probably at 33,000 feet somewhere.

So many of my memories of working with Lois are from being on the road, touring together in Europe, the States, South America, China, Australia.... You get to know people in a different way when you see how they behave in radically different environments. Lois is an ideal person to tour with for many reasons: she has been everywhere and can offer histories and perspective on places all over the world from the 1970s to the present; she is fearless about trying new things; she can do anything and talk to anybody. I remember a few years ago she stepped in and directed our plot and focus at the Sydney Opera House studio when our lighting designer couldn't make it – I had no idea she could read lighting plans, but she was a total pro. I got tired of having to rely on other people to translate for me, she said. In a crisis, she could probably land an airplane. She lives much more in the present than most people and is a brilliant social and political observer. One thing I've appreciated in seeing Lois in so many different situations from 'glamour gigs' to community projects around the globe is her ability to combine serious political commitment with a curiosity about and generosity of spirit towards people from far beyond comfortable or familiar circles. She is provocative in a uniquely approachable, seductive way.

To me the Tammy WhyNot character and her open naiveté about all the things she 'needs to know' is hugely ironic because Lois Weaver is a very sharp, hugely knowledgeable person. She has her own totally unique brand of praxis and critique. Once, between shows in Finland, I noticed her leafing through a theory book. I use theory like porn, she said, I just flip through 'til I get something I can use. This is typical Lois modesty and humour, but get into a conversation with her about cultural materialism or neoliberalism or research methodologies and you could well find yourself outgunned in terms of intellectual critique and holding a multitude of perspectives and experiences.

The significance of Lois's work is huge and this book is a tribute to that, but one of Lois's biggest contributions to the field is also in showing so many of us how to live, how to be artists, how to be political, how to be in the world, how to seize the moment, how to get older, how to stay on the road.

P. S. The title of this book, *The Only Way Home Is Through the Show*, has a special resonance for us, as we literally found our home through a show we did with Lois in San Francisco in 2011. The three of us were performing round the corner and decided to take a look at a house that was on the market. When we first walked into the entry hall, Lois opened the door to the double garage and exclaimed, 'It's got a theatre!'

Opposite: Snapshots on the road. Clockwise from top left: Debra Miller, Lois Weaver, and Peggy Shaw, Seattle, 1991; Lois warming up, Open Eye Theatre, Minneapolis, 2008; Domestic Terrorist in Union Square, NYC; Lois in dressing rooms: Drill Hall Art Centre, London, 1998; Dixon Place, NYC, 2009; and Theatre Offensive, Boston, 1999. Centre Photo of image painted by Karen Kvernenes, Amsterdam, 1983. All photos property of Lois Weaver.

Floods (from *Miss America*)

Lois Weaver[63]

I am standing neck deep in dirty water.
I can't see below the surface.
Things brush past me,
a torn oven mitt, a shoe dislodged from an owner.
This is more than a flooded basement,
ladies and gentlemen,
and we've lost the chance to go for higher ground.
There's only one small spot left here
on the tip of landfill,
the touchdown, the fire line, the fault line,
the fabric store of patchwork, melting
pot luck suppers across this great and worn out
sourced
country fried
sink hole
lot of shaking going on
and unless they finally give us the final word
on who wants to be a millionaire
and why not lose weight for fame
or fall down for glory
or ask the 64,000-dollar question
whose answer could be a case of life or death
or Budweiser just in time for the game.
Off. No play. Rained out,
upstaged, care free, care less, care more about
the skins of animals and the flight of bees

whose plight is still to be determined to win
no matter what the consequences.
And truth? Ladies and gentlemen, truth has
nothing to do with it.
And love? Love?
What's love got to do
with the borderline personality
whose pickin's are slim in the first place
with no way to get there without the airfare
and what if plane shadows were footprints
putting corn out of business
as usual
when the suspects
are few and far between those of us who know
for a fact
that this digital noise is a false wind that
blows our mind
and restricts the frequency of free speech
and free will and free lunches
for those who try but can no longer stand
in line for the cash back on a dream house.

I'm talking to keep from drowning.
Talking to keep the mud from sucking me down.
Talking so you won't see how scared I am.

172

You Never Told Me (from *Miss America*)

Lois Weaver[64]

You never told me
that your mother's smoke kept you from seeing the
kindness in her eyes

You never told me....
that you don't really love anyone

You never told me....
that the cherries in the neighbour's backyard
were sour
that your thoughts were poison

You never told me....
you want to be buried in the ground
that you want to deteriorate not pollute

You never told me....
that a maraschino cherry never deteriorates

You never told me....
that you rely on AOL for all your news
and have never admitted that before

You never told me....
Every time you need to do something important
you get lost on You Tube

You never told me what happened to you last night

You never told me....
that you don't like the guy upstairs

You never told me....
that you have a good time at the beach
but don't like to swim

You never told me....
you rented a car and never picked it up

You never told me....
that your desire is to be poor,
that you find wealth boring
that you romanticise poverty

You never told me....
that your sense of justice came from a father who
worked too hard

You never told me....
that you feel despair as you age
that this age is full of despair
that you think despair is a dark canyon where the
downdraft pushes your own voice back down your
own throat

You never told me....
that you have lost the belief that things happen
for a reason

You never told me....
that all countries have a hard edge of steel
at their hearts
that a soft heart has no place in this world

You never told me....
that you could not make a list of things you care
about because you can't remember

You never told me....
that you want to stand on this rubbish heap and
stamp your feet until something changes

You never told me....
that the flood came once when you didn't notice
so that when it returned the ground was already full
of water and refuse

You never told me....
that refuse and refuse are spelled the same

You never told me....
that when you are in the audience
you think you are alone

1   Marilyn Stasio, 'Split Britches', *New York Post*, 24 February 1981, p. 18.

2   Bette Bourne, Paul Shaw, Peggy Shaw, and Lois Weaver, *Belle Reprieve: A Collaboration*, in *Split Britches: Lesbian Practice/Feminist Performance*, ed. by Sue-Ellen Case (London: Routledge, 1996), pp.149-83 (p. 183). Italics original. The play is also printed with a brief introduction and some interviews conducted by Kate Davy in the behemoth teaching text, *Modern Drama: Plays/Criticism/Theory*, ed. by W.B. Worthen (Fort Worth, TX: Harcourt Brace College Publishers, 1995), pp. 990-1002.

3   For readers who want to explore more approaches to understanding Lois's work, especially with Split Britches, please see the citations in the conclusion to this essay and in the bibliography at the end of this book, which demonstrate the extensiveness of the literature.

4   For example, Lois's article 'Performing Butch/Femme Theory', which outlines a performance-making workshop, is perhaps less about performing butch or femme in particular as it is about trying to evade self-censorship. Lois Weaver, 'Performing Butch/Femme Theory', *Journal of Lesbian Studies* 2.2-3 (1998), 187-99; and simultaneously in *Acts of Passion: Sexuality, Gender and Performance*, ed. by Nina Rapi and Maya Chowdhry (New York and London: Haworth Press, 1998), pp. 187-99.

5   Lois Weaver in Peggy Shaw, Lois Weaver, and Kate Davy, 'Peggy Shaw and Lois Weaver: Interviews (1985, 1992, 1993)', in *Modern Drama: Plays/Criticism/Theory*, ed. by W. B. Worthen (Fort Worth, TX: Harcourt Brace College Publishers, 1995), pp. 1003-08 (p. 1005); interpolated text original to source text.

6   Peggy Shaw, 'How I Learned Theater', in *Cast Out: Queer Lives in Theater*, ed. by Robin Bernstein (Ann Arbor: University of Michigan Press, 2006), pp. 25-9 (p. 28).

7   Weaver in Shaw, Weaver, and Davy, 'Interviews', p. 1006.

8   Deb Margolin, Peggy Shaw, and Lois Weaver, *Beauty and the Beast*, in *Split Britches: Lesbian Practice/Feminist Performance*, ed. by Sue-Ellen Case (London: Routledge, 1996), pp. 59-86 (p. 60).

9   Deb Margolin, Peggy Shaw, and Lois Weaver, *Little Women: The Tragedy*, in *Split Britches: Lesbian Practice/Feminist Performance*, ed. by Sue-Ellen Case (London: Routledge, 1996), pp. 119-48 (p. 122).

10   Margolin, Shaw, and Weaver, *Little Women*, p. 132.

11   Margolin, Shaw, and Weaver, *Little Women*, p. 130.

12   Shaw, 'How I Learned Theater', p. 26.

13   Vivian M. Patraka, 'Split Britches in *Split Britches*: Performing History, Vaudeville, and the Everyday', *Women and Performance: A Journal of Feminist Theory*, 4:2 (1989), 58-67 (p. 59); Patraka cites a conversation with Split Britches in January 1989.

14   Charlotte Canning, *Feminist Theatres in the USA: Staging Women's Experience* (London and New York: Routledge, 1996), p. 141.

15   Split Britches in conversation in January 1989 as cited by Patraka, 'Split Britches in *Split Britches*', p. 59.

16   Patraka, 'Split Britches in *Split Britches*', p. 59.

17   Canning, *Feminist Theatres*, p. 141; Canning also quotes Patraka, 'Split Britches in *Split Britches*'.

18   Lois Weaver in Patraka, 'Split Britches in *Split Britches*', p. 60; Patraka cites an unpublished 1986 interview with Split Britches and Rhonda Blair.

19   Margolin, Shaw, and Weaver, *Little Women*, p. 127. Ellipsis original.

20   Margolin, Shaw, and Weaver, *Little Women*, p. 128.

21   Margolin, Shaw, and Weaver, *Little Women*, p. 140. Ellipsis and italics original.

22   Bourne, Shaw, Shaw, and Weaver, *Belle Reprieve*, p. 151.

23   Margolin, Shaw, and Weaver, *Little Women*, p. 140.

24   Notably, it is plays that foreground women's self-abnegation that Split Britches has selected to workshop with students: in 1989, at Hampshire College, they worked on Euripides' *Alcestis*, 'women's erasure within the home and society, women's silencing, and a literal self-sacrifice a woman makes to save her husband'; Rhonda Blair, 'The Alcestis Project: Split Britches at Hampshire College', *Women & Performance: A Journal of Feminist Theory*, 6.1 (1993), 147-50 (p. 148). In 1993 they worked on Henrik Ibsen's *A Doll's House* at the University of Hawaii at Manoa. For detail on *Valley of the Dolls' House*, see Juli Burk, '*Valley of the Dolls' House*: Split Britches Did It with Feminism in the Sitting Room', in *Constructions and Confrontations: Changing Representations of Women and Feminisms, East and West: Selected Essays*, Literary Studies East & West, vol. 12, ed. by Cristina Bacchilega and Cornelia N. Moore (Honolulu: University of Hawaii Press, 1996), pp. 274-85.

25   Lois Weaver in Alisa Solomon, 'The WOW Cafe', *The Drama Review*, 29.1 (1985), 92-101 (p. 100).

26   See, for example, the version printed at the end of this book.

27   Lois Weaver, unpublished interview with Jen Harvie, London, 20 May 2015.

28   Sue-Ellen Case, 'From Split Subject to Split Britches', in *Feminine Focus: The New Women Playwrights*, ed. by Enoch Brater (Oxford: Oxford University Press, 1989), pp. 126-46 (p. 143).

29   Shaw in Shaw, Weaver, and Davy, 'Interviews', p. 1004.

30   Deb Margolin, Peggy Shaw, and Lois Weaver, *Upwardly Mobile Home* [1984], in *Split Britches: Lesbian Practice/Feminist Performance*, ed. by Sue-Ellen Case (London: Routledge, 1996), pp. 87-118 (p. 91).

31   Patraka, 'Split Britches in *Split Britches*', p. 66.

32   Deb Margolin in Lisa Merrill, 'An Interview with Lois Weaver, Peggy Shaw and Deb Margolin', *Women & Performance: A Journal of Feminist Theory*, 6:1 (1993), 151-67 (p. 161).

33   Peggy Shaw in Merrill, 'An Interview', p. 161.

34   Merrill, 'An Interview', pp. 161-3.

35   Weaver in Merrill, 'An Interview', p. 163.

36   Shaw in Shaw, Weaver, and Davy, 'Interviews', p. 1005.

37   Bourne, Shaw, Shaw, and Weaver, *Belle Reprieve*, p. 167.

38   Justin Hayford, 'Women in Love', review of Split Britches' *Anniversary Waltz* at Randolph Street Gallery, *Chicago Reader*, 21 June 1990 <http://www.chicagoreader.com/chicago/women-in-love/Content?oid=875897> [accessed 16 April 2015].

39   Deb Margolin, 'Interview', *Amherst Bulletin*, 25 October 1989; cited in Burk, '*Valley of the Dolls' House*', pp. 274-85.

40   Peggy Shaw, Lois Weaver, and James Neale-Kennerley, *Lust and Comfort* (1995), in *Split Britches: Lesbian Practice/Feminist Performance*, ed. by Sue-Ellen Case (London: Routledge, 1996), pp. 225-72 (pp. 270-1).

41   See, for example: Sue-Ellen Case, 'Toward a Butch-Femme Aesthetic', in *Making a Spectacle: Feminist Essays on Contemporary Women's Theatre*, ed. by Lynda Hart (Ann Arbor: University of Michigan

Press, 1989), pp. 282-99. Reprinted in *The Lesbian and Gay Studies Reader*, ed. by Michèle Aina Barale, David M. Halperin, and Henry Abelove (New York: Routledge, 1993), pp. 294-306; and Case, 'From Split Subject to Split Britches'.

42 Kate Davy, 'Constructing the Spectator: Reception, Context, and Address in Lesbian Performance', *Performing Arts Journal*, 10.2 (1986), 43-52.

43 Jill Dolan, *The Feminist Spectator as Critic*, 2nd edn (Ann Arbor: University of Michigan, 2012).

44 Jill Dolan, *Presence and Desire: Essays on Gender, Sexuality, Performance* (Ann Arbor: University of Michigan Press, 1993); Vivian Patraka, 'Split Britches in *Little Women: The Tragedy*: Staging Censorship, Nostalgia, and Desire', *The Kenyon Review*, 15.2 (1993), 6-13; Deanna Shoemaker, 'Pink Tornados and Volcanic Desire: Lois Weaver's Resistant "Femme(nini)tease" in *Faith and Dancing: Mapping Femininity and Other Natural Disasters*', *Text and Performance Quarterly*, 27.4 (2007), 317-33.

45 Case, 'Toward A Butch-Femme Aesthetic'; Kate Davy, 'Fe/Male Impersonation: The Discourse of Camp', in *Critical Theory and Performance*, ed. by Janelle Reinelt and Joseph Roach (Ann Arbor: University of Michigan Press, 1993), pp. 231-47; Paul Menard, 'The (Fe)Male Gays: Split Britches and the Redressing of Dyke Camp', in *We Will be Citizens: New Essays on Gay and Lesbian Theatre*, ed. by James Fisher (Jefferson, NC, and London: McFarland & Company, 2008), pp. 185-93.

46 Elin Diamond, 'Mimesis, Mimicry, and The "True-Real"', in *Acting Out: Feminist Performances*, ed. by Lynda Hart and Peggy Phelan (Ann Arbor: University of Michigan Press, 1993), pp. 363-82.

47 See Lynda Hart, 'Afterword: Zero Degree Deviancy – *Lesbians Who Kill*', in *Fatal Woman: Lesbian Sexuality and the Mark of Aggression* (Princeton: Princeton University Press, 1994); and 'Identity and Seduction: Lesbians in the Mainstream', in *Acting Out: Feminist Performances*, ed. by Lynda Hart and Peggy Phelan (Ann Arbor: University of Michigan Press, 1993), pp. 119-37.

48 Patraka, 'Split Britches in *Little Women*', and 'Split Britches in *Split Britches*', p. 58.

49 This is a handwritten draft of text by Deb Margolin that would later appear in a revised form in Peggy Shaw, Deborah Margolin, Lois Weaver, *Split Britches: A True Story*, in *Split Britches: Lesbian Practice/Feminist Performance*, ed. by. Sue-Ellen Case, pp. 35-57 (pp. 56-57).

50 Rebecca Schneider, 'Remembering Feminist Remimesis: A Riddle in Three Parts', *TDR: The Drama Review*, 58.2 (2014), pp. 14-32 (p. 22). Emphasis original.

51 All citations from *Split Britches: The True Story* are from *Split Britches: Lesbian Practice, Feminist Performance*, ed. by Case, (London and New York: Routledge, 1996), p. 57.

52 The performance group consisting of Weaver, Margolin, and Shaw. After 1992, only Weaver and Shaw performed as Split Britches.

53 Sue-Ellen Case, 'Introduction,' in *Split Britches: Lesbian Practice, Feminist Performance*, ed. by Sue-Ellen Case (London and New York: Routledge, 1996), pp. 1-34 (p. 22).

54 All citations from Deb Margolin, Peggy Shaw, and Lois Weaver, *Upwardly Mobile Home* (1984), in *Split Britches: Lesbian Practice, Feminist Performance*, ed. by Sue-Ellen Case (London and New York: Routledge, 1996), pp. 87-118 (p. 99).

55 Margolin, Shaw, and Weaver, *Upwardly Mobile Home*, p. 103.

56 Margolin, Shaw, and Weaver, *Upwardly Mobile Home*, p. 99.

57 Margolin, Shaw, and Weaver, *Upwardly Mobile Home*, p. 106.

58 All citations from *Belle Reprieve* in *Split Britches: Lesbian Practice, Feminist Performance*, ed. by Sue-Ellen Case (London and New York: Routledge, 1996), pp. 150-1.

59 In the programme from the original show which opened in New York in 1991, Deb Margolin is credited with the Cassandra monologue.

60 Lois Weaver, 'Domestic Terrorism: Hang Your Laundry in Public', 2013, *Public Address Systems*, <http://publicaddresssystems.org/projects/domestic-terrorism-hang-your-laundry-in-public/> [accessed 7 January 2015].

61 Weaver, 'Domestic Terrorism: Hang Your Laundry in Public'.

62 A version of this lecture is included in this collection. See Lois Weaver, 'Diary of a Domestic Terrorist', below, pp. 262-5.

63 This text is adapted from Peggy Shaw and Lois Weaver, *Miss America* (2008), in *Theatre in Pieces: Politics, Poetics and Interdisciplinary Collaboration, An Anthology of Play Texts, 1966-2010*, ed. by Anna Furse (London: Methuen, 2011), pp. 317-51 (pp. 348-9).

64 This text is adapted from Shaw and Weaver, *Miss America*, in *Theatre in Pieces*, ed. by Furse, pp. 320-3.

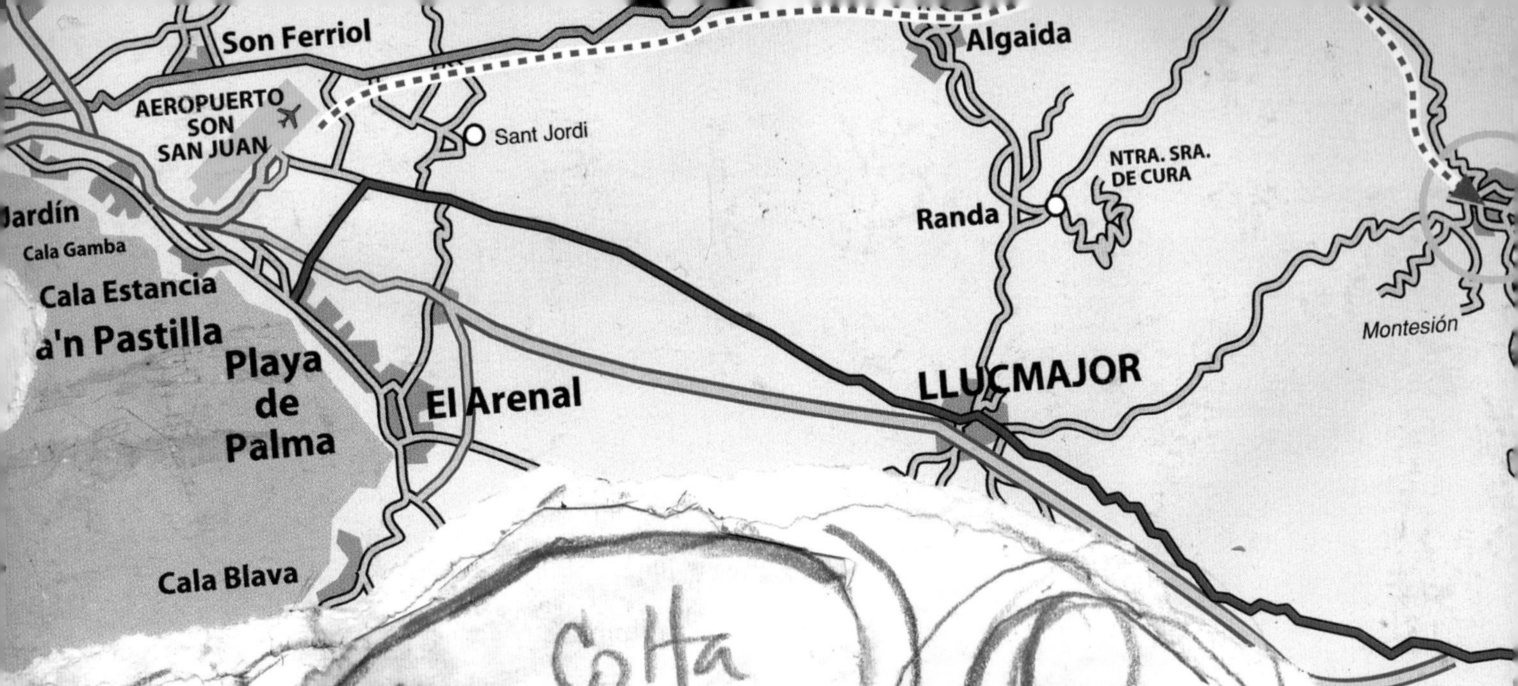

Son Ferriol

Algaida

AEROPUERTO SON SAN JUAN

Sant Jordi

NTRA. SRA. DE CURA

Jardín

Cala Gamba

Randa

Cala Estancia

a'n Pastilla

Playa de Palma

El Arenal

LLUCMAJOR

Montesión

Cala Blava

Terra Cotta

...gressive views.. They are conservative ...
...d ....uking. Again this
....ms to drive on t...
....ship and even th...
....al upheaval. ...
....ness or Naïveté [when is my
... I need it. I have lost what little a...
spell] This 200 year old house sits on
a farm and these women have soaked
of history, moved through the dust of
soil. They've seen it before.

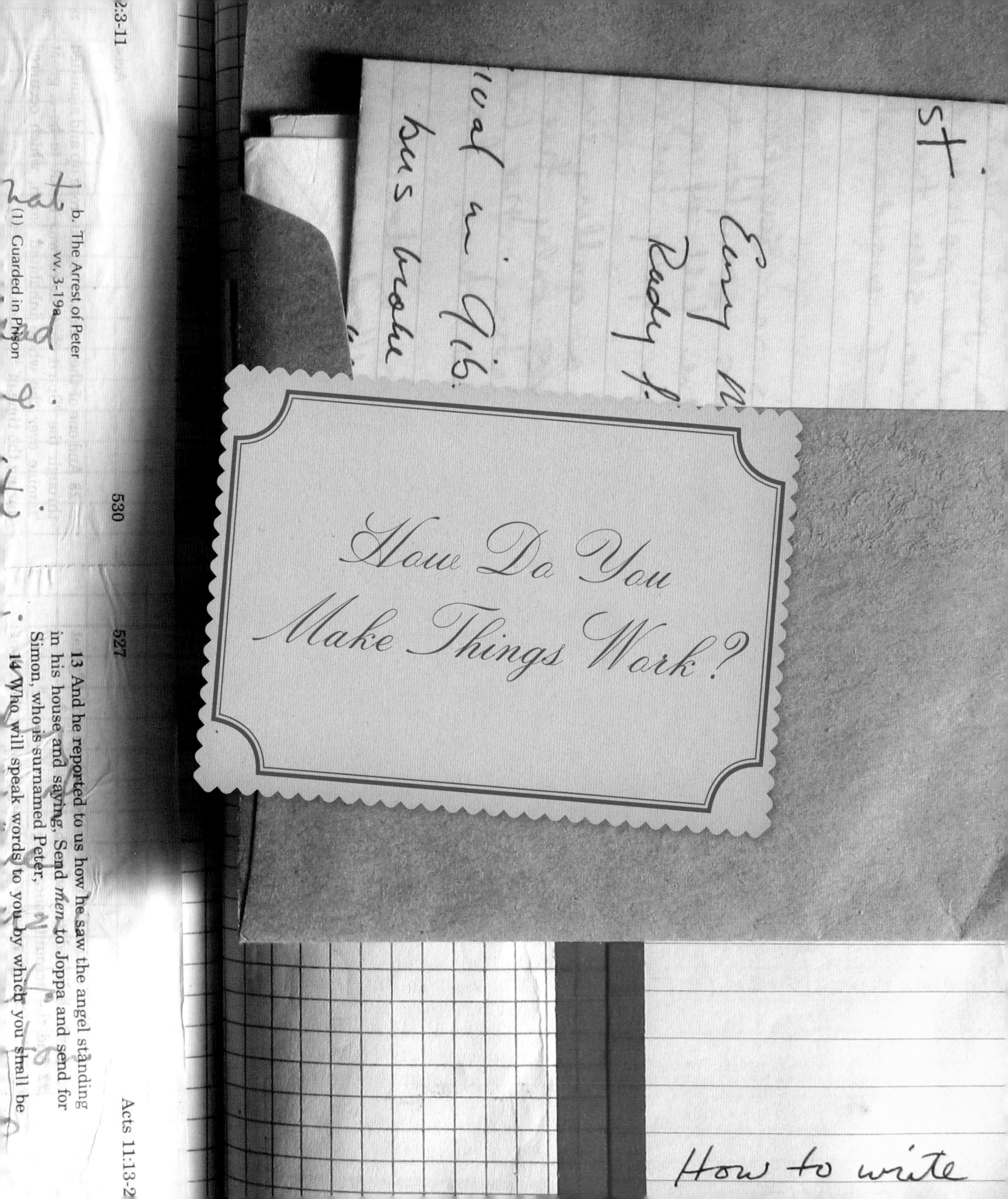

b. The Arrest of Peter

vv. 3-19a

(1) Guarded in Prison

530

527

13 And he reported to us how he saw the angel standing in his house and saying, Send *men* to Joppa and send for Simon, who is surnamed Peter; **14** Who will speak words to you by which you shall be

How Do You Make Things Work?

How to write

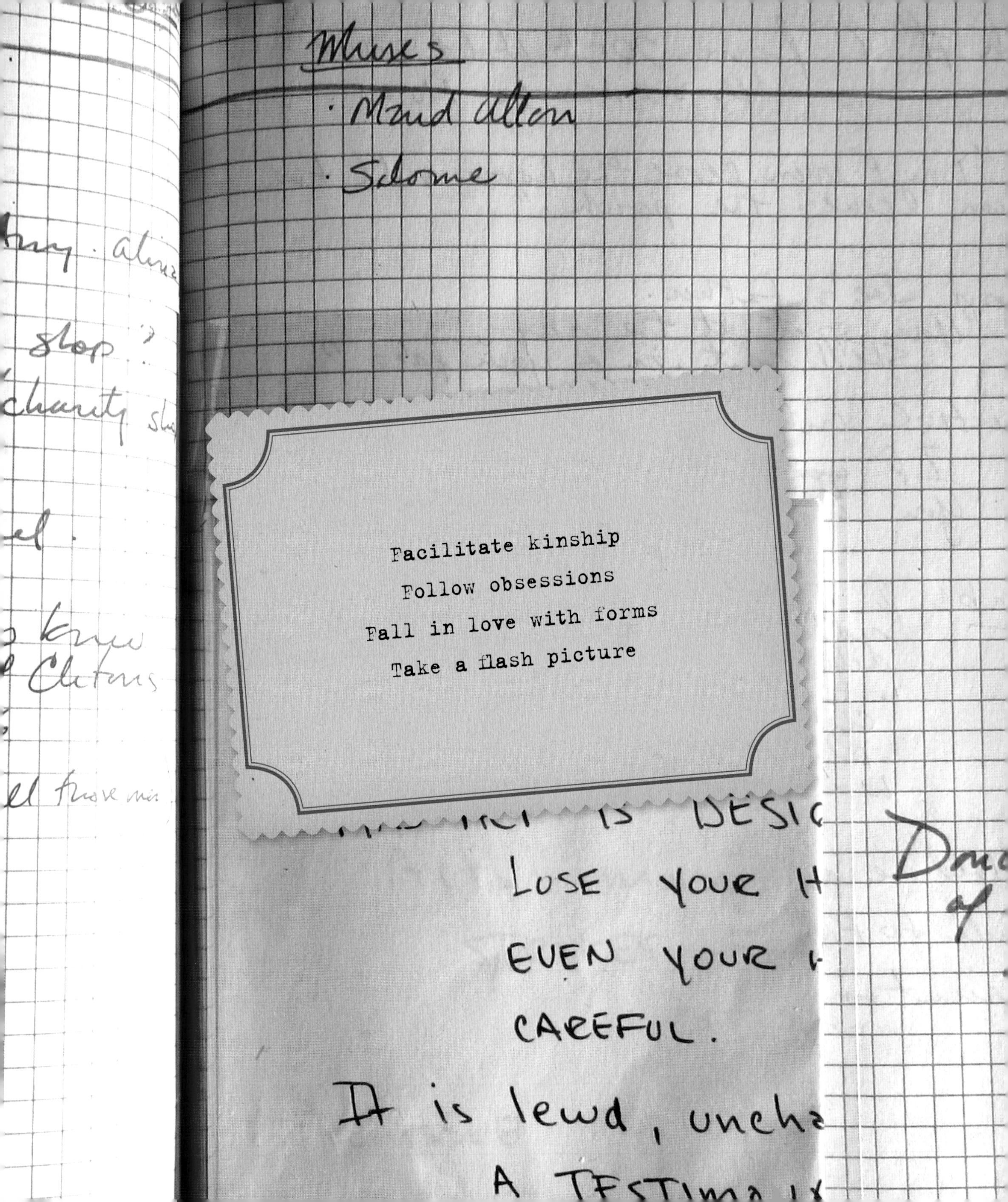

Muses
· Maud Allan
· Salome

Facilitate kinship
Follow obsessions
Fall in love with forms
Take a flash picture

any . alin...

stop ?

charity sh...

...el .

...know

...Clitoris

...el those mi...

... IS DESIG...
LOSE YOUR H...
EVEN YOUR ...
CAREFUL .

It is lewd, uncha...

A TESTIM...

Dro...
of

The good guide for creating a non cooperative; or, how to organise a collective that will last for more than 30 years

Lois Weaver

Find a place to do something

Hold weekly meetings

Invite everyone to attend, even the green grocer

Give everyone a key

Do not elect a board, appoint a director or even hold an election

Do ask someone to facilitate meetings

Sit in a circle

Have the same discussions over and over.
For example, 'How do we feel about men in a women's space?'
Try to grow with the growing vocabulary

Try to reach a consensus

If you can't come to a consensus, remember that the decision will probably rest with the person who is willing to do the work. Don't forget, everyone has a key!

In other words, be prepared to accept that the colour of the ceiling might be dictated by the person willing to paint it.

Go away together once a year to programme a year's activities

Do this by going around the circle and asking people to state what they want FROM the group not what they want FOR the group

Go around again and ask what they want to DO or MAKE

Try to fit as many of those things onto a year's calendar as possible

Do try to help everyone understand that in order to take up space, you have to put in some time

Try to live with the chaos

Have parties regularly to raise the rent money or just to raise spirits, and give them funny or ironic titles such as Freudian Slip Party and XXX Rated Xmas.

(Note: This process began sometime in 1983 just after we started the WOW Café on East 11th Street, New York. A group of about 10-15 women ran it as a café, serving food and producing small events in the evenings. However, we quickly reached a crisis point because women who were waitressing during the day did not necessarily want to be volunteer waitresses at night. Could we continue? How? And mostly, was it worth it? We held a meeting and I remember saying that in order to survive we needed to stop thinking what we are sacrificing FOR the space and start articulating what we want FROM the space. That was a turning point. As we went around the circle, we began to see how we might be able to survive on the resources of our own desires. In that moment we established a unique structure that I like to call 'a go around of desire' that is still in operation at WOW more than 30 years later. Obviously, some things have been altered over the years but the framework is mostly the same and the discussions are most definitely the same, although some languages may have changed.)

Imagine it, make it, change it

Jen Harvie

'If you can imagine it you can make it. If you can make it then you can make it *change*.'
Lois Weaver[1]

'Don't wait for funding, don't wait for permission, don't wait to be asked, make work in your bedroom, in your living room, don't wait for it to be finished, show people five minutes, ten minutes, let your audience help you shape it.'
Lois Weaver[2]

'To participate simply take a seat at the table'
Excerpt from 'The *Long Table* Etiquette' by Lois Weaver[3]

Activist for, and architect of, imagination

Lois Weaver is not only a feminist theatre and performance maker and activist herself. She is also, equally importantly, a trailblazing, pioneering, charismatic performance-making leader, especially for generations of lesbians and feminists but also for other marginalised communities. Furthermore, she is an activist and advocate. Where received 'understandings' of expertise and legitimacy exclude many people from participating in public discourse, Lois works with and creates structures for those people to help them imagine, articulate, and promote their own opinions, interests, and desires. Lois believes strongly that '[a]rt enables us to imagine ourselves out of current situations',[4] so she champions imagining.

Lois leads powerfully through example, by continuously making her own lesbian feminist performance with Split Britches and also solo, as Tammy WhyNot and in shows such as *Faith and Dancing*. However, she enhances and significantly extends that informal leadership through practices such as teaching, and through formal structures which facilitate participation in performance-making and public discussion. These structures include performance schools, venues, and companies, and her multifarious Public Address Systems for public engagement. Lois's commitment to democratic participation and expression is not, in other words, merely the *message* of her performance work; it is the underlying *principle* of all of her work. She enacts that principle powerfully in performance, but also in teaching, hosting, leading, and organising others, and in imagining, establishing, building, curating, and promoting events and structures in which she and others can pursue their desires, make work, and be very powerful marginal majorities.

In what follows, I start by attempting a semi-chronological romp through the history of some of the many courses Lois has taught and important structures, events, and companies she has created and co-created. My aim in providing this condensed history is to give a flavour of the range and longevity of Lois's advocacy, activism, and initiatives in this area while not consigning the whole capacity of the book to this particular set of stories and their juicy sub-plots. I then summarise some of the key principles that these initiatives share, and I summarise their effects.[5] Some of the very greatest benefits of Lois's practical and structural endeavours to foster imagination and democratically extend expression are, precisely, their reach, often well beyond even unconventional theatrical spaces, to people who might rarely otherwise be exposed to their opportunities, and often well into new generations of performance making and makers.

Leading, teaching, curating, and socialising

Lois has been a feminist leader at least since her teens, when she was the first female President of the Virginia Baptist Student Union. She has been enabling other people's participation in performance at least since her College days, when she first worked as a director. These early demonstrations of pleasure in, and commitment to, feminist leadership reappear across the whole of her career. She consistently explores and experiments with ways of expanding participation in performance and public engagement through teaching, co-founding companies, establishing venues and festivals, curating events, and developing mobile structures for performance making and social engagement.

WOW

Not long after she arrived in New York, Lois was already teaching as an artist in schools and then at Emerson College. She was also soon involved in the founding of Spiderwoman Theater and then Split Britches. Drawing on positive experiences touring with Spiderwoman in Europe, and the contacts they'd established there, in 1980, Lois and Peggy Shaw along with Pamela Camhe and Jordy Mark[6] founded the Women's One World (or WOW) Festival of performance that ran in New York for two years. 'WOW came about from desire,' Peggy Shaw writes. 'There was nowhere to perform.'[7] In some quirk of serendipity, they found the Electric Circus (by this point called the Allcraft Center)[8] 'that Andy Warhol had done his stuff in. It seated 500 people.'[9] WOW couldn't offer its international visitors much; they had to fund their own travel, and slept on friends' floors. Kate Davy records that '[o]ut-of-town groups received three hundred dollars and local artists one hundred dollars per performance. The producers were not paid, nor was any other form of labor remunerated. Scholarships were available for women willing to work in exchange for admission.'[10] The first Festival was launched with 'approximately a thousand dollars from a series of fund-raising events – evenings of music, cabaret, and comedy called "Summer Nights". By the second festival they had "amassed" three thousand dollars.'[11] What WOW couldn't offer in funds it could offer in its venue, and in an army of volunteer support. 'We had two hundred volunteers', Peggy writes. 'And we had thirty-six shows from eight countries in eleven days. The next year we did it we had one hundred shows from ten countries, four shows a night for eighteen days.'[12] Lois has emphasised, further, that 'just having a spot to perform in New York was a great deal for them. And they got some press. That actually generated enough interest that they could come back on their own later.'[13] The 1981 Festival attracted performing groups from 'Finland, Sweden, New Zealand and all over Europe'.[14]

The WOW Festivals exposed women performance makers in New York to a great range of European feminist performance and fuelled their own desire to make more. Feminist theatre historian Charlotte Canning writes, '[a]fter the second festival in 1981 the organizing group did not want to lose the momentum generated by the festival and decided to continue the festival as a local community gathering place and performance venue. Through community dances and benefits they funded theater, poetry, movies, and art. The space was named the WOW Cafe 330 and opened in March 1982.'[15] From 1982-85, the café theatre occupied a storefront at 330 East 11th Street in Manhattan's Lower East Side, 'before the collective moved to its current location at 59-61 E. Fourth Street', according to WOW's first major historian, Kate Davy.[16]

Solomon recounts that the first venue was named '"WOW at 330" to signify both its address and the hour, as Weaver puts it, "when girls get out of school and go out looking for fun."'[17] As well as producing women's performance, WOW was a crucially important social venue. Solomon quotes Lois: 'But what we really wanted... was a woman's performance space. We also wanted a hangout, a girls' social club.'[18] WOW also hosted performance workshops, often run by Lois; later in this book, Anne Tallentire writes about participating in some of Lois's workshops there. Peggy and Lois have described WOW as 'a performance space dedicated to producing works by and for women',[19] and its approach was promiscuous, sometimes with multiple shows a night in what one WOW member vividly describes as 'hit-and-run theatre'.[20] Davy claims that between 1982 and 1985 alone, 'hundreds of shows were presented'.[21] Her book's extensive WOW Production History appendix cites literally hundreds more up until 2002,[22] despite the very partial records that are, for Davy, a residue of WOW's 'anarchic approach'.[23] More history is forthcoming in the eagerly anticipated book, *Memories of the Revolution: First Ten Years of the WOW Café*,[24] co-edited by two of WOW's early 'alumni' Carmelita Tropicana and Holly Hughes plus Jill Dolan. The WOW Café Theatre is still running strong at the time of writing in 2015.[25] WOW has always been quite small spatially. Solomon notes that the stage at 330 E. Eleventh,

> like the entire space, is barely 10 feet wide. With its floor of octagonal ceramic tiles, patterned along one side, the rooms [sic] seems like it might have been someone's vestibule or, even earlier, half of a dining room. Now, impossibly narrow and maybe 20 feet long, it hardly contains a dozen or so rows of folding chairs. The homemade lightboard of household dimmers sits in the center of the room, controlling a handful of small, outdoor-type reflector lamps.[26]

Despite its diminutive physical proportions, WOW has also been disproportionately productive as well as psychically immense in the landscape of feminist and lesbian performance in ways that I'll consider below, following this summary history of Lois's enabling activities, events, and structures.

Teaching

Lois and Peggy's feminist leadership and outreach work were not limited to WOW. However enormous its impact, it didn't generate the kind of secure income that practices such as teaching could. One of their most enduring leadership practices has been teaching, partly due to this economic reality, but also because they love it, are great at it, and have had exciting invitations to do it. Along with fellow Split Britches co-founder Deb Margolin they ran major performance workshops in 1989 on Euripides' *Alcestis* at Hampshire College,[27] and in 1993 partly on Ibsen's *A Doll's House* at the University of Hawaii at Manoa (where they met performance maker Stacy Makishi).[28] In a testament to Lois's teaching abilities, one of the Hampshire College participants observed about her, '[s]he's great at getting people to work without them even realizing just how hard they're working.'[29] Peggy and Lois have also taught in the UK at the University of Lancaster.[30] In 1997, Lois taught 'Theatre 479: Re-

Queer School 'encouraged artists to get out of their living rooms and on to the stage; not wait for someone to cast them in a play but create their own work'.

inventing the Southern Voice' at Virginia's College of William and Mary.[31] Since 1997, she has taught performance-making part-time at Queen Mary University of London (QMUL), notably in her long-running module Performance Composition, which features a regular weekly performance night hosted by Tammy WhyNot. Soon after starting at QMUL, Lois co-founded with Lois Keidan of the Live Art Development Agency London's annual live art training and emerging performance festival, East End Collaborations, which included the workshop *Everything You Wanted to Know About Live Art But Were Afraid to Ask*.

Gay Sweatshop

In 1991, the English Arts Council granted revenue funding to Gay Sweatshop, which Sue-Ellen Case has described as 'the most prominent theatre in London for gay and lesbian performance'.[32] The company advertised posts for two Artistic Directors, one male, one female, and in 1992, James Neale-Kennerly and Lois were appointed. While he took up directing major productions – including Split Britches' *Lust and Comfort* in 1994 – she set about instituting the kind of wide, democratic access to politicised performance-making which she and others had pioneered at WOW. Sue-Ellen Case writes:

> During the years 1992-3 [at Gay Sweatshop], Weaver initiated a number of outreach projects to encourage independent lesbian and gay performers, called *One Night Stand, Club Deviance*, and *Queer School. One Night Stand* was a series which invited solo performers to produce their work in a cabaret format. The series enjoyed packed houses and enthusiastic audiences, especially in London and Manchester. *Club Deviance* was a similar project, bringing together the sense of lesbian and gay club life and an underground performance tradition. *Queer School* helped to prepare performers for a professional life, offering courses in technical and business skills along with acting and interpretation. Weaver was interested in reaching out to a younger generation of queers who did not go to the theatre, but who did frequent clubs. She was developing both new performers and new audiences. For Weaver, the form which suited this enterprise was the solo act.[33]

In interview with Sandra Freeman, Lois has elaborated on her aims at Gay Sweatshop. She was interested in pursuing explicitly queer theatre, which she identifies as 'very politically based, it's very urgent, it comes out of a necessity around issues of the AIDS crisis for one, and censorship for another'.[34] She describes it as 'much more agit-prop, not in style but in content, experimentation with form and space'.[35] She also reports that she wanted to take Gay Sweatshop back to its street roots and 'shake those foundations that had been built up over the sixteen or seventeen years and make it much more grass roots and community oriented and community based'.[36] Gay Sweatshop's revenue funding offered Lois the extraordinary opportunity to work 'with a funding base' to do '[a]ll that kind of stuff that I'd been doing at WOW in the States' – queer school, platform performance series, and 'encourag[ing] artists to get out of their living rooms and on to the stage and not wait to be funded, not wait for someone to cast them in a play but create their own work'.[37] Ultimately, Lois's objectives for Gay Sweatshop clashed with those of some of its Board members and funders, who wanted more conventional theatre outcomes and forms. Gay Sweatshop was disbanded by its Board in 1997 due to 'lack of funding'.[38]

Portraits of James Neale-Kennerly and Lois Weaver as Co-Directors of Gay Sweatshop, London, 1993. Photo by Gordon Rainsford.

She works not only to facilitate performance and performers, but also to develop the skills and workers who make performance possible.

Curation

Part of what Lois did at both WOW and Gay Sweatshop was curate programmes of performance, even if one of her key curatorial principles was to include as much as possible along the lines of a WOW rule: 'whoever shows up for rehearsals gets to be in the play'.[39] In East End Collaborations and its successors at QMUL, AiR Supply and Peopling the Palace(s), Lois and collaborators, including Lois Keidan, continue to curate short festivals of live art, especially by emerging artists, often in collaboration with more established ones. At Peopling the Palace(s) in 2013, she commissioned and, as Tammy WhyNot, emceed an evening of performance duets by the likes of mid-career and early career live artists Lauren Barri Holstein and Julia Bardsley, Forced Entertainment founder Tim Etchells, and Hester Chillingworth, Artistic Director of younger feminist company GETINTHEBACKOFTHEVAN. In 2011, Lois curated FeMUSEum, with installations by four generations of femme live artists – Lois herself, Amy Lamé, Carmelita Tropicana, and Bird la Bird – to 'pay tribute to the lineage and legacy of femininity and performance'.[40] When QMUL hosted the major performance festival and academic conference Performance Studies international #12 (PSI #12) *Performing Rights* in 2006, Lois was the Artistic Director of the massive international performance programme which included work by Coco Fusco, Karen Finley, Rabih Mroué, and Guillermo Gómez-Peña. She also formed and curated for PSi#12 *The Library of Performing Rights*, an installation archive of materials documenting international performance about human rights that has since toured to various sites including Glasgow, Vienna, and Montreal in 2014 for the Hemispheric Institute. Furthermore, she works in these contexts not only to facilitate performance and performers, but also to develop the skills and workers who make performance possible: the technicians, producers, hosts, and other facilitators. At QMUL, this endeavour has helped to develop generations of emerging producers under the umbrella name AiR Supply which represents the scheme's origins at QMUL as part of the artists in residence (AiR) programme, AiR Supply, which started around 2009.

Public Address Systems

Finally, Lois has cultivated a variety of portable and adaptable practices designed to enable democratic audience engagement in a range of situations and discussions. She calls these her Public Address Systems, each of which variously 'creates spaces that are hospitable and open, where alternatives can be modelled and critical questions staged',[41] and they are detailed on a dedicated website, www. publicaddresssystems.org.[42] They routinely adapt domestic social forms such as sitting together around the supper table, playing cards, sitting on the porch, and hanging laundry; sometimes they adapt slightly more formal scenarios such as a cocktail party. In Lois's incarnations of all of these recognisable forms, audiences are invited to practise the familiar in slightly unfamiliar contexts: the supper table is in a theatre studio; or the cocktail party is a cocktail seminar. Audiences are also invited to engage in somewhat unfamiliar ways – the topic of conversation is set and it is, for example, 'feminism and live art' or 'getting older and having sex'.[43] Lois's adaptations draw on the familiarity and, for many, comfort of their source forms to help participants feel both at ease and expert, enabled to speak out and address the topic of conversation however austere, embarrassing, difficult, daunting, or even insignificant it may initially feel.

Lois Weaver in 'Dance of the Seven Wigs', in Gay Sweatshop's *Club Deviance*, WOW, NYC, 1996. Photo courtesy of Gay Sweatshop.

Principles

I hope it's clear by now that there are key principles that underpin all of these diverse facilitating activities and structures that Lois and her collaborators practise and create. Foremost amongst these principles are inclusivity and participation. Davy might find WOW's approach anarchic but it was deliberately non-hierarchical and collective, even when 1980s Reaganism was rendering such values profoundly unfashionable, even perverse, as it exponentially intensified competition in American culture. In interview with Davy, Lois has commented,

> I think WOW's politics is in the way it operates, the way it has maintained its operation in the face of all kinds of influences to do otherwise. That's what defines the politics: the way we run it by town meeting, the way everyone has a voice, the way it's open, there are no administrators. [...] When I sit back and look at the things to be proud of as far as WOW is concerned, I'm proud of all the personal achievements that people have made, but I'm mostly proud of how WOW has operated as a sociological, political entity in a world where the whole idea of a collective is not necessarily supported. I mean, here it is the beginning of the 80s and it was all about the individual; collectivity wasn't anything anyone was aspiring to. But WOW worked on certain principles that enabled it to evolve into something really political.[44]

This collectivism was not only administrative but artistic as well. According to Lois, a related WOW principle was that 'anyone can play a part when you get into production; whoever shows up for rehearsals gets to be in the play. That's one of the things we try to do so we don't exclude people based on talent at WOW;' 'everyone that wants to work gets a chance. That's really enough for us. We try to encourage more people to get involved'.[45] Beyond *permitting* participation therefore, Lois and Peggy actively *encourage* it. 'Pushing people on to the stage, that's something Peggy and I have been committed to', says Lois. 'People in general haven't been encouraged because the concept of theatre has been Broadway, stardom. That's what I like about the community aspect of WOW, everyone can be in it, including the audience.'[46]

This approach to performance which prioritises participation necessarily de-prioritises conventional ideas of excellence, though that doesn't mean it lacks excellence, and it often means it recalibrates ideas of what excellence is. Furthermore, this approach informs not only Split Britches' performance-making and performance-facilitation but also their teaching. Reflecting on teaching with Split Britches at Hampshire College, Rhonda Blair remarks admiringly, '[t]he emphasis was not on getting a particular show up or teaching students to have technically polished skills, but on class and rehearsal as exploration – of an issue and of the self.'[47] As I discussed in this book's 'For the Love of Work' section, Lois and her collaborators foster participants' ability to talk and perform, and to do so from personal experience, especially their gendered experience.

Perhaps Lois's most important principles are her radical faith in imagination, and her commitment to fostering everyone's imagination, whatever their circumstances. 'If you can imagine it you can make it', she says, and, 'If you can make it then you can make it *change*.'[48] With a worldview characterised by such potential, capability, and empowerment, why would anyone hesitate to

'That's what I like about the community aspect of WOW, everyone can be in it, including the audience.'

Top: Moe Angelos, Peggy Reynolds, Beverly Bronson, and Peggy Healey sell refreshments at WOW's Tenth Anniversary, P.S. 122 , NYC, 1990. Photo by Morgan Grenwald.

Bottom: Cathy Coray, Lois Weaver, Peggy Shaw, Terrence Diamond, Claire Moed, and Lisa Kron marching with Lesbian Herstory Archive in NYC, Gay Pride March, 1986. Photo by Morgan Grenwald.

XX ~~RATED~~ **XMAS**

FOR WOMEN ONLY

AN EROTIC EVENING
of hoochie cooch dancing, sensual
acrobatics, exotic tapping, high &
low comedy & wild abandon

BENEFIT FOR WOW SOCIAL CLUB

It seeks to develop people's
skills, even if they are
such humble – but crucial
– skills as speaking up and
speaking out.

start making? Long before 'just do it' ever became Nike's slogan it was Lois's. 'Don't wait for funding, don't wait for permission, don't wait to be asked', Lois commands, 'make work in your bedroom, in your living room, don't wait for it to be finished, show people five minutes, ten minutes, let your audience help you shape it.'[49]

Effects

Fundamentally, Lois's commitment is not just to her own work but to others' too. It is particularly about facilitating creation by and participation of women and lesbians as well as others who are socially marginalised. It aims to enable the voices of women, lesbians, queers, older people, and people from underprivileged class backgrounds, ethnic minorities, and non-western backgrounds. It seeks to raise people's consciousness about the conditions that constrain them; to raise people's confidence to speak out, create, and perform; and to develop and exercise people's skills, even if they are such humble – but crucial – skills as speaking up and speaking out. It advocates for collectivism in a long series of decades heralded by Reaganism in the USA and Thatcherism in the UK that have championed selfish individualism. It is a powerful democratising project.

The many strategies of facilitation deployed by Lois and her collaborators have undoubtedly made a difference – as the many contributions to this book attest. WOW was a crucial home and incubator for many feminist and lesbian artists and audiences. For Kate Davy, writing in 1989, '[t]he WOW Café is a context that presumes a lesbian worldview. In this context, WOW artists create a theatre *for* lesbians, a theatre that responds to lesbian subjectivity.'[50] For historian Sara Warner, '[...] WOW Café produced some of the most audacious, sex-positive feminist artists of the 1980s and 1990s, who titillated audiences

Previous pages: Tammy WhyNot and Carmelita Tropicana (centre) work the crowd for WOW's Tenth Anniversary, P.S. 122 , NYC, 1990. Photo by Morgan Grenwald.

Left: Flyer for WOW benefit party, NYC, 1983.

with their hilarious and witty gender-bending productions.'[51] For Alisa Solomon, writing in 1985, '[t]he WOW Cafe is a force more than a place.'[52] The Five Lesbian Brothers, of which Moe Angelos is a member, got their start there. Playwright and performer Holly Hughes comments that Peggy and Lois 'were role models in a sense in the beginning' at the WOW Café Theatre and that 'they encouraged' many WOW regulars including performance maker Carmelita Tropicana, technician-writer-performer Alice Forrester, and Hughes herself.[53] Kate Davy reports that 'Carmelita Tropicana was telling me that she wouldn't be performing if it wasn't for that kind of approach and process' that Lois and Peggy practised at WOW.[54] British lesbian performer and playwright Sue Frumin pays enormous credit to Lois and Split Britches:

> Although I'd done quite a lot of work, I'd never had much confidence about that work and how to do it. I did some workshops with Lois and Split Britches and it completely affected how I did my work and gave me an awful lot of confidence. She's one of those people who teaches you that you should actually trust your ideas, which made a great change because most lesbians go around, like most teenagers I work with, saying what crap they are and that's a very British thing.[55]

Furthermore, what feels like the lion's share of the library of feminist performance criticism – by the likes of Case, Dolan, Davy, Aston and Harris, and many more – has used Split Britches' and WOW's work as its exemplary material and preferred territory,[56] in turn influencing new generations of theatre students, scholars, and audiences. As noted above, the WOW Café Theatre is still going strong. As the *Public Address Systems* website begins to illustrate, Lois's open access provision of instructions for forms such as the *Long Table* has helped them spread globally, from Brazil (as Paul Heritage notes in his entry in this book), to London, New York, Bogota (Colombia), Brisbane, Melbourne, Vienna, Montreal, and St Catharine's, Ontario. Finally, Lois and her collaborators have cultivated generations of performance makers, producers, and speakers, and they have encouraged probably many thousands more people simply to speak, watch and/or listen, in a legacy that is unquantifiable.

Perhaps Lois's greatest continuing legacies are her commitments to ethics of collectivism, coalition,[57] inclusivity, and imagination.

FESTIVAL PRESENTS

"SUMMER NIGHTS"

EVERY THURSDAY IN JULY AND AUGUST
8 P.M UNTIL? $4
23 ST. MARKS PL.

JULY

3rd plus 30'S MOVIES OF GREAT WOMEN COMEDIANS
LIVE STAGE SHOW FEATURING "THE SCHLOCKETTES"

10th EDWINA LEE TYLER AND
A PIECE OF THE WORLD

17th A MID-"SUMMER NIGHTS" SURPRISE PARTY

24th SQUARE DANCE WITH THE N.Y. WOMEN'S STRING BAND
plus HAYRIDES ON THE HOUR AROUND THE CITY

31st SPIDERWOMAN THEATER IN "FITTIN' ROOM"

Incandescence: the early years at WOW

Cynthia Carr

I had never seen lesbians be so daring and glam and full of themselves before.

'Do you know the way ...', Lois Weaver began to warble, a bit off-key and a bit off-kilter, into a cardboard mic, and – hell *yeah*, we knew the way to San Jose! It was 1982 or maybe 3, another incandescent evening at WOW Café. This was a storefront about the width of an airplane with a stage that looked crowded when three women stood on it. But always in my writing about the place I said 'incandescent', as I tried to describe the fervent joyous energy connecting the (mostly) lesbian performers and the (mostly) lesbian spectators, especially on the nights when the resident old pros from the Split Britches Company performed: Weaver, Peggy Shaw, and Deb Margolin.

Under Weaver's direction, their *Beauty and the Beast* had become a fractured fairy tale that could hold the above-mentioned pop song, a sprinkle of Shakespeare, a quasi-rabbi doing stand-up, a glimpse at the shooting of Ronald Reagan, a Katharine Hepburn imitation, a Perry Como imitation, a little vaudeville, and a proudly outspoken butch wearing a dress. They were gleefully deconstructing various theatre tropes and gender identities but – who knew? Or perhaps I should say – who cared? It was all so entertaining. Weaver's performance of Lady Macbeth's 'unsex me here' monologue? Hilarious. Inevitably Beauty (Weaver) found her happily-ever-after with the Beast (Shaw), and that was more of a plot than most of their performances had. As a rule, certain threads got tied together – others dangled – yet the shows always held together, rather like a pair of split britches.

It's difficult to overstate how startling this work was at the time. The 'womyn's culture' attached to 1970s lesbian/feminism had been so earnest and often so dreary, so prissy – with butch/femme deemed politically incorrect and sex not discussed. We'd been through 'liberation', but how much had it really changed our lives? Then suddenly at WOW, we saw it acted out onstage. I had never seen lesbians be so daring and glam and full of themselves before. The work done at WOW was rude and raunchy and... queer. Split Britches set that tone.

The troupe's name actually originated in the rural south where Weaver grew up, where women wore trousers open along the bottom so they could kneel and urinate easily while working in the fields. The first piece Weaver-Shaw-Margolin created together, a play called *Split Britches*, was based on Weaver's three eccentric aunts who lived in the Blue Ridge Mountains in the 1930s. Still, the style and direction of this work fit right in with 1980s schizo-culture, built on alternating currents of postmodern theory and nightclub energy. WOW fit in with the vibrant but short-lived East Village club scene (Limbo Lounge, 8BC, the Pyramid Club, et al.) that was rewriting performance art history. I'm not sure the word 'postmodern' was ever uttered within the humble confines of WOW. Then

Flyer for events to benefit the first Women's One World Festival (WOW), held in the Electric Circus, St Marks, NYC, 1980. Flyer design by Peggy Shaw.

I'm not sure the word 'postmodern' was ever uttered within the humble confines of WOW. I knew that Derrida would not be showing up. Neither would a critic from *The New York Times*.

again, I knew that Derrida would not be showing up. Neither would a critic from *The New York Times*. This was Off-Off-Off Broadway.

Weaver had gravitated to the experimental before her career even began. While still in college in Virginia, she did her own adaptation of Jean-Claude van Itallie's *The Serpent*, a play directed originally by Joe Chaikin of the Open Theater. Their approach was what galvanized her – ensemble work that broke with dramatic conventions like narrative and naturalism. As she described the Open Theater, '[t]hey used impulse and images and abstractions to build worlds that weren't necessarily logical psychological worlds, and I just fell in love with that.'[58]

Weaver arrived in New York in 1973, in time to see the Open Theater's last production. One of the company's original members, Muriel Miguel, then went on to create the feminist multiracial Spiderwoman Theater, built around a core of Native American women. 'Muriel learned from the Open Theater but she broke with them in lots of ways', says Weaver, who joined Spiderwoman after they formed in 1976. 'Their use of fantasy and personal stories and a belief in the mundane – that came from her.'[59] Shaw joined Spiderwoman in 1978 after leaving Hot Peaches, a drag troupe in which she'd been the only woman, a troupe from a whole other section of the avant-garde theatre spectrum. All of it fed the work done by Split Britches when they began in 1980.

As a director, Weaver has specialised in pieces that don't or won't move forward in a straight line. Split Britches worked by creating characters first, then finding scenarios and words for them. The relationships among the characters mattered but narrative? Not so much, or not at all. Weaver's recent work with the *Long Table*, where she orchestrates a dialogue among people seated as if at a dinner party seems a natural outgrowth of this approach. It's about community, and back in the 1980s that's what was so crucial and so magical at WOW Café. This self-proclaimed 'home for wayward girls' was a refuge from a world that scorned lesbian theatre along with lesbian anything.

Left: Close up of Tammy WhyNot and Carmelita Tropicana at WOW's Tenth Anniversary, P.S. 122 , NYC, 1990. Photo by Morgan Grenwald.

Right: Shara Antoni, Lois Weaver, Peggy Reynolds, and Peggy Shaw in chorus line for Erotic Night WOW benefit. Photo by Saskia Scheffer.

This self-proclaimed 'home for wayward girls' was a refuge from a world that scorned lesbian theatre along with lesbian anything.

Weaver, Shaw, and Margolin also became role models to a bevy of younger artists, who either didn't have much theatre experience or had never created their own work: Holly Hughes, Lisa Kron, Alina Troyano, and Moe Angelos among them. Weaver taught a class at WOW called School for Wayward Girls where they learned what she called 'story building'. And the café became a safe place to make that crucial first piece.

Weaver's character Tammy WhyNot was another revelation. She's a big-haired blonde who gave up country western stardom to become a lesbian performance artist. Though she first appeared when Weaver was part of Spiderwoman, this character really began to blossom in the Split Britches show called *Upwardly Mobile Home*. She sang Tammy Wynette's 'Your Good Girl's Gonna Go Bad'. And did she ever. Tammy WhyNot is hyper-femme in the Nashville style, and she'll speak to y'all in that Dolly Parton twang, but she does tend to be rather salacious. In a sweet way. And often in a humorous way. Holly Hughes was inspired to write some lyrics for Tammy WhyNot. 'You put the cunt back in country', goes one of the lines least likely to invite censorship. The unspoken motivation behind Tammy is that certain things ought to be talked about, and she'll function as their unlikely emissary.

Over time, she has become more than just a character. Weaver refers to Tammy as 'my superhero – because she does things that I wouldn't have the nerve to do as Lois. One of them is to fail. Tammy can "not know" in public, and I can never "not know" in public'.[60] This allows Tammy to work without a script – which just might be the definition of *persona*. A character would need a script.

But Weaver has also spoken about the ways in which playing a character can bring something out of the performer that she didn't know was there. While part of Spiderwoman Theater and their *Evening of Disgusting Songs and Pukey Images*, Weaver chose to create a sinister, slithery, vampirish character and later said, '[t]hat's what really enabled me to come out. It opened up a new life in me and that's when my real life began.'[61]

WOW: an uncooperative cooperative

Holly Hughes

When I entered the door at WOW on East 11th Street in 1982, I was lost in every sense of the word. I had left the Midwest a few years before, to attend the New York Feminist Art Institute, my dreams of sisterhood and art-making informed by listening endlessly to the Pointer Sisters, Sister Sledge, all the pop music sisters. The Institute was founded by women from the Heresies collective, artists and second wavers who were bucking it all – the patriarchy and the puritanical streak that had sucked the air out of feminism. There was a grand opening ceremony that was covered by the press; am I wrong to think the mayor was there? Or a significant underling? So much fanfare attended the opening, much was hoped for in the name, particularly in staking claim as an 'Institute', but the programme I enrolled in was gone in six months. We insisted on our sisterhood; we had no language for the many ways we were different; our giant collective dream of uncomplicated sisterhood left us feeling erased and betrayed.

But WOW is still going strong after 30 plus years. You do the math. It's queer years, like dog years; some years were decades long and some passed in a blink.

An accusation hurled at WOW from some disgruntled parties – and we were all disgruntled some of the time – was that it was little more than a cult of personality, centred around Lois and Peggy. Maybe that's not entirely wrong. Or bad. Obviously the place has continued after they ceased to be central presences, but the psychic space they created outlasted their daily presence. Many other spaces led by charismatic figures collapsed when those people left; how did WOW survive?

We were, as someone joked, an uncooperative cooperative. Though Lois facilitated our weekly staff meetings, and contributed other organisational skills that were unsung but necessary, she also recognised that we were a motley crew of square pegs. We were prickly and difficult as well as funny, resourceful, committed, and driven, we were weird as shit and it was hard to tell what was genius and what was scar tissue; whatever structure that held us together had to have enough give in it, there had to be no pressure to be someone we weren't. Lois removed the gatekeeping associated with most theatre; auditions were out, you didn't need a contact, you just needed to show up and do the work, which meant not only your creative expression, but doing the work of supporting someone else's dream.

I remember more than once when we hit a snag, when Lois would remind us that no matter what, we all loved each other. It did not mean we were the same, it did not mean, certainly, that we liked each other; it meant something else, something larger. We needed the elastic sense of community, we were people who had thought we were crazy because no one could understand us, until we entered this space. Lois had had a religious background, and something of that expansive, mystery of love that is central to faith remained in her, passed through the prism of feminism, of deep commitment to social change, to the risk of art and sex. The love she preached was larger than any vision of sisterhood; it made WOW able to continue for over 30 years, it shines through all of her projects to this day.

We were weird as shit
and it was hard to tell
what was genius and
what was scar tissue.

Top: Women of WOW pose for a group
picture at the 1987 retreat in upstate
New York. Photo by Debra Miller.

Bottom: WOW contingent at Gay Pride
Parade. Photo by Peggy Shaw.

Lois Weaver makes the world a less scary place

Rosana Cade

Being a young queer feminist performance maker can be scary. It's scary to put your life out there in front of an audience. It's scary to talk about what you feel is important in a world that can regularly sideline your issues, place you on the outskirts. It's scary to experiment with different modes of performance, to work with trashy personas as well as owning a socially engaged practice and to hope that people will understand the importance of both.

But Lois Weaver makes the world a less scary place. I'm sure I'm amongst so many artists who have been encouraged by her generosity and enthusiasm to continue down the tricky paths we are making for ourselves.

However, the first time I met Lois was definitely scary. It was scary because I had looked up to her for years, read her words, watched countless videos of her, imitated her, fantasised about her, and been influenced and inspired by so many aspects of her practice. I was meeting one of my idols and I was terrified! And yet, within a few minutes she had invited me over, asked me about myself and my work, and before I knew it we were holding hands and giggling away together. This is a moment I will always remember and one that, for me, sums up so much of what is brilliant and unique about Lois as a person and a practitioner.

Lois spoke to me as an artist, an equal. She made me feel good about my work and broke down any weird barriers between us, any notions of the experienced and the inexperienced. She opened her hand and we had a drink, two lesbians flirting with each other.

Within feminist or artistic circles, I have often experienced people using binary ways of speaking about young and old, placing distance between the generations and making you feel insignificant as a younger person. Lois does the opposite, understanding what you need in order to feel good and make good work.

Over the past year my sister and I have been working together to make a show called *Sister*, which deals with our personal stories as a way of investigating female sexual identity and our relationship to each other and to feminism. When Lois agreed to work with us I was totally thrilled. This was a sensitive process, and Lois came into it at a crucial point. She shared tools for making and structuring performance which I know I will use for the rest of my life. Her incredible openness and insight allowed her to understand where my sister and I were at, and what we needed. She worked with us with humour and love. In the middle of a process that had felt stressful and scary, she renewed our confidence and determination *to make the work that we wanted to make*. And this was the most important thing we could do.

> She made me feel good about my work and broke down any weird barriers between us, any notions of the experienced and the inexperienced.

Opposite: Lois Weaver prepares for a protest at the 2004 Republican National Convention, NYC. Photo by Lori E. Seid.

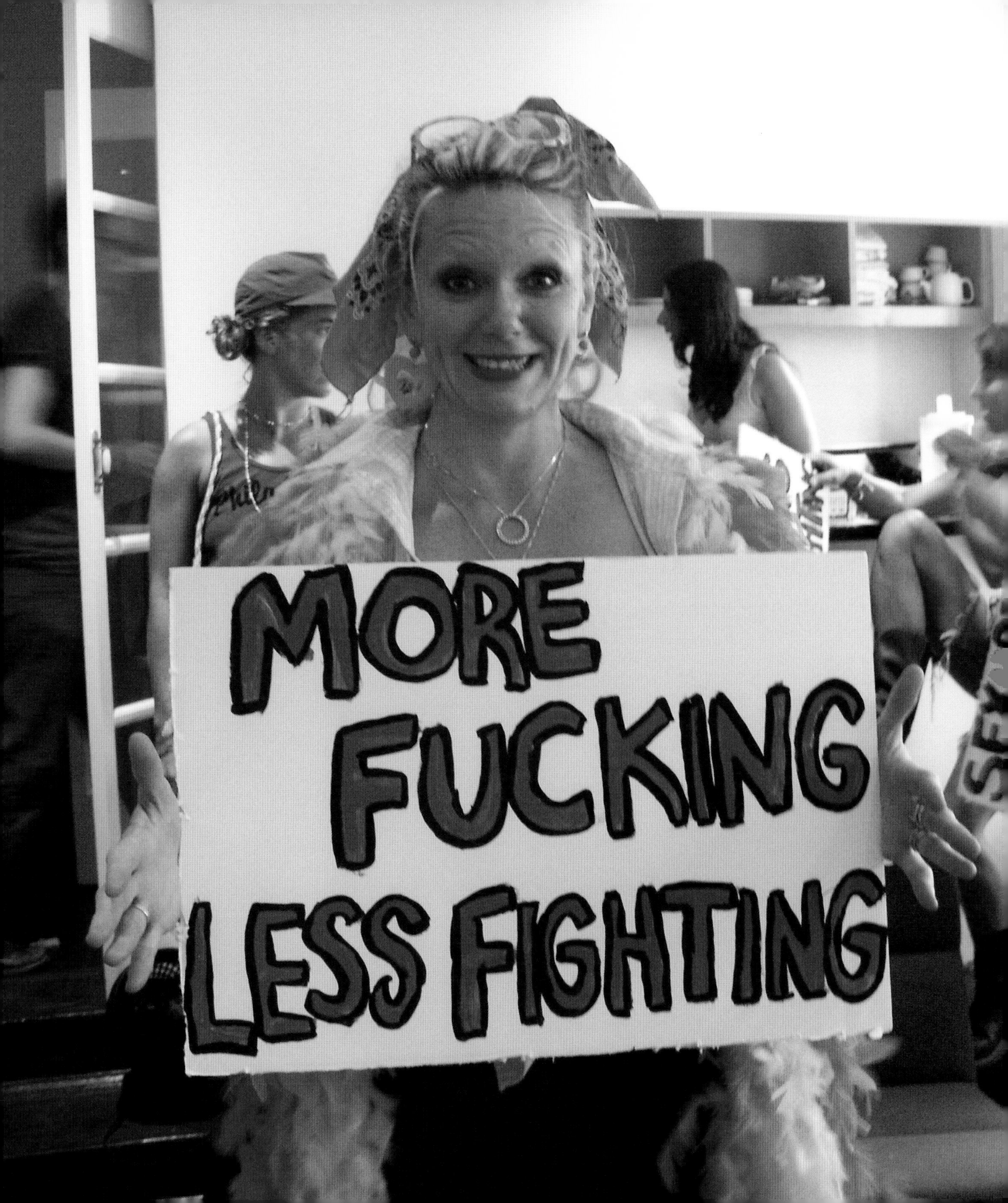
MORE
FUCKING
LESS FIGHTING

Taking a seat at the Table

Deirdre Heddon

The *Long Table*, best described as an aestheticized social practice for prompting dialogic interaction and public debate, was first installed by Weaver in Rio in 2003, a component of the project *In the House*.[62] Since then, the *Long Table* has been set in a number of places, from the Hemispheric Institute in Colombia, to Performance Studies international gatherings in London, Zagreb, and Stanford University, and festivals in Manchester and Plymouth. Each *Long Table* holds – or hosts – a particular subject for discussion, with topics to date ranging from Labour, Live Art, and Feminism to Gender and Citizenship, Democracy and Technology, Performance and Community, and Social Justice and Performance. The components required for a *Long Table* include a large table with 12 chairs around it and up to 40 at a distance from it, microphones and a recording device, a tablecloth and fabric marking pens. Accompanying – framing, guiding, supporting – all *Long Tables* is 'The *Long Table* Etiquette', a sheet of 'instructions' placed on each chair around the *Long Table* offering reassurance by making the protocols of participation explicit. The performers in the *Long Table* are simply those who choose to take a chair at the table and contribute to the discussion.

Attending a number of *Long Table* installations – both as a participant and as an observer/listener (sitting close to the table but not at it) – I am struck by its capacity to cultivate revised democratic practices. In some senses, the *Long Table*, a space for public debate, takes its place within Jürgen Habermas's framework of democracy, functioning as an example of 'the public sphere', a 'theatre in modern societies in which political participation is extended through the medium of talk'.[63] However, its form and content challenge some of Habermas's presumptions, not least that of a single, liberal public sphere. As Nancy Fraser has so powerfully asserted, the idea and practice of an idealised 'public sphere', one rhetorically promoted as 'accessible', was constituted from multiple exclusions based on gender, class, and race. Though such exclusions might have been formally eliminated, Fraser emphasises that the persistence of structural inequality continues to affect participation (in terms of who and how). Recognising differential access to 'the material means of equal participation', Fraser asks what 'institutional arrangements will best help narrow the gap in the participatory parity between dominant and subordinate groups?'[64] Though Fraser posed this question in 1990, the fact of deepening structural inequality renders it still timely.

> I am struck by its capacity to cultivate revised democratic practices.

Right: Handout that establishes the rules of etiquette at a *Long Table*. Designed by Charlie Cauchi.

The Long Table Etiquette

This is a performance of a
dinner table conversation

Anyone seated at the table
is a guest performer

Talk is the only course

No one will moderate

But a host may assist you

It is a democracy

To participate simply take
an empty seat at the table

If the table is full you
can request a seat

If you leave the table you can
come back again and again

Feel free to write your
comments on the tablecloth

There can be silence

There might be awkwardness

There could always be laughter

There is an end but no conclusion

The relationship mobilised
between private and public
is an important, feminist
tactic of empowerment.

Weaver admits that her dialogic arts practices offer ways of her coming to terms with her own idea of what democracy is: 'everyone deserves a voice and everyone deserves a place at the table'.[65] Marleen Gorris's film, *Antonia's Line* (1995), is credited as the inspiration for the *Long Table*. In the film, Antonia continues to extend her dinner table in order to accommodate those excluded from the local community, constituting a new community in turn. The dinner table, then, has performative potential. Hannah Arendt's insights resonate here too: the table gathers people together, functioning as an in-between that simultaneously relates and separates.[66] However, Arendt's table is not explicitly a dinner table and for Weaver, the relationship mobilised between private and public is an important, feminist tactic of empowerment. The dinner table, presumed a private and domestic space and therefore historically the excluded outside of political debate, is here made the medium *for* that debate, also allowing topics that might be considered marginal to politics to be, literally, tabled. What is put on the table is determined by those who choose to gather around it, whilst the table itself – a prop dressed in a tablecloth – signals conviviality and congeniality rather than neutrality or impersonality, acting as a magnet for participation and the performance of a counterpublic.[67]

Political theorist Romand Coles asks that we re-imagine democratic processes by dislodging a central figure of democratic politics, 'the political *table*', that political space 'around which members of a polity are to deliberate and exercise judgement'.[68] Coles proposes developing 'practices of more receptive tabling' which represent and perform the 'tensional promise' between 'representations of commonality and representations of difference', the agonistic alongside the consensual.[69] Such tensional promise is the very essence of democratic politics. As Coles proposes, '[d]emocracy will not be or become solely or primarily at a central table of fixed being and location, but only from tables that let themselves move and move us to very different spaces and modes of relation'.[70] The *Long Table*, in form and function, offers one version of more democratic and receptive, relational, tabling. It intends a generous, non-intimidating space, with participants hailed by the dining table to contribute in their own voices, with no presumption of a single public, a 'we', to be addressed. Whilst broad topics of focus are chosen at the outset, the matters of concern or issues to emerge from these and to be deliberated – and indeed to come and go, as performers change – are unknown. What is 'tabled' expands as a result. The people joining and leaving over the duration of the discussion literally and symbolically render the table an ever-shifting site of debate between ever-shifting representatives. Where Coles re-imagines the practice of tabling by presenting a table which moves – to other places and other people – the *Long Table*, by contrast, offers a political table productively unsettled not just by its strategic domestication and welcome, but by the movement around it.[71]

Left: *Long Table* on Violence and the Politics of Representation, Hemispheric Institute Encuentro 2007, Buenos Aires, Argentina.

Entertaining discussion:
The *Long Table* and *Porch Sitting*

Geraldine Harris

The last time I saw Lois (at this moment of writing, not 'ever' I hope) was in June 2014 at Queen Mary University of London when I had the pleasure of taking part in a 'Coffee Table Talk' which featured coffee and cake, and a 'Cocktail Seminar' which to my delight featured *real* (as in alcoholic) cocktails. Lois was co-curating and facilitating these two events as part of the Live Art Development Agency's (LADA) *Restock, Rethink, Reflect Three* project on feminism, live art, and archives.

The re-purposing of the cosy feminine homeliness of the coffee klatch and the louche glamour of the cocktail party as a means of framing and encouraging dialogue between artists and academics, aligns the idea of the Coffee Table Talk and the Cocktail Seminar with some of the more developed strategies that Lois has designed over the years to stimulate 'open ended, non-hierarchical discussion'.[72] These include formats such the *Long Table* (which Lois also used within the LADA project), *Porch Sitting*, the Card Table, and *Domestic Terrorism: Hang Your Laundry in Public*, all of which Lois collects together under the category of the 'everyday' on her *Public Address Systems* website. However, like *all* of the various activities she details on this website, as Lois puts it in regard to the *Long Table*, within these everyday strategies 'theatrical craft and political commitment are mutually supporting'.[73] This means that the everyday is quoted within structures that have both the status of performances and are (socially and politically) performative. I want to explore how this is achieved and to what potential effect with specific reference to the *Long Table* and *Porch Sitting*. In doing so I intend to borrow from Helen Molesworth's article on 1970s women artists entitled 'House Work and Art Work'(2000)[74] in a way that connects back to Lois's work on the LADA project.

The *Long Table* (outlined by Dee Heddon in this volume, above) is the best known of these 'everyday systems' and has been used by others as well as by Lois in a wide range of artistic, academic, institutional, and community contexts to explore a diverse menu of topics. As indicated in the model 'etiquette sheet' for these events provided by Lois, this is a '*performance* of a dinner party conversation' in which all participants have equal status as 'guest performers'.[75] This etiquette sheet also underlines that 'there may be awkwardness' and 'there can be silence' and Lois has stressed elsewhere that if people 'allow' these things to happen, 'something will come, people will talk with each other'.[76] Bearing in mind the distinction between talking *with* as opposed to talking *to*, in my experience of the *Long Table*, this particular guideline can sometimes prove surprisingly challenging. Some participants will do their best to avoid awkwardness and silence, especially those (academics, for example) used to leading (some people might say *dominating*) public discussion. *Porch Sitting* might be seen as a strategy for circumventing this problem.

Some participants will do their best to avoid awkwardness and silence, especially those used to leading public discussion.

Long Table awaiting participants at Hemispheric Institute's Encuentro, Bogota, 2009. Photo courtesy of the Hemispheric Institute.

This first *Porch Sitting* was performed at La MaMa Experimental Theatre Club in New York on New Year's Eve 2013, where Lois remarks 'as it turned out' the conversation was about the future of queer and feminist performance and led directly to a new initiative designed to support emerging queer artists.[77] This format could be perceived as a performance of an *after* dinner conversation, although this may be just be the way I imagined it when I took part in it later in 2014. As with the *Long Table*, participants are usually free to swap from being 'on stage' to 'off stage' and silence, laughter, and raucous singing as well as conversation are all welcome.[78] However, in this instance guest performers sit in irregular lines facing the same way as if on a porch (or a balcony, or the space in front of any kind of shelter). This spatial relationship is key to its dynamic in that a side-by-side configuration is less highly charged than the face-to-face, less likely to make people feel they have to fill a silence and, in reducing the visual 'cues' passing between participants, it places more emphasis on *listening*.

How to behave at a *Porch Sitting*

Lois Weaver

Porch Sitting is an alternative model for public conversation conceived and developed by Lois Weaver. The project takes seriously the idea that public dialogue can happen side-by-side, rather than face-to-face. It makes space for the things we wonder about rather than providing a platform for the things we know. *Porch Sitting* is a space to sit, think, dream, or get involved in the ongoing conversation.

A few notes on how to behave at a *Porch Sitting*

1. Imagine this is a shared household.

2. The household might have two areas: the Kitchen and the Porch.

3. The Kitchen is where you can get your drinks, your snacks, and your gossip. You can just hang out in the kitchen if you want and behave whichever way you please.

4. The Porch, however, has a few guidelines:

- It is where you sit, think, and dream or get involved in the ongoing story or conversation.

- You can come and go when and if you please. Just pay due respect to the silence or the flow of conversation.

- If you can't think how you should think on the Porch, put yourself in the mind of a porch sitter with phrases like:

  I wonder whatever happened to...

  Who do you think that is...

  I have a feelin' it's going to...

  Or just about any phrase that begins...

  I imagine... I wonder... I think... I feel...

- Try not to worry if it all goes quiet for a spell, or if it gets a bit raucous for a time, or if somebody just bursts into song. The Porch can handle it.

- Let everyone know ahead of time just how long you think you might be sitting on the porch, and when the time comes, find a way to turn the porch light on and wish everybody a safe journey home.

5. After a spell, visit the Soapbox on: publicaddresssystems.org, to post on the Facebook page, to send an email to let us know how it went or to upload photos to the Flickr site.

This side-by-side configuration is less highly charged than the face-to-face, less likely to make people feel they have to fill a silence, and places more emphasis on listening.

Lois suggests a series of prompts for the conversation such as 'when was the last time you saw?', 'what is coming down the road?', or phrases beginning 'I imagine, I wonder, I think, I feel'.[79] These prompts set the scene for an event that revolves around 'an implicit question, or an implicit rumination, rather than a display of knowledge'.[80] They also recall the instructions Lois used for writing exercises in a four-day workshop for performance makers to learn about Split Britches' devising process, in which I participated in 2006 and subsequently documented in *Performance Practice and Process: Contemporary [Women] Practitioners*.[81] Indeed, in general the structure of Lois's everyday systems very much reflects the principles and techniques she and Peggy identified during this event as guiding the creation of their shows.

Two of these techniques are 'juxtaposition' and 'layering' and both are designed to produce highly condensed images or 'moments' that convey multiple meanings. I would suggest that the *Long Table* and *Porch Sitting* operate in this manner, so that while described as 'formats' they may seem straightforward, as *performances* they are multi-layered in their potential political/philosophical implications. Indeed, they offer themselves to be analysed in relation to theories that have recently energised performance studies criticism, such as Jacques Derrida's thinking on the 'ethics of hospitality'[82] or the discourse around 'socially engaged art' as developed under the influence of thinkers including Nicolas Bourriaud, Jacques Rancière, and Claire Bishop.[83] What makes me reluctant to undertake this analysis is that firstly, in the course of such debates the manner in which practices are used to illustrate arguments can obscure the fact that 'theory' usually comes down the road *after* and is inspired by radical, cutting-edge practice (theatrical, political, or everyday) rather than vice versa. Secondly, and perhaps relatedly, it is noticeable that within these particular debates, feminist, queer, and anti-racist ideas and practices are often either overlooked or dismissed as 'identity politics' of a type no longer useful to the task of re-conceptualising democracy in the face of the problems created by twenty-first century global capitalism.

As Molesworth demonstrates in 'House Work and Art Work', the habit of seeing ground-breaking feminist projects (and those arising from queer, anti-racism, and similar political movements that intersect with feminism) as 'separate from', or peripheral to, 'the putatively "dominant" conversations being held in the art world' (or those of philosophy and politics) is long established.[84] Hence the necessity for the LADA feminist live art archive project; in the spirit of which, rather than attempting to place Lois's everyday systems *within* the scholarly debates cited above, I'd like to borrow aspects of Molesworth's essay to situate these systems in *advance* of these theorisations, as part of an established but still leading and vital trajectory of feminist art practice.

The works Molesworth analyses include Judy Chicago's *The Dinner Party* (1979), Mary Kelly's *Post-Partum Document* (1979), Mierle Laderman Ukeles's *Maintenance Art Performances* (1973-74), and Martha Rosler's videos *Semiotics of the Kitchen* (1973) and *Domination and the Everyday* (1978), a list that might be extended geographically and temporally to embrace works by artists as diverse as the UK's Bobby Baker, Malaysian artist Simryn Gill, or the US's Liza Lou to name but three. As Molesworth acknowledges in regard to the works she explores, there are important conceptual, formal, and *political* differences between all of these artists. Nevertheless, in most cases there is a tendency towards humour. But their most striking affinity is the public and overtly theatrical re-purposing or 're-presenting' of aspects of the private and the domestic, a realm that traditionally has been regarded as 'feminine'. While overall marked by continual innovation and response to differing social and cultural contexts, this is also a trope evident in Split Britches productions going back to their first show in 1980, *Split Britches*, as well as in Lois's everyday systems.

As Baker has attested[85] these features are often misrecognised as lack of *seriousness* and Molesworth argues that in the 1970s the 'domestic/maintenance content of such works was read as equivalent to their meaning'.[86] By this (I think) she means that they were taken as being 'about' the domestic, the female or the feminine with no relevance to wider political and/or artistic economies. In response, Molesworth contends that 'what has not been appreciated' is the way this material not only permits an engagement with 'questions of value and institutionality' in relation to *art*, a central concern of the avant-garde at the time, but simultaneously allows for a critique of 'the conditions of *everyday life*'.[87] She asserts that by submitting 'public space to the pressures of what it traditionally excludes or renders invisible', in terms of both subjectivities and genres of work (house work *and* certain kinds of art work), these pieces raise issues about the relationship between art and life, private and public, the domestic economy and, as she puts it, the broader 'democracy-capitalism covenant'.[88] However, Molesworth is at pains to stress that these works

> [H]ave not collapsed the distinction between art and life; rather, they have used art as a form of legitimated public discourse, a conduit though which to enter ideas into public discussion. So while all the works expose the porosity between public and private spheres, none call for the dismantling of these formations. Fictional as the division may be the private sphere is too dear to relinquish, and the public sphere as a site of discourse and debate is too important a fiction for democracy to disavow.[89]

Instead, she contends that these works operate on the basis of 'what if', representing exercises in 'speculative feminist utopic thought', with each one offering a proposition of how the world might be organised differently.[90] In developing this analysis Molesworth is touching on themes and tropes still central to current debates on 'socially engaged' practices.[91]

Lois's everyday systems do not exactly 'fit' all aspects of Molesworth's argument but this article is useful in helping to identify some of the 'layers' in the *Long Table* and *Porch Sitting*. On a simple level these formats import the codes and conventions of domestic hospitality and sociability into public, institutional spaces to promote a more open, inclusive and convivial atmosphere for discussion. However, in bringing the private into the public a juxtaposition is created that puts these spaces 'under pressure' in regard to what they traditionally 'exclude or render invisible'. In addition, being cited as both 'out of place' and under the sign of 'art', as self-conscious theatrical *performances*, also (potentially) opens these codes and conventions themselves to critical scrutiny. This might prompt consideration of the way that the laws of hospitality are imbricated in structures of exclusion, whether in the context of the domestic economy (who is welcome or 'entertained' in the home) or the broader socio-political economy (who is welcome or 'entertained' in the community/institution/nation-state/global contract). As Judith Still points out, the social codes of hospitality are rooted in patriarchal

They can (and frequently do) embrace disagreement and contestation, the life blood of drama and of democracy.

structures and in 'property rights' and on this point it is important that there is no formal 'hostess' or 'host' in either the *Long Table* or *Porch Sitting*. Historically, the position of host has been coded as masculine with 'hostess' being generally a denigrated term with ambiguous connotations.[92] Meanwhile, the invisible embodied *labour* of delivering the material signs of hospitality has usually fallen to those placed under the sign of the feminine.

On a more *explicit* level, citing these codes and conventions as a performance, an exercise of the imagination that does not have to conform to the 'rules' of everyday life, gives the 'guest performers' licence to imagine beyond the limits and constraints of the current economies of hospitality, so that alternative possibilities may be envisioned and invented.

As *performances*, then, the *Long Table* and *Porch Sitting* (and to some extent the Coffee Table Talk and Cocktail Seminar) extend the possibilities of *what* it might be considered 'legitimate' to discuss in the public spaces in which they occur, *how* it might be 'legitimately' discussed and by *whom*. In the process they implicitly pose questions about 'value and institutionality' in regard to both the world of art and/or the academy (or other institutions depending on their context), as well as about everyday life. At the same time, they stage a feminist/queer utopic proposition of how the world might be organised differently, creating a space for guest performers to explore their own ideas of 'what if?'

All this is achieved by playing on but not collapsing the distinction between private and public, 'on' and 'off' stage, life and art, performing and not-performing, entertaining and being entertained. Keeping these distinctions 'in play' means that the *Long Table* and *Porch Sitting* do not necessarily posit a stable and inevitably exclusive concept of 'community', the part of the guest being marked *as* a theatrical role limited to the time of the performance. Neither do these strategies necessarily imply an ideal of 'harmony' (there may be awkwardness, there is an end but no conclusion); rather they can (and frequently do) embrace disagreement and contestation, the life blood of drama *and* of democracy. As such, they point to the connections between what Rancière refers to as the politics of aesthetics and the aesthetics of politics[93] while avoiding some of the tendencies that have produced what Molesworth refers to as an attitude of 'frustration or dismissal' towards feminist utopian thought,[94] and indeed towards the utopianism of some recent 'relational' and 'socially engaged art', as critiqued by Rancière and Bishop.[95]

Lois Weaver and the ethics and etiquette of the *Long Table*

Diana Taylor

Take a seat. Let's listen and talk to each other. This poetic, bare-bones invitation to sit and dialogue, proffered by Lois Weaver's *Long Table* has given thousands of artists, scholars, and activists not just the opportunity but the structure within which to speak to each other across linguistic, geographic, and disciplinary boundaries to engage in difficult and conflictive topics. Developed by Weaver in 2003, the *Long Table* looks like a banquet table complete with a paper tablecloth and chairs, although microphones have been added. Coloured pens lie on the table, waiting for people to write or doodle as they listen and talk. The *Long Table* is all potentiality. 'An experimental public forum that is a hybrid performance-installation-roundtable discussion-dinner party designed to facilitate dialogue'[96] has been a regular event at the Hemispheric Institute ever since Weaver introduced it at the Encuentro in Argentina in 2007. Back then, participants cautiously approached it as they would a panel, formally introducing themselves and their work. Hemi, as always, provided translation. Soon, however, it became a necessary space for sharing intimate feelings about everything from hair texture and race, to what it meant to be 'queer' or 'cuir,' to how discrimination and neo-imperialism play out in the Americas not only in our various social contexts but also at the *Long Table* itself.

In June 2014, during the Hemispheric Institute's Encuentro (eight-day conference/performance event) in Montreal, a very heated dispute erupted in the assembly of some one thousand participants. Jesusa Rodríguez and her wife Liliana Felipe, two of Mexico's most radical performance artists and activists, had presented a play, *Juana la Larga* (*Long Juana*), developed from archival documents unearthed by queer Mexican historian, María Elena Martínez of University of Southern California (USC). Juana Aguilar, an eighteenth century intersex person from Central America, was accused by the Inquisition of committing 'abominable sins' with women.[97] Depicted onstage as an anatomical model, Juana's genitals were examined and transposed by a physician, Narciso Esparragosa y Gallardo, played by Jesusa, who declares that Juana has no sex at all ('se es nada'), and is therefore a nothing, and cannot be prosecuted and executed by the Inquisition. While the designation saved Juana's life, the 'nothingification' of women, the play suggests, reflects how they have been treated as non-humans in Mexico for a very long time.

Juana la Larga was humorous as almost all of Jesusa's work is, at times pushing (some would say exceeding) the boundaries of acceptable taste. Using caricature, vaudevillesque gags, over-simplifications, double entendres, and other forms of word play the performance makes its point, and the point is sharp. The two artists call out the continued and escalating violence and nullification of women. Feminicide, a term coined in Mexico to describe the gendered nature of the viciousness, continues to escalate. 2,764 women were murdered in 2012 alone. Throughout the play the tension oscillates between the desire to destabilise gender and sexual categories by showing the violence of medical and archival categorisation that historically cemented current notions of 'difference', and, at the same time, the desire to make an urgent point: that 'women', products of that systematic and violent differentiation, are being targeted and killed for being women. The play attempts to resolve this tension between 'women' and unsettling gender in the last line with a celebration of 'women of all sexes'.

The next morning, on Facebook, we learned that some transsexual members of the audience felt humiliated and laughed at during the performance. One said it had brought him to the point of tears and that he had resisted the temptation to walk out.

The next hours were full of discussions, accusations, and demands for clarification. In a brief impromptu town hall meeting that I called that same day in the midst of a packed performance schedule, Jesusa explained that her intention had never been to make fun of trans people. On the contrary, her artistic and performance work has always pushed for gender rights, sexual rights, and other forms of human rights. A tall, strong, trans woman dressed in pearls and high heels came up to the three of us on the raised platform and thrust her hand within inches of my face. 'It's not their fault', she shouted at me: 'It's your fault.' I let the

gesture pass, even as I felt physically attacked. For all the talk in the audience of the need to create 'safe' spaces, I did not feel safe. Again, Jesusa reiterated that the violence against women, including trans women, in Mexico is so virulent that she and Liliana had wanted to bring it to the foreground. She apologised if they had inadvertently hurt people in the audience.

The conflicts remained unresolved. Lois Weaver then offered to organise a *Long Table* for the next day at the Library of Performing Rights that she created for the Encuentro. The *Long Table* would clearly enable an alternative form of discussion to the escalating name-calling in the town hall meeting. Seated at the *Long Table* the following day required that we look at people as we spoke to them. This is a far cry from Facebook communication. Jesusa sat at the table, and Liliana chose not to. The trans man who posted on Facebook sat next to Jesusa but did not speak. The trans woman who confronted me did not participate, and let it be known through others that she would not talk to any of us. Others, non-trans queer activists and theorists made some points: the trans community bears the burden of always having to explain itself – we should not contribute to that burden; there were language issues and points of untranslatability. Was the audience laughing at what the artists said, or at the translation that kicked in a minute or so later? Some pointed out the dangers of censorship; others re-iterated that Jesusa should have explicitly referenced the trans population as she played with genitals; others felt uneasy with artists being called on to apologise for their work. Larry La Fontaine, a queer theorist from Puerto Rico who is a professor at the University of Michigan, pointed out the dangers of mis-translation and misrecognition around terms and concepts combined with the challenges of engaging historical documents. The play after all, he stressed, dealt with the eighteenth century Spanish Inquisition! 'I understood it was a parody and that Jesusa was opening a space for conversation,' he said. But he added that 'it sounds to me like the white people from the North are once again telling the women of colour from the South how to do their work'. The Jamaican artist/scholar

Sitting around the table, looking at each other, hopefully even hearing each other, it was clear that everyone spoke from a place of partial understanding and limited expertise. Weaver was right; it was uncomfortable. The silences were painful. But it felt necessary.

Honor Ford-Smith agreed that the discussion reflected a North/South divide, 'the huge gap between what Jesusa was trying to get at' and the attitude that 'those backward Third World people need to be taught things'. Was this another form of Inquisition? If so, I wondered, who would be called in to adjudicate? Queer performance artist Peggy Shaw expressed her position succinctly: 'If you have a problem with a show, go make your own fucking show.' She added that women have never been safe, and women have had to explain themselves for centuries and get used to seeing themselves objectified and ridiculed onstage and off. For the first time, a self-identified trans person spoke, saying, 'the only person I can speak for is myself', and told Jesusa, 'I want to be in solidarity with you.'

And so it went.

Sitting around the table, looking at each other, hopefully even hearing each other, it was clear that everyone spoke from a place of partial understanding and limited expertise. Weaver was right; it was uncomfortable. The silences were painful. But it felt necessary.

Jesusa repeatedly asked for someone to explain the specific thing/image that had offended them.

At the end of the hour and a half *Long Table*, the trans man who had posted on Facebook leaned over to Jesusa and asked her quietly if he could have time to speak with her.

Weaver had warned us, there was no 'conclusion'. The discussion did not end there.

So what did the *Long Table* reveal? Among many possible responses I would highlight only a few. One has to do with the difficulties of communicating across languages and cultures. The people at the *Table* did not all understand each other. The interaction was powerful because it was grounded in actual exchange with other people in the here and now. Reactions and feelings had to be taken into account in real time. People needed to find the words. Areas of miscommunication or misunderstanding became evident immediately and were subject to debate. Pontificating participants risked performing a Polonius. This was not a utopian vision of intelligibility – interactions tend to be incomplete and messy. These general issues were complicated by the additional challenges Martínez called 'historical anachronism', such as 'trying to make [Aguirre] a part of "gay and lesbian history"'. 'Succumbing to a classificatory impulse', she adds, is 'not unlike that which is present on Esparragosa's investigation'.[98] Translating humour, of course, poses yet other problems. I would argue that the disconnect was less about the important trans movements and more about the ways that identity struggles and power inequalities can blind us to related forms of violence. We were all talking about violence – the violence trans communities face every day; the violence against women; the violence of refusing to discuss one's ideas and positions in a public setting; and the fear of violent repression that can lead to self-censorship. Turning something into a personal grievance puts it beyond discussion (I cannot argue with your feelings). But talking about violence as relational and multi-directional allows us to develop strategies of resistance. Women have always been explaining themselves; feminists have always been explaining themselves; people of colour have always been explaining themselves; queer, transgendered, and transsexual groups have always been explaining themselves. Surely, as the one 'out' trans person who spoke at the *Table* noted, there are grounds for solidarity. As Peggy Shaw reminded us, if we are going to cast everything as a war, we need to remember who our enemy is. Behaviours can, I believe, be modified by this performance, which has its own conventions and correctives. Modifying behaviours and finding other words in order to sustain an interaction might be just the thing to build hemispheric solidarity and coalitions. But first, we need to take a seat at the table.

Collaboration

Lois Keidan

Lois was the first other Lois I ever met. I knew there were lots of Loises out there, including the most famous of them all, Lois Weaver, but I didn't meet her until 1992 when she moved to London to become joint Artistic Director of Gay Sweatshop, and we worked together on *Fierce: Sex, Art and Censorship, US style* at the ICA. It was over 20 years ago, but I can clearly remember the moment I was introduced to this Other Lois, and the moment someone said 'our' name and we both turned around. It was the first time I'd ever had that experience, and it turned out to be the first of many other 'firsts' I've experienced working with Lois.

I could talk about that ICA programme – the first time that so many fiercely politicised artists emerging from the heat of the US culture wars had been seen in the UK – and how it was a catalytic moment for Live Art. I could talk about the UK performance scene at that time – the tensions between traditional theatre and emerging new performance based practices – and how Lois's appointment at Gay Sweatshop so vividly exposed and tested those relations, just as Neil Bartlett's arrival as Artistic Director at Lyric Hammersmith did a few years later. I could talk about her shift into academia, her groundbreaking work as a teacher and researcher, and her impact on a generation of artists, producers, and thinkers who have grown up under her influence. I could talk about her visionary role as Artistic Director of Performance Studies international #12 *Performing Rights* (2006), bringing theorists and artists together to consider the responsibilities of performance to issues of human rights, or as creator of the instrumental East End Collaborations and Fresh development programmes for new artists and ideas at Queen Mary University of London. I could talk about her inspirational approach to research for the Live Art Development Agency's *Restock Rethink Reflect* project, mapping and marking neglected feminist performance histories. I could talk about

her work as an artist – a dazzlingly brilliant performer and performance maker. But what I really want to talk about – and what is implicit in all the roles she has played – is Lois as a collaborator.

Collaboration is an 'art'. I didn't realise this until I first worked with Lois, and it is an art in which she excels. Collaboration has become a bit of a cliché in modern artspeak – it's a word that's easy to write (usually into funding applications), but a concept that's difficult to truly grasp and even more challenging to put into action. I've worked with Lois on many different collaborations since 1992, and each has required us to develop new kinds of relations, new methodologies, new modes of production and new frameworks for research, discourse, and practice.

All of these have been possible because of Lois.

Her innate generosity, her smartness (street and book), her commitment to social justice and grass roots politics, her curiosity and thirst for new ideas, her willingness to get her hands dirty and do the grunge work, her belief in the young and faith in the old, and her capacity to take all kinds of risks and have fun while doing so, are all active ingredients in a good collaborator. What makes Lois a great collaborator is something else – it's her *understanding* of the different kinds of needs that different kinds of artists have, of the necessity for radical new frameworks for radical new forms of art, and of the possibilities for new affinities and relationships between practice, research, and discourse and between institutional and independent contexts. These, coupled with her *ability* to bring all her diverse experiences and responsibilities as an artist, activist, researcher, producer, educator, and host to bear to create new ways of working that can make a real difference, are what make Lois Weaver a fearless and peerless collaborator.

Friends, family and collaborators, left to right: Coney Island Christmas with Lori E. Seid, Ian Antoni, Peggy Shaw, and Lois Weaver; Muriel Miguel, Gloria Miguel, and Lisa Mayo of Spiderwoman; Lois Weaver and Lois Keidan; Susan Young, Holly Hughes, and Lois Weaver at WOW; Vick Ryder, Lois Weaver, Melanie Hope, Stacy Makishi; Peggy Shaw, Lori E. Seid, Lois Weaver, Vivian Stoll, and Stormy Brandenberger at Desperate Archives; Lois and Virginia Weaver with Shara and Ian Antoni in Virginia's back yard; Karena Rahall, Alice Forrester, Peggy Shaw and friends.

Kinship

Lois Weaver[99]

A kin-ship is a strange little vessel. She is small yet seaworthy and abides by a comforting yet troubling set of codes that determines who gets in and who stays out of the boat. Like most ships, she lists. She lists between a company of kin that can sit down to breakfast with one mother or two fathers and their brood of loved but unrelated ones, and one that holds fast to blood that draws a line at the family table; between a block that parties and a party that blocks; between unruly affinity occupying all streets and the systematised sameness that holds office.

Those of us who work in theatre have our own fleet of kinships. The moment we embark on the *Process* by sitting down for the first rehearsal or standing in the circle of an early workshop, the habits of family slowly crawl out of the hold and start chatting up the mother, brother, sister, wife, husband, father and, more often than not, the lover in the room. When it works well, we experience all the benefits of family and none of the angst of ancestry. The rehearsal dynamic and the after-show camaraderie can be like a love boat cruise that ends with everyone sharing photos and promising to do this again. When it doesn't work, we throw on our teenage jumpers patched with rivalry and paranoia and slink into our rooms alone or with our equally sulky best friend and slam the door. However, in all cases there is the moment when we realise that this was not the lifetime family cruise we thought it was going to be, and that none of these people is likely to show up for Christmas dinner, and that we are again, happily or not, adrift.

Collaboration is a crafty racing boat, complex in design, capable of speedy manoeuvres, offering a thrilling ride but most assuredly a more treacherous voyage. We make quick, intuitive decisions about the who and how of working with other artists. We are attracted to the shine of their sharp spiky points or their spirited high gloss, and we convince ourselves that in spite of some rough edges, we will bond. We will become a perfectly compatible, highly creative team. Delighted to have the company, we jump into the creative process full of excitement and head directly into some very dangerous, uncharted waters. The storms are inevitable. Sometimes we weather them. In fact, we are glad the rain cleared the air. But once in a while it's a fatal tempest. Our beautiful streamlined collaboration races straight for the rocks. The project is shipwrecked, the boat irreparable, the cargo badly damaged, if not destroyed, and bodies are scattered all over the island. Stranded with the provision of hindsight, we realise we should not have taken this kinship for granted, we should have agreed on the way to disagree. We should have drawn up a simple contract, a map that pointed to what we hoped to achieve, outlined emergency measures for maintaining our sense of humour, and clearly articulated a procedure for bailing out or staying the course.

Built not for speed but for strength, the *Community* is a vast freighter. Her sheer size accommodates passengers of all classes: performers, designers, directors, singers, dancers, academics, activists, artists, colleagues, co-workers, participants, spectators, audience, stakeholders, and critics alike. She carries the goods of all kinds: cultural celebration, ethnic identification, geographic and sexual orientation, and aesthetic passions and prejudices. While this kinship is not as prone to dramatic shipwreck, she can be known to sink from the weight of the responsibility of representation. Her passengers can drown in a sea of assumptions of sameness or shared vision, or in the singular notion that this is our one and only community. She is hard working and we depend on her various labours and yet she is not welcome in all ports, often relegated to shipping docks and excluded from the marinas of high culture.

To avoid some of these perils I suggest we rebuild and rechristen. I propose we find a way to salvage the good materials of kinship and recycle them into a more sustainable craft and rechristen her with a term made unpopular by governments and popular by movements for change. Let's call our kinship a *Coalition* and build on the strengths of that definition: Coalition – a group of individuals who come together for a specific amount of time to achieve a common goal. Let's adopt this term for the work of the theatre and state loudly and clearly that we are a kinship of diverse individuals who achieve a closeness without necessary affinity or family resemblance, who come together without ownership and separate without anxiety and who commit ourselves not just to the potential of our extraordinary imaginations but to the careful articulation and fulfilment of our common goals.

215

1   Lois Weaver, unpublished interview with Jen Harvie, London, 20 May 2015.

2   Lois Weaver in Elaine Aston and Geraldine Harris, 'Imagining, Making, Changing', in *Performance Practice and Process: Contemporary [Women] Practitioners* (Basingstoke: Palgrave Macmillan, 2008), pp. 100-18 (p. 102).

3   Lois Weaver, 'The *Long Table* Etiquette', *Public Address Systems* http://publicaddresssystems.org/wp-content/uploads/2013/05/takeawaylongtableprotocol.pdf> [accessed 21 April 2015].

4   Weaver, 'Afterword', in *The Routledge Reader in Gender and Performance*, ed. by Lizbeth Goodman with Jane de Gay (London: Routledge, 1998), pp. 303-04 (p. 304).

5   Inevitably, there is some bleed across these three categories of history, principles, and effects.

6   See Kate Davy, *Lady Dicks and Lesbian Brothers: Staging the Unimaginable at the WOW Café Theatre* (Ann Arbor: University of Michigan Press, 2010), pp. 27-30.

7   Peggy Shaw, 'How I Learned Theater', in *Cast Out: Queer Lives in Theater*, ed. by Robin Bernstein (Ann Arbor: University of Michigan Press, 2006), pp. 25-9.

8   Alisa Solomon, 'The WOW Cafe', *TDR*, 29.1 (1985), 92-101 (p. 93).

9   Shaw, 'How I Learned Theater', p. 27.

10   Davy, *Lady Dicks and Lesbian Brothers*, p. 63.

11   Davy, *Lady Dicks and Lesbian Brothers*, p. 63.

12   Shaw, 'How I Learned Theater', p. 27.

13   Lois Weaver in Charlotte Canning, *Feminist Theatres in the USA: Staging Women's Experience*, (London-New York: Routledge, 1996), p. 75.

14   Solomon, 'The WOW Cafe', p. 95.

15   Canning, *Feminist Theatres*, p. 75.

16   Davy, *Lady Dicks and Lesbian Brothers*, p. viii.

17   Solomon, 'The WOW Cafe', p. 95.

18   Weaver in Solomon, 'The WOW Cafe', p. 96.

19   *Honey, I'm Home: The Alcestis Story* programme, Hampshire College, 1989, in Split Britches Archive, Fales Library, NYU, MSS 251, Series 1, Box 1.

20   Cited in Davy, *Lady Dicks and Lesbian Brothers*, p. ix.

21   Davy, *Lady Dicks and Lesbian Brothers*, p. viii.

22   Davy, *Lady Dicks and Lesbian Brothers*, p. 185-200.

23   Davy, *Lady Dicks and Lesbian Brothers*, p. viii.

24   *Memories of the Revolution: First Ten Years of the WOW Café*, by Holly Hughes, Carmelita Tropicana, and Jill Dolan (Ann Arbor: University of Michigan Press, forthcoming 2015).

25   See <http://www.wowcafe.org> [accessed 21 April, 2015].

26   Solomon, 'The WOW Cafe', p. 96.

27   See Rhonda Blair, 'The Alcestis Project: Split Britches at Hampshire College', *Women & Performance*, 6.1 (1993), 147-50; Sabrina Hamilton, 'Split Britches and the Alcestis Lesson: "What is this Albatross?"', in *Upstaging Big Daddy: Directing Theater as if Gender and Race Matter*, ed. by Ellen Donkin and Susan Clement (Ann Arbor: University of Michigan Press, 1993), pp. 133-50; Lisa Merrill, 'An Interview with Lois Weaver, Peggy Shaw and Deb Margolin', *Women & Performance*, 6.1 (1993), 151-67.

28   See Juli Burk, '*Valley of the Dolls'* House: Split Britches Did It with Feminism in the Sitting Room', in *Constructions and Confrontations: Changing Representations of Women and Feminisms, East and West: Selected Essays*, Literary Studies East and West vol. 12, ed. by Cristina Bacchilega and Cornelia N. Moore (Honolulu: University of Hawaii Press, 1996), pp. 274-85.

29   Ericka Jennings in *Honey, I'm Home*.

30   For details, see Aston and Harris, 'Imagining, Making, Changing', pp. 100-18; and their *Split Britches Workshop*, Women's Writing for Performance Project (on DVD) <http://bit.ly/1HGBTvT>

31   Ann Elizabeth Armstrong, 'Building Coalitional Spaces in Lois Weaver's Performance Pedagogy', *Theatre Topics*, 15.2 (2005), 201-19.

32   Sue-Ellen Case, 'Lesbian Performance in the Transnational Arena', in *The Cambridge Companion to Modern British Women Playwrights*, ed. by Elaine Aston and Janelle Reinelt (Cambridge: Cambridge University Press, 2000), pp. 253-67 (p. 255). The archives of Gay Sweatshop are held at the Royal Holloway Archives and Special Collections <http://bit.ly/1CTgO25> [accessed 19 June 2015].

33   Case, 'Lesbian Performance in the Transnational Arena', p. 255.

34   Weaver, interview with Sandra Freeman, Brighton, May 1996, cited in Freeman, *Putting Your Daughters on the Stage: Lesbian Theatre from the 1970s to the 1990s* (London: Cassell, 1997), p. 42.

35   Weaver, interview with Sandra Freeman. p. 42.

36   Weaver, interview with Sandra Freeman. p. 43.

37   Weaver, interview with Sandra Freeman. p. 43.

38   Ray Malone, 'Gay Sweatshop Theatre Company', *Unfinished Histories: Recording the History of Alternative Theatre*, November 2013 <http://bit.ly/1ee8H4I> [accessed 21 April 2015]. See also Catherine Silverstone, *Shakespeare, Trauma and Contemporary Performance* (New York and London: Routledge, 2011), p. 107.

39   Lois Weaver in Peggy Shaw, Weaver, and Kate Davy, 'Peggy Shaw and Lois Weaver: Interviews (1985, 1992, 1993)', in *Modern Drama: Plays/Criticism/Theory*, ed. by W. B. Worthen (Fort Worth, TX: Harcourt Brace College Publishers, 1995), pp. 1003-08 (p. 1003).

40   FeMUSEum, commissioned by the AHRC-funded *Performance Matters* for the *Trashing Performance* symposium, presented in London and New York. See 'FeMUSEum', http://publicaddresssystems.org/projects/femuseum/> [accessed 21 April 2015].

41   Weaver, *Public Address Systems* <http://publicaddresssystems.org> [accessed 21 April 2015].

42   Lois describes them in detail in Weaver and Caoimhe McAvinchey, 'Lois Weaver: Interview and Introduction by Caoimhe McAvinchey', in *Performance and Community: Commentary and Case Studies*, ed. by McAvinchey (London: Bloomsbury, 2014), pp. 21-32 (pp. 26-7).

43   Weaver hosted two *Long Tables* on live art and feminism as part of *Restock Rethink Reflect Three: On Live Art and Feminism* at LADA 2013-15 (see <http://bit.ly/1CNq6NF> [accessed 22 June 2015]) and two on sex as part of the Wellcome Collection's 2015 exhibition *The Institute of Sexology* (see <http://bit.ly/1ee7har> [accessed 19 June 2015]).

44   Weaver in Shaw, Weaver, and Davy, 'Interviews', p. 1007.

45   Weaver in Shaw, Weaver, and Davy, 'Interviews', p. 1003.

46   Weaver in Shaw, Weaver, and Davy, 'Interviews', p. 1003. See also Weaver on WOW in Weaver and McAvinchey, 'Lois Weaver', pp. 29-31. WOW alumnus Lisa Kron has achieved huge Broadway success and says, '[t]he greatest thing that happened to me in my career was

finding the WOW cafe (in the 80s), a lesbian theater collective that was my creative home.... We were authoring the world with ourselves as the cultural center.' Kron cited in Eric Sasson, 'Why Broadway's "Fun Home" Reflects a Growing Tolerance', *Wall Street Journal, Speakeasy*, 29 April 2015, http://blogs.wsj.com/speakeasy/2015/04/29/why-broadways-fun-home-reflects-a-growing-tolerance/ [accessed 25 May 2015].

47   Blair, 'The Alcestis Project', p. 148.

48   Lois says a version of this in Split Britches workshop for the Women's Writing for Performance Project (2003-06). Cited in Aston and Harris, *Performance Practice and Process*, p. 2. Italics original.

49   Weaver in Aston and Harris, 'Imagining, Making, Changing', p. 102.

50   Davy, 'Reading Past the Heterosexual Imperative: *Dress Suits to Hire*', *TDR*, 33.1 (1989), 153-70 (p. 154).

51   Sara Warner, *Acts of Gaiety: LGBT Performance and the Politics of Pleasure* (Ann Arbor: University of Michigan Press, 2012), p. 24.

52   Soloman, 'The WOW Cafe', p. 92.

53   Rebecca Schneider, 'Holly Hughes: Polymorphous Perversity and the Lesbian Scientist', *TDR*, 33.1 (1989), 171-83 (p. 174).

54   Davy in Shaw, Weaver, and Davy, 'Interviews', p. 1003.

55   Sue Frumin, interview with Freeman, February 1996, cited in Freeman, *Putting Your Daughters on the Stage*, p. 98.

56   See many examples in this book's bibliography.

57   Lois advocates for coalitional relationships in theatre-making in 'Kinship', *Contemporary Theatre Review*, 23.1 (2013), 43-44; reproduced below.

58   Weaver, unpublished phone conversation with Cynthia Carr, 11 November 2014.

59   Weaver, phone conversation with Carr.

60   Weaver, phone conversation with Carr.

61   Weaver, Interview with Carr, May 1987, cited in Carr, 'The Lady is a Dick: The Dyke Noir Theater of Holly Hughes', *The Village Voice*, 19 May 1987, pp. 32-4.

62   *In the House* was an installation focusing on women in prison. See Weaver and McAvinchey, 'Lois Weaver', pp. 21-32.

63   Nancy Fraser, 'Rethinking the Public Sphere: A Contribution to the Critique of Actually Existing Democracy', *Social Text*, 25/26 (1990), 56-80 (p. 56).

64   Fraser, 'Rethinking the Public Sphere', pp. 65-6.

65   Weaver in Weaver and McAvinchey, 'Lois Weaver', p. 29.

66   Hannah Arendt, *The Human Condition* (Chicago: University of Chicago Press, 1958), pp. 52-3.

67   See Fraser, 'Rethinking the Public Sphere', pp. 66-9.

68   Romand Coles, 'Moving Democracy: Industrial Areas, Foundation Social Movements and the Political Arts of Listening, Traveling, and Tabling', *Political Theory*, 32.5 (2004), 678-705 (p. 692).

69   Coles, 'Moving Democracy', p. 693.

70   Coles, 'Moving Democracy', p. 694.

71   One organisation to have adopted The *Long Table* format to facilitate discussion is Motherlodge's Live Arts Exchange, see 'The Long Table', *Motherlodge* <http://motherlodge.com/the-long-table/>.

72   Weaver, 'Everyday', *Public Address Systems*, 2013 < http://bit.ly/1Ok149g > [accessed 1 June 2015].

73   Weaver, 'Long Table', 2013 <http://tinyurl.com/ndou7q6> [accessed 1 June 2015].

74   Helen Molesworth, 'House Work and Art Work', *October*, 92 (Spring 2000), 71-97.

75   Weaver, 'The *Long Table* Etiquette', 2013 <http://bit.ly/1Szw2eH> [accessed 1 June 2015].

76   Weaver in Weaver and McAvinchey, 'Lois Weaver', p. 24.

77   Weaver in Weaver and McAvinchey, 'Lois Weaver', p. 28.

78   Weaver, 'Long Table', 2013.

79   Weaver, 'Porch Sitting', 2013 < http://bit.ly/1SzvUfj > [accessed 17 June 2015].

80   Weaver in Weaver and McAvinchey, 'Lois Weaver', p. 28.

81   Aston and Harris, 'Imagining, Making, Changing', pp. 100-18.

82   For an example of how Derrida's thinking on hospitality has been used in performance studies, see Benjamin D. Powell and Tracy Stephenson-Shaffer, 'On the Haunting of Performance Studies', *Liminalities*, 5.1 (2009) < http://bit.ly/1MFviTz > [accessed 13 September 2014].

83   See for example: Claire Bishop, *Artificial Hells: Participatory Arts and the Politics of Spectatorship* (London: Verso, 2012); Nicolas Bourriaud, *Relational Aesthetics* (Dijon: Les Presses du Réel, 2002); and Jacques Rancière, *The Emancipated Spectator*, trans. by Gregory Elliot (London: Verso, 2009).

84   Molesworth, 'House Work and Art Work', p. 75.

85   See Aston and Harris, *Performance Practice and Process*, p. 23 and p. 28.

86   Molesworth, 'House Work and Art Work', p. 81.

87   Molesworth, 'House Work and Art Work', p. 81. Italics added.

88   Molesworth, 'House Work and Art Work', p. 82, p. 76. Italics added.

89   Molesworth, 'House Work and Art Work', pp. 95-6.

90   Molesworth, 'House Work and Art Work', p. 95.

91   Significantly, Shannon Jackson places Laderman Ukeles's *Maintenance Art* within current debates about 'socially engaged art' alongside more recent works. See Jackson, *Social Works: Performing Arts, Supporting Publics* (London and New York: Routledge, 2011).

92   Judith Still, *Derrida and Hospitality: Theory and Practice* (Edinburgh: Edinburgh University Press, 2010), p. 21.

93   See Jacques Rancière, *The Politics of Aesthetics The Distribution of the Sensible*, trans. by Gabriel Rockhill (London: Continuum, 2004).

94   Molesworth, 'House Work and Art Work', p. 97.

95   See Bishop, *Artificial Hells*.

96   'A Series of *Long Tables*', *Wellcome Collection* <http://bit.ly/1ee7har> [accessed 19 June 2015].

97   See María Elena Martínez, 'Archives, Bodies, and Imagination: The Case of Juana Aguilar and Queer Approaches to History, Sexuality, and Politics', *Radical History*, 210 (Fall 2014), 159-82 for segments from the archival accounts of the case.

98   Martínez, 'Archives, Bodies, and Imagination', p. 174.

99   Adapted version of Weaver, 'Kinship', *Contemporary Theatre Review*, 23.1 (2013), 43-4.

Embody your worst nightmare

Develop a persona

Tammy interviews Lois

Lois Weaver

London, June 2015

Tammy: Do you remember when we first got together?

Lois: I remember sitting in my apartment on East 11th Street with Spiderwoman, and we were working on *The Lysistrata Numbah!* (1977). We were talking about the characters in the play: there were the Athenian women, who are the more sophisticated city women, and then there were the Spartan women, who were obviously the 'country' women. It soon became clear that I would be playing a Spartan woman, and that seemed natural to me because I came from the rural American South. I identified with what it means to be 'inferior' from not being raised up north and in the city.

As we began to develop the piece, Muriel asked what everyone's performance fantasy was and how we might want to attach those fantasies to the characters. I probably said that I could play the part as a sort of stereotypical blonde, country western singer, knowing that I didn't want to because I was shamed by this characterisation, that it's a part of my past that I didn't necessarily want to represent. But at the same time I knew full well that I was going to. And that's how you came into being, Tammy. It was sort of like you were an unwanted child; there I was, I knew I was pregnant, and there was nothing I could do but give birth.

Tammy: Does that mean you never really liked country music?

Lois: Well, to be perfectly honest, no, I didn't listen to country music. It was something that I was aware of but kept myself somewhat separate from. At some point I must have wanted to differentiate myself from a conservative, racist, culturally backwards, working-class South. All of that seemed wrapped up in country music. So the fact that I would start to take you on, Tammy, had very little to do with the music itself; it had a lot more to do with my desire to occupy the space, of possibility if not reality, that I imagined lay beneath the fake exterior of the female country and western singer. I had seen glimpses of the fierce mind, strong will, and murderous sense of humour of certain Southern women who dressed themselves in synthetic hair and plunging necklines. I wanted other people to see that. And in fact, I didn't even consider myself a singer; you know I wouldn't be caught dead singing in public. It's you, Tammy, who does the singing.

Tammy: Why are you so afraid of singing?

Lois: I think it relates to the fact that singing is so closely linked to what it means to have a voice. In order to sing you have to actually commit yourself – to hit the note, keep the tune, stay in key; you have to commit yourself to being heard. I think I've had an ambivalent relationship to being heard. I am committed to both audibility and visibility. That's very important for all of us and for women in particular. I advocate for that around different kinds of issues – femme visibility, lesbian audibility, etc. But I think over the years it's been hard for me to actually take responsibility for that voice. I remember when I first started working with Peggy at WOW, I had loads of ideas but I didn't have the right amplification system for them. I didn't know how to blast them, make them heard, announce or even enact them. Peggy was a perfect amplification system. I would mention that I was thinking of something that we ought to do and immediately, with her unfailing sense of confidence and belief that together we could do anything, she would get going, and we'd make it happen. This carried on for years; people used to say, 'You whisper and Peggy shouts'. But at a certain point I felt like I didn't have my own voice, that I couldn't take credit, or even responsibility, for my own ideas. So I began to find ways in which I could make myself heard. That meant changing a habit and a pattern with Peggy, and it also meant me going solo. That's where you came in, Tammy. You didn't replace Peggy but you definitely assisted me in getting my ideas heard, and when I felt insecure about an idea, I always relied on you Tammy to help me work it out and get it out. Now, of course, I've established some things called Public Address Systems, which I think are purely mechanisms for, not just me being heard, but for all of us to have a voice, and a say, and a place at the table.[1]

Tammy: Is that your greatest fear?

Lois: The word fear makes me think of that feeling you get when you go out after dark to get the laundry in, and you have to make that journey from the back porch to the laundry line. You're fine when you start out, but you take the first couple of steps, and then you feel something start to creep up from the bottom of your spine, a kind of cold phosphorescence that lights up every nerve on its way to the small hairs on the back of your neck until it reaches your brain with the realisation that you are out in the yard, alone, in the country, in the dark night.

I guess my greatest fear is being afraid that you aren't the thing that you appear to be and being found out. Maybe that's the thing that makes me afraid of singing. It's an unmistakable test; either you get the note or you don't, whereas with a lot of other things, you can dance around the tune, make it appear as if you actually hit the note.

So if my greatest fear is of being found out, then it makes sense that you are my greatest source of courage. You are not afraid of being found out because you are exactly what you are. There's no pretence: in fact, you are pretence. The wigs, the lashes, the accent all are fake, and you can't be found out for being a fake because you already are. I think that's the fear that holds a lot of us back, the fear of actually being our own true, authentic, divine, incapable selves, and just putting that out there without feeling judged.

Tammy: I like that you think I make you brave but what else do you think you get out of hanging out with me?

Lois: I'd like to say that you give me the permission to be ridiculous. But I think it's more than that, I think it's because you have a great sense of wonder and a curiosity. And you're not embarrassed by your curiosity nor by what you may or may not know. I seem to approach a situation feeling as if most people know a lot more than I do and I should have known some of that already. I'm never quite able to approach a situation out of pure wonder, pure curiosity, and without the fear or the shame of being uninformed.

Thinking is trying to formulate ideas that have a kind of structure, background, purpose... whereas wonder can just sit with you.

One of the many things that we have in common, Tammy, is that you and I are both pretty much self-taught artists. I did go to university and I did study theatre, and I learned quite a bit about that context. However, in terms of carrying on and developing myself as an actor or even as a director – and particularly as a writer – I didn't study. I cut and pasted the things I knew in order to make things work. And that's one of the things that I always regret, is that I haven't had the discipline to actually engage properly with a discipline. I feel like we're similar in that way. However, I feel like you don't apologise or worry about that. You are perfectly happy to take on board the knowledge and information that you need, and can make it work for you right then and there. I have a little bit of reluctance to show myself, so that makes you my show woman.

Tammy: Well then what is the use of wond'rin'?

Lois: Well Tammy, I think wonder is absolutely essential to life and to thinking. For me, thinking is trying to formulate ideas that have a kind of structure, background, purpose… whereas wonder can just sit with you. Like sitting on a porch and wondering who's coming down the road, or wondering what's happening next, or wondering how other people feel about things. That's what you are particularly good at, Tammy – you really want to know what other people think. When you set out to ask questions, it's not because you have something that you want to prove, it's because you are genuinely curious about what and how other people are thinking. And what you want is to hear people think out loud. You have a great sense of wonder and curiosity, and you want to act on that, but you are absolutely determined to do that in public.

Tammy: How'd you get the idea for my outfit?

Lois: Well Spiderwoman, a fairly dressed-down feminist theatre company, was starting to experiment and re-appropriate aspects of glamour. That's something that we'd picked up from Hot Peaches: our costumes hadn't arrived to our gig, and they were in the same town, so we asked them if we could borrow some costumes. Of course, they were all very high-femme, high-glam kinds of things. From that beginning, we wanted the characters in *Lysistrata Numbah!* to be crazy-glamorous – sort of 'glamour clowns'.

Tammy: Is that how you think of me, as a clown?

Lois: One of the things that Muriel Miguel, the director of Spiderwoman, often talked about alongside personal fantasy was 'personal clown'; 'clown' as in that part of you that allows you to be ridiculous. I think I've transferred her term to the term 'persona'. And that's what I consider you, Tammy – you are a persona. You're that part of me that allows me to be ridiculous and to take on serious subjects in a humorous way.

Tammy: Does that mean that you disappear when I come on the scene?

Lois: Not at all. That's what I mean by persona. I don't really call you my alter-ego, I don't call you my clown, you're not even what I would call a character. For me a character is personality that is so developed that you cannot see the actor or the performer within them. With persona, I think you can actually see the outer characteristics of an outrageous, utterly different, or an extreme personality, but deep inside those characteristics you can actually see the personality of the performer who's carrying, developing, or dressing-up in those characteristics.

I think or at least hope that you can always see Lois inside the pink and orange chiffon, blonde wigs and sling-back heels. I'm visible. I'm just a bit quiet.

I feel like your curiosity and your wonder is... . Ok, this is me now, Lois, analysing you slightly, Tammy, I feel like you're not all that interested in what people say. I think what you're mostly interested in is getting people to say it, and getting the act of conversation going is the thing that gives you the most pleasure. And of course within that act of conversation a lot of things get exchanged. Information, emotions, affinities get established or differences become celebrated, and I think your love of the question, or maybe your love of what you call 'research', is really about the act of talking to somebody and getting somebody to talk back to you.

Tammy: What do you think you could teach Tammy?

Lois: That's an interesting question because I think it gets right to the heart of the fact that there's no real division between me and you, Tammy. I feel that together we have learned quite a lot and it's been that combined effort of educating ourselves and making ourselves – literally making ourselves, as in constructing ourselves – and that's been a combined effort. So that is probably the most symbiotic aspect of our relationship, the ways in which we seek and learn and then share, probably, what we've learned. But if you pushed me, I think I'd probably say I can teach you to take your time. I think, Tammy, sometimes you get overly excited, and you move a little too fast, and you move on, sometimes, before the moment is complete. So I might teach you to do that, or I might encourage you, or encourage us, together, to do that. I also think I might encourage you to investigate the ephemeral nature of what we do. I think you believe that the most important thing is the interaction, the thing that happens between people in that moment. I think there's something to be gleaned from that interaction, something to be gathered, maybe something to be recorded and then passed on. I think that perhaps you're the knowledge gatherer; whereas maybe Lois can teach you how to make good use of the things that you gather, to make them into something concrete that could in some way I suppose be passed on beyond the moment of interaction. I think that's a question for both of us to ponder: the value of what we have in the moment, and enact in the moment, in relation to the value of something that gets kept and passed on. And I think that Tammy, you and I could have that conversation about the importance of an archive of conversations.

Tammy: When I have on my wig and accent, I know I'm Tammy; how do you know you're Lois?

Lois: I think I know I'm Lois when I'm listening. Or actually in that space between hearing something and knowing what to say next, what question to ask. It's those in-between spaces when I feel like I am most myself. Between thought and action – I often call that an impulse space. When I feel I am operating on impulse, when I am hearing the voice of my own instinct and moving in that direction, when I'm listening to someone else and can breathe in between that to process what I'm being told, or what I'm hearing, so that I know where to go with that information: either to continue the conversation, or to take action, or to make something. I often also feel the most like I'm Lois when I'm on my own within a creative process such as commonplace book-making. That is when I am at my truest. I

When I grew up, I wanted to make sure that I lived in a place where there would be people awake when I went to bed.

know it's not for anyone but me, and that it doesn't need or ask for any kind of acceptance or approval. It's a pure creative act and not an act that is subject to another person's or institution's opinion, not linked to any cultural, professional, or gender identity. It's not subject to anything; it's only related to the desire to make. And I think that's when I feel most like myself.

Tammy: Why do you think you left Virginia?

Lois: As a kid I used to say that when I grew up, I wanted to make sure that I lived in a place where there would be people awake when I went to bed. I grew up in the rural South and was usually the last person to turn off my lights. I hated that – if I opened my eyes in the middle of the night I wouldn't know if I was dead or alive because I couldn't see anything in front of me. I also was in love with the theatre and I knew I would have to leave Virginia to do it. But mostly I think it was the sense that I was somehow different from most of the people around. For one thing, I was a lesbian. I wasn't aware of that at the time, but I had a sense of something that wasn't replicated in any other people that I had seen around me, and probably subconsciously I was looking to find my 'tribe'.

But I never really left Virginia, actually. I mean, for years after I left I went back constantly, and I felt completely drawn to that red soil and to those habits and customs and people. It was in me, and I didn't know how to separate myself from it or bring it with me. I remember once I had a residency at the College of William and Mary in Williamsburg, Virginia, and I had this overwhelming sense that I understood every molecule of how the world around me functioned. Whereas in New York, and now in London, I *still* feel in a slight state of translation. Even in the same language, with similar customs, or customs that now have become totally mine, I'm still translating them from what was my home language. And that was a very subtle language. Right down to how and what people ate, how they moved and talked.

After all these years of having kept some distance between myself and where I was born, you, Tammy, are the thing that keeps me tied there. When you and I step on stage together, I feel like I'm at home.

I Got into the Wrong Car in Memphis

Lyrics by Lois Weaver and Paul Clark, Music by Paul Clark [2]

It was in the afternoon, the Tennessee glare of
mid July
I opened the door of a lavender Ford
Looked just like mine
A woman with big hair asleep at the wheel
Woke up and said
Hello sweetheart
It's your lucky day
Come on get in

Chorus
It was the wrong car in Memphis
I knew right then I'd be payin' a toll
I got in to the wrong car in Memphis
Summer heat and cheap perfume had
repossessed my soul

I'd come here with a letter to mail
But was still holding it in my hand
She laughed at me and said
Oh honey don't ya know
There's not enough stamps for your discontent
It's just one of those letters that never get sent

Chorus
I got in to the wrong car in a parking lot
    in Memphis
I knew in that instant that I was outta control
I got in to the wrong car in the parking lot
    in a post office in Memphis
Summer heat and cheap perfume
    had repossessed my soul

She touched up her lipstick
Turned on the radio
And said, are you ready to ride?

I eased into drive. In the rear view
Everything looked like a sign
Firestone Tires
Krispy Kreme Doughnuts
Pearl's Psychic Reading
And Sister Hope's Beauty Salon
When we turned off Superstition Freeway
    and onto Bona Venture Highway
I knew there was no going back
I knew there was no going back

Chorus
I got in to the wrong car and I pulled out of the
parking lot of the post office in Memphis
Fate pulled me over, what could I say
I got in to the wrong car with the right girl and
I pulled out of the parking lot of the post office
    in Memphis
I'll tell you right now it was my lucky day

That is how Tammy was born again, again.
It was like Saul on the bus to Damascus
She saw a blinding light and she knew she could
no longer be a famous country western singer.
She had to turn herself around and become a
lesbian performance artist. And all because of
the wrong car with the right girl in a parking lot
of the post office in Memphis.

Chorus
It was the right car in Memphis
I knew in an instant that I'd lost control
I got in to the right car in Memphis
Summer heat and cheap perfume
    repossessed my soul

229

Demented Forsythia, a Love Song

Lyrics by Lois Weaver and Amy R. Surratt, Music by Amy R. Surratt [3]

Oh, I Fell In Love with a woman that was crazy
I fell in love with Forsythia when
she finished her encore, left them wanting more
walked back on stage to start all over again –

She was headlining the county fair
a shock of wild silver hair
singin' country blues
and I wanted to, too

Oh I fell in love with a woman that was 80
I fell in love with Forsythia when
she caught sight of my rapture,
said I love an amateur
I'll take you back places you've never been

I wanted her to be my wife
but she said, just get a life
pulled me down on the floor
Do I need to say more?

Oh I fell in love with Demented Forsythia
I fell in love with Forsythia and
when I told her one day that I thought
she was crazy
she said, well get yourself an old
chrysanthemum then

She's scrappy in wintertime
the very first to spring to mind
blooms, then re-blooms
makes me half-crazy, too

Oh I fell in love with Demented Forsythia
I fell in love over and over again when
she climbed out the window of the
hospital cryin'
'They'll never hold me – or put me back in!'

When I see her tomorrow
she'll have forgotten my name
but I know that she loves me
just the same

'Cause –

Forsythia finds Eden
in a world full of sin
she rebuilds tomorrow
and she lets me back in

Oh, I would do anything, Forsythia,
Forsythia,
I would do – anything – for you.

FAMOUS COUNTRY WESTERN SINGER TURNS . . .

LESBIAN PERFORMANCE ARTIST

REMEMBER to use the POST CODE!

Dear Tammy,

Hello! I am going to tell you a little story, that I have heard in the village of Tressos, it circulates as a rumour, and, it has scared at night, made me look nervously around, here and there. They say there is on the island a special and very rare species of pre-historic spider. It is called "tetrangathos" which means that which has four fangs, or thorns. It is named like that because, apparently, it has 4 very distinctive fangs protruding, people say it moves extremely fast, it looks the colour of a scorpion - light brown/reddish and its bite is extremely painful, more than a scorpion's. Very. It has become very rare, and very few people have seen it - some old people from the old days. On few rare occasions, one has been sighted in the village, and everybody has run away in panic. It likes the dark, and it is drawn to fires. Sometimes, at night, I look around, and wonder ... will revisit. Take care. Big Hug ♡

My heart is yours

Tammy WhyNot
151 First Ave. Suite 59
New York, NY 10003
USA

PEELING PEARLS

Please PRINT the Postcode

Dear Tammy,

'Pearl trading calls for special skills and a good deal of courage. Natural pearls form in oysters in warm waters, and they are found in commercial quantities in various corners of the tropical and sub-tropical world. [...] the value of a raw pearl is not easily guessed. Pearls are laminated like onions - that is to say they consist of layer upon layer of minutely thick skin. [...] Since a pearl can no more be put back together again than can a peeled onion, the decision requires courage. By peeling the right number of layers of tightly compacted pearl skin, an expert pearl peeler pearler can transform something dull and barely saleable into an object worth a hundred times more. By peeling when he should not, however, or by peeling too much, he may ...

(from Georges Perec: A Life in Words by David Bellos, p 19-20)

Tammy WhyNot
151 First Ave. Suite 59
New York, NY 10003
USA

2-13-0?
13 FEB 2006

Dear Tammy,

I was glad that I could pass on the info on Dolly's mother. I don't have the obituary anymore so I'm not sure of the exact date.

I really enjoyed your show; especially from a fellow Virginian! I'm always so surprised at the amount of Virginians here in NYC. I still love it with all my heart but I had to venture out ... but I return often.

Sincerely,
Topher Corbett

P.S. I love written correspondence too!

Tammy WhyNot
151 First Ave. Suite 59
New York, NY 10003

POST CARD

Dear Tammy,

I heard that in Japan red is considered as traditionally feminine colour. They must feel pretty odd watching Chicago Bulls games.

Tammy WhyNot
151 First Ave. Suite 59
New York, NY 10003
USA

POST CARD

BLACK HERITAGE

Dear Tammy,

Once I went to Charlie Johnson's oyster farm. It is in an exquisite landscape North of San Francisco. The land is flat and there is sea water from the Pacific. ... Very cinematic.

fondly,
Andi

Tammy WhyNot
151 First Ave. Suite 59
New York, NY 10003

How Do You Sing a Broken Song?[3]

Lyrics by Lois Weaver, Music by Vivian Stoll [4]

Mend a teacup
Set a broken bone
Break a locked silence
Repair bad dreams
...with sweet tones
Fix up an old house
Right a wretched wrong
But how do you sing a broken song?

You can
Run and catch the wrong bus
Show up late for a kiss
Your legs can retreat from dancing
'Cause your feet betray the wish

You can lose your keys
And still sing along
You can run out of time
And force the rhyme
But how do you sing a broken song?

Mend a teacup
Set a broken bone
Break a locked silence
Repair bad dreams
...with sweet tones
Fix up an old house
Right a wretched wrong
But how do you sing a broken song?

Tammy WhyNot: stage/life superhero

Jen Harvie

Tammy WhyNot

Tammy WhyNot has been Lois's theatrical alter ego since the late 1970s – that's almost 40 years as I write this. In that time, Lois herself has become an assured, even suave, queer metropolitan New Yorker and part-time Londoner. Nowadays, Lois's metropolitanism manifests in an accent barely inflected by the south; a wardrobe styled principally in monochrome black and white; smart, thick-framed glasses; an architectural platinum blonde haircut; and an intellectual and political savviness that she has built up over decades of critical and creative engagement with innovations in performance, feminism, and other movements for social justice and social pleasure.

Tammy, meanwhile, has allowed Lois to continue to express herself in the Blue Ridge Mountain drawl and patter of her youth. Tammy possesses an unsophisticated, unconcealed gossipy awe that always answers the question, 'Why', with the intrepid, fearless, and perhaps sometimes naive reply, 'Why not?' She shares with Lois the kind of eager wonder that the assimilated metropolitan is supposed to have overcome, or simply never been afflicted by. Tammy helps Lois to hybridise her selves, to combine and even balance parts that are educated, informed, street-smart, and queer, with parts that are innocently ignorant, curious, fuelled by gut instinct, and graced with no-nonsense common sense. Lois-Tammy is a powerful hybrid who permits these contrasting characters not only to exist simultaneously, but to conspire and collaborate. She is a stage/life superhero who can achieve much more than either of her two parts ever could alone.

In what follows, I start to introduce Tammy in the kind of rhinestone detail she deserves, as one of the most infamous and enduring alter egos in contemporary live art and politically engaged performance. I then explore whom she helps Lois to encounter and work with, and what she and Lois do together, especially in their pursuit of both social justice and, importantly, social pleasure.

Who Is Tammy WhyNot?

Tammy WhyNot introduces herself as a famous country singer who gave up that successful career to become a lesbian performance artist.[5] She still looks a lot more like the former than the latter. Her head is capped with a bright blonde wig, its crown rising high and its loose curls cascading over her shoulders. Long, false eyelashes frame her eyes, and bright lipstick her mouth. Her favourite colours are orange and pink, and she bedecks herself in suitably-hued accessories, from bangles to feather boas. Teetering on high-heeled cowboy boots or sling-backs, she usually wears tight-fitting black jeans and a cowboy shirt, embroidered and studded with flowers and stars. Unlike Lois she speaks with a strong Southern drawl, she has an unfiltered chattiness, and her wide-eyed, full-frontal mode of flirting is unimpeded by any silly proprieties of butch/femme protocol or queer sophistication. Most crucially, Tammy wears an expression that combines gleeful curiosity and cheery optimism, shaded slightly with

Opposite: Portrait of Tammy WhyNot for Split Britches' *Upwardly Mobile Home* (1984). Photo by Eva Weiss.

234

unselfconscious naivety. She is an intrepid explorer, clearly out of her familiar territory but excited at the prospect. She is seeking how to be a lesbian performance artist but she's easily distracted by lots of other (important) investigations along the way, most recently for example, regarding what she needs to know about getting older and having sex.[6]

Lois invented Tammy around 1978, when she appeared in Spiderwoman Theater's *The Lysistrata Numbah!* as the Spartan Woman, in other words, the country hick. Lois revived her in Split Britches' 1984 show *Upwardly Mobile Home*,[7] where she fronted the band Tammy WhyNot and the Expectations, with Peggy Shaw and Deb Margolin as backing singers. One of Tammy's favourite activities remains singing, though in her new life as an aspiring lesbian performance artist she knows she needs to adapt her material to context, hence song titles such as 'Stand *on* Your Man'; the tale of discovery, 'I Got into the Wrong Car in Memphis'; and the frisky, 'This Lemon's Still Got a Whole Lotta Juice'.

Ever since *Upwardly Mobile Home*, Tammy has been Lois's fellow traveller, especially as a hostess and MC at cabaret nights at the WOW Café and Gay Sweatshop and then at weekly performance nights with Lois's students in Performance Composition at Queen Mary University of London (QMUL). From that higher education/performance context, from 2004 on Lois began to develop shows built specifically around Tammy and *her* research. These shows' titles generally begin, *What Tammy Needs to Know about...*, and each explores a different topic. For example, in her early days at QMUL, Tammy held sessions with academic colleagues enquiring *What Tammy Needs to Know about Proust and Feminism*. Tammy frequently hosts or co-hosts *Long Tables* (discussed in the previous section), appearing, for example, at conferences to enable discussions on what are often difficult topics. In a *Long Table on Why Sex Matters* as part of the Wellcome Collection's *Institute of Sexology* season in London in January 2015,[8] Lois was the host but she placed Tammy's wig on the table, just in case the conversation seriously stalled and Tammy needed conjuring to jumpstart it back to life in her inimitable style.

Finally, Tammy assembles interested communities of fellow investigators who are often socially marginalised. She gathers these co-investigators to help her to explore, but likely more importantly to help *them* explore, and to help them speak out on their own behalf to societies which otherwise resist hearing them. In recent years, Tammy has often worked in this capacity with older people on such issues as what they want from technology,[9] and, of course, what they want from sex.

What Does Tammy Do?

Tammy helps Lois to operate across different registers, and in ways that audiences might not expect from a seasoned avant-garde performance maker and live artist such as Lois. Tammy is a playful, funny alibi through whom Lois reanimates herself with exaggerated femininity and Southern styling. Like a favourite character from an old television show, or a country music form considered out of fashion, Tammy is a familiar time-traveller from a bygone age. The attitudes of the age might be slightly misogynist, or the music somewhat corny, but negative history seems not to touch Tammy. Despite the exaggeration of her performance of gender, for example, it provokes no fear that she'll suffer for it. Her elaborate costume is perhaps something of a *visibility* cloak, allowing her to trample into dangerous territories apparently without exhibiting fear or encountering mishaps. Her exaggeration liberates her from

As a poor, white, Southern, 'trailer trash' belle, Tammy does occupy and invoke slightly uncomfortable categories of class, ethnicity and gender.

having to fulfil expectations about psychologically realistic behaviour, so she's free to challenge assumptions about what's realistic anyway, to try out fantasies, and to erase boundaries of (gendered) expectations and protocols.

That said, as a poor, white, Southern, 'trailer trash' belle, Tammy does occupy and invoke slightly uncomfortable categories of class, ethnicity and gender.[10] But her wit, charm, and downright attractiveness demonstrate that neither the categories nor Tammy herself are wholly or inherently *bad*. Furthermore, her exaggeration foregrounds her social construction, and her active, direct engagement with the audience and its gaze interrupts visual economies that fetishise women. If anything, Tammy fetishises herself, in a feather-boa loop of self-pleasure that keeps her outside of patriarchal visual economies.[11] Most importantly, the affection Lois demonstrably has for Tammy averts any risk that her portrayal of 'trailer trash' might be satirical, superior, or judgemental. Like the femme whom Lois recuperates from dismissive suspicion, Tammy recuperates her 'trailer trash' predecessors and cousins, demonstrating that they merit recognition at the very least, and likely also credit, appreciation, and gratitude. Lois too gets to reclaim some of the things about her background that have embarrassed but also drawn her, such as the sincerity of country music, and working class culture's intolerance of patronising pretence.

Tammy is adaptable and open. As Sue-Ellen Case has observed, with specific reference to Lois's Tammy,

> The *persona* offers a pliable and adaptable form of performance. It is well suited to 'found' performance spaces, sometimes without a stage, or theatrical lighting. It can appear in the midst of a variety of occasions which might create something like an audience, from a party to a political rally. In one sense, the *persona* could be seen as a shell for improvisation. The *persona* can be improvised within and is open to interaction with the audience – particularly in the act of sexual flirtation. The club-type atmosphere of these performances encourages flirting, or the sense that a kind of available sexuality could promiscuously travel through the crowd.[12]

Tammy works with some pre-scripted material, and the 'script' of her persona, but largely she improvises, responding in the moment to things, ideas, and importantly people she encounters. She has a remarkable openness articulated through curiosity, warmth, fun, and effervescent friendliness. This openness provokes her interlocutors to respond with tolerance at least, and usually with affection and delight. She provokes and engages in genuine dialogue, conversation, and enquiry. She never fills a show or scene with her own opinions or ideas but always coaxes input and wisdom from her collaborators through a combination of gentle teasing, humour, and tenderness. Her engagement in potentially difficult conversation about, for example, people's sex lives, has a fleet-footed dexterity that allows her to take individual discussants in and out of sensitive areas as they are able, but also in exciting ways they might not anticipate. She shares her joy in discovery with her collaborators. Furthermore, her dexterous facility for engagement helps stimulate and manage public debate, discussion, and dialogue *between* individuals and groups, even when those discussions involve conflicts or disagreements. She makes no claims to resolve conflicts; but she will actively support their airing and expression.

Tammy's work supporting speaking in public and public dialogue is especially socially important given that she tends to work with collaborators, audiences, and

Tammy is, in other words, a crucial character in Lois's experimental dramaturgy for democracy.

loosely formed communities who are often socially marginalised, under-appreciated, and/or neglected – the old, the queer, the working class, and the non-academic – in societies preoccupied with the privileged and the normative – the young, the beautiful, the 'straight', the elite. And she engages them in discussion about issues that, although important, are also neglected, often burdened by social assumptions and myths. She is concerned with *everyone*'s human rights. In societies which are ageist, she works repeatedly with older people to bust myths about their presumed ignorance and obsolescence. For example, she has worked with older people on both their *access* to digital technology but also their own *designs* for it. And she is currently working with older people to explore their attitudes to, relationships with, and desires around sex.

Tammy is, in other words, a crucial character in Lois's experimental dramaturgy for democracy. She pursues issues of social justice that are themselves often marginalised. And she does so with people who are frequently ignored or neglected, not so much by design as, more often and insidiously, by accident and routine. To stretch one of my earlier metaphors, Tammy shares her cloak of visibility with her collaborators, supporting them not only to speak but to do so in front of audiences and in public fora, where others will not only hear them but might be affected by them and might act to change their own behaviour and to support Lois's collaborators too.

How Does Tammy Do It?

Tammy's built-in exaggeration allows her to make fun of herself while also being herself, in all her loud, fun, flirtatious, playful, attention-demanding ways. Her assurance legitimates her enquiries while her naive curiosity encourages her collaborators to feel safe in those enquiries and to contribute to them. Tammy allows Lois to explore aspects of herself and her own autobiography which she feels ambivalent about, and to play with different perspectives and behaviours.

Many performing artists use exaggerated alter ego or personas. A handful of examples includes Israeli-born, London-based feminist artist Oreet Ashery's Hasidic male alter ego Marcus Fisher; American William Talen's evangelising anti-consumerism eco-preacher Reverend Billy; feminist performer Lauren Barri Holstein's The Famous Lauren Barri Holstein; and queer London-based performer and compère David Hoyle's former persona The Divine David. These alter egos share a lot with Tammy. They often point up social problems in pursuit of social justice. And they often feature exaggerated characteristics which can be somewhat uncomfortable because they are apparently complicit with retrograde ideologies, or simply because the personae are mean, as is sometimes the case with The Famous and The Divine David, both of whom may certainly have good cause to be angry.

In the pantheon of performance personae, Tammy stands out for the strength and security of her character – thanks to the strength and security of Lois's character, no doubt. Without getting too grand about it, which neither Tammy nor Lois would likely be happy with, Tammy also stands out for her magnanimous humanity, her interest in seeking out those whose voices are unjustly subdued, in exploring the issues that matter to them on their terms, and in flirting, playing, and seeking with them to make the world a better place, with more blonde wigs and pink accessories, more fun, and more social justice.

Opposite: Tammy WhyNot in dressing room preparing for Spiderwoman's *The Lysistrata Numbah!* (1977). Photo courtesy of Spiderwoman Theater.

1970s

1980s

2000s

2010s

1990s

2010s

What Tammy taught me... about surviving as a poor girl in the Academy

Kim Solga

Tammy WhyNot didn't realise she was destined to be a famous Lesbian Performance Artist until she got into the right car (a lavender-coloured Ford) with the wrong girl in a post-office parking lot in Memphis, Tennessee one hot, bright July afternoon. Until then she was just a crooner, another piece of trailer trash, a big-haired Southern gal busy doing the stuff that people expect big-haired Southern gals to do. The (right) wrong girl dozing in the steamy sun of the driver's seat in Memphis told Tammy to step outside of what she thought she knew about who she was supposed to be, and to step into the car in order to start catching up on all the stuff she didn't yet know about the world and her place in it. She broke Tammy open and spilled out the smart and sassy locked up inside.

I didn't realise that I might be a scholar and a feminist – I didn't even really know what a feminist was! – until about a year after I took my compulsory Shakespeare course at the University of Alberta with Linda Woodbridge, who happened to be the most important feminist Shakespeare scholar of her generation. During her class I had no idea who Professor Woodbridge really was, or what she had to offer me; she was, perhaps, the right teacher at the wrong time. I also knew nothing about Shakespeare – except that I had written some really good essays about him in High School. My teachers all thought I was smart, a natural reader of Shakespearean things; I alone knew the truth.

Most of my friends were lifelong readers of all kinds of books, and especially of things like Shakespeare. I was not. I mostly read just what I needed to in order to get by, to pass as a smart kid at school. Unlike my friends' parents, mine were not readers, and reading didn't come naturally to me. There were a few books in our house – on a shelf in the basement along with a bunch of knick knacks – but they weren't anything I would ever want to crack open: Pearl S. Buck, a history about the Third Reich, something about Winston Churchill. My mom and dad took me to the library occasionally, but it wasn't a significant part of our lives. Instead, we watched a lot of television: I have vivid memories of looking at the screen with them, seeing the Ewings, the Cosbys, the CBC and NBC reporters march by. I remember the characters, the stories, where and how we sat as we watched, how it felt to be together that way.

Previous pages: Tammy Timeline
Photos by Uzi Parnes, Gordon Rainsford, Lori E. Seid, Angela Stewart Park, Peggy Shaw, and Claire Nolan.

Opposite: Tammy WhyNot in *What Tammy Needs to Know* (2003), Drill Hall, London. Photo by Lori E. Seid.

Tammy loves questions and will bombshell into any room in order to ask the assembled experts what makes them so special.

My parents were good, hard-working people who did their best to make opportunities for me, to make sure I was well fed and loved and that I could go to school with my head held high. I did really well there, won scholarships to university, went to grad school on a full ride. I'm so grateful for all they made possible for me. But a book-reading, essay-writing smarty-pants was nothing mom and dad had ever seen on their horizon, let alone planned for as parents: nobody in either of our families had ever gone to university, and in fact I'm still the only one who has. My career is something I more or less stumbled into, and there are plenty of days when I still wonder how I actually got to where I am now. When I look back at my high school years, I remember my good fortune, but also my shame at the apparently obvious things I seemed to know nothing about, when everyone around me was so cultured and savvy.

Tammy WhyNot might not call herself 'cultured' (that's a pretty highfalutin word, after all), but she sure is savvy. Savvy, in fact, precisely because she is thoroughly unashamed of what she does not know. Tammy loves questions and will bombshell into any room in order to ask the assembled experts what makes them so special. She will gladly turn her microphone on any audience in order to ask spectators what they think *she* needs to know: about being a lesbian, about sex and ageing, about joy and pleasure, about philosophy, about politics, and about the way art and culture works (or doesn't work) to allow ordinary people to see themselves, their own smarts and know-how, reflected on stage or screen or canvas. Although she began her theatrical life first with Spiderwoman Theater and then alongside Peggy Shaw and Deb Margolin in Split Britches' *Upwardly Mobile Home* (1984), Tammy is now best known for her extensive public engagement. For well over a decade she has been working on a performance research project called *What Tammy Needs To Know...*, which gives life to her motto that 'everyone is an expert in some way'. As Lois Weaver puts it on the website that documents Tammy's work, publicaddresssystems.org, 'Tammy's own expertise is in asking questions, specialising in questions other people might be afraid to ask, because they seem too basic, or personal, or not well enough informed.'[13] Tammy never cares if she's not yet well enough informed; she knows she will get there in the end. Armed with bags of artefacts drawn from her personal, professional, and imaginary past lives she travels to academic conferences, regional theatres, community centres, prisons, and university campuses to draw elders, children, students, inmates, friends, hetero- and homosexuals, old lovers, liberals, conservatives, and everyone in between into unexpected conversations – chats that inevitably lead to fresh learning for all concerned.

The thing Tammy *already* knows, and what knowledge she brings to every conversation she hosts, is how to survive and thrive as two women in one body. One half of Tammy is a brazen, charming, platinum blonde behemoth who would never shy away from hanging her laundry in public; the other half is a bob-haired, neatly-dressed full professor at Queen Mary University of London called Lois Weaver, a teacher, mentor, and friend to scholars, artists, and students across the globe. I didn't realise that Lois was meant to be *my* friend and mentor until I met her for the first time (in the shape of a sexy monster called Michigan, acting in a play called *Dress Suits to Hire*) at the Throws Like A Girl festival in Austin, Texas in March 2005. I was on a postdoctoral fellowship, working with the famous and brilliant Jill Dolan, and I'd just landed a tenure-track job back

Opposite: Tammy WhyNot and Carmelita Tropicana in *Cheet Chat with Carmelita*, Club Chandelier, NYC, 1984. Photo by Uzi Parnes.

Tammy helped me to see
that being simultaneously
brilliant and put together,
naïve and ignorant
and vulnerable isn't
at all uncommon, and
doesn't need to be an
embarrassment.

in Canada. In theory I'd hit the academic jackpot. I didn't feel like a high roller, though; surrounded by the clever students and faculty at the University of Texas Department of Theatre and Dance, I felt more than ever my lack of well-readness, my persistent fear that I'd somehow fooled the scholars around me into thinking I belonged among them.

All academics suffer from imposter syndrome; it's in our DNA. (DNA is something else Tammy knows all about. Just ask her.) But it's especially hard being a poor kid at the beginning of an academic career. When I say poor I don't necessarily mean dirt-poor, no-money, no-stuff poor, though of course those scholars work among us, too (and deserve way more respect than we give them, if we even realise how much they've accomplished in just getting through the door). I mean working class kids, kids without a taken-for-granted amount of cultural privilege behind them. Kids whose families now struggle to talk to us, who know they are proud of what we've accomplished but who also no longer know who we are. I've met a lot of us over the years, enough to guess that we're a silent majority in many universities. Meeting Lois and Tammy in 2005 was, as it turns out, a revelation at exactly the right time: they helped me to see that being simultaneously brilliant and put together, naive and ignorant and vulnerable isn't at all uncommon, and doesn't need to be a handicap or an embarrassment. They helped me realise that holding two people inside myself at once – the girl not born to the academy, and the girl who now belongs there – could be a gift, an opportunity to take a different view of what it means to learn, and to teach, for a living.

Lois Weaver became my friend that March in Austin; in August 2012 she became my trusted colleague at Queen Mary. When I landed at Heathrow one rain-splashed summer day she was still in New York, working on a new show with Peggy Shaw. (Called *Ruff*, it's a cabaret about surviving a stroke, losing control

Left: Spiderwoman's *The Lysistrata Numbah!* (1977). Left to right: Lisa Mayo, Pam Verge, and Lois Weaver. Courtesy of Spiderwoman Theater.

Opposite: Polaroid of Tammy WhyNot's boots. Photo by Lois Weaver.

TAMMY

of your body, and figuring out how to learn all over again.) But when I opened the door to my new office, I found a message from Lois: Tammy's sofa was in the middle of the room. It's a greeny-blue two-seater with an old-fashioned pattern and traditional lines – not a looker but really comfortable. Lois asked me if I might keep it in my room because her office was a tight squeeze, and I had space. I said (of course!) that I'd be happy to share space, and well-earned down-time, with Tammy. Happy to have an excuse in the middle of our hectic days to stop, breathe, sit. Maybe think a bit. Or maybe just doze in the sunshine.

Since they first came to Queen Mary in the 1990s, Lois and Tammy have asked a lot of research questions to support their performance interventions and give them academic 'cred'; these questions begin in Tammy's naivety, her curiosity, driven by her sequined history as a working class woman from backwater Southern America, but they end in Lois's scholarly dossiers, sounding just like the questions all UK academics must produce every few years in order to 'measure' the 'value' of their research. Lois and Tammy's questions are at once illuminating and very funny, profound and powerful and yet utter self-parodies; they could be nothing less, emerging as they do from the shared yet contradictory public roles the two women inhabit. Theirs are the kinds of research questions the institutions that employ Lois want to know the answers to, rather than the kinds of questions *Tammy* wants to know the answer to; they thus needle gently but persistently, just as Tammy always does, academic assumptions about what constitutes useful knowledge, about who gets to be in charge of that knowledge, and about where that knowledge should live. In my favourite of these questions, Lois asks: 'Can the performance of hyperfeminin[ity] interrupt expectations of "what a serious artist and academic looks like"?' You're damn straight I can, says Tammy from beneath her fake blonde curls. Just pull up a chair and let's talk it out.

In March 2012, exactly seven years after I met her for the first time and three months before I would land on her doorstep, Lois Weaver was invited to offer her inaugural address at Queen Mary in celebration of her promotion to full professor, the highest rank in the school. She arrived on stage – of course – as Tammy WhyNot, big hair and strong accent announcing her 'lack' of 'culture', her refusal to pretend that her new title speaks to her ownership (finally!) of a special, privileged, elite kind of knowledge. Presenting *What Tammy Found Out*, discoveries from a lifetime of field research into what constitutes ordinary human expertise – knowledge about the kinds of things academics typically discount as unimportant or not properly intellectual – Tammy revelled, teased, invaded her audience, surprised more than a few of them, and threw cupcakes at the lot with glee, scandalising some while others hooted with pleasure. Everyone got a bit of frosting on them.

Here's to the power of not yet knowing.

Making fun and making time: pedagogical principles

Erin Hurley

I first met Lois Weaver in June 2012 during Queen Elizabeth II's Diamond Jubilee celebrations, a season of glittering festivities marking the monarch's 60 years on the throne. Lois had taken her own rather sparkly alter ego, Tammy WhyNot, down to Battersea Park in southwest London to talk to people about this event. She wanted to know about *their* jubilees, their milestones and memories. As a Canadian whose national news media had produced splashy, colour inserts in newspapers and special, extended (some might say doting) television coverage of the Jubilee celebrations, I was tickled by the idea of the Southern Tammy democratising the event with collaborator Stacy Makishi from their 'Tourist Information Wanted' booth. But I was also struck by the mix of satire and warmth in the piece in Lois's description of it. Although it certainly 'took the piss' out of the Jubilee hullaballoo, 'Tourist Information Wanted' did so by asking what participants cared about, what they celebrated about their own lives, and it did so by listening to their responses, as graphed on timelines Lois and Stacy invited them to make and as recounted to the performers.

I mention this particular performance of site-based intervention and conversation as it brings together two ways in which Lois and her work are important to me, particularly as a teacher. First, Lois creates work out of desire and curiosity; in the case of 'Tourist Information Wanted' she asked people to tap into their own wants and wishes, as well as their histories. She is committed to the interrogative mode as a means of knowledge production. This mode is especially fostered in her Tammy WhyNot persona, whose last name is itself a question and who, Lois has said, can sustain a sense of wonder longer than Lois herself is able to. Tammy's series of performances prefixed with *What Tammy Needs to Know...* embodies this aspect in her unending quest for knowledge generated through talk with other people. She is dedicated to the burning question and to its various responses. How might this model of structured conversation (with some serious wigs) be activated in my classes as well? 'What would Tammy do?' is the operative question here.

Second, longevity. It is not just that Lois has been making performance, staging conversations and making space for new voices for more than four decades (which merits a Ruby Jubilee celebration). Tammy has been with her since about 1978, a formidable run for a 'famous lesbian performance artist' whose quest is to discover how to be a lesbian (practice is all!) and how to be a performance artist (an almost equally worthy pursuit, she tells us). It's also that Lois seems to *make* time – for example, her *Long Tables* seem to extend temporality in their topical and sometimes pointed but not necessarily linear discussions around the table, as you literally sit with an idea, a question, in the company of others equally compelled by it. It's the time it takes to work collaboratively as at the WOW Café, to mentor junior artists and scholars as she does at Queen Mary and at Montreal's Studio 303, to name only two of the many places she has done this work.

Desire and time. Lois weaves them into her work and wraps her audiences in the material that results. What better pedagogical structures and goals?

Opposite: Publicity image of Tammy WhyNot for *Club Deviance* (1996), Gay Sweatshop, London. Photo by Gordon Rainsford.

Cupcake velocity: the subversive expertise of Lois Weaver and Tammy WhyNot

Johanna Linsley

It's late in the night at a London venue for queer club performance, a space that also functions as 'a Real East-end Working Men's Club'. Lois Weaver is performing *What Tammy Found Out*, a 'front line report from the back porch, the schoolyard and the dinner table'.[14] In this performance, armed with 62 cupcakes, she counts the years of her life, and traces a journey into feminism, activist politics, and queer identity, stopping in rural Virginia, downtown New York City, and East London. To punctuate crucial moments and events, Lois tosses cupcakes into the crowd. Near the end of this show, I watch the arc of a particularly joyful projectile until it terminates in my face. I'm silly with pleasure as I wipe the pink icing from my forehead, and lick this ammunition for a radical femme research project off my fingers.

I've seen this performance before, during Lois's Inaugural Lecture as a Professor at Queen Mary University of London. In the lecture hall, as in the club, flying cupcakes sailed through the air, but there they also seemed to puncture, gently, the mechanisms of authoritative discourse that surrounded the whole proceeding. Lois is an expert. She was being both honoured and interpellated as such by this institution of higher education. Yet one of the many skills for which she is so justly celebrated is her ability to reconfigure the assumptions of institutional authority, especially when it comes to what counts as knowledge or research. In this case, her intervention was literally sugar-coated, but nevertheless designed for impact (as I would find out).

Lois has a canny understanding of how power is constituted in the production of knowledge, and how this type of power acts on bodies – what Foucault might term 'power-knowledge relations',[15] and what Lois's persona Tammy WhyNot might call 'gettin' it' (innuendo intended). As Tammy, Lois undertakes research into sex and ageing, human rights, feminism, and other big questions.[16] The knowledge that is produced through this research is real, but the authority of the researcher and the separation between her and her subjects is gleefully dissolved. Similarly, when it comes to disseminating her research, Lois has developed structures to open up – and call into question – dominating or hierarchical forums for knowledge distribution. The best known of these is the *Long Table*, a riff on the dinner party where 'talk is the only course'. There is also *Porch Sitting*, where the face-to-face encounter is turned into a space for side-by-side contemplation, and variations include the Card Table, the Cocktail Seminar, and the Coffee Table Talk. In each of these, domesticity complicates the authority of public discourse, even as it underlines the importance of talking in public.

Lois's take on her position as a researcher is both serious and subversive. Her seriousness is not that of the strategic over-identification found often in activist performance.[17] Rather, she cultivates a slant perspective, allowing unexpected associations and opportunities to veer off course – like a cupcake hurtling through the air, destination unknown.

Opposite: Tammy WhyNot with Bill Cogswell in *What Tammy Needs to Know about Getting Old and Having Sex* (2014), La MaMa, NYC. Photo by Lori E. Seid.

Portrait of Lois Weaver for *Desperate Archives* (2014), La MaMa La Galleria, NYC, in dress as worn by Tammy WhyNot in 1984 (see photo on p. 235). Photo by Eva Weiss.

Stay Gone

Lyrics by Lois Weaver and Paul Clark, Music by Paul Clark [18]

You can't trust a late blooming flower
They show up and die on the vine
Like love gone wrong
I am not interested in the promise of flowers

A garden is too hard to keep
I'd get there too late in the spring
Then, there's the fall
By then, I'll be gone
And I'm gonna stay gone

[Chorus]
Stay gone
I've never been one who could
stay home
before the grass grows
I'm long gone
And I stay gone

My winter is measured in miles
Summer's just too fast for the road
Sun's got not enough time for effect
But effect is not a good word for a song

[Chorus]
Stay gone
I've never been one who could
stay home
before the grass grows
I'm long gone
And I stay gone

But I didn't start out writing a song
I wanted to tell you how much I love the road
and have spent my whole life just trying
    to stay on it
I'm happy when my suitcase is packed, my
closets are empty and there's nothing between
    me and the highway

But sometimes when you write one thing it
    comes out something else.
Like February, you can't trust the month
    of February
Things bloom unnaturally, forced in a hothouse
of false hope like hyacinth in clay pots, hearts
    in plastic wrap,
Valentines advertised too soon, sold
prematurely, then forgotten when the
    time comes
They're gone and they stay gone
Like the rain in Boulder, the clouds in Sante Fe
There briefly, then gone
Like the cruel 'carryin' me back to ole
Virginny' or 'across the wide Missouri'[19]
Leaving behind the white crystals of a Salt Lake
    and dry grass of a fertile coastal marsh
where the sand of memory and the brackish
    backwater of tears
cultivate the most delicate and unwanted pearl.
I am talking now about loss and a late falling in
love, like late fall falling in love with the sun
There's not enough heat to balance the effect
    of the coming cold
but effect is not a good word for a song

I'm stuck in this terrible verse
Putting miles between the garden and me
Miles and miles
Diggin' myself out of this winter love
    gone wrong

Stay gone
I feel better when I
stay gone
gonna stop singing this love song
And stay gone

253

1   See 'About', *Public Address Systems* < http://publicaddresssystems.org/about/> [accessed 23 June 2015].

2   Words by Lois Weaver and Paul Clark, music by Paul Clark; from Lois Weaver, *What Tammy Needs to Know*, 2004.

3   Words by Lois Weaver and Amy R. Surratt, music by Amy R. Surratt; from *What Tammy Needs to Know about Getting Old and Having Sex*, 2014.

4   Words by Lois Weaver, music by Vivian Stoll; from *What Tammy Needs to Know about Getting Old and Having Sex*, 2014.

5   Lois Weaver, 'Performing the Persona', *Public Address Systems*, 2013 <http://publicaddresssystems.org/projects/performing-the-persona-3/> [accessed 9 May 2015].

6   Lois Weaver, *What Tammy Needs to Know…about Getting Old and Having Sex* (2008).

7   Deb Margolin, Peggy Shaw, and Lois Weaver, *Upwardly Mobile Home* (1984).

8   *Long Table on Why Sex Matters* took place on 31 January 2015 as part of the Wellcome Collection's *Institute of Sexology* exhibition and season. As part of this season, Lois/Tammy also hosted *Long Table on the Ins and Outs of Sex* (26 March 2015), presented *What Tammy Needs to Know about Getting Older and Having Sex* (21-23 May 2015), and trained a platoon of mini-me Tammy WhyNets (featuring pink hairnets) who spent several afternoons in the exhibition facilitating audiences' engagement with it. See 'Past Events', *Wellcome Collection* <http://wellcomecollection.org/events/past>, and 'The Institute of Sexology', *Wellcome Collection* <http://wellcomecollection.org/exhibitions/institute-sexology> [both accessed 9 May 2015].

9   This work was part of a larger QMUL-based research project over 2007-08 titled *Democratising Technology*. See its website, *Democratising Technology* <http://www.demtech.qmul.ac.uk/index.html>, and Lois Weaver, 'Performance as Methodology: Democratising Technology', *Public Address Systems*, 2013 <http://publicaddresssystems.org/projects/performing-the-issue/> [both accessed 9 May 2015].

10   Weaver, 'Performing the Persona', 2013.

11   Emily Underwood, 'Confusing Gender: Strategies for Resisting Objectification in the Work of Split Britches', *Platform,* 2.1 (2007), 25-37 (p. 25) <https://www.royalholloway.ac.uk/dramaandtheatre/documents/pdf/platform/21/confusinggender.pdf> [accessed 9 May 2015].

12   Sue-Ellen Case, 'Lesbian Performance in the Transnational Arena', in *The Cambridge Companion to Modern British Women Playwrights*, ed. by Elaine Aston and Janelle Reinelt (Cambridge: Cambridge University Press, 2000), pp. 253-67 (p. 256). Italics original.

13   Weaver, 'Performing the Persona', 2013.

14   Lois Weaver, 'Inaugural Lecture: Professor Lois Weaver', 21 March 2012, *Queen Mary University of London* < http://www.qmul.ac.uk/events/items/2012/60464.html> [accessed 4 October 2014]. The lecture Lois performed at QMUL was a version of what she performed at the Bethnal Green Working Men's Club near the same time.

15   Michel Foucault, *Discipline and Punish: The Birth of the Prison* (New York: Knopf Doubleday Publishing Group, 2012), p. 26.

16   Weaver, 'Performing the Persona', 2013.

17   For a recent example, see Michael Shane Boyle, 'The Ironic Manifesto in an Age of Austerity', in *Manifesto, Now!: Instructions for Performance, Philosophy, Politics*, ed. by Laura Cull and Will Daddario (Bristol: Intellect, 2013), pp. 23-36. The term 'overidentification' in this context is often associated with Slavoj Žižek, in 'Why are the NSK and Laibach Not Fascists?', *M'ARS*, 5.3/4 (1993), 3-4.

18   Words by Lois Weaver and Paul Clark, music by Paul Clark; from *What Tammy Needs to Know*, 2004.

19   Tammy is sampling iconic American folk songs, 'Carry Me Back to Ole Virginny', written by African American James A. Bland in the late-nineteenth century, and 'Across the Wide Missouri', also known as 'Oh Shenandoah', likely from the early nineteenth century. Lois explains that 'the cruelty is in the line itself, the cruel sentimentality of the song' (email correspondence with Jen Harvie, 14 June, 2015).

Opposite: Tammy WhyNot in Spiderwoman's *The Lysistrata Numbah!* (1977). Courtesy of Spiderwoman Theater.

Kup...

EXOTIC
WORLD

EXOTIC
KRISTA?
WORLD

Ribot-
goat
Island?

(Clean Break!

TAMMY

Book

Web site · Archives

Ps

What Would You
Hang on the Line?

olive tree
and ate
uncontrolable

slice

I had to draw my tongue
from wrist to fingertip
before I could pick
up my pen.

Provence
August 1998

PROJECTS

* MY BOOK

* TAMMY'S ALBUM

* COMMONPLACE HERIONES

* RRR#3

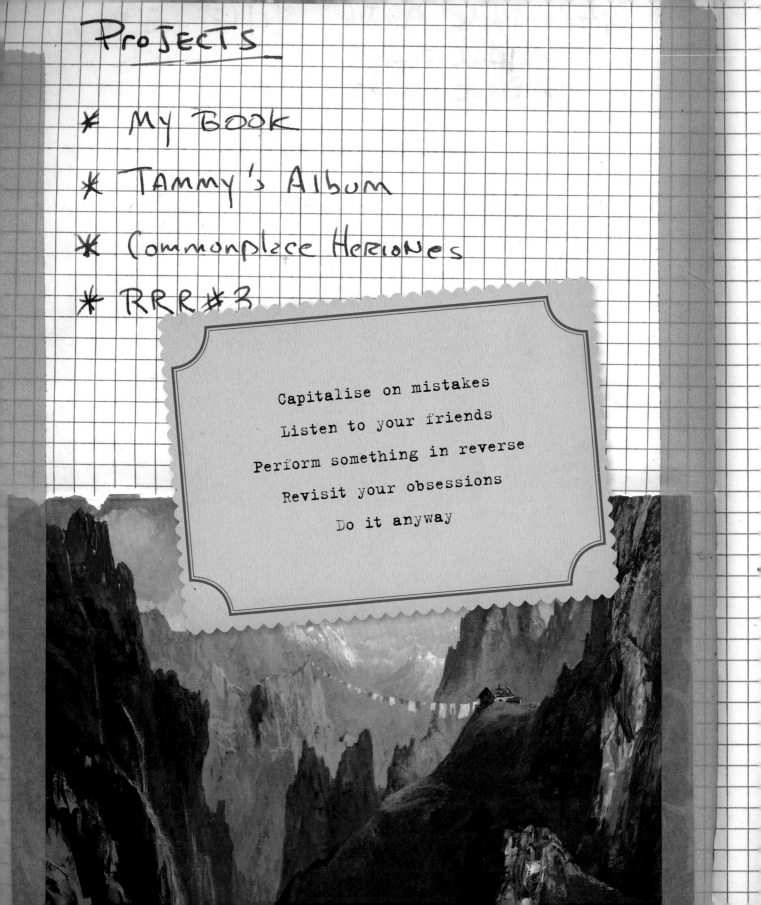

Capitalise on mistakes

Listen to your friends

Perform something in reverse

Revisit your obsessions

Do it anyway

String of Lights (adapted from *Salad of the Bad Café*)

Lois Weaver[1]

It was a cold November night. The last show of the season. Dark already. You were stringing lights. Hammer in hand, mouth full of tacks. Some people cover every available straight line and right angle of an otherwise dark face with lights that blink and sing. But you chose carefully one kind of bulb, several strands and many colours. You hung them with a dip and curve ignoring the straight and narrow. Hung them loosely like a cheap necklace at the throat of a gentle lady. I held you there on the ladder in that dark night. The light and sway of those many coloured bulbs burned into that part of the brain that gives birth to desire. For who were you doing this for? If not for me? Why else would you adorn the face of this tired, dark place if not for me? And what could have been gayer than this string of coloured lights. What more could have signalled the gathering together for the sake of pleasure or good company? How else advertise our local honky tonk, sideshow, queer bar, than with this string of lights swinging in the breeze.

How else would we find a place to gather, yes, gather and wait until there would come a moment when we would act in unison. And no one would hold back. And whether this would result in some senseless acts of violence or... the start of a friendly neighbourhood cafe would depend on destiny.

Documentation from *Commit an Act of Domestic Terrorism, Hang Your Laundry in Public*, Art in Odd Places, NYC, 2012. Photo by Lori E. Seid.

Diary of a Domestic Terrorist

Lois Weaver[2]

Dear Diary,

I am not home. I am away. I have travelled a long way to talk to people from around the world about what I think about home and away, about the local and the global.

In New York I take the local whenever I can because I like to stop at all the stops. Like 18th Street, for instance. No one I know ever has to go to 18th Street but it stops there so you don't have to walk from 23rd or 14th. I prefer the local, the small, the curious, the untraveled, and curiously, I will travel miles to find it. The local, the domestic, the intimate, and close to home has always been my house and home.

Home grown, like tomatoes.

Is it true all tomatoes grown in Italy are exported?

Home grown, like terrorists.

Do you think we, here, in what we call the West, have contributed enough to the health, welfare, and education of our immigrant populations to actually call them 'home grown'?

And home town like targets,

like flea markets, shopping malls and theme parks.

Do you think we are at risk in the heartland?

The homeland ...Security?

In the days following 9/11/2001 signs appeared all over the US asking citizens to report suspicious activities. 'If you see something, say something.'

Do you see anything?

Can you say?

As the dust settled and fear climbed up the 110 stories of a phantom national spine it seemed as if the list of suspicions might include some of our most private and mundane activities like:

hanging out laundry,

packing suitcases,

taking photographs,

writing letters,

disagreeing with dinner guests,

gossiping in gyms,

bearing breasts ....

In the interest of national security it was probably best that they cut to an aerial view of the Super Bowl stadium the second Janet Jackson's breast aired prime time, then filed a class action lawsuit against Jackson and Timberlake on behalf of 'all American citizens who watched the outrageous conduct', and in the aftermath, demanded the re-edit of scenes on *ER* in which an elderly woman's breast could be seen non-explicitly in the context of her injury and treatment.

It was a matter of national security.

But when I feel insecure, I TAKE OFF MY CLOTHES. I strip down, reveal all, show the flaws, capitalise on the failures. I have been doing it for years. I do it before they do it to me.

Dear Diary,

I am standing in my slip in front of a room full of people from all over the world. They look relatively well fed and well groomed and seem to make a decent living back home by writing, talking, researching the great and beautiful detail of the wide world of theatre. I am wondering if they are wondering what in the world this has to do with theatre. I am wondering if they are going to be able to SEE something that they cannot read, if they see something they cannot say.

They will no doubt assume a few things:

She is American,

or more accurately, North American,

Southern, white, female,

and feminist.

Oh yes, Mr McCarthy, I am now and have for some time been a feminist. I am still.

Because, Dear Diary,

We have to keep working at it. I am here in this moment because of the work of feminists who might be sitting right there beside you.

Can you see them?

If so, would you say?

Where are you? Would you raise your hands?

No, don't raise your hands. Stand up!

And those who are willing to stand beside these standing women, will you stand too?

Thank you.

It is always good to know who you are talking to.

Yes, I have been a feminist, femme feminist, a lesbian feminist, a lesbian femme, a resistant femme, and possibly even a para feminist, which, according to Amelia Jones, is not something that comes after as in post but stands beside as you are now

shoulder to shoulder.

Although Dear Diary,

I am afraid that under the current unbearable, despicable, terrifying, but yet oh so comfortable for us here in the locality of this room,

in this lovely city,

after such a delicious lunch...

What was I saying?

Oh yes, under the horror of current global circumstances,

I want to add another identity to my growing list.

I want to call myself a terrorist.

A home grown,

home town

Heart felt and homeland

Domestic terrorist.

Dear Diary,

I like to think of Janet Jackson as one of our early Domestic Terrorists. Known of course for Nipplegate, the qirl-illa action in which her wardrobe malfunction exposed more than her single naked breast. It exposed the American culture's selective outrage.

What's worse?

Thousands of Iraqi civilians dead,

or Janet Jackson's naked breast?

Children seeing a naked breast,

or men watching the violent contact of American football?

Ok I have to admit Dear Diary,

Sometimes I get so mad, I would love to blow something up. I fantasise about sacrificing myself in order to put an end to the men who have put us all in this situation. And in this fantasy, I can see how I might employ my theatrical skills and imagination to achieve such an aim. And if some of my simplest actions

like hanging laundry,

standing up for what I believe in,

taking off my clothes,

are going to place me under suspicion, then I would rather do it before they do it to me.

So yes, Mr. President, I am a domestic terrorist.

Ok Dear Diary,

I know that calling oneself a terrorist, even the clothes-pin irony of my domestic terrorism, is problematic. But my tactic has always been to appropriate and subvert the thing that could cause me harm. So I have taken on this intervention and, to some extent, act of civil disobedience called domestic terrorism by simply hanging my laundry in public.

I like laundry because in some ways it is the most visible work that women do and yet it is often the most forgotten and overlooked. Laundry hanging on a line can suggest the gender, class, and aesthetic principles of the person doing the laundry. It can disclose the population and income of a household. It reveals personal taste and bad habits; betrays acts of insurrection and indiscretion. How laundry is hung can be a statement of pride or an expression of modesty. It can be a violation of housing codes in certain communities or perceived as a national threat in times of war. It can be a form of communication between prisoners. In prison, laundry is one of the most hopeful things about the yard. It is a constant display of individuality and sometimes a secret language encoded with messages to prisoners in other parts of the prison that can be seen but not heard.

So Dear Diary,

As a Domestic Terrorist, I intend to use laundry to make public the visual evidence of private domestic work. I will encourage the use of private detail as a means of public resistance. I aim to encourage these researchers who spend their time contributing to a universal body of knowledge to:

Join me in exploring the intimate mind of the personal and travel with me to the land of the home

Imagine theatrical interventions and performance strategies that use private local details as a means of public global resistance and to explore how intimate everyday objects can play a small part in discussions of worldwide subjects.

Have intimate, detailed, local conversations about our global concerns

Talk about theatre and the power of the imagination

Talk about theatre and activism

Talk about ways in which the global, the historical, the factual can not only archive but activate, can make things change.

Dear Diary,

Theatre for me is about imagination and a local imagination is crucial in these global times

and if we can imagine something we can make it, if we can make it, we can make it change.

Take the local, find ways to risk the personal, let your slips show and hang out your laundry, however you can.

Opposite: Clockwise from top left: Stacy Makishi, Claire Nolan and Tammy WhyNot, *Tourist Information Wanted*, London 2013. Photo by Jo Palmer; Lois Weaver, Republican National Convention, NYC, 2004. Photo by Lori E. Seid; Tammy WhyNot, *FeMUSEum*, London, 2011. Photo by Helaine Gawlica; Domestic Terrorist, Union Square, NYC 2004. Photo Lori E. Seid; Lois Weaver, Republican National Convention, NYC, 2004. Photo by Lori E. Seid; Lois Weaver, Hong Kong, 1999. Photo by Peggy Shaw.

Hidden Treasures

Jen Harvie

When the Tide Is Out (2000)

Lois Weaver and Stacy Makishi are down on a mucky beach revealed by the retreat of the Thames River at low tide. It is morning on New Year's Day, 2000. A new millennium has dawned; it is overcast and cool. The night before, this stretch of river in central London played host to a colossal fireworks display before a live audience of thousands, and a television audience of millions. The pavements and sand are still littered with the festivities' detritus: poppers' plastic shells and spent ribbons of coloured paper; empty bottles, corks and caps; abandoned bits of fancy dress costumes; and broken, discarded novelty eyeglasses spelling out the digits 2-0-0-0.

Lois is dressed in warm clothes and wellington boots, in role as her Domestic Terrorist (whom I'll come back to, below). She is hanging a clothesline down there in the sand along the tide line. Stacy is progressing along the beach, placing tangerines in its dull, damp sand. In many traditional Eastern cultures, tangerines and oranges are harbingers of New Year's good luck and good fortune. Here along the Thames, the fruits' bright colour punctuates this New Millennium's Day morning like a series of triumphant little sunrises, or a line of expectant ellipses, or the exhalations 'oh', 'oh', 'oh', uttered perhaps with fatigue, trepidation, or maybe excitement.

A small audience gathers. Many, like me and my partner Deb, are out for fresh air, and happily stumble across this curious, hospitable little event by these artists and friends whom we know but will come to know much better. Some members of the audience have been summoned by invitation, issued on rice paper, and accompanied by a written recipe for the Southern rice and black-eyed pea dish Hoppin' John, also purported to bring good luck, and being served here and now on the beach by Lois and Stacy. The women also offer their audiences bits of rice paper on which to write our wishes for this new millennium. We write, and pin our papers to the clothesline. As the day progresses, the tide gradually, inevitably, advances. Piecemeal, it covers... the tangerines... then the clothesline... and the rice paper wishes.... When the tide next retreats, all evidence of Lois and Stacy's New Millennium's Day intervention are, of course, gone, thoroughly collected by the surging embrace of the lunar tide.

This was *When the Tide Is Out*, which Lois and Stacy describe in more detail in their discussion which follows. I describe *When the Tide Is Out* in some detail because it provides a vivid example of the huge range of work that Lois makes, solo and with collaborators, which is small-scale, temporary and, for everyone but a very few, hidden. Making this kind of work is crucial to Lois and to her artistic, social, and political ethos because it fundamentally recalibrates dominant systems of value.

The fruits' bright colour punctuates this New Millennium's Day morning like a series of triumphant little sunrises, or a line of expectant ellipses.

Screen shots from *When the Tide is Out* (Lois Weaver and Stacy Makishi, 2000), London. Film by Vick Ryder.

267

Small Acts for Now, Here, and You

Such work is important to Lois and her collaborators not because it aims to be rare and exclusive (it does not), but because it aspires to respond to the world in ways that are socially important to the performance's particular time, its place and – importantly – its people or audiences. After all the hype of the millennium build-up, and all the apocalyptic paranoia about the so-called Millennium Bug, *When the Tide Is Out* deliberately lowered the hysterical pitch, slowed things right down, and invited participants to recalibrate their sense of what's important. Its small rituals focused attention down, onto personal wishes, everyday interpersonal domestic activities of sharing food and doing laundry, and the human scale of friendship. And its rituals focused attention out, onto the tides, as part of a global ecology and a galactic set of forces. The work was aimed at Lois and Stacy's invited friends, but also at lucky passers-by, welcomed to participate – or not, as we chose – in the little surprise of these special but deliberately modest events. *When the Tide Is Out* was thus specific and particular – designed for that day, that site, and those audiences only. But the work was also typical of Lois and her collaborators, because it used its curious particularity to leverage a small but potentially powerful intervention into an ideological juggernaut, in this case, the millennium.

Lois makes this kind of intervention across her work. Earlier in this book, Erin Hurley writes about Lois and Stacy's 'Tourist Information Wanted' booth set up in London's Battersea Park during Queen Elizabeth's Diamond Jubilee celebrations in 2012.[3] Here, Lois and Stacy slowed down and re-directed the juggernaut of the Jubilee by inviting passers-by to recount *their own* personal and familial milestones and memories.

Across her work as a Domestic Terrorist, Lois hangs her laundry in public, for example, in her contribution to the event Art in Odd Places in New York City in 2011.[4] As part of this work, Lois engages passers-by in conversation about attitudes towards laundry and what this most banal human activity says about class, gender, labour, bodies, cleanliness, civility, propriety, inter-neighbourly competition, and more. She disrupts dominant assumptions about public propriety and public space by inserting the activity of hanging laundry, with its significations of domesticity, the private, and 'the memories of mothers' hands'.[5]

As discussed briefly in the fourth part of this book, in 2011, Lois curated *FeMUSEum*,[6] first in Toynbee Studios in East London, then in New York. *FeMUSEum* incorporated two rooms. The first was Toynbee's imposing wood-panelled Court Room and was empty save a sign saying, 'Exit to the Gift Shop'. The 'Gift Shop' was a live installation crammed in a small-ish back room. Lois and three other queer femme performers – Amy Lamé, Bird la Bird, and Carmelita Tropicana – each occupied a space in the room and, in their various ways, summoned their femme muses. In Lois's case, this included displaying tiny bells and old silk gloves, mementoes of her femme muses, La MaMa Experimental Theatre Company founder Ellen Stewart in the case of the bells, and long-gone Aunt Edna in the case of the gloves. Again, the work inserted the domestic into a public space, this time a gallery. It also brought in the outsider femme, and it legitimated clandestine affection for and attraction to that femme. 'The *FeMUSEum*', says Lois, 'was about the lack of feminine within the museum

Carmelita Tropicana, Bird la Bird, Amy Lamé, and Lois Weaver planning for FeMUSEum, New Jersey, 2011. Photographer unknown.

'The FeMUSEum was
about the lack of the
feminine within the
museum or within the
repositories of culture.'

or within the repositories of culture. It was a response to institutional male dominated museums and it looked at women's work, the commodification of women's work and the place women often occupy in institutional spaces.'[7]

This is just a small sample of some of Lois's 'hidden' work. It is not so much deliberately *hidden* as it is deliberately focused, designed as an experiment for a particular audience at a particular time to make a particular social intervention. There is plenty more. And there are plenty more examples of work by Lois and collaborators that has been 'hidden' by its comparatively small critical afterlife (for example, plays such as *Little Women: The Tragedy*).

And there is plenty more work by Lois that is just emerging. As I write in spring 2015, Lois is performing *What Tammy Needs to Know about Getting Old and Having Sex* across the UK, in Manchester, Brighton, Glasgow, and London. She has funding to tour it more extensively in 2016. She is hosting *Long Tables* around the UK. She has trained up a cohort of mini-me Tammy WhyNets (like swans' baby cygnets?) to facilitate audiences' engagement with the Wellcome Collection's *Institute of Sexology* exhibition.[8] Developing from their collaboration on *Ruff*, written and performed by Peggy Shaw and directed by Lois, the two are collaborating on a series of public service announcements about ageing and health; they have recently filmed one on recognising the signs of stroke.[9] This summer, Peggy and Lois travel to Tasmania to collaborate with Matt Delbridge on green screen multimedia performance experiments. The list goes on. As Tammy sings proudly, 'This lemon's still got a whole lotta juice'.

Lois Performs in Aotearoa New Zealand

Catherine Silverstone

On a visit to Aotearoa New Zealand I stopped by The Women's Bookshop on Auckland's Ponsonby Road. While checking out the Lesbian section, I came across Doreen Agassiz-Suddens' 24-page booklet, *The History of Lesbian Theatre in New Zealand*.[9] The booklet caught my attention for the boldness of its titular claim in relation to its slim format, though the relative paucity of lesbian theatre was far from a surprise given my experiences of growing up in New Zealand and reading, studying, and watching local theatre and literature. Still, little history does not mean no history. Agassiz-Suddens charts close personal and professional relationships between women in the early twentieth century; the work of dancer Freda Stark in the 1940s (famous for her semi-naked performances and relationship with Thelma Trott); consciousness-raising political theatre in the 1970s and 1980s, especially in the context of women's and gay and lesbian rights; performances that recuperated lesbian lives; the emergence of openly lesbian writers and performers in the 1980s and 1990s, including Renée, Lorae Parry, Amanda Rees, sisters Jools and Lynda Topp, and Carmel Carroll; and the diversification of performance forms including contemporary dance, comedy, and cabaret.

Half way through reading Agassiz-Suddens' booklet, my attention was arrested by an image of a promotional flyer for Split Britches, which reproduced the steamy, uncompromising image of sexual desire between women in the iconic photograph of Lois and Peggy embracing as Stella and Stanley in *Belle Reprieve* (1991). The barely visible print on the flyer reveals that Split Britches visited New Zealand (one of their lesser known destinations) to perform as part of the Magdalena Aotearoa International Festival of Women's Performance in Wellington and Paekakariki in March 1999, preceded by a performance of Peggy's show *Menopausal Gentleman* (1996), in Christchurch.

The website of the Magdalena Aotearoa Trust – a branch of The Magdalena Project, an international network of women in contemporary theatre – records that Lois and Peggy performed their solo shows – *Faith and Dancing* (1996) and *Menopausal Gentleman* respectively – during the festival at Circa Theatre in Wellington; they also participated in workshops held by Māori women at Paekakariki. Lois Weaver gets everywhere, including Aotearoa New Zealand, which is a long way from Virginia and New York and about as far from London as you can get.

It tickles my fancy that Lois was in New Zealand just before I emigrated to the UK (though I didn't know that's what I was doing at the time), generating a phantom nostalgia for a performance I didn't see, a body of work I didn't know existed and a person I hadn't yet met. Lois's presence in New Zealand and in Agassiz-Suddens' *History* also, and more importantly, speaks to her commitment to travelling and performing internationally, to participating in international and local networks that promote work by and for women, and to being out in cultures where it might not always be safe or even possible to articulate same-sex desires. There's less homophobia in New Zealand than some of the places Lois has visited, worked, and effected change – discrimination on the basis of sexual orientation was outlawed in 1993 and same sex couples have been able to form Civil Unions since 2005 and marriages since 2013. It's worth remembering, though, that homosexual law reform decriminalising sex between men didn't occur until 1986 amidst strong opposition. Lois's and Peggy's performances in New Zealand along with the image used to advertise their work offers a brief, sexy contribution to lesbian visibility and history in bars, bookshops, and theatres, and elsewhere besides, in Aotearoa New Zealand.

'Everything's breakable', or what I learned from Lois Weaver

Benjamin Gillespie

We live in times defined by proliferation and destruction. In moments of desperation, hopeful acts can inspire us to reposition the world, giving newfound motivations to strive for something different in the scenes of crisis that envelope us. Hope can push us to construct the new presents and futures we dream of. Lois Weaver's life is an embodiment of this kind of hope, and her artistic and pedagogical legacies exemplify what can be accomplished when innovation, collaboration, and love combine to refute threats posed by conservatism and normativity.

For more than three decades, Lois has thrived as a maker of experimental, feminist, and queer performance, offering unique creative processes that help her and others to articulate important critiques of the status quo. As a lesbian and feminist, questions related to gender, sexuality, and identity are always central to her work, inspiring generations of theatre makers and activists in developing collaborative strategies for artistic exploration around these issues. Lois's performances are much less about fixed aesthetics and narratives than about social and political engagement, and they are always informed by active desires and marginalised cultural perspectives. We can see activist practices in her work, especially when she purposefully breaks into the audience during performances to see how we are feeling; despite being on stage, she never distances herself from the real world.

The stage allows Lois a place to reconfigure the troubling normative beliefs that she can't directly change in the world. Instead, in the span of her experimental career, she has implicated these beliefs through performing acts of resistance toward them. Significantly, when she reflects upon her influential career, she is not overly precious or sentimental about the past. Instead, Lois foregrounds the breaking down of history to see how it can be restructured for the here and now. This was highlighted during a *Long Table* discussion at the *33 x 3 Festival: A Split Britches Reunion*, held at La MaMa Experimental Theatre Club in New York in April 2012, where Lois considered what about Split Britches' past pieces still worked effectively for current audiences, as well as what didn't. I found this impressive, and when I helped curate the 2014 *Desperate Archives* exhibition at New York's La MaMa Galleria with Lois and Peggy, I once again experienced this fearless and unpretentious approach to the past, evidencing a true investment in the future.

With her characteristic humour and grace, Lois remains interested in how performance can be broken down and put back together in meaningful ways. She has reiterated to me that it is important to foresee that things never go as planned; she says, in fact, that life (and performance) would be pretty boring if they did. In Lois's view, everything in performance is *breakable*. Nothing remains static; if something isn't working, she remakes it, adjusts it, and learns from it. As a profound sounding board for creative experimentation, Lois never settles for what seems easy or predictable – just what seems right for telling the story and finding a new way forward. Though she makes her creative process look easy in performance, behind the scenes – and behind her distinctive eyeglasses – Lois is a truly engaged critical thinker, inspired by unwavering political convictions and her readings in critical theory. Driven by her motivation to care for others and an unwavering hospitality for the world around her – always making me feel so at home – Lois never fails to inspire audiences, colleagues, and collaborators alike.

The worlds that Lois curates expand with the presence of her collaborators and audiences, allowing her to break apart the present as we know it in order to yield new and better futures, while not forgetting the difficult work it takes to get there. More than three decades into her career, she is still breaking perceived limitations apart to reconfigure them, and it is my hope as a fan, friend, and collaborator that she will continue doing so for a long time.

Talking about *When The Tide Is Out*

Lois Weaver and Stacy Makishi
2 June 2015, London.

LOIS: I wanted to talk about *When the Tide Is Out*, the project you and I came together to do right at the Millennium.

STACY: What I remember is we wanted to do something for 'Small Acts for the Millennium',[10] which was a commissioned programme of work by Live Art Development Agency in London and we missed the boat, as we often do. But we tried to catch the tide anyway and said, let's just do something. We wanted to make some kind of rite of passage, ceremony, ritual to open up a whole millennium and mark it with something that was really important to us. We didn't care if this was going to be documented, if we were going to get paid, if we were going to be a part of some kind of anthology. It was just that we needed to do this and nothing could stop us.

LOIS: I think the thing we both were attracted to in the call for proposals was the fact that it said 'small acts for the millennium'. I remember being terrified by the magnitude of this idea of 'the millennium', both the hype of it and the reality of it. The idea that we could create some small act was absolutely delicious for us – but we just couldn't get it together to put in the application for the project! I have a lot of joy thinking that even though we didn't get the grant we decided to go ahead and do it anyway.

STACY: I remember that I wanted to use tangerines, to mark the new millennium and my new 'home' with something old and familiar. To celebrate the new year in Japanese culture, tangerines are placed upon hard mochi[11] on an alter; Hawaiians also stack significant stones onto each other in sacred places. I suppose tangerines placed onto stones was a ritual that signified this momentous moment in time... a bunch of people bearing witness to time moving like a river through us, and ritual is a way for us to somehow feel it move through us.

LOIS: And at that point I was beginning to get obsessed with hanging laundry. The idea of hanging something on a laundry line along the riverbank, below the tide line, so that when the tide came up, the river would take whatever it was – that was something that appealed to me, just like the tangerines somehow appealed to you. I also liked the idea of just standing on the riverbank with a laundry basket and a laundry line. So we put those two ideas together.

STACY: And that was around the time I was doing *On The Street Where You Live*,[12] and people were putting prayer flags in my mailbox and in my garden. I think we both wanted to involve people, people passing by, but also to invite our friends to a ceremony. So I remember we decided to put up a laundry line on which people could air their wishes. Do you remember the prompt that was used for the hanging of their wishes?

LOIS: We gave everybody a piece of rice paper and told them to write their wish for the new millennium and we would hang it on the line. And then when the tide came the wishes would be taken down river. We sent out a little pack of instructions to everyone as an invitation – and in that invitation was the piece of rice paper.

STACY: I think we also gave them a plastic bag and told them to capture some breath from the old millennium to bring into the new millennium.

LOIS: And then we told them to come down to the riverbank at two o'clock or something on New Year's Day.

STACY: We told them to come at low tide

LOIS: Of course, and when they got there, you were way up the riverbank and I was standing with my laundry basket next to a laundry line at edge of the river. I came up and collected their wishes then walked down to hang them on the line as you walked up into view. As you walked, you placed these beautiful orange objects, which were the tangerines, in the grey mud of the Thames. It was beautiful.

After you joined me at the laundry line, we joined everyone up on the promenade and fed them Hoppin' John, a Creole rice and black-eyed pea recipe for good luck in the New Year. We were standing amongst the biggest pile of champagne corks and confetti from the biggest New Year's celebration ever. It was awful, but there was something wonderful about how grungy it was.

STACY: It was. It was like we were standing in the detritus of the last millennium.

LOIS: It was one of my favourite performances ever that

I remember being terrified by the magnitude of 'the millennium' and the idea that we could create some small act was absolutely delicious for us.

Previous pages: Images from various *Domestic Terrorist* interventions, Parksville, Manhattan and Brooklyn NY, 2004-2013. Photos by Morgan Grenwald and Lori E. Seid.

Top: Flyer for *When the Tide Is Out*
(Lois Weaver and Stacy Makishi) London, 2000.

we've done together, I think.

STACY: I'm so glad that we missed it. There's something great about missing it but then still showing up. We could have just been, 'Oh, we missed it', and it won't count, but it did matter and it did still count. We were all there, we were all counted, all of our hopes, all of our wishes that we were pinning on the line, pinning on the next millennium.

LOIS: I was thinking about the difference between the kind of self-started project like *When the Tide Is Out* – that arose out of a spiritual connection to the millennium – and *Tourist Information Wanted*, the commissioned project that we did for the Jubilee and for which we had no real emotional connection. I think we did some similar things, had some similar aims but it just didn't have the same satisfaction or something about it. Do you know what I mean?

STACY: Yeah, because the millennium happened for all of us, but then the coronation was, you know... just about... well you know, if no one had paid us, we wouldn't have done it.

LOIS: No, we wouldn't have done it. However I do think we came at it with the same desire to communicate with the audience, the same desire to let the audience communicate their own sense of what this occasion meant to them but this time with an element of irony, no, not really irony, but an element of appropriation. We wanted it to be everybody's Jubilee, not just the Queen's Jubilee. It came with the same kind of interactions but it just didn't have the same sweetness that, although we got absolutely no support, *When the Tide Is Out* did.

STACY: I know it was like the tide: it came, it went, and it left a few glimpses of people that you would never see again. I've never seen some of these people since then. I mean, it was emotional, and it was so true, wasn't it? Everything about that piece was true.

LOIS: It's almost like it never happened. It's like a dream.

STACY: It is like a dream, I feel really dreamy about it.

Lois's hidden treasures:
What Tammy Needs to Know About Prison

Caoimhe McAvinchey

Between 2001 and 2003, Lois was a partner in *Staging Human Rights*, an international research project directed by Paul Heritage and produced by People's Palace Projects. During this time, I worked with Lois and Peggy Shaw exploring human rights with women in four prisons in England and Brazil. Lois and Peggy's particular and eclectic methodology for making their own work together underpinned their approach to making work with women whose lives were shaped by societal structural disadvantage both within and beyond the prison walls. This work was charged with a commitment to biography, fantasy, and an imperative to witness the lives of women who gave testimony through the performances they made together. Central to this process was the arrival of Tammy. The following is an account of Tammy's first encounter with life in prison, revealing the radical playfulness that informs Lois's practice.

HMP Highpoint. 4 April 2002. Day 3

It is another grey morning. Lois says that she would like to introduce someone to the group. As she sits, as Lois, on a chair in the circle with the women, she begins to describe Tammy. She takes off her boots and slips on a pair of sparkly mules. As she takes off her jumper and puts on a sheer leopard-skin-print blouse her voice begins to change, morphing from educated East Coast to a more cascading, playful Southern drawl. She moves from talking about Tammy in the third person to talking *as* Tammy in the first person. She leans forwards and when she snaps her head back, Lois's short blonde bob has been replaced by a river of white-blonde locks.

Tammy tells us all about the trailer where she lives and the songs she likes to sing as she glues on her eyelashes and swipes a dash of lipstick across her mouth. Her orange bangles clack as she waves hello to the women who are transfixed by this metamorphosis from the drama teacher who gets them to do annoying warm-ups to this effervescent creature with a mischievous look in her eye. Who is she? Where did she come from? Where is Lois?

How is that possible? There is a hiatus of disbelief and pleasure as we all recognise that Lois's fantasy character has become a reality. Tammy explains that she is in the process of educating herself and has never been to a women's prison before. She asks the women to host a session called *What Tammy Needs to Know About Prison*. Women who previously had to be gently encouraged to speak are now talking over each other in an attempt to tell this woman all she needs to know about prison – how it works and how to survive it.

The room has been transformed. It is no longer a glaringly lit aircraft hanger with monochrome aspirational prints on the wall, humming with sounds spilling over from the painting and decorating workshop next door. It is now a salon of curious and opinionated women, hosted by the most delightful, irreverent, provocative, and engaging hostess.

There is laughter and coy disbelief as Tammy sings her manifesto for loving life, a call to put 'the cunt back in country', encouraging the women to join in the chorus. They respond, quietly raucous, shooting nervous glances towards the door. Tammy WhyNot is a gregarious and generous-spirited character who flicks her peroxide curls out of the way as she takes a closer look at life. Within these prison walls, she is a delightful anathema. Tammy gathers her things and says:

Well, I just love you all to pieces and I'm telling you what, I would love for you all to come on tour with me. In fact, one of the things I'm going to do is buy a bus that is so big and so strong that I'm just going to drive that bus straight through the front gate and load you all up and take you just everywhere!

At the end of the session Tammy thanks the women for her education and grins before sliding off her wig. Lois then asks the women to think about the props and costumes they want for their fantasy characters. We set off at lunchtime with a shopping list for gold bustiers, trench-coats and tutus.

Meeting Lois Weaver

Anne Tallentire

December 2014

Looking for a place to live drew me to the Women's One World Café (WOW) in the East Village, New York sometime in late February or early March, 1983. I was refiguring my life, studying print-making at the School of Visual Arts (SVA) and looking for a home. Someone at the school suggested I check out the café. There on the notice board I found an advertisement for a place in Brooklyn that became my home and a few weeks later, encouraged by my flatmate who knew the café well, I signed up to one of Lois Weaver and Peggy Shaw's acting workshops.

Not long before travelling to New York I had begun to consider movement in relation to space and time in an attempt to construct my art practice that was moving away from painting. Apart from attending the course at SVA I had had no formal art education. However I was reading feminist theory and looking at political performance practices and conceptual art that would inform my work to this day.

The Split Britches classes taught me technical skills related to voice and movement. Years later I would incorporate these skills into performance workshops for undergraduate students at Byam Shaw School of Art and Central Saint Martins in London, and into aspects of my own practice. More importantly I learnt from the women at WOW that there were many ways to imagine an affective political practice on one's own terms. I did not want to pursue theatre as such but here a group of artists and actors such as Holly Hughes, Lois Weaver, and Peggy Shaw were affirming their sexuality and rights imaginatively and powerfully through radical theatre to create a context for other women to explore and assert who they were.

Although I followed the class instruction diligently I was also beginning to draw together an idea for my first public performance (as I understood it to be; in reality it might have been no more than a staging of class work). Most of the others performed narrative works based on evocations and interpretations of texts we had engaged with in class; however, emboldened by the experimental dynamic that the café embodied and the visual art performances I was able to see in New York at that time, I decided to test and risk a work that reflected the direction I was determined to uncompromisingly follow from then on. Standing very still, facing rows of women in the long narrow space looking back at me, I looked into the eyes of all the women in the room one by one until they made eye contact back. It was a minimal gesture, yet this work with its pretentious title *Returning the Gaze* signalled the beginning of a transformation for my practice.

Years later, living in London, I went to see Split Britches a few times over the years at the Drill Hall and did think to make contact with Lois at Queen Mary University of London to at least say how meeting her work had affected a change for me, but I never did. Then just some months ago we found ourselves in a workshop at Queen Mary (at the invitation of the Live Art Development Agency) and I was delighted to be able to tell.

Dear Carmen

Paul Heritage

Rua São João Batista, 105
Botafogo
Rio de Janeiro
1 April 2015
To Carmen Miranda
- *a pequena notável*[13]

Dear Carmen,

Let me introduce Lois Weaver. At 1.62m she stands just 10 cm taller than you, but in your patented platform heels, Carmen, I guess you and Lois would almost brush eyelashes if you ever got close. And I wish you could. Both of you know so well how to enunciate your physique and articulate your curves – to dress your body up (and down) so that it speaks before you and in languages that go beyond words. You should have met in New York, although neither the years nor your addresses really match. Taking up residence at 25 Central Park West in the 1940s Carmen means that you and Lois would never have been close neighbours in the city that Lois has made her half-home with London. Being half-home is something that the two of you might understand about each other. Did you ever call New York home, even as you spent the last 16 years of your life there? Home must have been a complex place for a Portuguese immigrant to Brazil, who by 1945 had become the highest paid women in the United States by constantly performing a *latina* of no fixed abode. Brazilian? Argentinean? Mexican? Cuban? What did it matter? Home seems to have become seriously unfixed for you, which is something Lois understands well. She has dug out that territory so often in her performances. I wish you could have seen how home could go impossibly, upwardly mobile in her collaboration with Holly Hughes, Peggy Shaw, and Deb Margolin at New York's WOW Café in 1984[14] and then become a small but infinitely expandable house when Lois and Peggy joined forces with Suzy Willson and Paul Clark at the Clod Ensemble in 1999.[15] Lois has honed home to be the goal and purpose of every performance, as this book itself reminds us in its title. Just as for you Carmen, home has always been a complex place for Lois, intensely so in the last two and a half decades as a native Southerner navigates a life lived and performed between New York and London. Displacement is something Lois feeds on and provokes in her performances. You two should work together.

You never met in Rio de Janeiro. When you waved goodbye to the multitudes on the quayside to set sail for New York in 1939, Carmen, you were hardly ever to return. I first invited Lois to come here in 1999 but she was rejected at the border as she had no visa. She turned round, took the same plane back to London, got a visa and was here again in the blink of a costume change. A life spent touring with Spiderwoman, Split Britches, and Bloolips brings resilience and the ability to turn misfortunes into perfect timing. Lois has shown time and again how refusal, denial, and negation at frontiers can be the incentive for the creative act to follow. From a number of significant projects and workshops that Lois has undertaken in Brazil over subsequent years, there is one performance event that I want to share with you now, Carmen. Called *In the House*, it took place in 2003 in an almost derelict building at 31, Avenida Mem de Sá in the Lapa neighbourhood of Rio de Janeiro. There Lois staged her first *Long Table*, just round the corner you turned every day 80 years ago as you left your parents' house at 53, Rua Joaquim Silva to study with the nuns at the Santa Teresa College or, unbeknownst to your parents, sweep the floors of a local brothel.

Other writers in this book will describe much better than I can what the *Long Table* became but I want to share with you how it started. Lois goes to where women are, so it was no real surprise when she accepted my invitation to return to Rio de Janeiro in 2003 with Peggy Shaw and Caoimhe McAvinchey[16] to run workshops in Nelson Hungria, a women's prison in the Frei Caneca Penitentiary Complex. How often did you move quickly past those nineteenth-century walls in the centre of the city when you lived here? They must have cast only a passing shadow on the tropical Rio de Janeiro, whose image and sound you came to embody as you rose from the poverty of an immigrant merchant family to become Brazil's first national star of radio and film. Frei Caneca was the first prison establishment I visited when I arrived in Rio de Janeiro in 1991, and 12 years later it was where I invited Lois to spend two weeks playing with lesbian, queer, dyke, butch, and femme identities with 20 women prisoners.

Carmen, your fabricated self-characterisation fixed a national cultural identity that would later trouble as much as celebrate Brazil. Lois unstitches identity as she fabricates performances that resolutely celebrate trouble. The external forces that seemed to determine the identities of 20 women in Nelson Hungria Prison met their match in 2003 when Lois began to reveal their pleasures, desires, fantasies. Resistance was enacted every time Lois and Peggy (and sometimes Tammy) walked down the corridors with bodies, gestures, words, smiles, looks, smells, and a presence that confused and defied the whys and the hows by which a prison is constructed. Even behind bars that seem to refuse the multiple possibilities of identity as much as they confine the body, Lois led workshops that liberated alternative ways of being and of playing being. Was that still true for you, Carmen, as your home-spun turbans rose to impossible architectural heights, as the bangles climbed ever higher up your arm, as your eye brows arched and winked yet another invitation to the Technicolor tropics, as your gravity-defying platform heels senselessly interchanged sambas and rumbas, cha cha chas and mambos? As you conquered North American stages, screens, and magazine pages were you still able to control the fabrication of your body? Only five years after arriving in New York, you were rightly proud to have become the highest paid woman in the USA, Carmen, but what was the price you paid as you continued to accentuate your English over the next 16 years so that it would forever speak of a land that was far from the one you had supposedly conquered?

In the unadorned concrete bunker of a museum that now holds your outward show in Rio de Janeiro, Lois looked as always for a woman that was not imprisoned in her own image. In the awkwardly lit display cases, Lois saw the Carmen Miranda who authored, designed, dressed, and invented herself in the 1930s. There amongst the sequins, feathers, and plastic fruits she also saw the masculine jackets you pioneered as womenswear in Rio as early as 1933. Lois has a thing for dress suits. Or really for anything that mixes up what we might assume about gender and sexuality. Carmen, even though in the USA you became forever associated with an iconography which left little room for the sort of doubt, irony, and confusion that Lois can inspire, in those first few years in Rio de Janeiro you knew how to play multiple, nuanced, and powerful versions of self. As you stepped into Vitor & Lupovici's tailor's shop on Avenida Rio Branco in 1933, you became their first woman customer to be measured for a suit. Worn over skirts or with baggy trousers, those suits were as remarkable (and desired) in Rio de Janeiro at the time as your baubles, bangles and beads were to become on New York's Fifth Avenue.

I have become distracted by clothes, which is something that always seems to happen whenever I think about either of you. Distraction – the drawing away, the pulling apart or disturbance of the mind – is an essence of the art which both of you practise, so perhaps I shouldn't be surprised. You both distract. I want to tell you about how Lois made what she discovered during her workshops with those women prisoners in Rio into the performance event *In the House*. It wasn't a play or a film, but an extension of the art of cabaret within which Lois has forever framed her performances. Cabaret was also your world, Carmen. Whatever the story of a particular film, you and your character – as indivisible as any of the performers and characters in a Split Britches show – were never far from the cabaret stage, however improbable the bend in the narrative.

That night in Rio, in a crumbling, abandoned house in Lapa in 2003, Lois created an environment that was as far as could be imagined from the New York cabaret scene which you dominated in the 1940s. Come with me now as the audience enters the cavernous, lofty, and dusty hall that comprises the central ground floor of the house, long white tablecloths hanging like the sails of Bahian *jangadas* or fishing boats. The gloom of the space is put into relief by the projections that catch the floating cloths, showing photographs and video sequences from the workshops that Lois, Peggy, and Caoimhe had been running for the previous two weeks. Fragments of emotion, flashes of fury and passion, dance across the white sheets before being lost again on the distant, dark walls.

Criss-crossing the space are high-hung washing lines with paper cut-outs of fantasy clothing, bearing words, hopes, accusations, challenges, and visions of a future that was not prescribed by the imprisonment of the women that had written them. A soundtrack mixes North American Southern music with South American *sertaneja:* country meets country. In the middle of the room, a long table. Covered by a white tablecloth with six microphones on stands, the table has space for ten guests to be seated. Tammy WhyNot gently encourages, cajoles, and seduces the first guests to come to the table, while the others fill up the 50 chairs scattered around the room. Tammy explains the rules, which remain the same today as on that first night, and the participants begin to serve up and digest a rich debate on human rights and women in prisons. The first speakers at the table include special guests from the legal profession, human rights activists, prison guards, and artists, together with Julita Lemgruber who, in the 1990s, had been the first female director of a Brazilian state prison system. There is an empty chair, but you cannot sit there Carmen. It has been left for the women prisoners who are not present. Although their attendance had been negotiated carefully, at the last minute the logistical operation has been compromised for security reasons (or possibly just by plain resistance) and the women who Lois has led towards the sharing and performing of their intimacies, ecstasies, and tragedies are not with us for this final event. Their absence beats a *batucada* – a rhythm of exclusion – on that first *Long Table* and I know that Lois hears it again every time the table is laid in theatres, conference halls, parks, and public spaces around the world.

You achieved international fame through creating and living by your own persona, Carmen. Nothing can diminish the power of what you made for and of yourself, but that performance trapped you in exile, which is why I

want to introduce you to Lois Weaver, the most remarkable escape artist Lois has used performance to reveal that identity is not a frontier to be defended but is rather a place of encounter, of relations and transactions to which she is deeply and actively committed. She has constantly sought out complex narratives of interaction that iterate the importance of the exchange and not the permanence of any particular identity.

You never found your way back Carmen, dying within hours of a live show on North American television in 1955. Your knees give way at the end of a five-minute frenzy of foxtrot, samba, tango, and mamba as the heart attack that will kill you in the early hours of the next morning breaks through your body. But you know the only way home is through the show. Your eyes roll back, your words blur as your mouth begins to twist but you do not desist. Neither your consummate artifice nor your indefatigable charm is lost as somehow you pull yourself back up for the end of the routine, perfectly executing the last pulsating steps. A few moments later you take your final bow, dancing backwards out the door, waving goodbye, and blowing kisses to all. Within five hours you have fallen dead on your bedroom floor, clutching your hand-mirror as you removed your make-up for one last time. Lois would never have left you lying there. Melodrama was only ever a gesture in Split Britches, not an ending.

Rio de Janeiro, 1956. The city that had only recently resisted and resented your long delayed return, opened its arms, fell to its knees and wept as your coffin made its tumultuous way to the São João Batista cemetery, here at the end of the street from which I am writing today. Recognition. You were known again, Carmen.

Recognition. You were recalled to the minds and hearts of Brazil. Recognition. The knowledge that you identify with someone, sense something you have felt before. Lois insists on recognition, even as she reveals its impossibility. Those women she worked with in Nelson Hungria Prison recalled, identified, sensed, knew again, were known again as they moved into and beyond identification. Their absence at that first *Long Table* urged recognition of who they are as prisoners, as women, and as Maria, Jorginha, Nair, Aparecida, Dalva, Josefa, Mirela, Luciene, Janeilma....

Carmen, do you recognise Lois? Is it possible that there might be a hint of seduction, or at least a mascara-loaded wink, as the two of you face each other across the years? Femme with a twist, you launched yourself in January 1930 with a hit that has been cheered and chanted at every Rio carnival ever since: 'Eu fiz tudo pra você gostar de mim'/'I did everything to make you love me'. Abject words, resisted and overcome by the euphoric rhythm and utter joy that marches through your voice. For women who have done too much to make others – husbands, lovers, bosses, fathers, mothers, sons, and daughters – adore them, Lois brings the possibility that performance can resist such abjection. She brings them to a place that they can begin to define for themselves as home.

You both have done everything I could have ever wanted to make me love you.

Saudades!

Paul

Images from *In the House* installation,
Staging Human Rights, Rio di Janeiro, 2003.
Photos by Lois Weaver, Peggy Shaw, and Barbara Bickert.

Laundry (from *Faith and Dancing*)

Lois Weaver[17]

I used to sit in the wicker clothesbasket
under the clothesline
just behind the lilac bush
while Virginia would hang out the wash.
She wore pants on those days.
I guess it was because the clothesline was on a hill
and she thought her dress might blow over her head.
And she never did, except on Sunday, wear any underwear.
Maybe that's what I was thinking sitting there in that basket.
I wanted to see.
I wanted her to have on a dress
and I wanted it to blow over her head.
And Virginia used to say
that a woman is judged by how she hangs out her laundry.
She didn't actually say it.
She never directly said very much at all.
But she did instruct.
Be economical with the clothespins.
Let the panties share the pins.
Sheets are doubled and hung with at least three pins.
They too must share.
Towels are not folded in any way but hung straight
and together with all the other towels.
Shirts are hung from their tails at the side seams.
It is more difficult to share pins with shirts
but may be necessary to save space and equipment.
Pants are hung front on at the waist,
Although some hung them from the cuff.
Some even dried them on stretchers creating a peculiar effect
of an army of workers floating like kites at the end of the yard.
The most important thing to remember is category.
Hang things in groups.
Sheets with sheets, towels with towels
and underwear together, always on the back line.
Keep in mind that people can see these details of your life.
What I mean is, people can see how you manage your private affairs
in the way you hang out your laundry.
The other women will notice if the sheets are smooth and stretched
and if there are gaps in the underwear.

1   This is an adapted version of text from Stacy Makishi, Peggy Shaw, and Lois Weaver, *Salad of the Bad Café*, first produced in 1999, unpublished; versions of this text are archived in the Split Britches Archive at Fales Library, MSS 251, Series 1, Box 2.

2   This is an adapted excerpt from a text presented by Lois Weaver as a Keynote address at the 15th World Congress of the International Federation for Theatre Research, 'Global vs Local', hosted by the University of Helsinki, 11 August 2006. See 'Global vs Local' Programme, IFTR, University of Helsinki, 7-12 August 2006 <http://www.helsinki.fi/theatreresearch/infofiles/FIRT/firt/CongressSchedule.pdf> [accessed 13 June 2015].

3   *Tourist Information Wanted* was commissioned by Home Life Art as part of their Alternative Village Fete that took place on 3 June 2012, in Battersea Park, London, as part of the Diamond Jubilee Festival. See Home Live Art, 'Diamond Jubilee Festival: The Alternative Village Fete', *Home Live Art* <http://www.homeliveart.com/event/the-alternative-village-fete-at-the-diamond-jubilee-festival-in-battersea-park/> [accessed 13 June 2015]. The performance is described briefly on Lois Weaver, 'Tourist Information Wanted', *Public Address Systems*, 2013 <http://publicaddresssystems.org/projects/performing-the-persona-3/> and pictures are gathered on a blog titled 'Tammy and Stacy's Jubilee', 2013, *TravelPod* <http://www.travelpod.com/travel-blog-entries/starwanderings/1/1339082531/tpod.html#album> [both accessed 18 May 2015].

4   Lois Weaver, 'Domestic Terrorism: Hang Your Laundry in Public', *Public Address Systems*, 2013 <http://publicaddresssystems.org/projects/domestic-terrorism-hang-your-laundry-in-public/> [accessed 18 May 2015].

5   Weaver, 'Domestic Terrorism', 2013.

6   *FeMUSEum* was commissioned by the AHRC-funded programme *Performance Matters* for the *Trashing Performance* symposium and was presented in London and New York: Lois Weaver, 'FeMUSEum', 2011. See 'FeMUSEum', Public *Address Systems*, 2011 <http://publicaddresssystems.org/projects/femuseum/> [accessed 21 April 2015]. Lois describes *FeMUSEum* in detail in Lois Weaver and Caoimhe McAvinchey, 'Lois Weaver: Interview and Introduction by Caoimhe McAvinchey', in *Performance and Community: Commentary and Case Studies*, ed. by McAvinchey (London: Bloomsbury, 2014), pp. 21-32 (pp. 23-4).

7   Weaver in Weaver and McAvinchey, 'Lois Weaver', p. 24.

8   See 'Past Events', *Wellcome Collection*, 2015 <http://wellcomecollection.org/events/past> and 'The Institute of Sexology', *Wellcome Collection,* 2014-15 <http://wellcomecollection.org/exhibitions/institute-sexology> [both accessed 9 May 2015].

9   Doreen Agassiz-Suddens, *The History of Lesbian Theatre in New Zealand* (Auckland: Charlotte Museum Trust, 2009).

10   'The performance series *Small Acts at the Millennium* was conceived by Tim Etchells and curated and produced by a consortium of Tim Etchells and Verity Leigh of Forced Entertainment, Lois Keidan, Adrian Heathfield, and Hugo Glendinning. The project was funded by the Millennium Commission and the Arts Council of England's Live Art Commissions Fund'. *Small Acts: Performance, the Millennium and the Marking of Time*, ed. by Adrian Heathfield (London: Black Dog Publishing Limited, 2000), p. 190.

11   Japanese rice cakes.

12   Stacy Makishi, *On the Street Where You Live*, 1999. Footage of the performance is held by the Live Art Development Agency: <http://www.thisisliveart.co.uk/resources/catalogue/on-the-street-where-you-live> [accessed 13 June 2015].

13   The small, notable one, an affectionate and common nickname for Carmen Miranda in Brazil.

14   Split Britches, *Upwardly Mobile Home*: dir. by Lois Weaver; written by Deb Margolin, Peggy Shaw, and Weaver; performed by Weaver, Shaw, and Margolin. First performance: Wow Café, New York, 1984.

15   *It's a Small House and We Lived in It Always*: Created by Peggy Shaw, Lois Weaver, Suzy Willson, and Paul Clark; performed by Shaw and Weaver; produced by Clod Ensemble. First performance: Southbank Centre, London, 2000.

16   For further details of this project, see elsewhere in this book, Caoimhe McAvinchey, 'Hidden Treasures: *What Tammy Needs to Know About Prison*', p. 276.

17   This text is adapted from Lois Weaver, *Faith and Dancing: Mapping Femininity and Other Natural Disasters*, an excerpt of which is reproduced in Lizbeth Goodman (selected and introduced by), *Mythic Women/Real Women: Plays and Performance Pieces by Women* (London: Faber and Faber, 2000), 287-300 (pp. 298-9).

List The Things to guard
Against

Then + Now

1. ____ at ____ ____ ____ by Suzy
____ ____ place of

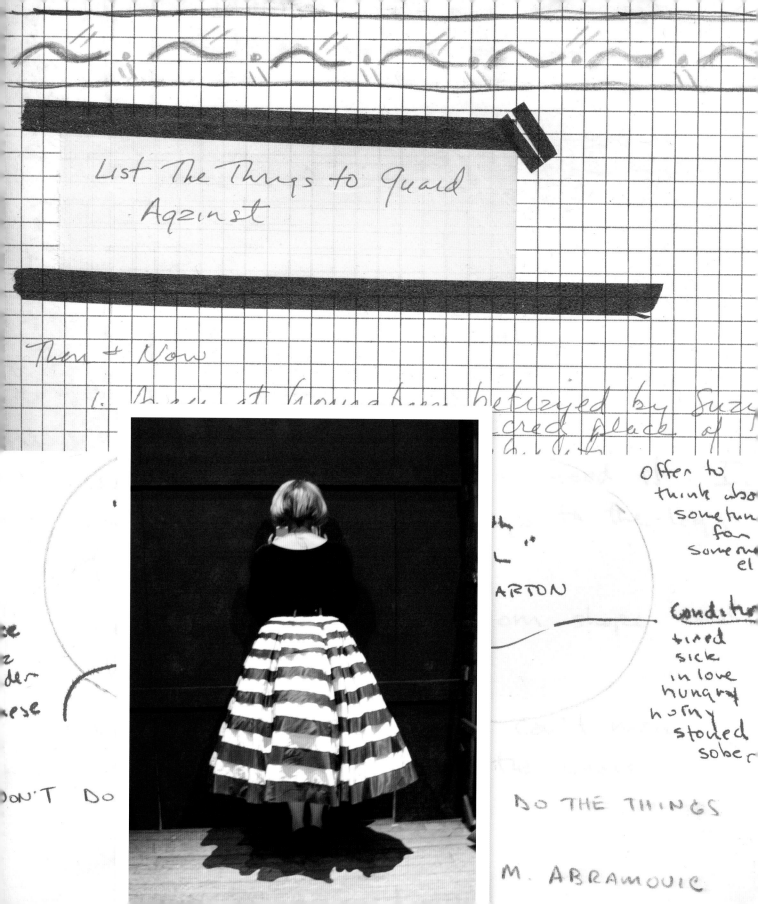

Offer to
think abou
somethin
for
someon
el

ARTON

Condition
tired
sick
in love
hungry
horny
stoned
sober

DON'T DO

DO THE THINGS

M. ABRAMOVIC

New Thoughts.
read Ms. Dalloway.
unique.
escape artist.

plucking eyebrows
" hello nice attractive
lady "

woman lifting curtain
on 3rd st.

red wine Running up
sleeve.

2.

news weeks
9:30

MAKE WORK
IN THE SPACE
YOU HAVE

to your ....tion

Afterwards

·hop

· a cm fits

Pochsitting
Find yr Due

· Bags & doy

Photo booth

· Pins (badges)

Diary Session(?)

· Wigs

· Costumes (?)

· Cameras (2)

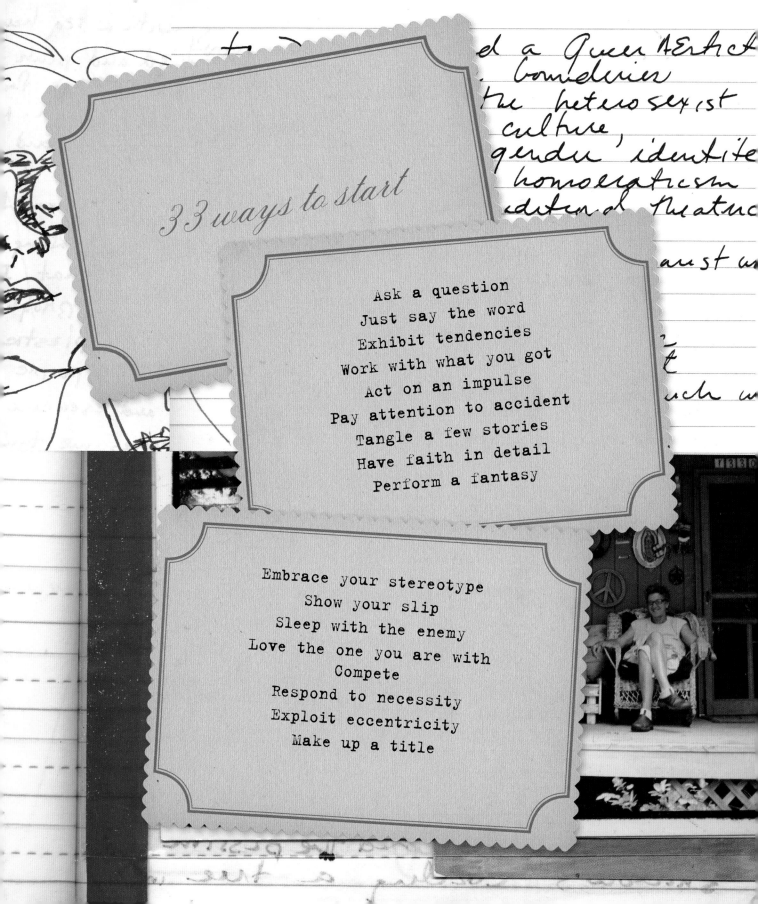

33 ways to start

Ask **a** question
Just say the word
Exhibit tendencies
Work with what you got
Act on an impulse
Pay attention to accident
Tangle a few stories
Have faith in detail
Perform a fantasy

Embrace your stereotype
Show your slip
Sleep with the enemy
Love the one you are with
Compete
Respond to necessity
Exploit eccentricity
Make up a title

TAMMY'S F WORDS

A CHORUS f TAMMY'S

ST IT

S. NO LAUNDRY

INK

SHELF

zlome

eils

e Clitoris

Spread a rumour
Do what scares you
Take something apart
Reveal a guilty secret
Ease a pain or two
Facilitate kinship
Follow obsessions
Fall in love with forms

pornograp
at affects you to sex.
obsession is the substitute

Consensual Pervert

Take a flash picture
Embody your worst nightmare
Develop a persona
Capitalise on mistakes
Listen to your friends
Perform something in reverse
Revisit your obsessions
Do it anyway

Still counting

Lois Weaver

1

2 At

3 I sat in the lap of Virginia and marvelled at the curvature of the earth. Virginia is the name of a state in the Southern United States but it was also the name of my mother and it was in her lap that I felt my girl body lean, lengthen, and mould itself against the voluptuous and humid flesh of her Blue Ridge Mountains.

4 When I was

5 I stood on the dining room table, holding the hem of my dress in both hands, and sang 'How Much Is That Doggie In the Window'. We could analyse that. 'How much is that Doggy In the Window.' Maybe consider the capitalist imperative sung in the voice of such a young consumer, the objectification of the 'waggedy tail', the subliminal message of commodification of core values in the 'I do hope that doggy's for sale'. However the development of these critical faculties came at a much later stage and probably at a much greater cost. That solid oak table in the middle of a room sandwiched between the living room and kitchen was the unintentional kindergarten of my theatrical training. It's where I learned first and foremost that it was crucial to have a stage and it didn't matter where or what it was as long as there was an audience. And by the age of

6 I had discovered longing. I kept my lavender patent leather purse in the top drawer of a chest full of Aunt Edna's oversized corsets and Virginia's extra tablecloths. Edna wore costume jewellery and tail-biting neck furs and rode the train with a matching set of luggage. Aunt Edna came to live with us after her second husband died. She took me to town on the bus once a week. Dressed and ready to go one Saturday, I ran back for my purse. I tiptoed and reached my hand into the hiding place but it was gone. Gone, and with it every trace of my little girl liberty. Virginia had decided I was too big for such a tiny purse and it was too dangerous to encourage a love for lavender patent leather.

7

8

9 was the year I spent most of my just before bedtime in front of the mirror, practising: my kisses, my tantrums, and my striptease. I wanted to be Miss America, or rather I wanted to participate in the pageant and I figured my best

shot in the talent competition would be to do a striptease. So I stood in front of the mirror with my pajamas and a towel and worked on my routine. I was going to STRIP for Miss America! But I never got to study dance. Although I did pay a lot of attention to the weather. I looked it up in the Yellow Pages once. Dance that is. Just like I looked up the word lesbian in the dictionary after I heard two boys spelling it out behind me in a voice that made me think it must be written on my back. I was only

10 and couldn't find the definition. But I got my answer. Without asking I got my answer, 'How can you be a good Christian and think about being a... dancer?' Virginia just didn't know what else to say. She would have had to admit then and probably too soon that I had a body and that body could take flight and leave the state of Virginia.

11 was my favourite number, a perfect parallel, impossible to reverse and heaven for a dyslexic who, instead of falling in love with God, fell in love with the preacher's wife. Her creamy skin, perfectly drawn lips, and teased hair teased me, until I had no choice but to sit next to her and *Softly and Tenderly* attempt to play *Just As I Am* on the upright piano in the front room of the parsonage. She coached me and coaxed me, from a shining Sunbeam for Jesus, to a cardboard-crowned and plastic-sceptred Queen Regent of the Girl's Auxiliary of the Mount Pleasant Baptist Church. Praise God for a chance to be queen.

12

13

14

15 Sweet

16 and bored stiff, sweet Jesus, with no other choice but to become a cheerleader. I wasn't pretty but they said I had a good personality, which made up for homemade clothes and a complete lack of eyebrows. Plus I had good thighs and a mother who could sew. So Virginia – my mother – was put to work making 12 very different girls look exactly alike. Cheerleading was my first experience with physical training and is where I learned how to keep spirits up even when your team was losing. But as much as I liked the belonging, I hated being the same and was constantly at risk of busting out of uniform. My release came in the form of a job in the Deb Boutique of a local department store where I was outfitted with the first and only Mary Quant mini dress

Lois Weaver in 1955 on her way for a
swim in the creek, Roanoke, Virginia.
Photographer Virginia A. Weaver.

and pair of white Courreges Go-Go boots the Blue Ridge Mountains had ever seen. I took Virginia off homemade uniform duty and put her to work on homemade Mod and vowed never to wear a Villager shirtwaist again.

17

18 When I was

19 I left the world of mothers and sisters but not Virginia. I crawled deeper into the lap of the Blue Ridge to attend a university founded in 1910 as the Radford Normal School for Girls. I went there with 4000 women – over half of whom were physical education majors. 'What do you want to major in?', they asked me. 'Drama', I answered, not realising that most of the drama took place in dormitory hallways where the future volleyball coaches wooed the future primary school teachers of America. My theatre training was a conservatory of conversion: converting the Home Economics lab into a theatre, classics into contemporaries, and girls into men. I got to play all the parts including Vershinin in *Three Sisters* and Childie in *The Killing of Sister George*. I wasn't a lesbian but I had a 'best friend' who was a softball major, drove a red convertible, and filled my room with roses every morning. I wasn't a lesbian but my heart skipped a beat each time I heard Sister George describe how she felt when she stepped into the wet and talcum-powdered footprints left by Childie after her bath. I wasn't a lesbian but if I had known then what I know now... . By now I'm

20 The faint porous lines of a blueprint are starting to emerge from the developing solutions of workshops on collective process, articles on women's liberation in *TIME Magazine*, a friend's just on the verge of legal abortion, Antigone's rage against the state, Kent State, bellbottomed cords, embroidered undershirts and *Hair*, '[L]ong beautiful hair; Shining, gleaming, streaming, flaxen, waxen; Give me down to there, hair'!

21 and by

22 I was so bored by the possibility of playing Nora in her doll's house for the rest of my life that I cancelled the flights to my postgraduate acting auditions and thereby narrowly escaped the complexity of being in the same graduating class as Meryl Streep... and Sigourney Weaver and Glenn Close. I intended to abandon my love for theatre which was – in the words of a

23-year-old – 'clearly a luxury of the middle class', and throw myself at the soup kitchens, halfway houses, and daycare centres of the poor. Instead, I ran headlong into the poor and open theatre of Jerzy Grotowski and Joe Chaikin, where I learned I could mix my theatre with my worldview. At the age of

24 I became a feminist. I took the long road to New York City through inner city Baltimore where I had gotten my hippie hair tangled in the jeans and t-shirts of the peace and justice movement. Virginia forgot to tell me about lots of things. Menstruation was one of them. Another was the unbridled patriarchy of the Left. So I left Baltimore in search of sisterhood. I scoured the *Village Voice*, sat alone in the Women's Coffee House on Seventh Avenue and on the back pew of feminist meetings at Washington Square Church. I spoke to no one. I couldn't break the code.

25 I was finally rescued by a group of women, who simply wanted to talk about the mundane details of their exquisitely complicated lives. After a year of meetings, where we were always leaving early and starting late, we became Spiderwoman: Native American, African American, and white working class women making theatre out of the rags and tags of our everyday. Spiderwoman was the name of the Hopi goddess of creativity who taught her people to weave and encouraged them to leave a flaw in their design so that her spirit could come and go. With these women, I learned to love the mistake and perform the fantasy. We could be whatever we wanted to be – regardless of age, race, class, talent, or size. We were both the princess and the frog. We wove stories of untold violence and family disappointments, appropriated dirty jokes, and wrung new meanings out of the old songs of romance. We were liberated feminists for those who had never seen such wanton display but we were women in need of liberation for those who were feminists with a capital F, who were shocked when they saw us put on our make-up and high heels for life, not for the show.

26

27 I became a femme feminist at the age of

28, just after Spiderwoman made friends with the drag artists Hot Peaches. We were due to perform in Berlin within days of each other but when Spiderwoman arrived, our trunk of costumes did not. This was the seventies and we had become a feminist company who made our costumes from children's toys and cooking utensils. Hot Peaches came to the rescue with a suitcase filled with feather boas, sequined gowns, vast wigs, and sparkling platform shoes.

As we immersed ourselves in this forbidden finery, we knew we would never again make a performance that did not involve glitter, false eyelashes, and some drag queen attitude. Like Venus from the clamshell, Tammy WhyNot was born from this trunk. I couldn't sing or keep a beat but the great pile of synthetic blonde hair, the push-up bra, the familiar hillbilly accent, the thrill of performing fantasy enabled me to embrace my childhood distaste for country music and my fear of my trailer trash roots. Tammy started work on her remix, 'Stand ON Your Man'.

29 By the time I was

30 I had been pushed up against the wall by a few prominent lesbian feminists asking me didn't I realise that Tammy's push-up bra was offensive, that I was just titillating and tempting the men in the audience, and wasn't I REALLY a lesbian? I liked the feeling of my back against the wall and knew for a fact that it wasn't the men that I wanted to tempt. So in *An Evening of Disgusting Songs and Pukey Images* I created a fake-blood-sucking, soft-shoe-dancing bouncer in blue lamé who slithered against the dark wall before pouncing into the light and onto the necks of the unsuspecting female audience. This coming out performance of predatory lust and sweet contamination left a blue lipstick kiss on the necks of a long list of victims and the taste of real blood on my lips. I was finally a lesbian at

31 Cue the entrance of the butch lesbian and the beginnings of my lesbian femme career. She was George Jones to my Tammy WhyNot, Spencer Tracy to my Katharine Hepburn, and I was Barbra Streisand to her Neil Diamond. We mined everything we knew: movies, television, rhythm and blues, working class parents, old-school lesbian friends, to find the precious metals we needed to build our altar to the blessed binary and the foundation of a new theatrical company: Split Britches. It was an old formula with a new twist. We played and displayed butch-femmeness in order to disrupt the norm, unsettle the status quo. It was both sex toy – according to Sue-Ellen Case – and work ethic – according to us – and one of the keys to the theatrical success of the company. Playing femme mixed my business with my pleasure.

32

33

34 When I turned

35 I bleached my hair all over and for good. I sat up in the stylist's chair, looked in the mirror and knew this was what I had been born to be: a blonde femme.

36 We called it WOW. Some called it a theatre, some a café. I called it a home for wayward girls. We were bleached blonde feminist outlaws. Making it up as we went along...

37 We held Butch Nights, Femme Nights, XXX Rated Xmas's, Freudian Slip Parties. We did shows like: *Fear of Laughing on the Lower East Side, Well of Horniness, Pair a' Dykes Alley*.

38 It was not so much a community as a coalition. Coalition – a group of individuals that come together for a specific amount of time to achieve a common goal.

39 Turning

40 wasn't nearly as difficult as being

41, femme, and sharing the stage with a drag queen in a performance that grew out of my obsession with Tennessee Williams. I loved my drag queen brothers and benefited from their delicious theatricality and femme expertise. But I also struggled with the assumptions that they knew more about being women than women themselves and envied their overwhelming strength and power when it came to taking stage. I could see that their strength was in the performance of resistance. They were resisting society's idea of what it meant to be a man just like butches were resisting the expectations of what it meant to be a woman and the power of both the drag queen and the butch lay in the space between, between the norm and the resistance to the norm. I wanted that space for myself: to both resist and embrace the feminine, to be a woman impersonating a woman and to take stage as a femme on her own, without the signifying arm of a butch. I set about trying to define and create the resistant femme. So at

42, after classic and exhaustive attempts at impersonating the likes of Stella Kowalski and Marilyn Monroe, Tammy WhyNot came back to the rescue. Her love of pink and orange chiffon, her invincible sense of wonder, and her ability to fail gloriously and without shame were her superpowers and she became my super-femme superhero. The wisdom of her Why Not gave me the definition I was searching for: resistant femme, (n.) a highly competent woman who just looks like she needs a little help. And at

43 I learned to embrace accident and surrender to necessity. At

44 Tammy helped me get my first real job. I heard that Gay Sweatshop in London was looking for an artistic director. Tammy told me she kinda liked the idea of living close to a queen but thought that was a long way to go just to work in a sweatshop. I assured her this would be different. I found this opportunity tempting because I had been frustrated by the Unofficial – that's what Tammy calls leadership in a collective (especially a collective like WOW). So, wanting to make it official, I proposed that I would return this Gay Sweatshop to the rough and rubble of its roots as an activist organisation. I would call it queer and start a Queer School to teach all those lonely heart artists sitting at home waiting for the phone to ring that they could do it on their own. I declared that I would programme otherness as the given and not the exception. But at

45 there was a small kink in that plan of mine. It was called funding. The Arts Council of England had given the company funding to tour conventional gay plays across the United Kingdom, not to conduct a series of international one night stands called queer performance. So at

46 I had a real taste of failure. It was something to do with the word 'work'. I was truly the milkman's daughter. And like my father, the milkman, I thought that since I was getting a paycheque, I ought to do what was expected. I did not listen to my own little voice, I did not fight bravely for my vision, did not follow my impulse – the very things that, ironically, would have made the work work. So at

47 I ran away but only got as far as a university just a mile down the road.

For someone who had cancelled her flights to a postgraduate education, I had ended up spending an awful lot of time in universities. Now that was due, I think, to my complicated love affair with performance and gender studies and well... teaching had always been a river that ran under my ground. I love teaching because it combines thinking, writing, directing, and performing into one very exquisite moment. Teaching at a university in London was perfect for Tammy's project *What Tammy Needs To Know*. But while she fed her voracious appetite for knowledge, my roots got longer, my heels lower, and my clothes looser. I entered my low maintenance/highly professional femme phase. However, Tammy kept watch, ever ready with sling-backs, wigs, and lashes. She showed up every Tuesday night for *Tammy's Art and Beauty Salon* and used her country music background to help me share all I had learned – not only about making the work but making the community to make it in and the place to perform it. At

48 Tammy became a researcher and embarked on her research project, *What Tammy Needs To Know*. By now she had found out a few things, but Tammy needed to know a whole lot more.

49 Reaching

50 wasn't such a big deal but it was a big number and to prove it I made a performance in which I counted it out slowly, one number at a time, stopping occasionally to reflect silently on one number's story or another year's significance. I finished by pointing out that if I were a piece of furniture, I would be a cherished and valuable mid-century antique.

51 At

52 I went to prison, because somebody told me that's where a lot of women live. So I went to work with a lot of women in prisons in England and Brazil. In the context of working in prisons I developed a methodology, one that I had to give up on at a moment's notice because you never really knew what was going to happen next.

Working with words like desire, obsession, fantasy were so volatile for women who had lived in fear of the roles they were forced to play in other people's desire, obsessions, and fantasies – and attempts to recast those roles were met with 'Lady we don't do drama here, we do time'. The woman who would speak those words most often was a famous pickpocket who was about my age and had been incarcerated 39 times. She told me that she – like me – was just looking for information. She could slip her hands into a bag and come out with everything she needed to know about being somebody else. It was just a question of confidence and timing, she said. Nobody ever told me that performance was so much like picking pockets. Just like it did for me, a suitcase full of wigs and boas could provide these women with a possible Tammy who could allow them to fearlessly fail or succeed without consequence. And I found so much laundry hanging everywhere that laundry became our common language for performance. Together we hung out the underwear of the abuse of having been used by systems both legal and illegal; the sheets of frustration of having been put in jail for trying to feed their family; the tattered shirts of isolation of seeing family disintegrate in their absence after having worked so hard to keep it together in the absence of their men. As a result of all this and at the age of

53 I became a Domestic Terrorist.

I obsessed about hanging my laundry in inappropriate places... on the streets of London, New York, Rio di Janeiro. I searched the everyday for more methods like the clothesline that crossed the boundary between public and private. I obsessed on the film *Antonia's Line* that features a dinner table that gets longer and longer to accommodate the unwanted and uninvited until it is so long it has to be moved out of doors. Finally at

54 I would create my own *Long Table*.

I would invite everyone to come to the table. The phrase 'come to the table' produced such beauty of embodiment. We could find a way to turn a hierarchy of experts into a table of conversationalists. We could discover a way for expertise to flow easily between statistics and story, between fact and fiction, between spectator and participant, and we would find that the ability to actually come and go from the table could be such a beautiful choreography of experience. If we had an hour or two, we could sit there and have conversations on subjects like autobiography, gender, citizenship.... At

55 I started looking everywhere for methods of exchange. I squatted the idea of a library for human rights, appropriated a museum for the feminine influence, co-opted card games in order to crack the institutional safe and spread the wealth.

I snuck up on technology at the age of

56 and talked to people a lot older than me about how to design technology for a future that wasn't ours. And that's how I found the most effective research methodology of all: intense porch sitting. I found out that if you sat long enough and easy enough and listened hard enough, you would know the context of your work, you would get what you needed to formulate your question, you'd be sitting squarely in the rocker of your methodologies, and with a little help, you would find out the things you need to know... and that no matter what, it seemed the subject would always come around to sex.

Now, let's talk about sex. I was a late bloomer but still, as an ageing femme of

57 I have celebrated 25 years of divine, magnificent, outstanding, assorted, and sordid lesbian sex. Listing the brevity and longevity, dominance and passivity would require a separate performance of counting: 1, 2, 3, 4, and counting... each lover, each tender nudge or sharp request, each hurdle of fear that, once crossed, gave way to safe surrender and then more urgent desire. 5, 6, 7, 8 –

58 And I am both hungry and satiated. I craved the violence of the grab, the relentless touch, the soul-penetrating thrust, and yet I often retired to my gentle and complete solitude. The occupation of my age was to build a graceful bridge between the two. Bridge-building is a dangerous occupation. There are always casualties: the lost dreams of a latent adolescence, the bruised butch's entreaty, 'but what about me?', and the femme's stronghold on her blessed and enduring vanity. But at

59 I found the experience and skills developed from a lifetime of longing. And I had some tools in my chest: gratitude for those who have loved me well, tenderness for my own fragile and eccentric need, energy that is challenged by the young ones and safeguarded by the older, and the belief that I will never be too old for the seduction, the courtship and the descent into the sweat and discovery of passion. At

60 Tammy begins her new research on *What Tammy Needs to Know about Getting Old and Having Sex*. And at

61 I start celebrating what Tammy found out

And she – Tammy – asked me to leave you with a list of key words:

education happens

class does make a difference

autobiography is not a dirty word

the political is personal

performance helps

participation matters

stories are key

the details are delicious

kinship is flexible

and spending time is essential

and being face to face is a pleasure.

62

63

64

65 And still counting.

challenging the boundaries

...

Eleanor Savage

Dear Eleanor
What about the laundry?
Love Lois

Dear Lois,
The laundry was hung out to dry on the line
You know the line...
out that screen door in the back.
That line...
between black lace slips and cotton shirts,
lovers and friends, bourbon and thirst; between
Macon and Big Lick, heartache and song, sweet
kisses and sweet surrender; between the need to
know and the need to run, sugar magnolias and
salty dogs, midnight howls and morning doves;
between storms a-brewin' and downpours, peach
fields and cast iron, where ya at now and where'd
you come from; between tides and salt marshes,

porch swings and old pickups, ink stained
letters and tattoed skin.
Yes the laundry is on the line.
Ain't it a wonder that anything dries in
this heat.
Love, Eleanor

---

to ... ...

+ ... ...

Jo Palmer

+

Dear Jo
how do you fold a library?
love Lois

+

Dear Lois
It will be done by hand.
We start by making a score in something solid.
It takes more than one to decide where it
starts and where it ends.
What comes in between and enables the fold
will not be straight
It will definitely not be perfect
Inside these folds is where we relinquish control
And what falls into them are the genuine parts
of people
Revealed or even discovered when they begin
to interact
This is why you make the score to make the fold.
Love Jo

Dear
Mi

Score (skôr)
v. 4. Music a) to orchestrate
7.a.

Joni Wong

Dear Joni
How can you help us end a show?
Love Lois

Dear Lois,
The short answer is: I could go to black.
The longer answer is that across all these years,
I have realized that that is one of the hardest
questions to answer. How do you ever know when
something is done? I can only help by asking
questions. What did you want to say? Have you said
it? Does it feel like you are holding a balloon
that you've just blown up? Is there is enough air in
there for the balloon to hold its shape, the tension
felt in its skin? Will it will float in the air when
you tap it instead of flopping to the ground? If you
blow any more air into it, will it explode? Then
you've found the end of the show.

love, Joni

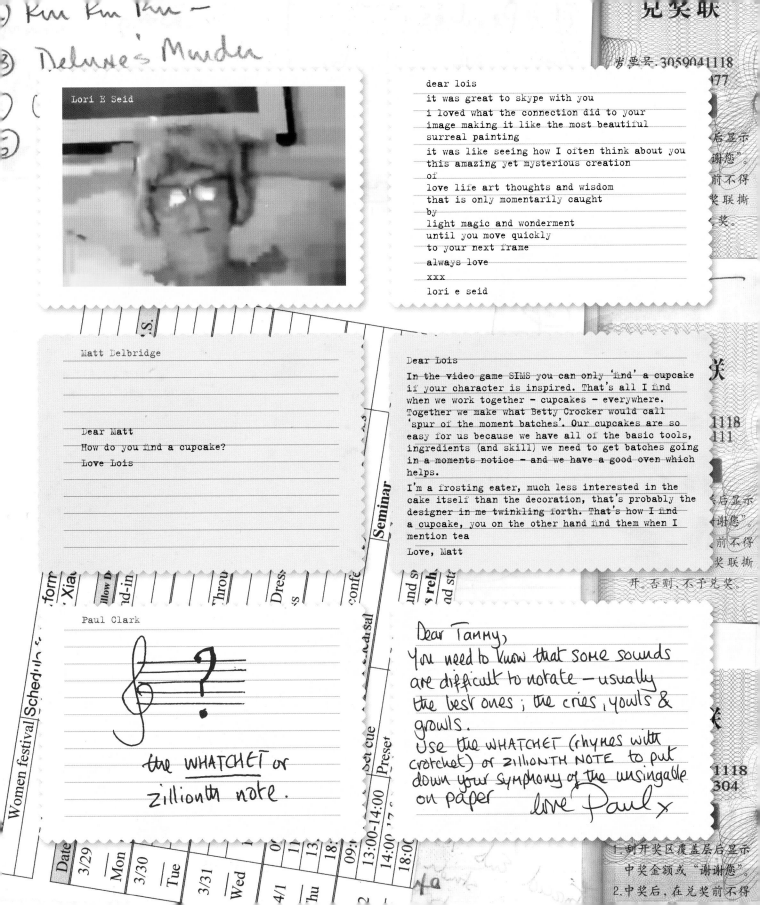

Lori E Seid

dear lois

it was great to skype with you

i loved what the connection did to your
image making it like the most beautiful
surreal painting

it was like seeing how I often think about you
this amazing yet mysterious creation
of
love life art thoughts and wisdom
that is only momentarily caught
by
light magic and wonderment
until you move quickly
to your next frame

always love

xxx

lori e seid

Matt Delbridge

Dear Matt
How do you find a cupcake?
Love Lois

Dear Lois

In the video game SIMS you can only 'find' a cupcake
if your character is inspired. That's all I find
when we work together – cupcakes – everywhere.
Together we make what Betty Crocker would call
'spur of the moment batches'. Our cupcakes are so
easy for us because we have all of the basic tools,
ingredients (and skill) we need to get batches going
in a moments notice – and we have a good oven which
helps.

I'm a frosting eater, much less interested in the
cake itself than the decoration, that's probably the
designer in me twinkling forth. That's how I find
a cupcake, you on the other hand find them when I
mention tea

Love, Matt

Paul Clark

the WHATCHET or
zillionth note.

Dear Tammy,
You need to know that some sounds
are difficult to notate — usually
the best ones ; the cries, yowls &
growls.
Use the WHATCHET (rhymes with
crotchet) or ZILLIONTH NOTE to put
down your symphony of the unsingable
on paper
love Paul x

Seminar

Women festival Schedule ... form ... Xia ... llow D ... nd-in ... Throu ... Dress ... s ... confe ... nd s ... s reh. ... d str ... ursal ... Set cue ... Preset

Date	Mon 3/29	Tue 3/30	Wed 3/31	Thu 4/1						13:00-14:00	14:00	18:0
	09:	11.	13.	18:	09:							

Vivian Stoll

Dear Viv
How do you sing a broken song?
Love Lois

Dear Lois,
Here's one way to sing a broken song:
Go someplace between holding it all together
and letting it all fall apart.
Fragments dangle between absurdity and
disaster, lost and found, old and new,
past and future.
Not too loud and heavy, not too soft and light.
Stay suspended there for a while...
Then stop thinking at all and let your voice
come out.
Love, Viv

Debra Miller

Dear Debra
How do you paint a lunch lavender?
Love Lois

Dearest LoLo,

Well the first thing I would do is send everybody
staying at the Lexington art camp away for the
day. After a week of real work, those gals from
WOW deserve a break, after all!

Then I would find some very old paint, preferably
the color of a well known spring flower. Next
I would have two fabulous, femme inclined
individuals decide to take up arms against the
current boring color.

BEST
KNICKERS
DAY!

The Intrepid Two would have a great time thinking
of all the meals that would be made for the upcoming
summer acting camp and performances. We know how
much making art makes one hungry. Did I mention
that the paint should be old and possibly toxic? (it
was 1985 what did we know about toxicity!)

Finally, I would awake the next morning to find that
both of the "artists" in question spent the night
praying over the porcelain throne.

And that's how I would paint a lunch lavender.

Love and smooches, Debra aka Dub

Beccy Trowler

Dear Beccy
How do you know what's true?
Love Lois

Dear Lois
By being real. If you can be real, even for a
moment, you can feel what is and isn't true.
Love, Beccy

Bette Bourne and Paul Shaw

Dear Bette and Paul
What about the strangeness of stranagers?
Love Lois

Dear Lois
My most strangely delightful memory was our
travelling to Majorca to begin our writing
process via the farmhouse of Madame Paul
Eluard on the outskirts of Paris and having
the biscuits for our tea served on real Picasso
plates and her saying, when she noticed my
amazement, that she uses them because they will
only go to a museum when she dies.

I also remember that strangely wonderful
rehearsal when Bette took us through a whole
dance routine and when we got to go back over it
no one could remember a single step and we spent
the next half hour in complete hysterics with
Peggy rolling around on the floor.
Love, Bette and Paul

Stormy Brandenberger

Dear Stormy
How do you move a mountain?
Love Lois

Dear Lois
I quietly watch and wait for the mountain
to move me. Once I understand its rhythm
and force, we dance through new and unknown
territory.
Lois, "moving a mountain" was very difficult
for me to think about. I cannot approach a
choreographic work with the thought that I
must change the performer in front of me
rather than see fresh possibilities that
might allow me to think creatively. The joy
and challenge in risking "chance" is a more
powerful force than the fear of failing.
All My Love,
Stormy

Lois Weaver Timeline

Jen Harvie with Lois Weaver

We have attempted here to list much of Lois's professional work, as well as a handful of important personal events, chiefly to help readers navigate her long career and contextualise events referred to throughout the book. However, this timeline is necessarily incomplete. For example, we have not attempted to list all productions on a tour, or all revived and revised productions of each show that Lois and her collaborators have worked on (there are many of these). Furthermore, her career is ongoing. The timeline also almost certainly includes inaccuracies or flaws. Within any given year, for example, we have tried to place events in their proper sequence, but this may not always be accurate. More broadly, as Lois and Muriel Miguel note in their interview included earlier in this book, flaws are both part of real life, and can be opportunities for creativity to take seed. In other words, some flaws are welcome in Lois's work and story.

1949 26 October: born in Roanoke, Virginia, to Virginia (38) and Russell Weaver (38). Elder siblings are Coy Lee Weaver (14) and Judy Ann Weaver (9).

1964 As a high school student, plays the part of Polly Ann Podger, a poor relation, in the Lions Club Annual Review at Mount Pleasant Elementary School, Roanoke County.

1968 Awarded Good Citizen award by the Daughters of the American Revolution; is proud of this at first for its recognition of her good citizenry, but later embarrassed by its connection to the Daughters of the American Revolution.

Graduates from William Byrd High School, Vinton, Virginia.

Goes to Radford College (now University).

1969 Tours with Virginia Baptist Drama Team.

1970 Spring: performs title role in Sophocles' *Antigone* at Radford College.

Performs in summer stock theatre at Mill Mountain Playhouse, Roanoke, Virginia, as The Bride in Jean Cocteau's *The Eiffel Tower Wedding Party*, and in a devised show titled *US* in which she recounts a dream about having sex with Jesus (see her 'Jesus Wept', above).

Starts activism in Southern Baptist Convention. Over the course of the next few years speaks twice at Conventions to 13,000 Southern Baptist preachers and their wives about issues of social justice in the church.

Autumn: performs at Radford College in *The Killing of Sister George*.

1971-72 Becomes first female president of the Virginia Baptist Student Union.

1971 Becomes radicalised by reading *Newsweek* on feminism with Gloria Steinem on cover.

Performs summer stock theatre at Mill Mountain Playhouse, Roanoke, Virginia, as Baby Roo in *Winnie the Pooh* and as Nellie Ewell in Tennessee Williams' *Summer and Smoke*.

1972 Directs Jean-Claude van Itallie's *The Serpent* on Radford College's main stage as her graduating project.

Graduates from Radford College with an honours degree in Theatre and Education.

After graduation: receives audition invitations for postgraduate study in acting at Florida State University, Yale University, and New York University (Tisch School of the Arts). Has what she's described as 'a bit of a drop out summer', being slightly disaffected with conventional acting, discouraged by costs of further study, and disturbed by her brother Coy's heart attack at age 38 (with three kids) as well as the death, caused by a heart condition, of a friend from the Virginia Baptist Drama Team.

1972 Moves to Baltimore: involved in peace and social justice work; gets involved with Baltimore Theatre Project and studies with members of Open Theater; decides to come back to theatre.

1973 Moves to New York City.

1974 Does a lot of theatre workshops, including with members of the Open Theater and the Performance Group.

Works in a fish market, as a bike messenger and at lots of other jobs in New York.

First public appearance of the group of women who will later form the core of Spiderwoman Theater in a short piece entitled *Storyweaving*.

1975 Teaches at a residential school for girls with emotional disorders.

Appears in professional performance in New York City for the first time, in Amiri Baraka's *The Sidney Poet Heroical*, directed by Baraka himself.

Performs in Karen Malpede's *Rebecca*, a play about the Triangle Shirtwaist Factory fire in New York City in 1911.

Co-founds Spiderwoman Theater.

Attends Naropa Institute in Boulder, Colorado, a Tibetan institute of spiritual and cultural study where many artists and cultural gurus offer workshops.

Performs in *Women in Violence*, Spiderwoman Theater. Show opens in New York City, tours USA and Europe.

1977 Teaches for the first time at a university, Emerson College. Salary is $1000. Observing that students arrive drowsy after lunch, Lois institutes a 20-minute nap at the start of each class.

Meets Peggy Shaw in Europe on tour.

1977-78 Co-creates and performs in Spiderwoman Theater's *The Lysistrata Numbah!*, directed by Muriel Miguel. Tammy WhyNot (originally Whynot) is born in this show.

1978 Peggy Shaw joins Spiderwoman Theater.

Co-creates and performs in Spiderwoman Theater's *Cabaret: An Evening of Disgusting Songs and Pukey Images*.

1979 Appears in Spiderwoman's *Cabaret: An Evening of Disgusting Songs and Pukey Images* at Vrouwenfestival [Women's Festival], the Melkweg, Amsterdam; idea of WOW is conceived here with Peggy Shaw, Jordy Mark, and Pamela Camhe.

Gets together with Peggy Shaw.

Plays Dorothy Parker in Hot Peaches' production of *Parker, Ms*, a retrospective of the life and poetry of Dorothy Parker, at Hot Peaches' loft.

1980 Co-creates *Split Britches: A True Story* with Naja Beye, Peggy Shaw, Pam Verge, Cathy Gollner; first produced in a rough workshop version at WOW Festival, New York City.

WOW International Festival is held in one of Andy Warhol's old spaces, the Electric Circus. Each evening performance is opened by the Schockettes (a play on the Rockefeller Center's show-opening Rockettes), a can-can line of eight performers in tights, white shirts, a tie, and white sneakers.

1981 *Split Britches* produced by Spiderwoman Theater Company with texts by Deb Margolin, performed by Pam Verge, Peggy Shaw and Lois Weaver.

Second WOW International Theatre Festival is held, mostly in the Ukrainian National Home, East Village, New York.

Split Britches at the WOW Festival, New York City, with Deborah Margolin, Peggy Shaw, and Lois Weaver, then toured to the Boston Women's Festival.

Leaves Spiderwoman Theater.

Co-founds Split Britches with Peggy Shaw, and Deb Margolin.

1982 Happens to walk past Barnard College on Manhattan's Upper West Side on her way to teach a performance workshop for children at the Riverside Church. Notices Barnard is hosting the famous conference 'Towards a Politics of Sexuality'. Returns after her workshop in time to hear author and activist Amber Hollibaugh's pro-sex, anti-censorship talk in response to the anti-pornography protests going on outside on the street.

Co-directs *Bustin' out the Box: A Folk Play of Stereo-types*, produced by Children's Theatre Video Workshop, presented by American Folk Theatre, conceived and written by The Company, directed by Cristobal Carambo and Lois Weaver, set design by Maureen (Moe) Angelos.

Co-creates Split Britches' *Beauty and the Beast*, first performed at University of the Streets, Avenue A at 7th Avenue, East Village, New York.

Performs *Split Britches* at the Oval House, London, booked by Kate Crutchley who also helps book a tour with Third Eye (Glasgow), Midland Arts Centre (Birmingham), Midland Group (Nottingham), Chapter Arts (Cardiff), and a venue in Manchester. Pay in London was approximately £250/night upstairs or £100/night downstairs which Lois describes as pretty good. Later performed *Split Britches* at ICA (London).

Performs *Split Britches* at the Melkweg, Amsterdam, and at the Copenhagen Fool's Festival as well as Italy and Germany in Split Britches' first European tour.

1983 With Peggy Shaw and others co-founds WOW Café Theatre at 330 East 11th Street, New York City, a performance space dedicated to producing works by and for women.

Split Britches perform *Split Britches* at the Nat Horne Theatre, off-Broadway, New York City.

Split Britches is invited to perform *Split Britches* at the Women and Theatre Programme Pre-conference of the Association for Theatre in Higher Education (ATHE), Minneapolis. Lois describes this as 'the beginning of the beginning of people paying attention to us'.

Split Britches' *Beauty and the Beast* (script by Deb Margolin, additional text by Peggy Shaw and Lois Weaver, directed by Lois Weaver) performed at WOW Café, New York City.

1984 *Upwardly Mobile Home*; Deb Margolin, Peggy Shaw, Lois Weaver; directed by Lois Weaver; first produced at WOW Café, 330 East 11th Street, New York City.

Directs *Sappho and Aphrodite*, written by Karen Malpede.

Lois's father, Russell Weaver, dies.

Directs *Tennessee Waltz* at WOW on East 11th Street.

Adapts and directs a version of Hans Christian Andersen's *The Snow Queen*, designed by Peggy Shaw, for their briefly formed company Working Girls Repertory at WOW on East 11th Street.

Performs in *Patience and Sarah*, by Isabel Miller, adapted by Joyce Halliday, directed by Kate Crutchley; produced at the Ovalhouse then the Cockpit, London.

1985 WOW Café moves to 59 East 4th Street, New York City.

Directs *St Joan of Avenue C*, written by Deb Margolin, Peggy Shaw, Lois Weaver, in collaboration with the company; about housing and gentrification on Manhattan's Lower East Side.

Spends summer upstate in Lexington, NY, at Art Awareness Inc., based in an old hotel. Many WOW women attend and convert an old kitchen into a cafeteria; provide technical and production support to other groups; run the cultural programme and present summer performances. Lois runs weekend workshops called *Acting Up and Out* with Linda Putnam and Emma Missouri.

Split Britches wins a *Villager* award for Best Ensemble.

Split Britches members re-unite with Spiderwoman to perform *Cabaret: An Evening of Disgusting Songs and Pukey Images*.

December (to January 1986): directs Cheryl Moch's *Cinderella: The Real True Story* at the WOW Café.

1986 Directs Eugène Ionesco's *The Chairs*, presented by Present Stage, Northampton Centre for the Arts, Massachusetts.

Collaboratively creates, directs, and performs in *Dress Suits to Hire*, text by Holly Hughes; first presented as a reading at the WOW Café.

Split Britches wins an OBIE cash award.

Works on *Queer Justice* at WOW in which 12 lesbian 'jurors' tell stories based on their own lives/fantasies.

1987 Stars as filmmaker Jo in Sheila McLaughlin's feature film *She Must Be Seeing Things*.

Directs *Patience and Sarah* at WOW and the Women's Interart in New York City.

Premiere of *Dress Suits to Hire*, at P.S. 122 at the Veselka Performance Festival, New York City.

December-February 1988: *Dress Suits to Hire* produced at Women's Interart, New York City.

1988 Plays undertaker Sue alongside Peggy Shaw as dentist Rory in Giovanna Manana's soft porn film, *Long Awaited Pleasure* (Pop Video productions).

UK premiere of *Dress Suits to Hire*, Ovalhouse, London.

Dress Suits to Hire tours the midwest including the University of Michigan.

Little Women: The Tragedy; Deb Margolin, Peggy Shaw, Lois Weaver; directed by Lois Weaver; first produced this spring at WOW Café, 59 East 4th Street, New York City.

Split Britches premiers on public television in a version directed by Mathew Geller in association with WGBH/WNET Television and the New York Foundation for the Arts' 'Artists and New Works Programme'.

1989 *Little Women: The Tragedy* at Interart Theater, New York City, which included a performance for the Women & Theatre Pre-conference at the Association for Theatre in Higher Education (ATHE), New York.

Autumn: Split Britches are in residence at Hampshire College and teach on the course Feminist Theatre/*Alcestis*, instructors Rhonda Blair and Sabrina Hamilton, in which the class produces a show based on Euripides' *Alcestis* entitled *Honey, I'm Home: The Alcestis Story*. Created by the Split Britches Company in collaboration with Theatre Three, directed by Lois Weaver, with Lois as Alcestis, Peggy as Admetus, and Deb Margolin as Death. Show performed 8-11 and 15-18 November.

1990 First performs at La MaMa Experimental Theatre Club [E.T.C.], New York City, in The Club with *Anniversary Waltz*, celebrating Lois and Peggy's tenth year Anniversary.

1991 Co-directs with Peggy Shaw the American premiere reading of Ginka Steinwachs' *Monsieur-Madame* as part of the programme Postmodernism and Feminist Theatre, Goethe House, New York, 23 September, at The Club at La MaMa. Sue-Ellen Case arranges the event and Lois and Peggy invite collaborators to perform. Lisa Kron plays the publisher with a crocodile hat; Peggy Shaw appears as George Sand; the Five Lesbian Brothers sing 'Hey There Georgie Girl'; Laka Daisical appears as Chopin with a red mouth coil which she pulls out as blood when she coughs. The next day the artists attend a panel on postmodernism and feminism; Peggy Phelan talks about the decapitation of capitalism represented by Peggy's removal of Lisa's crocodile hat in order to do a swing dance.

Directs, co-creates, and performs in *Belle Reprieve*; commissioned by La MaMa E.T.C., New York City and Drill Hall, London, co-produced by Split Britches and Bloolips. Show tour includes London, March 1991; La MaMa E.T.C., April 1991; Double Edge Theater, Boston; Alice B Theatre, Seattle and Theatre Rhinoceros, San Francisco January-March 1992; Britain and Ireland 31-performance tour, including, Arts Centre, University of Warwick; The Leadmill, Sheffield; The Green Room, Manchester; The Junction, Cambridge; Gardner Arts Centre, University of Sussex, Brighton; Phoenix Arts Centre, Leicester; Grand Theatre, Blackpool; Old Museum Arts Centre, Belfast.

Co-wins *Village Voice* OBIE Award with Peggy Shaw, Bette Bourne, and Paul Shaw for ensemble acting in *Belle Reprieve*.

1992 Split Britches premieres *Lesbians Who Kill* at La MaMa E.T.C., New York City.

1993 Becomes Joint Artistic Director of Gay Sweatshop. Moves to London part-time.

Co-curates with Lois Keidan international performance festival *Queer Bodies*, co-produced by Gay Sweatshop and the ICA, London.

During a one-semester residency at the University of Hawaii at Manoa, at the invitation of Juli Burk, Split Britches co-creates with 28 students *Valley of the Dolls' House*, based on Ibsen's *A Doll House*, Jacqueline Suzanne's *Valley of the Dolls*, Angela Carter's *The Loves of Lady Purple*, together with the personal stories and experiences of the students in the company.

Stars in Tom Eyen's *The White Whore and the Bit Player*, at La MaMa E.T.C., New York City, directed by Eric Concklin.

1994 Co-curates with Lois Keidan UK performance festival *It's Not Unusual*, co-produced by Gay Sweatshop and the ICA, London.

Co-creates and performs *Femme Lecture Dem* with Peggy Phelan at the ICA, London.

Premier of *Lust and Comfort*, a Split Britches/Gay Sweatshop production hosted by It's Queer Up North, Manchester.

1995 Lois's mother Virginia Weaver dies.

1996-97 Tours solo show *Faith and Dancing: Mapping Femininity and Other Natural Disasters*, co-commissioned by Gay Sweatshop and It's Queer Up North; first performed at the Green Room, Manchester, UK, as part of the It's Queer Up North festival, 1996; US premiere at La MaMa, E.T.C., May 1997; subsequently toured more widely; excerpts appear in *Mythic Women/Real Women* (2000), selected and introduced by Lizbeth Goodman.

1997 Awarded the 1997 Hunt-Scammon Distinguished Artist Residency at the College of William and Mary, Virginia. Teaches 'Re-inventing the Southern Voice' and produces a devised performance entitled *Be Nice or Leave*.

Takes up a part-time post in Drama, Queen Mary University of London (then, Queen Mary and Westfield College, University of London).

1999 Performs *Salad of the Bad Café*, co-created with Stacy Makishi and Peggy Shaw, many versions and many places, including at the Drill Hall, London; Dance Theatre Workshop and BAX and La MaMa E.T.C., New York City; Wellesley College, and UC Berkeley and Riverside. There are two fully different versions and videos of both.

Performs at International Festival of Women's Performance, New Zealand, an event Lois describes as 'really important to us, mostly because of the bicultural partnership with a group of Maori women'.

Directs Holly Hughes in Hughes' show *Preaching to the Perverted*.

In collaboration with the Live Art Development Agency (LADA), London, launches East End Collaborations (EEC), a series of events supporting graduates and emerging artists working with Live Art; EEC runs annually until 2009 and is followed from 2010 with Fresh AiR. EEC includes a professional development programme entitled *Everything You Wanted to Know about Live Art but Were Afraid to Ask....*

1999-2000 Co-devises *It's a Small House and We Lived in It Always* with Peggy Shaw and the Clod Ensemble (Suzy Wilson and Paul Clark), commissioned by the Southbank Centre, London; first performed at the Purcell Room in 1999 as part of the British Festival of Visual Theatre. Revised version performed at Performance Studies international (PSi), Tucson, Arizona, 2000. Tours US, UK, and Brazil.

2000 Creates *When the Tide Is Out* with Stacy Makishi, London.

With Peggy Shaw and many other women, participates in Eeo Stubblefield's performance ritual *Women Walking with Chairs*, in and near Phoenicia, New York.

2001 Co-devises *Miss Risqué*, with Peggy Shaw and the Clod Ensemble, which tours with *It's a Small House and We Lived in It Always* as *Double Agency*.

Salon de la Femme, a community performance performed at Dyke Night at the Walker Art Center during Gay Pride in Minneapolis, using the structure of *Miss Risqué*.

2002-03 Participates in *Staging Human Rights*, a performance and human rights project working in criminal justice systems. With Peggy Shaw and Caoimhe McAvinchey, designs and runs workshops in four women's prisons in the UK and Brazil.

2003 Produces *Junkyard Cabaret* at the Roxbury Arts Center in upstate New York, conceived and curated by Lois Weaver and Peggy Shaw; hosted by Lois Weaver as Tammy WhyNot, featuring music by Terry Dame's Electric Junkyard Gamelan; including guest performances by Helen Paris and Leslie Hill.

Produces first *Long Table* as part of *In the House*, an installation with and about women in prison, in Rio de Janeiro.

Co-creates *On the Scent* with Curious (Leslie Hill and Helen Paris). *On the Scent* premiered at the Fierce Festival, Birmingham in June 2003 and has toured the UK, US, Europe, China, and Australia.

2004 With Peggy Shaw creates a workshop version of *Dress Suits to Hire* with 16 women as part of the Women Theatre Festival in Taipei, Taiwan.

What Tammy Needs to Know... premiers at Dixon Place, New York City, and then the Drill Hall, London, Warsaw, Poland, and Helsinki, Finland.

First performs *Domestic Terrorist: Hanging Your Laundry in Public* in New York City during the Republican National Convention.

2005 Performs in re-staged version of *Dress Suits to Hire* at the University of Texas at Austin, La MaMa E.T.C., New York City, and the Drill Hall, London.

2006 Is Artistic Director of Performance Studies international #12: *Performing Rights*, Queen Mary University of London.

Co-develops the Library of Performing Rights with the Live Art Development Agency.

Performs *Dear Diary – Diary of a Domestic Terrorist* at the International Federation for Theatre Research 15th World Congress, Helsinki, Finland.

Awarded the Martin Luther King, Jr.-Cesar Chavez-Rosa Parks Visiting Professorship, University of Michigan, Ann Arbor, Michigan.

2007 Collaborates on *Democratising Technology* with Queen Mary University of London colleagues in the Department of Computer Science. Project explores ways of facilitating people's engagement with digital design and includes workshops led by Lois/Tammy, a DVD, an exhibition, and a symposium.

Hosts *Long Tables* on 'Manufacturing Bodies' and on 'Violence and the Politics of Representation' (Hemispheric Institute for the Study of Politics and Performance, Encuentro 2007, Buenos Aires, Argentina).

2008 *What Tammy Needs to Know about Getting Old and Having Sex* is commissioned by and premiers at Chelsea Theatre, London.

Split Britches' *Miss America* premiers at La MaMa E.T.C., New York City; written and performed by Peggy Shaw and Lois Weaver; developed in collaboration with Stormy Brandenberger.

2009 Creates and performs in *Performing in Agony*, based on Miroslav Krleza's *Behind the Mask*, created through an international collaboration with Croatian academic, Dr. Lada C. Feldman, and British director Julia Bardsley; Rijeka, Croatia, as part of a PSi regional conference.

UK Premier of Split Britches' *Miss America* at the People's Palace, Queen Mary University of London.

Split Britches' *Retro(per)spective* begins to tour US Colleges and Universities.

Split Britches has a residency at the University of Richmond to create *Lost Lounge*, which premiers at Dixon Place, New York City.

Hosts *Long Tables* on Feminism (Red Room Platform: Women's Edition, London); Queer Autobiography (Queer Autobiography Conference, King's College London); Change in America (PSi, Zagreb, Croatia); Gender and Citizenship and Staging Citizenship (Hemispheric Institute for the Study of Politics and Performance, Encuentro 2009, Bogota, Colombia).

2010 Curates Outside AiR Festival at Queen Mary University of London.

With Live Art Development Agency, London, launches Fresh AiR, an initiative to support graduates and emerging live artists; this runs also in 2011 and as (Re)Fresh 2013, followed up by Peopling the Palace(s) from 2014.

Split Britches performs *Lost Lounge* at Queen Mary University of London and in Zagreb at the Performance Studies international Conference.

Card Table commissioned by the Affective Archives, Performance Studies international Conference regional conference in Italy.

Launches AiR Supply programme to support development of emerging performance producers.

Hosts *Long Tables* on Lineages, Memories, Legacies (at The Pigs of Today are the Hams of Tomorrow Symposium, Plymouth Arts Centre, Plymouth, UK); and The Artist, the People, the Place (Outside AiR Festival, Queen Mary University of London).

2011 *Lost Lounge* performed again at Dixon Place, New York City.

FeMUSEum commissioned by *Performance Matters* and installed at Toynbee Hall, London. Created with Bird la Bird, Amy Lamé, and Carmelita Tropicana.

First *Porch Sitting – Porch Sitting* for the New Year – held at La MaMa E.T.C., New York City.

2012 Split Britches' *Ruff*, co-written by Peggy and Lois, directed by Lois and performed by Peggy, commissioned by P.S. 122 and premiered at the Coil Festival, New York City.

Creates and shows *What Tammy Found Out*, as Inaugural Lecture for Professorship at Queen Mary University of London.

Split Britches given Edwin Booth Award for Contribution to American Theatre.

33 x 3: Split Britches' Reunion, Split Britches' anniversary celebrations at La MaMa E.T.C., New York City, with Peggy Shaw and Deb Margolin, featuring work of Stacy Makishi and Desiree Burch.

Porch Sitting at La MaMa E.T.C., New York City, on 'the future of queer and feminist performance'.

Hosts *Long Tables* on Labour (Performance Space, London); Lineages and Legacies (La MaMa E.T.C., New York City); Senses of Aversion (Sexuality Summer School, University of Manchester, UK); Performance as Research (Queensland University of Technology, Brisbane); State of the Field (ASTR Conference, Nashville, TN); Performance and Activism (Stanford University, California); What Does Queer Performance Want? (Hemispheric Institute, New York University).

2013 Co-curates Peopling the Palace(s) festival of performance and discussions at Queen Mary University of London.

Split Britches' *Ruff*, co-written by Peggy Shaw and Lois Weaver, directed by Lois and performed by Peggy, premiers at the Chelsea Theatre, London and tours UK.

Develops *Green Screening* a creative workshop format using green screen technology.

Hosts *Long Tables* on Women, Feminism and Austerity (Roehampton University, London); Gender and Drag (Women Festival, Slovenia).

Collaborates with Live Art Development Agency on *Restock Rethink Reflect Three: on Live Art and Feminism*. One outcome is *Are We There Yet? A Study Room Guide on Live Art and Feminism* curated by Lois Weaver in collaboration with PhD candidate Eleanor Roberts and the Live Art Development Agency (2013-15).

2014 Awarded a Guggenheim Fellowship.

Co-curates Peopling the Palace(s) festival of performance and discussions at Queen Mary University of London.

Hosts *Long Tables* on Live Art (Festival of Live Art, FOLA, Melbourne, Australia); Representing Bodies and Experience (Hemispheric Institute for the Study of Politics and Performance, Encuentro 2014, Montreal, Quebec).

Made Senior Fellow of the Hemispheric Institute for the Study of Politics and Performance.

Performs *What Tammy Needs to Know about Getting Old and Having Sex*, La MaMa E.T.C, New York City.

2015 Conducts 'Tammy in the House' residency for *The Institute of Sexology*, Wellcome Collection, London.

Performs *What Tammy Needs to Know about Getting Old and Having Sex* in Manchester, Brighton, Glasgow, and London, UK.

Co-curates Peopling the Palace(s) festival of performance and discussions at Queen Mary University of London.

Hosts *Long Tables* on Why Sex Matters, and The Ins and Outs of Sex, and Sex and Ageing (Wellcome Collection, London); How We Talk about Gender (Pink Fringe, Brighton); Decision, as a companion to the Carsten Höller exhibition, *Decision* (Hayward Gallery, Southbank Centre).

Tammy WhyNot and her NYC WhyNets,
*What Tammy Needs to Know About Getting
Old and Having Sex* (2014), La MaMa, NYC.
Photographer Lori E. Seid.

Acknowledgements

We have tried to acknowledge those who have made up this life that became a career that is now a book by naming them whenever possible and inviting them to continue the conversation. However, there will be some that we will have missed but who are still woven into the story as it is told this time and there are some names that will always need repeating:

Virginia mountains and Weaver family for making it hard to leave and easy to come back

Peggy Shaw for all the years of good times off stage and great timing onstage

Both Peggy Shaw and Deb Margolin who had the foolhardy courage to follow our most foolish impulses

Collaborators, who show up in the rehearsal room, still, after all these years: Stormy Brandenberger, Susan Young, Vivian Stoll, Lori E. Seid, Matt Delbridge. And those who work continually to help make things happen: Rose Sharp and Lois Keidan

Some friends, colleagues, lovers and places that occupy the spaces between love and work: Beccy Trowler, Ali Mears, Eleanor Savage, Stacy Makishi, Vick Ryder, Joy Tomchin, Karena Rahall, Cynthia Baker, Alice Forrester, Judy Rosen, Sue Baynton, Laka D., Bette Bourne, Paul Shaw, James Neale-Kennerley, Hemispheric Institute, La MaMa, Dixon Place, Berrybook Road, NY, and many more.

New energy and fresh inspiration for the future: Tracy Gentles, Jo Palmer, Hannah Maxwell, and Claire Nolan

And especially to Stacy Wolf and Deanna Shoemaker who originally set the idea of this book in motion

We thank Lois Keidan, CJ Mitchell, and Dominic Johnson for commissioning the book for the Intellect Live series. We thank those who contributed to the book's images, including Eva Weiss, Uzi Parnes, Morgan Grenwald, Lori E. Seid, and Christa Holka plus many others. We thank Catherine Silverstone and Kim Solga for responding to the book in draft, and all those who contributed text, including some already named above plus Moe Angelos, Rosana Cade, David Caines, Cynthia Carr, Sue-Ellen Case, Elin Diamond, Jess Dobkin, Jill Dolan, Lisa Duggan, Benjamin Gillespie, Gerry Harris, Charles L. Hayes, Dee Heddon, Paul Heritage, Leslie Hill, Lauren Barri Holstein, Holly Hughes, Erin Hurley, Johanna Linsley, Caoimhe McAvinchey, Muriel Miguel, Joan Nestle, Helen Paris, Peggy Phelan, Anne Tallentire, and Diana Taylor. Thanks also for technical and practical support at Queen Mary University of London (QMUL) from Harriet Curtis, Eleanor Roberts, Sarah Bartley, Charlie Cauchi, and Sarah Mullan (whose extensive bibliographic work ours draws on), and, at the Live Art Development Agency (LADA), Katy Baird, Aaron Wright, and Alex Eisenberg.

Our work has been further supported by colleagues in Drama and English at QMUL, including (besides those named above): Faisal Abul, Julia Bardsley, Katie Beswick, Jonathan Boffey, Julia Boffey, Shane Boyle, Ali Campbell, Richard Coulton, Nadia Davids, Maria Delgado, Jules Deering, Markman Ellis, Rob Ellis, Bridget Escolme, Jenny Gault, Patricia Hamilton, Tracy Hammill, Maggie Inchley, Suzi Lewis, Huw Marsh, Matthew Mauger, Michael McKinnie, Aoife Monks, Daphne Rayment, Nicholas Ridout, Kate Russell, Beverley Stewart, Martin Welton, and David Wright. We also thank staff at the British Library and at the Fales Library and Special Collections at Elmer Holmes Bobst Library of New York University.

Jen personally thanks: Julie Crawford, Liza Yukins, and Jonas and Maeve for New York love; Judy Harvie; and, as always, Deb Kilbride.

Some of the material which appears in this book has been published previously, usually in slightly different forms. We are grateful to these publishers and co-authors for material adapted from: Lois Weaver, *Faith and Dancing: Mapping Femininity and Other Natural Disasters*, an excerpt of which is reproduced in Lizbeth Goodman (selected and introduced by), *Mythic Women/Real Women: Plays and Performance Pieces by Women* (London: Faber and Faber, 2000), pp. 287-300; Peggy Shaw, Lois Weaver, and James Neale-Kennerley, *Lust and Comfort* (1995), in *Split Britches: Lesbian Practice/Feminist Performance*, ed. by Sue-Ellen Case (London: Routledge, 1996), pp. 225-72 (pp. 255-6); Peggy Shaw, Deborah Margolin, and Lois Weaver, *Split Britches: A True Story*, in *Split Britches*, ed. by Case, pp. 35-57; Peggy Shaw and Lois Weaver, *Miss America*, in *Theatre in Pieces: Politics, Poetics and Interdisciplinary Collaboration, An Anthology of Play Texts, 1966-2010*, ed. by Anna Furse (London: Methuen, 2011), pp. 317-51; Lois Weaver 'Still Counting', in *Femmes of Power: Exploding Queer Femininities*, by Del LaGrace Volcano and Ulrika Dahl (London: Serpent's Tail, 2008), pp. 140-5; and Lois Weaver, 'Kinship', *Contemporary Theatre Review*, 23.1 (2013), 43-4, reprinted by permission of Taylor & Francis Ltd, www.tandfonline.com. Thanks also to those who collaborated on previously unpublished material we include here, including songs – Paul Clark, Vivian Stoll, and Amy R. Surratt – and Stacy Makishi and Peggy Shaw for *Salad of the Bad Café*.

This book has been supported by a Lower Manhattan Cultural Council Governors Island Artist Residency; support from the School of English and Drama, QMUL; and financial contributions made through crowdfunding. Both of us, as well as our colleagues at the Live Art Development Agency, are grateful to everyone who gave. Crowdfunders include a number who preferred to remain anonymous, plus:

Aaron Wright
Adam Alston
Adelaide Bannerman
Adrian Heathfield
Alessandra Cianetti
Alex Eisenberg
Ali Campbell
Alice Carey
Alice Forrester
Alice MacKenzie
Alice Moore
Aliki Boots
Alisa Solomon
Amanda Finch
Andrea Blood
Andrew Shaw
Andrew Wilford
Andy Lavender
Angharad Wynne-Jones
Aniela Czajewska
Ann Pellegrini
Anna Birch
Anne Bean
Anthony Roberts
Antonia Aulee
Barbara Dean
Beki Pope
Ben Walters
Benjamin Gillespie
Betsy Harvie Aziz
Billy Zhao
Bird la Bird
Bobby Baker
Boudicca
Brian
Caoimhe McAvinchey
Cat Fallow
Cat Jones & Cate Hull
Catherine Silverstone

Cecilia Wee
Charlotte Bell
Charlotte Harris
Chris Mottram-Wooster
Christina Crosby
Christine Ahern
CJ Mitchell
    & Karen Christopher
Clod Ensemble
C.O. Moed
Colette Conroy
Cynthia S. Baker
Dan Rebellato
Dani d'Emilia
Daniel Monk
Daniel Oliver
David
Debbie Kilbride
Debra Miller
Dee Heddon
Diana Damian Martin
Diana Taylor
Dominic Johnson
Dominic Thorpe
Dorothy Holland
Edd Hobbs
Eirini
Eleanor Roberts
Eleanor Savage
Elin Diamond
Elizabeth Lynch
Elizabeth Zimmer
Ellie Covan
Ellie Stansbury
Emily Forman
Emily Puthoff
Emily Wiles
Emma Møller
Eric Eich

Erin Hurley
Eva Weinmayr
Eva Weiss
Eve Katsouraki
F
Felicity Hall
Fintan Walsh
Florrie Burke
Fred McVittie
Gaia Shaw
George Easterbrook
Georgie Hulett
Geraldine Harris
Geraldine Pilgrim
Gerry Harris's brother
Gianna Bouchard
Gill
Gilli Bush-Bailey & Jacky
Bratton
Giovanna Maria Casetta
Giulia
Greg Barnes
Haitch Plewis
Hannah Maxwell
Hannah Stephens
Harriet Curtis
Heike
Helen Iball
Helena Hunter
Hemispheric Institute of
Performance and Politics
Hilary Machell
Hrafnhildur Benediktsdottir
Jackie Rudin
Jackie Stacey
jamie lewis hadley
Janelle Reinelt
Janice Perry
Jason E. Bowman

JD Stokely
Jen Harvie
Jennie Klein
Jerid O'Connell
Jess Dobkin
Jessica Foley
Jill Lewis
Jinny Keatinge
Joe Kelleher
Johanna Linsley
Joni Wong
Joonas Lahtinen
Jordan McKenzie
Joseph Dexter
Joshua Sofaer
Judith Katz
Judith Knight
Judy Furrow
Judy Harvie
Judy Rosen
Juju Vail
Julia Bardsley
Julia Cort
Julie Vulcan
Jungmin Song
Karena Rahall
Karl Taylor
Kath Weston
Kathleen Laziza
Kathryn L Beranich
Katie Bridget O'Brien
Katy Baird
Katy Price
Kay Turner
Keren Zaiontz
Kim Irwin
Kira O'Reilly
Kirstin Smith
Kristine Altwies

Lara Shalson & Lis Austin
Laura Godfrey-Isaacs
Lauren Davis
Lee & Anita Weaver
Lena Simic
Leo Burtin
Lewis Church
Lisa
Lisa Duggan
Lisa Kaplan
Leah Dunthorne &
   Katie McCrum
Lois Keidan
Louise Mothersole
Louise Owen
Luke Pell
Lulu Belliveau
Lynnette Moran
Maggie B. Gale
Mamoru Iriguchi
Manuel Vason
Margaret Shaw
Margherita Laera
Margot Williams
   & Maggie Jochild
Marilena Zaroulia
Marina Abramović
Mark Jeffery
Martin Welton
Mary Hall
Mary Osborn
Mary Paterson
Mathias Danbolt
Mathilde
Meg Savilonis
Megan Hanley
Megan Macdonald
Melissa Negro
Mermer Blakeslee

Michael Atavar
Michael Barrie Layward
Mimi McGurl
Minty Donald
Mischa Twitchin
Moe
Monica Pearl
Monika Treut
Morag Shiach
Morgan Gwenwald
Nadia Atia
Nanette De Cillis
Nao Bustamante
Natasha Davis
Needless Alley Collective
Nicholas Holden
Nicholas Ridout
Nicole Eschen
Noemie Solomon
Nora Jaffary
o_cesario
Oliver
Omar Kholeif
Oreet Ashery
Owen Parry
Patricia Ybarra
Paul Hamilton
Paul Murphy
Paula Grant
Penelope Woods
Peter Dickinson
Peter Harholdt
Philippa Barr
Rachael Longmire Hunt
Rachel
Rachel Beck
Rachel Clements
Rachel Lennox
Rachel Porter

Rachel Zerihan
Ramon Rivera-Servera
Rebecca
Rebecca French
Rebecca Schneider
Rhiannon Armstrong
Ricky Leach
Rob Ellis
Robert Gillett
Roberta Mock
Roewan Crowe
Rosa
Rosana Cade
Rosie Hunter
Roxanne Sutton
Ruth Ahnert
Ruth Fletcher
Ruthann Robson
Ruth Turner
Sam Scott Wood
Sara Warner
Sara Wolf
Sarah Dey Hirshan
Sarah East Johnson
Sarah Feinstein
Sarah Gorman
Sarah Maxfield
Sarah Miller
Sarah Mullan
Saskia Scheffer
Siena Oristaglio
Silas Howard
Sophie Nield
Stafford
Sue-Ellen Case
Sue Harris
Susan Thames
Susie Hewlett
Suzanne

Theresa Cirnigliaro
Theron Schmidt
   & Rajni Shah
Thomas John Bacon
Tim Hopkins
Trish Reid
Vendetta Vain
Vicky Ryder
Vincent Murphy
Vivian Stoll
Will Harvie
Yuhui Fu
Zerelda Sinclair

Contributor biographies

Moe Angelos has been a member of NYC's WOW Café since 1981 and is one of The Five Lesbian Brothers. Moe has performed with The Builders Association since 2000 and many other Off-Broadway luminaries. To hear more of what she has to say about show business, visit http://madehereproject.org/ and browse the artists.

Rosana Cade is an artist who mainly works in live performance. She roots her identity, practice, and politics in a queer discourse. Along with her best friend, Nick Anderson, she is co-founder of live performance festival //BUZZCUT// http://glasgowbuzzcut.wordpress.com.

David Caines is a graphic designer and visual artist based in London. His communications and design work include projects for the Live Art Development Agency, PRS for Music Foundation, and the British Film Institute. Other books he has designed include *Pleading in the Blood: The Art and Performances of Ron Athey* (2013), *Double Exposures* (2014) by Manuel Vason, and *Out of Now: The Lifeworks of Tehching Hsieh* (2009). David also makes paintings, and in 2015 was shortlisted for the East London Painting Prize.

Cynthia Carr was an arts writer for *The Village Voice* from 1984 until 2003 and is the author of three books – most recently, *Fire in the Belly: The Life and Times of David Wojnarowicz* (2012). Her work has also appeared in *Artforum*, *The New York Times*, *Modern Painters*, and other publications. She was awarded a Guggenheim Fellowship in 2007.

Sue-Ellen Case is Distinguished Professor and Chair of the PhD in Theater and Performance Studies and Director of the Center for Performance Studies at UCLA. She has published numerous books and articles in the fields of feminist/lesbian performance. A fan of Split Britches, she edited the publication of their first anthology.

Elin Diamond is Professor of English and Comparative Literature at Rutgers University. She is the author of *Unmaking Mimesis: Essays on Feminism and Theater* (1997) and *Pinters Comic Play* (1985), co-editor of *The Cambridge Companion to Caryl Churchill* (2009) and editor of *Performance and Cultural Politics* (1996). Her essays on drama, performance, and feminist theory have appeared in *Theatre Journal*, *English Literary History*, *Discourse*, *TDR: The Drama Review*, *Modern Drama*, *Kenyon Review*, *Art and Cinema*, *Maska*, and *Cahiers Renaud-Barrault*, and in numerous anthologies in the USA, Europe, and India. She is currently at work on a book on mimesis, modernism, and performance.

Jess Dobkin's performance and curatorial projects are presented at museums, galleries, theatres, universities, and in public spaces internationally. She lives in Toronto where she teaches as a Sessional Lecturer and is currently in residence to develop a new performance project at The Theatre Centre. For more about her work visit www.jessdobkin.com.

Jill Dolan is the Annan Professor of English and Theater and directs the Program in Gender and Sexuality Studies at Princeton University. Among other books, she is the author of *The Feminist Spectator as Critic* (1988, re-released in a 2012 anniversary edition) and *Utopia in Performance: Finding Hope at the Theatre* (2005). Her blog, *The Feminist Spectator*, won the 2010-11 George Jean Nathan Award for Dramatic Criticism.

Lisa Duggan is Professor of Social and Cultural Analysis at New York University. She is author of *Sapphic Slashers: Sex, Sensationalism and American Modernity* (2000) and *Twilight of Equality? Neoliberalism, Cultural Politics and the Attack on Democracy* (2003), co-author with Nan Hunter of *Sex Wars: Sexual Dissent and Political Culture* (1995), and co-editor with Lauren Berlant of *Our Monica, Ourselves: The Clinton Affair and National Interest* (2001). She is co-editor with Joseph DeFilippis, Kenyon Farrow, and Richard Kim of a special e-book issue of *The Scholar and the Feminist Online* titled *A New Queer Agenda*. She served as President of the American Studies Association during 2014-15.

Benjamin Gillespie is a PhD candidate in theatre at The Graduate Center of the City University of New York and a teaching fellow at Hunter College. His articles and reviews have been published in *Theatre Survey*, *Theatre Journal*, and *Canadian Theatre Review*, as well as in various anthologies on contemporary performance.

Geraldine Harris is Professor of Theatre Studies at Lancaster University. She has published widely on topics relating to gender, sexuality, and ethnicity in theatre and performance. Her most recent book (co-authored with Elaine Aston) is *A Good Night Out for the Girls: Popular Feminisms in Contemporary Theatre and Performance* (2013).

Jen Harvie is Professor of Contemporary Theatre and Performance and Lois's colleague at Queen Mary University of London. She is author of *Fair Play – Art, Performance and Neoliberalism* (2013), *Theatre & the City* (2009), and *Staging the UK* (2005); co-author of *The Routledge Companion to Theatre and Performance* (2006; 2nd edn 2014); and co-editor of *Making Contemporary Theatre: International Rehearsal Processes* (2010), and the Palgrave Macmillan series *Theatre &*.

Charles L. Hayes is Professor Emeritus of Theater and Cinema at Radford University in Radford, Virginia.

Deirdre Heddon is Professor of Contemporary Performance Practice at the University of Glasgow. She is the author of *Autobiography and Performance* (2008), co-author of *Walking, Writing and Performance* (2009), and *Devising Performance* (2005), and co-editor of *Histories and Practices of Live Art* (2012), and *Political Performances: Theory and Practice* (2009). She is also co-editor of Palgrave's series, *Performing Landscapes*.

Paul Heritage is Professor of Drama and Performance at Queen Mary University of London, International Associate at the Young Vic, Associate Producer at the Barbican, and International Adviser to the Brazilian Ministry of Culture on the *Cultura Viva* initiative. In 2004, the Brazilian government made him a Knight of the Order of Rio Branco.

Leslie Hill and Helen Paris are Associate Professors of Performance Making in the Department of Theater and Performance Studies at Stanford University and Artistic Directors of Curious theatre company, produced by Artsadmin, London, www.placelessness.com. Their most recent publication is *Performing Proximity, Curious Intimacies*, published in 2014.

Lauren Barri Holstein, also known as 'The Famous', is a contemporary feminist performance maker who has presented a substantial body of work in art, theatre, and dance contexts, including the Barbican, SPILL Festival, In Between Time Festival, The Arnolfini, Fierce Festival, and Duckie. Holstein is completing a PhD at Queen Mary University of London, and has authored a number of articles for *Performance Research*, *Feminist Times*, and *Dance Theatre Journal*, and a chapter in upcoming book *On Repetition: Writing, Performance, Art*, published by Intellect.

Holly Hughes is a writer and performer and the author of *Clit Notes: A Sapphic Sampler*, as well as editor of three collections: *O Solo Homo* (with David Román, 1998), *Animal Acts: Performing Species Today* (with Una Chaudhuri, 2014), and the forthcoming *Memories of the Revolution: The First Ten Years of the WOW Café* (with Carmelita Tropicana and Jill Dolan). Hughes' work has been presented internationally and she is the winner of awards including a Guggenheim Fellowship in 2011. She is currently a Professor at the Stamps School of Art & Design at the University of Michigan, where she co-founded the BFA in Interarts Performance.

Erin Hurley teaches courses in feminist and queer theatre, and in dramatic and performance theory at McGill University (Montreal). The author of *National Performance: Representing Quebec from Expo 67 to Céline Dion* (2011) and *Theatre & Feeling* (2010), and the editor of *Theatres of Affect* (2014), Erin is currently researching the history of English-language theatre in Quebec.

Lois Keidan is the co-Founder and co-Director of the Live Art Development Agency (www.thisisliveart.co.uk) which offers resources, opportunities, projects, and publishing for the support of Live Art practices and discourses. She has formerly worked at ICA, London; Arts Council England; Midland Group, Nottingham; and Theatre Workshop, Edinburgh.

Johanna Linsley is a researcher and artist. She has a PhD from Queen Mary University of London, and she works at the University of Roehampton. She is part of I'm With You, an international performance collective which deals with queer domesticity. She co-founded UnionDocs, a centre for experimental documentary in New York City.

Stacy Makishi is a Honolulu-born, independent artist based in London. Her work is the result of cross-fertilisation between theatre, comedy, film, and visual art. Her awards include ICA Attached Artist Award, Millennium Fellowship Award, Live Art Development Agency One to One and Artsadmin Bursary. Her work is produced by Artsadmin.

Deb Margolin is a playwright, actor, and founding member of Split Britches theatre company. She is the author of numerous plays, including *Imagining Madoff*, *Turquoise*, and *Bringing the Fishermen Home*, as well as ten solo performance plays which she has toured throughout the US, the most recent of which is *8 STOPS*, a comedy concerning the grief of endless compassion. Deb was honoured with an OBIE award for Sustained Excellence of Performance, the Kesselring Prize for Playwriting, and the Richard H. Broadhead Prize for teaching excellence at Yale University, where she is Associate Professor (Adjunct) in the undergraduate Theater Studies Program. She lives in New Jersey, which she denies.

Caoimhe McAvinchey is Senior Lecturer in Drama, Theatre, and Performance Studies at Queen Mary University of London. Publications include *Theatre & Prison* (2011) and, as editor, *Performance and Community* (2013). She is currently working on a monograph about Clean Break theatre company and an edited collection about international performance projects with women affected by the criminal justice system.

Muriel Miguel (Kuna/Rappahannock) is a founding member and Artistic Director of Spiderwoman Theater. She is a director, choreographer, actor, and educator and has worked in theatre in the United States and Canada for over 40 years. Her published plays include *Trail of the Otter* (in *Staging Coyote's Dream: Volume II*, 2009) and *Hot'n'Soft* (in *Two-spirit Acts: Queer Indigenous Performances*, 2013). Her awards include an Honorary Doctorate of Fine Arts from Miami University (1997), a Lifetime Achievement Award from the Women's Caucus for Art (2010), the Otto René Castillo Award for Political Theatre (2013), and a Rauschenberg Residency (2015).

Joan Nestle is co-founder of the Lesbian Herstory Archives (1974), author of *A Restricted Country* (1987) and *A Fragile Union* (1998), and editor of *The Persistent Desire: A Femme-Butch Reader* (1992) and, with Yasmin Tambiah, a special issue of *Sinister Wisdom* on 'Lesbians and Exile' (issue 94, autumn 2014). She entered public queer life in 1958 in Greenwich Village's working class bars, quintessential theatre where a good performance brought the yearned for touch or saved your life. In 2001, she left NYC to accompany her Australian lover, Di Otto, home to West Brunswick in Melbourne where she has lived ever since. Under different skies, she treasures the memories of community creations that gave her life for so many years. To all the women of Split Britches and WOW, thank you.

Peggy Phelan is the Ann O'Day Maples Chair in the Arts at Stanford University. She is Professor of Theater and Performance Studies, and English. She writes frequently about performance theory. Her books include: *Unmarked: The Politics of Performance* (1993); and *Mourning Sex: Performing Public Memories* (1997).

Peggy Shaw is a performer, writer, producer, and teacher of writing and performance. She has collaborated with Lois Weaver and Split Britches since 1980. Her book *A Menopausal Gentleman* (2011), edited by Jill Dolan and published by Michigan University Press, won the 2012 Lambda Literary Award for LBGT Drama. Peggy is a Senior Fellow of the Hemispheric Institute of Performance and Politics and was the 2014 recipient of the Doris Duke Artist Award.

Catherine Silverstone is Senior Lecturer in Drama, Theatre, and Performance Studies at Queen Mary University of London. She is the author of *Shakespeare, Trauma and Contemporary Performance* (2011) and articles on Duckie and queer films. She is also the editor of special issues on 'Derek Jarman and "the Renaissance"' for *Shakespeare Bulletin* (2014) and co-editor with Fintan Walsh of 'On Affirmation' for *Performance Research* (2014).

Kim Solga was Senior Lecturer in Drama at Queen Mary University of London from 2012 to 2014; she is now Associate Professor of English and Theatre Studies at Western University, Canada. She blogs about teaching, performance and activism at http://theactivistclassroom.wordpress.com. According to Peggy Shaw, she has excellent comic timing.

Anne Tallentire is a visual artist and Professor of Fine Art at Central Saint Martins, University of the Arts London. Her work across media is exhibited widely, including at the Venice Biennale, representing Ireland (1999); in a major retrospective at the Irish Museum of Modern Art, Dublin (2010); and in the survey show *Keywords* at Tate Liverpool (2014).

Diana Taylor is University Professor and Professor of Performance Studies and Spanish at New York University. She is the author of *Theatre of Crisis: Drama and Politics in Latin America* (1991); *Disappearing Acts: Spectacles of Gender and Nationalism in Argentina's 'Dirty War'* (1997); and *The Archive and the Repertoire: Performing Cultural Memory in the Americas* (2003; translated into Portuguese and Spanish). In 2012, she published *PERFORMANCE* in Spanish (forthcoming in English) and *Acciones de Memoria: Performance, Historia, y Trauma*. She is co-editor of *Estudios Avanzados de Performance* (2011), *Stages of Conflict: A Reader in Latin American Theatre and Performance* (2008), *Holy Terrors: Latin American Women Perform* (2004), *Defiant Acts/Actos Desafiantes: Four Plays by Diana Raznovich* (2002), *Negotiating Performance in Latin/o America: Gender, Sexuality and Theatricality* (1994), and *The Politics of Motherhood: Activists from Left to Right* (1997). She has edited five volumes of critical essays on Latin American, Latino, and Spanish playwrights. She has received a Guggenheim Fellowship (2005) and an ACLS Digital Innovation Fellowship (2013-14). She is Second Vice President of the MLA and will assume the presidency in 2017. She is founding Director of the Hemispheric Institute of Performance and Politics.

Works cited and additional citations of Weaver's work

Abrams, Josh and Gwendolyn Alker, 'Reflecting on ATHE's Silver: Archiving Conference Curation and the State of the Field in Theatre and Performance Studies', *Theatre Topics*, 22.1 (2012), 1-22

Allain, Paul and Jen Harvie, *The Routledge Companion to Theatre and Performance*, 2nd edn (London: Routledge, 2014)

Armstrong, Ann Elizabeth, 'Building Coalitional Spaces in Lois Weaver's Performance Pedagogy', *Theatre Topics*, 15.2 (2005), 201-19

Aston, Elaine, *An Introduction to Feminism and Theatre* (London: Routledge, 1994)

--, and Sue-Ellen Case, (eds.), *Staging International Feminisms* (Basingstoke: Palgrave Macmillan, 2007)

--, and Geraldine Harris, 'Imagining, Making, Changing: Split Britches', in *Performance Practice and Process: Contemporary [Women] Practitioners*, ed. by Aston and Harris (Basingstoke: Palgrave Macmillan, 2008), pp. 100-18

--, and Geraldine Harris (eds.), *Performance Practice and Process: Contemporary [Women] Practitioners* (Basingstoke: Palgrave Macmillan, 2008)

--, *Split Britches Workshop*, Women's Writing for Performance Project (Lancaster University, 12-15 January 2006 [on DVD]) <http://www.lancaster.ac.uk/depts/theatre/womenwriting/pages/publications.htm> [accessed 7 September 2013]

Ball, Katie Brewer, 'Cabaret Thoughts on Wow and Now', *Criticism*, 50.3 (2008), 543-9

Barnett, Claudia, '"In Your Dreams!": Deb Margolin's Fantasy/Drama', in *Staging a Cultural Paradigm: The Political and the Personal in American Drama*, ed. by Barbara Ozieblo and Miriam López-Rodríguez (Brussels: Presses Interuniversitaires Européennes, 2002), pp. 273-86

Bender, Felicia Aline, 'Girls Will Be Boys and Boys Will Be Girls: Gender Subversion in the Work of Split Britches Company and the Ridiculous Theatrical Company, 1967-1996' (unpublished doctoral thesis, University of Missouri, Columbia, 1997)

Bernstein, Robin, 'Staging Lesbian and Gay New York', in *The Cambridge Companion to the Literature of New York*, ed. by B. Waterman and C. R. K. Patell (Cambridge: Cambridge University Press, 2010), pp. 202-17

Blair, Rhonda, 'The Alcestis Project: Split Britches at Hampshire College', *Women & Performance: A Journal of Feminist Theory*, 6.1 (1993), 147-50

Blumenthal, Eileen, *Joseph Chaikin: Exploring at the Boundaries of Theater* (Cambridge: Cambridge University Press, 1984)

Bourne, Bette, Paul Shaw, Peggy Shaw, and Lois Weaver, *Belle Reprieve: A Collaboration*, in *Split Britches: Lesbian Practice/Feminist Performance*, ed. by Sue-Ellen Case (London: Routledge, 1996), pp. 149-83. Also published in *Modern Drama: Plays/Criticism/Theory*, ed. by W.B. Worthen (Fort Worth, TX: Harcourt Brace College Publishers, 1995), pp. 990-1002, and in *Gay and Lesbian Plays Today*, 33, ed. by Terry Helbing (Portsmouth, NH: Heinemann, 1993), pp. 1-39.

Burk, Juli, '*Valley of the Dolls'* House: Split Britches Did It with Feminism in the Sitting Room', in *Constructions and Confrontations: Changing Representations of Women and Feminisms, East and West: Selected Essays*, Literary Studies East and West vol. 12, ed. by Cristina Bacchilega and Cornelia N. Moore (Honolulu: University of Hawaii Press, 1996), pp. 274-85

Canning, Charlotte, *Feminist Theaters in the USA: Staging Women's Experience* (New York: Routledge, 1996)

-- 'The Beautiful Legs of Feminist Theatre: At the foot of the Mountain and Its Legacy', in *Restaging the Sixties: Radical Theatres and Their Legacies*, ed. by James Martin Harding and Cindy Michigan (Ann Arbor: University of Michigan Press, 2006), pp. 150-68

Carlson, Marvin, 'Alternative Theatre', in *The Cambridge History of American Theatre*, ed. by Don B. Wilmeth and Christopher Bigsby (Cambridge: Cambridge University Press, 2000), pp. 248-93

Carter, Jill, 'Processual Encounters of the Transformative Kind: Spiderwoman Theater, Trickster, and the First Act of "Survivance"', in *Troubling Tricksters: Revisioning Radical Conversations*, ed. by Deanna Reder and Linda M. Morra, Indigenous Studies Series (Waterloo, ON; Wilfrid Laurier University Press, 2010), pp. 263-87

Case, Sue-Ellen, *Feminist and Queer Performance: Critical Strategies* (Basingstoke: Palgrave Macmillan, 2009)

-- 'From Split Subject to Split Britches', in *Feminine Focus: The New Women Playwrights*, ed. by Enoch Brater (Oxford: Oxford University Press, 1989), pp. 126-46

-- 'Lesbian Performance in the Transnational Arena', in *The Cambridge Companion to Modern British Women Playwrights*, ed.

by Elaine Aston and Janelle Reinelt (Cambridge: Cambridge University Press, 2000), pp. 253-67

-- 'LGBTQ: An Alphabet of Interested Writing', *Theatre Journal*, 64.4 (2012), 607-16

-- 'Toward A Butch-Femme Aesthetic', in *Making a Spectacle: Feminist Essays on Contemporary Women's Theatre*, ed. by Lynda Hart (Ann Arbor: University of Michigan Press, 1989), pp. 282-99. Also published in *The Lesbian and Gay Studies Reader*, ed. by Michèle Aina Barale, David M. Halperin, and Henry Abelove (New York: Routledge, 1993)

-- (ed.), *Performing Feminisms: Feminist Critical Theory and Theatre* (Baltimore: Johns Hopkins University Press, 1990)

-- (ed.), *Split Britches: Lesbian Practice/Feminist Performance* (London and New York: Routledge, 1996)

Cave, Richard Allen, 'Engendering Confusion', in *Anthropological Perspectives*, ed. by Werner Huber and Martin Middeke (Trier, Germany: Wissenschaftlicher, 1998), pp. 19-43

Claycomb, Ryan, *Lives in Play: Autobiography and Biography on the Feminist Stage* (Michigan: University of Michigan, 2012)

-- 'Staging Psychic Excess: Parodic Narrative and Transgressive Performance', *Journal of Narrative Theory*, 37.1 (2007), 104-27

Davy, Kate, 'Constructing the Spectator: Reception, Context, and Address in Lesbian Performance', *Performing Arts Journal*, 10.2 (1986), 43-52

-- 'Fe/Male Impersonation: The Discourse of Camp', in *Critical Theory and Performance*, ed. by Janelle Reinelt and Joseph Roach (Ann Arbor: University of Michigan Press, 1993), pp. 231-47

-- *Lady Dicks and Lesbian Brothers: Staging the Unimaginable at the WOW Café Theatre* (Ann Arbor: University of Michigan Press, 2010)

-- 'Reading Past the Heterosexual Imperative: *Dress Suits to Hire*', *TDR: The Drama Review*, 33.1 (1989), 153-70

-- 'Peggy Shaw and Lois Weaver: Interviews (1985, 1992, 1993)', in *Modern Drama: Plays/Criticism/Theory*, ed. by W.B. Worthen (New York: Harcourt Brace, 1995), pp. 1003-08

Däwes, Birgit (ed.), *Indigenous North American Drama: A Multivocal History* (Albany: SUNY Press, 2013)

de Lauretis, Teresa, 'Sexual Indifference and Lesbian Representation', *Theatre Journal*, 40.2 (1988), 155-77

312

Diamond, Elin, 'Mimesis, Mimicry, and The 'True-Real'', in *Acting Out: Feminist Performances*, ed. by Lynda Hart and Peggy Phelan (Ann Arbor: University of Michigan Press, 1993), pp. 363-82

Dolan, Jill, 'Desire Cloaked in a Trenchcoat', *The Drama Review*, 33.1 (1989), 59-67

-- 'The Dynamics of Desire: Sexuality and Gender in Pornography and Performance', *Theatre Journal*, 39.2 (1987), 156-74

-- *The Feminist Spectator as Critic*, 2nd edn (Ann Arbor: University of Michigan, 2012)

-- 'Gay and Lesbian Drama', in *A Companion to Twentieth Century American Drama*, ed. by David Krasner (Oxford: Blackwell, 2005), pp. 486-504

-- '"Lesbian" Subjectivity in Realism: Dragging at the Margins of Structure and Ideology', in *Performing Feminisms: Feminist Critical Theory and Theatre*, ed. by Sue-Ellen Case (Baltimore: Johns Hopkins University Press, 1990), pp. 40-53

-- '*Lost Lounge*, Produced at Dixon Place, New York, NY, 2011', in *The Feminist Spectator in Action: Feminist Criticism for the Stage and Screen* (Basingstoke: Palgrave Macmillan, 2013), pp. 174-77

-- 'Practicing Cultural Disruptions: Gay and Lesbian Representations and Sexuality', in *Critical Theory and Performance*, ed. by Janelle Reinelt and Joseph Roach (Ann Arbor: University of Michigan Press, 1993), pp. 263-75

-- *Presence and Desire: Essays on Gender, Sexuality, Performance* (Ann Arbor: University of Michigan Press, 1993)

-- 'Seeing Deb Margolin: Ontological Vandalism and Radical Amazement', *TDR: The Drama Review*, 52.3 (2008), 98-117

--, *Theatre & Sexuality* (Basingstoke: Palgrave Macmillan, 2010)

Dolan, Jill (ed.), *A Menopausal Gentleman: Solo Performances of Peggy Shaw* (Ann Arbor: University of Michigan Press, 2011)

Duggan, Lisa, and Kathleen McHugh, 'A Fem(me)inist Manifesto', *Women and Performance*, 8.2 (1996), 153-59

Eschen, Nicole, 'Lois Weaver Performs Resistant Femme', in *CSW Newsletter*, January 2007 <http://www.women.ucla.edu/csw/Newsletter/Jan07/eschen.html> [accessed 7 September 2013]

-- 'Pressing Back: Split Britches', *Lost Lounge* and the Retro Performativity of Lesbian Performance', *Journal of Lesbian Studies*, 17.1 (2013), 56-71

Ferguson, Marcia, 'Menopausal Gentleman', *Theatre Journal*, 50.3 (1998), 374-75

Fliotsos, Anne and Wendy Vierow, *American Women Directors of the Twentieth Century* (Champaign, IL: University of Illinois Press, 2009)

-- 'Muriel Miguel', in *American Women Directors of the Twentieth Century* (Champaign, IL: University of Illinois Press, 2009) pp. 287-95

Freeman, Sandra, *Putting Your Daughters on the Stage: Lesbian Theatre from the 1970s to the 1990s* (London: Cassell, 1997)

Freeman, Sara, 'Gay Sweatshop, Alternative Theatre, and Strategies for New Writing', *New Theatre Quarterly*, 30.2 (2014), 136-53

Fowler, Catherine, '"Performing Sexualities" at Lancaster', *New Theatre Quarterly*, 10.38 (1994), 196-97

Geis, Deborah, 'Deconstructing (A Streetcar Named) Desire: Gender Re-Citation in *Belle Reprieve*', *American Drama*, 11.2 (2002), 21-31

Goodman, Lizbeth, *Contemporary Feminist Theatres: To Each Her Own* (London-New York: Routledge, 1993)

-- 'Introduction', in *Mythic Women/Real Women: Plays and Performance Pieces by Women*, selected and introduced by Goodman (London: Faber and Faber, 2000), pp. ix-xl

-- (selected and introduced by), *Mythic Women/Real Women: Plays and Performance Pieces by Women* (London: Faber and Faber, 2000)

Greer, Stephen, *Contemporary British Queer Performance* (Hampshire: Palgrave Macmillan, 2012)

Hall, Lynn, 'Performing, Playing, Politicking: Theatre as Dis(e)ruption', in *Making the Stage: Essays on the Changing Concept of Theatre, Drama and Performance*, ed. by Ann C. Hall (Cambridge: Cambridge Scholars Publishing, 2008), pp. 178-91

Hamilton, Sabrina, 'Split Britches and the Alcestis Lesson: 'What is this Albatross?', in *Upstaging Big Daddy: Directing Theater as if Gender and Race Matter*, ed. by Ellen Donkin and Susan Clement (Ann Arbor: University of Michigan Press, 1993), pp. 133-50

Harris, Geraldine, 'Double Acts, Theatrical Couples and Split Britches' *Double Agency*', *New Theatre Quarterly*, 18.3 (2002), 211-21

Hart, Lynda, 'Afterword: Zero Degree Deviancy – "Lesbians Who Kill"', in *Fatal Woman: Lesbian Sexuality and the Mark of Aggression* (Princeton: Princeton University Press, 1994)

-- 'Identity and Seduction: Lesbians in the Mainstream', in *Acting Out: Feminist Performances*, ed. by Hart and Peggy Phelan (Ann Arbor: University of Michigan Press, 1993), pp. 119-37

-- 'Lesbians Who Kill', *Theatre Journal*, 44.4 (1992), 515-18

-- (ed.), *Making a Spectacle: Feminist Essays on Contemporary Women's Theatre* (Ann Arbor: University of Michigan, 1989)

-- and Peggy Phelan, 'Queerer than Thou: Being and Deb Margolin', *Theatre Journal*, 47.2 (1995), 269-82

Harvie, Jen, *Fair Play – Art, Performance and Neoliberalism* (Basingstoke: Palgrave Macmillan, 2013)

Haugo, Ann, '"Circles upon Circles upon Circles": American Indian Women in Theater and Performance', in *American Indian Theater in Performance: A Reader*, ed. by Hanay Geiogmamah and Jaye T. Darby (Los Angeles: UCLA American Indian Studies Centre, 2000)

--,'Weaving a Legacy: An Interview with Muriel Miguel of the Spiderwoman Theater', in *The Color of Theater: Race, Culture, and Contemporary Performance*, ed. by Roberta Uno and Lucy Mae San Pablo Burns (London and New York: Continuum, 2002), pp. 218-34

Hughes, Holly, 'Faith Not Lost: Holly Hughes Interviews Lois Weaver About Split Britches' *Lost Lounge* (2009)', *Women & Performance*, 22.1 (2012), 135-40

Hughes, Holly, Peggy Shaw, and Lois Weaver, '*Dress Suits to Hire*: A Collaboration between Holly Hughes, Peggy Shaw, and Lois Weaver', *TDR: The Drama Review*, 33.1 (1989), 132-52

Hughes, Holly, Carmelita Tropicana, and Jill Dolan (eds.), *Memories of the Revolution: First Ten Years of the WOW Café* (Ann Arbor: University of Michigan Press, forthcoming 2015)

Jenkins, Linda Walsh, 'Spiderwoman', in *Women in American Theatre*, ed. by Helen Krich Chinoy and Jenkins (New York: Theatre Communications Group, 1987), pp. 303-05

-- 'Split Britches', in *Women in American Theatre*, ed. by Helen Krich Chinoy and Jenkins (New York: Theatre Communications Group, 1987), pp. 310-14

Klein, Emily B., 'Chapter 4 –Spinning Yarns: Spiderwoman Theater's *Lysistrata Numbah!* (1977)', in *Sex and War on the American Stage: Lysistrata in Performance 1930-2012* (Oxon: Routledge, 2014), pp. 87-107

Krasner, David, *American Drama 1945-2000: An Introduction* (Oxford: Blackwell, 2006)

Langworthy, Douglas, 'Deb Margolin: Take Back Your Proscenium', *American Theatre*, 13.5 (1996), 38-41

Loose Change Productions, Press Release for *Red Mother* by Muriel Miguel (New York, n.d. [2010]), <http://www.loosechangeproductions.org/PR_PDFs/RedMother_PR.pdf> [accessed 4 December 2014]

Margolin, Deborah, and Split Britches Company, *Little Women: The Tragedy*, conceived by Split Britches Company, scripted by Deborah Margolin, with additional text by Louisa May Alcott and Peggy Shaw, directed by Lois Weaver, and performed by Deborah Margolin, Peggy Shaw, and Lois Weaver, ed. by Vivian Patraka, *The Kenyon Review* 15.2 (1993), 14-26 [Note: this textual version is drawn from excerpts of its production at Interart Theatre, New York, 31 July 1989.]

Margolin, Deb, in collaboration with Peggy Shaw and Lois Weaver, *Lesbians Who Kill*, in *Split Britches: Lesbian Practice/ Feminist Performance*, ed. by Sue-Ellen Case (London: Routledge, 1996), pp. 185-224.

Martin, Carol, *A Sourcebook on Feminist Theatre and Performance: On and Beyond the Stage* (London and New York: Routledge, 1996)

McAvinchey, Caoimhe, 'Possible Fictions: The Testimony of Applied Performance with Women in Prison in England and Brazil' (unpublished doctoral thesis, Queen Mary University of London, 2007)

-- (ed.), *Performance and Community, Case Studies and Commentary* (London: Methuen, 2014)

Menard, Paul, 'The (Fe)Male Gays: Split Britches and the Redressing of Dyke Camp', in *We Will be Citizens: New Essays on Gay and Lesbian Theatre*, ed. by James Fisher (Jefferson, N.C. and London: McFarland & Company, 2008), pp. 185-93

Merrill, Lisa, 'An Interview with Lois Weaver, Peggy Shaw and Deb Margolin', *Women & Performance: A Journal of Feminist Theory*, 6.1 (1993), 151-167

Miller, Stephen, *Smart Blonde: Dolly Parton* (London: Omnibus Press, 2006)

Mohler, Courtney Elkin, 'Little (White) Women: Locating Whiteness in (De) constructions of the American Female from Alcott to Split Britches', *Platform*, 4.1 (2009), 60-78

Molesworth, Helen, 'House Work and Art Work', *October*, 92 (2000), 71-97

Mulvey, Laura, 'Visual Pleasure and Narrative Cinema', *Screen* 16.3 (1975), 6-18. Also published widely, including in Mulvey, *Visual and Other Pleasures* (1989), 2nd edn (Basingstoke: Palgrave Macmillan, 2009)

Nestle, Joan, 'The Femme Question', *The Persistent Desire: A Femme-butch Reader*, ed. by Nestle (Boston: Alyson Publications, Inc., 1992), pp. 138-46

Parnes, Uzi, 'Pop Performance, Four Seminal Influences: The Work of Jack Smith, Tom Murrin - the Alien Comic, Ethyl Eichelberger, and the Split Britches Company (New York)', (unpublished doctoral thesis, New York University, 1988)

Patraka, Vivian M., 'Split Britches in *Little Women: The Tragedy*: Staging Censorship, Nostalgia, and Desire', *The Kenyon Review*, 15.2 (1993), 6-13

--, 'Split Britches in *Split Britches*: Performing History, Vaudeville, and the Everyday', *Women and Performance: A Journal of Feminist Theory*, 4.2 (1989), 58-67

Patrascu-Kingsley, Ken, 'Masquerading Gender in *Belle Reprieve*: Adapting *A Streetcar Named Desire* for Transgendered Theatre', *Theatron*, (2004), 21-38

Pellegrini, Ann, 'From the Stage to the Page', *The Women's Review of Books*, 15.1 (1997), 22-23

Peterson, Jane, and Suzanne Bennett, 'Split Britches', in *Women Playwrights of Diversity: A Bio-bibliographical Sourcebook*, ed. by Peterson and Bennett (Westport: Greenwood Publishing Group, 1997), pp. 318-22

Porter, Rachel, 'Putting Feminism Back on the Table', *Exeunt*, 6 November 2013, <http://exeuntmagazine.com/features/ putting-feminism-back-on-the-table/> [accessed 1 October 2014]

Rademeyer, Philip, 'Gender Play in Performance as a Means of Enacting a Queer Utopia', *Crossing the Boundaries of Gender in the Performing Arts* (2012) <http:// www.inter-disciplinary.net/critical-issues/ gender-and-sexuality/femininity-and-masculinity/project-archives/2nd/session-10-crossing-the-boundaries-of-gender-in-the-performing-arts/> [accessed 7 September 2013]

Rapi, Nina, 'Hide and Seek: The Search for a Lesbian Theatre Aesthetic', *New Theatre Quarterly*, 34.9 (1993), 147-59

Schneider, Rebecca, 'Holly Hughes: Polymorphous Perversity and the Lesbian Scientist: An Interview with Rebecca Schneider', *TDR: The Drama Review*, 33.1 (1989), 171-83

-- 'See the Big Show: Spiderwoman Theater Doubling Back', in *Acting Out: Feminist Performances*, ed. by Lynda Hart and Peggy Phelan (Ann Arbor: University of Michigan Press, 1993), pp. 227-55

Senelick, Laurence, *The Changing Room: Sex, Drag and Theatre* (London-New York: Routledge, 2003)

Shalson, Lara, 'Creating Community, Constructing Criticism: The Women's One World Festival 1980-1981', *Theatre Topics*, 15.2 (2005), 221-39

Shaw, Peggy, 'How I Learned Theater', in *Cast Out: Queer Lives in Theater*, ed. by Robin Bernstein (Ann Arbor: University of Michigan Press, 2006), pp. 25-29

Shaw, Peggy, and Lois Weaver, *Miss America*, in *Theatre in Pieces: Politics, Poetics and*

Interdisciplinary Collaboration, An Anthology of Play Texts, 1996-2010, ed. by Anna Furse (London, Methuen, 2011), pp. 317-51

Shaw, Peggy, Deborah Margolin, and Lois Weaver, *Split Britches: A True Story*, conceived and directed by Lois Weaver, with additional contributions by Naja Beye, Cathy Gollner, and Pam Verge, WOW Festival, New York, 1980, in *Split Britches: Lesbian Practice/Feminist Performance*, ed. by Sue-Ellen Case (London: Routledge, 1996), pp. 35-57. Also published in *Women and Performance: A Journal of Feminist Theory*, 4.2 (1989), 68-95

Shaw, Peggy, Lois Weaver and Kate Davy, 'Peggy Shaw and Lois Weaver: Interviews (1985, 1992, 1993)', in *Modern Drama: Plays/ Criticism/Theory*, ed. by W. B. Worthen (Fort Worth, TX: Harcourt Brace College Publishers, 1995), pp. 1003-08

Shaw, Peggy, Lois Weaver, and James Neale-Kennerley, *Lust and Comfort* (1995), in *Split Britches: Lesbian Practice/Feminist Performance*, ed. by Sue-Ellen Case (London: Routledge, 1996), pp. 225-72

Shedd, Sally, 'Gender Traders/Gender Traitors: Staging Non-Traditional Gender Roles and Alternative Sexualities' (unpublished doctoral thesis, University of Kansas, 1998)

Shoemaker, Deanna, 'Pink Tornados and Volcanic Desire: Lois Weaver's Resistant 'Femme(nini)tease', in *Faith and Dancing: Mapping Femininity and Other Natural Disasters*', *Text and Performance Quarterly*, 27.4 (2007), 317-33

-- 'Queers, Monsters, Drag Queens and Whiteness: Unruly Femininities in Women's Staged Performances', (unpublished doctoral thesis, University of Texas, 2004)

Sinfield, Alan, *Out On Stage: Lesbian and Gay Theatre in the Twentieth Century* (London-New Haven: Yale University Press, 1999)

Silverstone, Catherine, *Shakespeare. Trauma and Contemporary Performance* (New York: Routledge, 2011)

Solomon, Alisa, 'It's Never Too Late to Switch: Crossing Toward Power', in *Crossing the Stage: Controversies on Cross-Dressing*, ed. by Lesley Ferris (London and New York: Routledge, 1993), pp. 144-54

-- 'The WOW Cafe', *TDR: The Drama Review*, special issue on *East Village Performance*, 29.1 (1985), 92-101. Also published in *A Sourcebook of Feminist Theatre and Performance: On and Beyond the Stage*, ed. by Carol Martin (New York: Routledge, 1996), pp. 42-52

-- *Re-Dressing the Canon: Essays on Theater and Gender* (London-New York: Routledge, 1997)

Solga, Kim, *Theatre & Feminism* (Basingstoke: Palgrave Macmillan, forthcoming 2015)

-- 'Dress Suits to Hire and the Landscape of Queer Urbanity', in *Performance and the City*, ed. by D.J. Hopkins, Shelley Orr, and Kim Solga (Basingstoke: Palgrave MacMillan, 2009), pp. 152-68

Steck, Rachel Kinsman, 'Laughing Lesbians: Camp, Spectatorship, and Citizenship' (unpublished doctoral thesis, University of Oregon, 2010).

Still, Judith, *Derrida and Hospitality: Theory and Practice* (Edinburgh: Edinburgh University Press, 2010)

Strand, Ginger, 'Split Britches', *High Performance*, 15.2-3 (1992), 76-77

Underwood, Emily, 'Confusing Gender: Strategies for Resisting Objectification in the Work of Split Britches', *Platform*, 2.1 (Spring 2007), 25-37

Velie, Alan R., and A. Robert Lee (eds.), *The Native American Renaissance: Literary Imagination and Achievement* (Norman: University of Oklahoma Press, 2013)

Warner, Sara, *Acts of Gaiety: LGBT Performance and the Politics of Pleasure* (Michigan: University of Michigan, 2012)

Weaver, Lois, 'Afterword', in *The Routledge Reader in Gender and Performance*, ed. by Lizbeth Goodman and Jane de Gay (London: Routledge, 1998), pp. 303-04

-- 'Doing Time', in *Applied Theatre Reader*, ed. by Tim Prentki and Sheila Preston (London: Routledge, 2008)

-- 'Faith and Dancing: Mapping Femininity and Other Natural Disasters', excerpt, in *Mythic Women/Real Women: Plays and Performance Pieces by Women*, selected and introduced by Lizbeth Goodman (London: Faber and Faber, 2000), pp. 287-300

-- 'Foreword', in Helen Freshwater, *Theatre & Audience* (Basingstoke: Palgrave Macmillan, 2009), pp. ix-xi

--, 'Kinship', *Contemporary Theatre Review*, 23.1 (2013), 43-4

--, 'May Interviews June', *Movement Research*, 1991

--, 'Performing Butch/Femme Theory', *Journal of lesbian studies*. 2.2-3 (1998), 187-99, and simultaneously in *Acts of Passion: Sexuality, Gender and Performance*, ed. by Nina Rapi and Maya Chowdhry (London-New York: Haworth Press, 1998), pp. 187-99

--, 'Sheila Dances with Sheila', in *Butch/Femme: Inside Lesbian Gender*, ed. by Sally R. Munt (London: Cassell, 1998), pp. 66-73

-- *Still Counting*, in *Femmes of Power: Exploding Queer Femininities*, ed. by Del LaGrace Volcano and Ulrika Dahl (London: Serpent's Tail, 2008), pp. 140-45

-- 'Writing and Performance', *PAJ: A Journal of Performance and Art*, 34.1 (2012), 138-39

-- and Jen Harvie, 'Beg, Borrow or Steal: Lois Weaver in Conversation with Jen Harvie', in *Theatre and Adaptation: Return, Rewrite, Repeat*, ed. by Margherita Laera (London and New York: Bloomsbury Methuen Drama, 2014), pp. 135-48

-- and Caoimhe McAvinchey, 'Lois Weaver: Interview and Introduction by Caoimhe McAvinchey', in *Performance and Community: Commentary and Case Studies*, ed. by Caoimhe McAvinchey (London: Bloomsbury, 2014), pp. 21-32

-- Helen Paris and Leslie Hill, *Getting On: A Backstage Tour: An Open Source Workshop Template*, n.d., no further publication information

-- with Peggy Shaw, 'MAKE SOMETHING: A Manifesto for Making Performance about Making Change', in *Staging International Feminisms*, ed. by Sue-Ellen Case and Elaine Aston (Basingstoke: Palgrave Macmillan, 2007), pp. 174-83

Williamson, Telory, 'Lust and Comfort', *Theatre Journal*, 48.1 (1996), pp. 102-10

Willis, Julia, 'The Splittin' Image', *The Lesbian Review of Books*, III.3 (1997)

Yarbo-Bejarano, Yvonne, 'The Lesbian Body in Latina Cultural Production' in *Entiendes?: Queer Readings, Hispanic Writings*, ed. by Emilie L. Bergmann (Durham: Duke University Press, 1995), pp. 181–200

Select relevant archives

Gay Sweatshop Theatre Company (1974-97) Archives, Royal Holloway, University of London, Archives and Special Collections, <https://www.royalholloway.ac.uk/archives/home.aspx> [accessed 19 June 2015]

Split Britches Archive, 1978-2000, MSS 251, The Fales Library and Special Collections, Elmer Holmes Bobst Library, New York University, <http://dlib.nyu.edu/findingaids/html/fales/splitbritches/> [accessed 19 June 2015]

Split Britches Hemispheric Institute, <http://hemisphericinstitute.org/hemi/en/modules/itemlist/category/245-britches> [accessed 2 September 2014]

Films/DVDs featuring Lois Weaver

Long Awaited Pleasure, dir. by Giovanna Manana, 1987.

She Must Be Seeing Things, dir. by Sheila McLaughlin, 1987.

Split Britches Video Collection, Hemispheric Institute Digital Video Library, <http://hidvl.nyu.edu/search/?start=0&fq=collectionId%3ASplitBritchesvideocollection&q=&facets=> [accessed 19 June 2015] Contains recorded versions/excerpts of:

The Anniversary Waltz
Beauty and the Beast
Belle Reprieve
Double Agency: Miss Risqué & It's a Small House and We Lived in It Always
Dress Suits to Hire
Faith and Dancing
Lesbians Who Kill
Little Women: The Tragedy
Lust and Comfort
Monsieur-Madame
Patience and Sarah
Peggy Shaw and Lois Weaver at Dixon Place
Salad of the Bad Café
Split Britches: The True Story
Upwardly Mobile Home
Valley of the Dolls House

Select relevant websites

Goat Island, Education/Workshops, Creative Response, <http://www.goatislandperformance.org/creativeResponse.htm> [accessed 24 November 2014]

Women's Writing for Performance, Lancaster University, <http://www.lancaster.ac.uk/depts/theatre/womenwriting/> [accessed 24 November 2014]

Split Britches, <https://splitbritches.wordpress.com> [accessed 19 June 2015]

Split Britches on *flickr*, <https://www.flickr.com/photos/splitbritches/> [accessed 7 January 2015]

Index

First published in the UK in 2015 by

Live Art Development Agency
The White Building, Unit 7, Queen's Yard
White Post Lane, London, E9 5EN, UK
www.thisisLiveArt.co.uk

and

Intellect, The Mill, Parnall Road,
Fishponds, Bristol, BS16 3JG, UK
www.intellectbooks.com

First published in the USA in 2015 by

Intellect, The University of Chicago Press,
1427 E. 60th Street, Chicago, IL 60637, USA

Edited by Jen Harvie and Lois Weaver, 2015

Contributions © the individual contributors, 2015

Front cover image: Lois Weaver as Beauty, played as a Salvation Army Sergeant, in Split Britches' *Beauty and the Beast*. Photo: Eva Weiss

Back cover image: Portrait of Lois Weaver for *Desperate Archives* (2014), La MaMa La Galleria, NYC. Photo by Eva Weiss

Lois's props and notebooks photographed by David Caines

Designed by David Caines Unlimited
www.davidcaines.co.uk

Printed and bound by Gomer Press, UK

ISBN 978-1-78320-534-9

Published with the support of Arts Council England.

Intellect Live

The Only Way Home is Through the Show: Performance Work of Lois Weaver is part of Intellect Live – a series of publications on influential artists working at the edges of performance. Intellect Live is a collaboration between Intellect Books and the Live Art Development Agency. The series is characterised by lavishly illustrated and beautifully designed books, created through close collaborations between artists and writers, each of which is the first substantial publication dedicated to an artist's work.

Series Editors: Dominic Johnson, Lois Keidan and CJ Mitchell.

ISSN 2052-0913